Acclaim for

NEVER SAY DIE

"[A] book that will change the way you think about growing old. . . . In the end, and in ways not recognized at the beginning of the book, *Never Say Die* is life-affirming."

—*Washington Independent Review of Books*

"Mixes rigorous reportage and tart-tongued criticism with memoir and history, slashing through romanticized versions of the golden years and delivering tough truths."

—*Newsday*

"Jacoby cuts through the fog of bromides and half-truths enveloping the discussion of aging, shines a light on issues long neglected and offers cogent solutions to pressing problems."

—*The Miami Herald*

"In this beautifully crafted book, [Jacoby] punctures the promises that aging will eventually be 'cured' either by a wonder drug or through positive thinking. The good news is that if we wake up from our delusions we may be better able to grow old with dignity."

—Barbara Ehrenreich, author of *Nickel and Dimed: On (Not) Getting by in America*

"Jacoby's book, which mixes the intellectual and the emotional, academic studies and personal anecdotes, is intentionally contentious. . . . That is just as it should be. Jacoby does not want to serve as a destroyer of hope. Thank goodness, however, that she is willing to be perceived as a destroyer of false hope."

—*The Seattle Times*

"Lively, carefully researched. . . . [Jacoby] writes with both passion and reason."

—*St. Petersburg Times*

"Eloquent. . . . [Jacoby] is courageously right. . . . One can hope that her impassioned, closely argued tract gains a serious hearing among her fellow boomers."

—*Columbia Journalism Review*

"*Never Say Die* is a beautifully written, clear-eyed, and deeply compassionate book."

—Sam Harris, author of *The Moral Landscape* and *The End of Faith*

Susan Jacoby

NEVER SAY DIE

Susan Jacoby is the author of nine books, most recently *The Age of American Unreason*, *Alger Hiss and the Battle for History*, and *Freethinkers: A History of American Secularism*. She writes The Spirited Atheist blog for *On Faith*, a website sponsored by *The Washington Post*. She lives in New York City.

www.susanjacoby.com

ALSO BY SUSAN JACOBY

Alger Hiss and the Battle for History

The Age of American Unreason

Freethinkers: A History of American Secularism

Half-Jew: A Daughter's Search for Her Family's Buried Past

Wild Justice: The Evolution of Revenge

The Possible She

Inside Soviet Schools

Moscow Conversations

NEVER SAY DIE

The Myth and Marketing of the New Old Age

Susan Jacoby

Vintage Books
A Division of Random House, Inc.
New York

FIRST VINTAGE BOOKS EDITION, FEBRUARY 2012

The Library of Congress has cataloged the Pantheon edition as follows:
Jacoby, Susan.
Never say die: the myth and marketing of the new old age / Susan Jacoby.
p. cm.
Includes bibliographic references and index.
1. Old age—United States. 2. Aging—United States.
3. Older people—United States. I. Title.
HQ1064.U5J324 2010
305.260973'09051—dc22 2010017123

Vintage ISBN: 978-0-307-45628-1

www.vintagebooks.com

Printed in the United States of America
10 9 8 7 6 5 4 3 2 1

In memory of Dr. Robert N. Butler
1927–2010

Can you imagine old age? Of course you can't. I didn't. I couldn't. I had no idea what it was like. Not even a false image—no image. And nobody wants anything else. Nobody wants to face any of this before he has to. How is it all going to turn out? Obtuseness is de rigueur.

—Philip Roth, *The Dying Animal*

Contents

Preface xi

ONE: Never Say Old 3

TWO: Youth Culture: An American Tradition 28

THREE: Boomer Beginnings and Age-Defying Denial 56

FOUR: Miracles of Modern Medicine and Other Half-truths 80

FIVE: A Mind Is a Terrible Thing to Lose 100

SIX: Women: Eventually the Only Sex 127

SEVEN: Greedy Geezers and Other Half-truths 155

EIGHT: The "Wisdom of Old Age" 180

NINE: Endings 210

TEN: The Ethics of Longevity: An Argument in Search of Facts 239

ELEVEN: Necessary Bedfellows: Bridges Between Generations, Old-Age Autonomy 265

Conclusion 282

Acknowledgments 297

Notes 299

Selected Bibliography 311

Index 315

Preface

Anyone who has not been buried in a vault for the past two decades is surely aware of the media blitz touting the "new old age" as a phenomenon that enables people in their sixties, seventies, eighties, nineties, and beyond to enjoy the kind of rich, full, healthy, adventurous, sexy, financially secure lives that their ancestors could never have imagined. Much of this propaganda is aimed at baby boomers now in their late forties, fifties, and early sixties, because marketers are betting that the boomer generation will spend almost anything on products that say "Hell no, we won't go!" to a traditionally defined old age. I too have read (and occasionally written) optimistic screeds on the joys and advantages of the new old age, also known as "young old age," also known as "successful aging." But I now regard the relentlessly positive vision promulgated by cheerleaders for the extension of longevity as more of an exhortation, even an ultimatum, than an evidence-based portrait of old age as it is today and is likely to remain for the huge baby boom generation. As the oldest boomers turn sixty-five, it is past time for a more critical and skeptical look at old age as it really is in America today, especially for the "old old"—those in their ninth and tenth decades of life. When I told a forty-something colleague that I was writing a book about the myth of young old age, she asked how old *I* was (a question still considered impolite in most contexts). I told her I was sixty-three. "Surely you don't think of that as old?" she asked in a horrified tone. Actually, being an American who came of age in the "forever young" decade, I do not usually think of myself as old. But when I recall how quickly the last two decades, packed with love and work, have sped by, I know how close eighty, or ninety, really is—as distinct from whatever subjective notions I cherish about my own youthfulness. Old, in America, always seems to be a decade or preferably two decades older than one's own age. The difference between forty and sixty is that, at sixty, the imaginative leap to old old age is not only possible but inescapable.

The idea that there is a new kind of old age, experienced in a radically different way from old age throughout history, is integral to the marketing of longevity. For who would want to live to be one hundred if, as individuals and as a society, we accepted or even suspected that the new old age, after a certain point, encompasses most of the vicissitudes of old-fashioned old age? There is a considerable amount of truth in the assertion that many old people today—if they are in sound financial shape, if they are in reasonably good health, and if they possess functioning brains—can explore an array of possibilities that did not exist even a generation ago. "If" is the most important word in the preceding sentence. The idea that we can control the future by aggressively focusing on and taking care of ourselves is an article of faith for baby boomers. Yet in many instances, successful aging—or the outward appearance of successful aging—means only that a person has managed to put on a happy face for the rest of the world; present an image of vigor and physical well-being even when bones are aching; smile even though a heart may be breaking with loss; do everything possible to conceal memory lapses; demonstrate a consistent willingness to try anything new; and scoff (with just the right, light touch of humor) at those misguided contemporaries who refuse to "live in the present."

Here's what one cannot do and be considered a person who is aging successfully: complain about health problems to anyone younger; weep openly for a friend or lover who has been dead more than a month or two; admit to depression or loneliness; express nostalgia for the past (either personal or historical); or voice any fear of future dependency—whether because of poor physical health, poor finances, or the worst scourge of advanced old age, Alzheimer's disease. American society also looks with suspicion on old people who demand to be left alone to deal with aging in their own way: one must look neither too needy for companionship nor too content with solitude to be considered a role model for healthy aging rather than a discontented geezer or crone. Successful aging awards are conferred only on those who have managed (often as much by biological good luck as effort) to avoid, or convince others that they have avoided, the arduous uphill fight that eventually consumes all who live too long to retain control over either the mundane or the important decisions of everyday life. It's great to be old—as long as one does not manifest too many of the typical problems of advanced age. The reality evaded by propagandists for the new old age is that we all are capable of aging successfully—until we aren't.

I hope that this book about the genuine battles of growing old will provide support for all who draw their strength and courage from reality, however daunting that reality may be, rather than from platitudes about "defying old age." This commonly used phrase in the annals of the so-called new old age fills me with rage, because the proximity of old age to death is not only undefiable but undeniable. Anger, by the way, is another emotion considered inappropriate in the old; the dubious notion of the "wisdom of old age" rests on the belief that elders can, and should, transcend the passions, vaulting ambition, and competitiveness of their younger adult lives and arrive at some sort of peace that passeth all understanding.

The capacity to negotiate between the past and the present, not transcendence of the emotions and desires that have made us who we are, is the proper definition of aging with dignity. The great Russian-born dancer Mikhail Baryshnikov, who once seemed to float above stage and earth as the preeminent male classical ballet star of his generation, bravely called himself a "dancing fossil" on the *Today* show. Having just turned sixty, he described the role of the older dancer as that of "a mediator between your memories and your [current] abilities as a human skeleton." This unromantic description of successful aging is applicable not only to nature's blessed exceptions, who figure so prominently in most prescriptions for age-defying behavior, but to anyone whose intense desire for meaningful experience remains undiminished by a realistic recognition of time's indelible, deepening imprint. The search for new, earthbound ways to express lifelong passions—not to transcend them in some mythical metamorphosis that seems more akin to a heavenly ascension—demands the most arduous efforts from and offers the most rich rewards for every aging human skeleton. Anyone who has outlived his or her passions has lived too long. Wordsworth got it exactly right, at the tender age of thirty-seven, in his "Ode: Intimations of Immortality from Recollections of Early Childhood": *O joy! That in our embers / Is something that doth live, / That nature yet remembers / What was so fugitive!*

Never Say Die

CHAPTER ONE

Never Say Old

The last time I saw my grandmother Minnie Broderick, in the summer of her hundredth year, we sat on a riverbank, ate turkey sandwiches, and watched children playing on the grass. A small boy tossed a beach ball in our direction. Gran tried to rise from her chair and throw the ball back, but she was too frail to stand without help. Collapsing backward, she said, in a soft voice devoid of either self-pity or anger, "The worst thing about having lived too long is you know you are of absolutely no use to anyone." It was agonizing for me to hear my grandmother say this, because she defined herself by her usefulness. She always seemed to know, without being told, what other people needed. When I was twenty years old and landed my first job as a reporter for *The Washington Post,* I did not have an appropriate workplace wardrobe or the money to buy new clothes. Gran took me to a chic store in Chicago and bought me a bright pink wool dress with a matching, businesslike jacket—an outfit that I wore for years because it made me feel like a combination of Jackie Kennedy and Nancy Dickerson (one of the few female correspondents on network television at the time). Gran was in her sixties then, but well into her nineties, she lived in her own apartment in East Lansing, Michigan, cooked her own meals, grew her own tomatoes, and did regular exercises every morning so that her bones and muscles would allow her to accomplish whatever tasks she had planned for the rest of the day. But eventually she did live too long to care for herself, and my mother, who was in her seventies and had significant health problems of her own, was physically unable to provide the extensive help that would have been needed to keep her mother out of a nursing home. Even while we were enjoying the beautiful August day by the river, Gran and I both knew that I would soon have to return her to a facility where she was one of only a handful of residents who still had a working brain.

A few months later, just short of her hundredth birthday, Gran died. Well-meaning people actually talked about what a tragedy it was that she had not lived long enough to blow out those hundred candles on a cake. I saw her death as a release from a purgatory much worse than any circle of hell. I wish that she had died while she was still living on her own, still taking walks, still baking her own blueberry muffins, still choosing what she wanted to eat, and still able to enjoy her meals without being surrounded by people barely able to feed themselves and too demented to carry on any kind of conversation. And yet, in many respects, my grandmother had what might be called a "good" old age and death. She had relatives who loved her and visited her regularly—foremost among them my mother, who was a tireless advocate for her mother with the nursing home's administrators. The home was then a relatively small, community-based facility with a compassionate staff. And many of the staff members paid special attention to Gran, in part because she was a lovable person and in part because she was one of the few inhabitants alert enough to take an interest in others and appreciate what they did for her. The tragedy was that she *had* outlived her usefulness—not only by other people's standards but, more important, by her own. She had lived too long to live well, and no assurances that she was loved could compensate for her own sense that she no longer made a difference in the lives of others. As more Americans live into their eighties, nineties, and beyond—if the actuarial tables are right and a social or ecological disaster does not intervene—my grandmother's fate awaits many of us whose lives are now so full of activities and obligations that we can barely imagine a time when too little rather than too much might be expected of us.

Only twenty years from now, when the oldest baby boomers will be eighty-five and the youngest sixty-seven, approximately seventy million Americans will be over sixty-five—with eight and a half million over eighty-five. By 2030, the U.S. Census Bureau predicts, those over sixty-five will make up 20 percent of the population—compared with about 13 percent today. Most important, the fastest-growing segment of the population is the over-eighty-five group. In 1975, Dr. Robert N. Butler, a pioneering gerontologist who later became the first director of the Institute on Aging at the National Institutes of Health, wrote a Pulitzer Prize–winning book, *Why Survive? Being Old in America,* in which he asserted that no one can know "whether we have already had the best years of our lives or whether the best are yet to come."[1] This was a welcome and necessary corrective to the dismal and monolithic stereotype of old age that had taken hold in mid-twentieth-century America, but it was based on a template that has much more validity for people in their sixties and seventies—the "young old"—than for the growing numbers of Americans who are now living into their late eighties and nineties, a group known to gerontologists and demographers as the "old old."

At sixty-five, the idea that the best years of our lives may still be ahead of us is certainly plausible even if it is not highly probable. At eighty-five or ninety—whatever satisfactions may still lie ahead—only a fool or someone who has led an extraordinarily unhappy life can imagine that the best years are still to come. As a people, we need to face reality and base both our individual planning and social policy on the assumption that by the time men and women reach their eighties and nineties, not the best but the worst years of their lives generally lie ahead. This is not to say that people in their ninth and tenth decades of life have nothing to look forward to or that they should give up on life, but that the difficulties of maintaining a purposeful and pleasurable everyday existence almost always increase—sometimes incrementally and sometimes, if catastrophic illness strikes, exponentially—with age. It is certainly possible that science may produce drugs—though not necessarily in time to help those already in their fifties and sixties—to alleviate some of the worst health problems of the old today. But to suggest that ninety may soon become the new fifty—the premise of a panel at the widely publicized annual World Science Festival held in New York City in 2008—is to engage in magical thinking. Such fantasies are far from harmless, especially to a baby boom generation whose sheer numbers are bound to strain the nation's social resources in ways that will be greatly exacerbated if boomers continue to underestimate the real difficulties of old age.

I am about to present a portrait of advanced old age that some will find too pessimistic and negative. The entire subject of old age is now surrounded by a fog of emotional correctness—a first cousin of political correctness and religious correctness—in which the very word "old" is seen as an expression of prejudice rather than a factual description of a stage of life. If this were a magazine or newspaper article, an editor would already have deleted the uncompromising three-letter word in favor of the less harsh-sounding *elderly* or *aging*. *Aging* is a particularly stupid euphemism for *old,* because while we are all aging, we are not all old. In the emotionally correct version of old age, superior wisdom supposedly compensates for any losses—whether of a beloved life partner or of one's own mental and physical powers. Dwelling on the inevitable losses of old age is considered a form of depression, to be treated in every case rather than respected, in some instances, as a realistic response to irremediable trouble, pain, and loss. I believe that an honest look at the prevalence of bad, worse, and worst-case scenarios is a precondition—*the* precondition—for figuring out how to improve those scenarios. We need to look at old old age as it is, not as the middle-aged and the young old would like it to be. In particular, we need to free ourselves from the all-too-prevalent baby boomer delusion that we can "beat this thing" (as one woman in her mid-forties declared at the conference devoted to proclaiming ninety the potential new fifty). Only when we abandon the fantasy of beating old age and feeling like a frisky fifty-year-old—or, better yet, a thirty-year-old—for the rest of our lives will we be capable of figuring out what needs to be done to enable mentally competent people like my grandmother to participate in society instead of being relegated to what amounted to a mental institution. And only then will we be able to develop more humane ways of caring for those whose mental and physical infirmities have made them totally dependent on others—those, to borrow the affecting phrase used by Senator Hubert H. Humphrey, in "the twilight of life and the shadows of life."

Since the 1960s, there has been a significant but bifurcated change in American attitudes toward old people. On the one hand, we recognize that many Americans over sixty-five—the now anachronistic age of retirement—are healthy, productive members of society. On the other hand, we refuse to think about the growing number of those who, in their ninth and tenth decades of life, are sick, removed from active intellectual and social life, and unable to take care of their most basic daily needs. When I was a child in the 1950s, old age was generally viewed as a dull and dreary time of life—something that began as soon as a man was forced to retire and returned home to bother his wife, whose main role was that of a babysitter for her grandchildren. If the image of parents having sex was unnerving, the image of grandparents having sex was unimaginable. Many of these attitudes began to change by the late 1960s, for two major reasons. First, Americans over sixty-five were influenced by the dissident spirit of the times. Plenty of grandparents marched for civil rights and against the Vietnam War; Dr. Benjamin Spock, the pediatrician and emblematic elder statesman of antiwar protest, had been born in 1903. The power of older voters played a major role in the passage of Medicare in 1965. By the early 1970s, when the Gray Panthers were founded by Maggie Kuhn, older Americans were becoming accustomed to using not only their votes but the tactics of younger social protesters. These new social activists coined the term "ageism" to describe discrimination against and negative stereotyping of the old.

The second and more important factor in the emergence of "gray power" was, of course, increasing longevity—attributable more to a general improvement in Americans' standard of living throughout the twentieth century than to specific medical advances. People born at the beginning of the twentieth century reached middle age before the first generation of antibiotics, and they survived childhood without any of the immunizations that would, in the second half of the century, all but eliminate once common killers like polio and diphtheria. The primary reason why so many babies born around 1900 reached their late sixties was not medical progress but social progress: they were better fed, better housed, and raised under better sanitary conditions than they would have been in the eighteenth and nineteenth centuries. When my grandmother was born in 1899, only about 4 percent of Americans were over sixty-five. By 1970, people over sixty-five accounted for 10 percent of the population. A critical mass had been reached, and the image of the old as a monolithic group characterized by inertia and often by senility began to change, albeit slowly and unevenly. In 1972, Kuhn shook up the General Assembly of the United Presbyterian Church (an institution for which she had worked many years before reaching compulsory retirement age and founding the Panthers to fight, among other practices, compulsory retirement) by telling the ministers that social activism and sex were the two most important components of a healthy old age. "Sex is a beautiful thing until rigor mortis sets in," Kuhn declared, adding that jokes about dirty old men and dirty old women were another manifestation of ageism.[2]

Today, received opinion insists that most of the problems associated with old age are not inevitable but the result of gerontophobia or ageism—the prejudicial and irrational exaltation of youth that devalues the wisdom, productivity, and usefulness of those who have lived beyond the biblical three score and ten. But the much needed debunking of stereotypically negative images of old age, which represents the positive side of attitudinal changes toward the old during the past four decades, has been accompanied by a new, more subtle, but no-less-pernicious form of ageism. American culture now exalts old people vigorous enough to shatter the stereotypes of the 1950s, but the fact that more people are managing to do so has driven us deeper into denial about the severe physical and mental infirmities frequently associated with the oldest phases of old age. The downplaying of these real disabilities, particularly the frightening explosion of cases of Alzheimer's disease, is coupled with an exaggeration of the capacity of science to perform medical miracles—if not this year, then surely next year. In this wishful scenario, a deus ex machina—embryonic stem cell research is cited most frequently—will soon intervene and produce a "cure" for Alzheimer's and other lethal age-related diseases. Then there will no longer be any reason to fear growing old.

At the June 2008 panel posing the question of whether nonagenarians might soon resemble middle-aged adults, the quivering enthusiasm of the audience in the sold-out hall was more reminiscent of a revival meeting than of a scientific discussion. The crowd was particularly excited after a presentation by David Sinclair, a Harvard Medical School researcher and cofounder of a pharmaceutical company, who was touting the life-extending and life-enhancing benefits of resveratrol, a substance found in red wine. When Sinclair showed a video of mice on resveratrol running harder and faster than untreated mice, he noted that the medicated mice had a lower incidence of Alzheimer's than ordinary mice. A woman next to me confided, "I'm about to wet my pants with excitement." She seemed not at all downcast when Sinclair acknowledged that the mice had received a daily dose of the substance equivalent to what, in a human, would be the amount of resveratrol in one thousand bottles of red wine. Sinclair's company, Sirtris Pharmaceuticals, was then testing compounds containing resveratrol for their impact on diabetes in humans. Such drugs cannot be tested for their anti-aging properties in clinical trials approved by the Food and Drug Administration because aging is not considered a disease by the FDA. In any case, a clinical trial lasting a few years could not, given the length of the average human life, reveal anything about whether a drug actually increases longevity. As it turned out, GlaxoSmithKline, the pharmaceutical giant that bought Sirtris for $720 million in 2008, stopped all tests on resveratrol-based drugs at the end of 2010 because the results in human clinical trials were unpromising. There is nothing surprising about the failure, because most drugs that work in mice do not work in men—a fact of which the crowd at the World Science Festival, excited by the possibility of endless youth and health, seemed blissfully ignorant.

That age ninety in the twenty-first century may turn out to be the same old ninety is a prospect that the hucksters of longevity refuse to entertain, and their refusal is dangerous in view of the demographic predictions of a major increase in the over-eighty-five population during the next two decades. "No one believes in the possibilities of science more than I do," Dr. Butler told me in 2008, "and I'd love nothing more than to wake up one morning and read a newspaper article announcing a cure for Alzheimer's. But we have to plan for aging as it *is*—not as it might be if a magic potion appears to wipe out the serious diseases associated with advanced old age."[3] Even more important, unquestioning faith in a medical "solution" to the "problem" of old age prevents realistic thinking about what can be done to ameliorate the economic and social conditions that impose additional burdens on old men and on even more old women who already suffer from serious health conditions. If we are counting on waking up tomorrow to the news that there is a cure for Alzheimer's, then there is no reason to seriously contemplate the changes we must make in health care in order to meet the needs of the oldest members of the enormous baby boom generation, who now are entering the age of high risk for this mind-shattering disease. Americans ought to think about making ninety not the new fifty but a better ninety than can be expected today. Furthermore, we need to pay less attention to expensive fantasies—from unending organ transplants to bionic replacement of every body part—to extend longevity for the few who will be able to afford such costly anti-aging measures and concentrate on improving the lives of the many who are ill-clothed, ill-housed, and ill-fed as soon as they are no longer able to hold a full-time job.

We cannot continue to base our image of old age on the extraordinary person, blessed by a combination of affluence and physiological hardiness, who remains "as sharp as a tack" and takes up a new, youthful hobby—say, skydiving—in her nineties. We cannot idealize the remarkable accomplishments of a few people who maintain their creative abilities and mental acuity into advanced old age as if those accomplishments were the norm. Yes, it was marvelous that Elliott Carter was still composing music at age 100 and was able to walk onstage at Carnegie Hall to enjoy the celebration of his centenary. It was splendid that the heart surgeon Michael DeBakey, who died in 2008 at age 99, still consulted on medical cases during his last decade; that the historian Arthur Schlesinger Jr., who died in 2007 at 89, was an active and influential public intellectual and prolific writer almost until the end; that Howard Zinn, an equally great historian who wrote about America from the perspective of the underdog, was exchanging quips with Jon Stewart on *The Daily Show* in the eighty-eighth and last year of his immensely productive life; that the abortion rights and voluntary euthanasia activist Ruth Proskauer Smith was teaching a course on the Supreme Court not long before she died at 102; that most of the centenarians who appear on the labels of Smucker's jam jars are still living independently and attributing their longevity to everything from faith to a daily glass of beer. Who does not admire and envy these fortunate old men and women who retain the physical and intellectual energy to play an active role in society throughout their lives? I call them fortunate because my grandmother's situation, as an ordinary person with serious health problems and ordinary financial resources, is more the rule than the exception for people who live into their tenth decade. For some years before her death, she was unable to do, even in attenuated form, most of the things that had given her life meaning. The iconic image of the sharp-as-a-tack, physically fit nonagenarian is the flip side of medical miracle stories about twelve-ounce premature babies who are saved by high-tech neonatal medicine and then go on to develop normally. Most of the tiniest preemies survive only with serious mental and physical disabilities, yet we invest disproportionate resources in medical efforts to save them while allowing millions of children to receive inadequate medical care simply because they are poor and because their parents have neither the education nor the money to provide their youngsters with a healthy start in life. Medicare will pay for surgery to keep a seriously ill ninety-year-old alive for a few more months, regardless of what quality of life she can expect, but it will not pay for regular at-home care from aides who might be able to help keep a frail but still-functional person the same age out of a nursing institution.

The selective diminution of ageism in recent years is ironically and inexorably linked with a social redefinition of people in their sixties and seventies as the "young old"—with the emphasis on "young." Betty Friedan, whose book *The Feminine Mystique* (1963) is rightly credited with the regeneration of American feminism, wrote *The Fountain of Age* (1993) in an effort to expose ageism as she had exposed sexism. Friedan conspicuously avoided the word "old" and noted that most Americans over sixty-five find it an objectionable term. That old people themselves dislike being called "old" attests only to the American fondness for euphemism; it does not make the term less accurate. No one objects to being called "young" unless the description is coupled with the modifier "too"—as in "too young to get married" or "too young to know what you're doing." For many Americans of all ages, the single, unmodified word "old" is enough to suggest disability—and they want no part of that suggestion. We apply the adjective "old" to family jewelry and trees with pride (does anyone call a redwood "elderly"?), but it is usually considered an insult to apply this perfectly honorable, precise description to a person. For the old themselves to avoid and denigrate the word "old" represents submission, not resistance, to cultural prejudice. In a massive work of 671 pages filled with hundreds of interviews, Friedan, who was seventy-two when her book was published, used almost no examples of people beyond their early seventies. (One exception was an interview with the octogenarian Maggie Kuhn.) Most of the hikers, mountain climbers—mountain climbing seems to figure prominently in books about the young old—and professionals enjoying active second careers were in their sixties. There is an endless list of coy terms intended to vanquish the idea that the old, however diverse their circumstances, share common problems simply because of their age. Harry R. Moody, the author of numerous books on the psychology and ethics of aging, came up with "wellderly" to describe the healthy old, as opposed to "illderly." What such distinctions do not acknowledge is that nearly all of the wellderly, if they live as long as my grandmother did, will turn into the illderly. Not even vast wealth offers real protection to the illderly, as demonstrated by the case of the renowned philanthropist Brooke Astor, who died of Alzheimer's at age 105. After her death in 2007, her 83-year-old son, Anthony Marshall, was indicted by a Manhattan grand jury for having taken advantage of his mother's mental condition to steal millions from her estate. Marshall, who may be as exceptional in his own way as a 100-year-old composer—given that the old are more frequently victims than perpetrators of crime—was convicted two years later after a lengthy trial.

In real old age, as opposed to fantasyland, most people who live beyond their mid-eighties can expect a period of extended frailty and disability before they die. Given the high proportion of illderly among the old old, the common boomer fantasy of dropping dead after a heart attack while making love at age ninety-five bears about as much relationship to the reality of old age as the earlier boomer fantasy of painless childbirth without drugs bore to the reality of labor as experienced by most women. Rosy predictions about the future of the wellderly depend on the statistically disingenuous practice of lumping together all people over sixty-five. We are told endlessly, for example, that Alzheimer's is not a part of normal aging but a disease—and the fact that only 10 percent of people over sixty-five have Alzheimer's is cited in support of this analysis. Alzheimer's is certainly a disease, but it is a disease, along with other types of dementia, that afflicts nearly half of Americans who live beyond eighty-five. There are more than seven times as many people over eighty-five with Alzheimer's as there are among the much larger American population between ages sixty-five and seventy-five.[4] How can a brain malady that affects nearly half of all people in the older age group *not* be considered a risk of "normal" aging? By calling Alzheimer's abnormal, we are really whistling in the dark and hoping that we will be in the lucky, dementia-free half. We are also assured that only 5 percent of Americans over sixty-five are confined to institutions. That's true, but anyone who lives beyond eighty-five has about a 50-50 chance of winding up in a nursing home—just as he or she has close to a 50 percent chance of developing dementia. The geriatrician Muriel R. Gillick, in *The Denial of Aging* (2006), describes the situation in unusually blunt terms. "The latest prediction is that if you are just now turning 65," Dr. Gillick explains, "you have nearly a 50 percent chance of spending some time in a nursing home before you die. Approximately

10 percent of these nursing home stays will be short-term, intended for recuperation after a hospitalization. The remainder will be for the long haul, with discharge to a funeral parlor, not to the family home."[5] This straightforward, clear-minded language is so rare among those in the "helping professions" that it startles a reader; Americans are much more accustomed to optimistic psychobabble assuring them that they can vanquish old age by taking the right supplements, discovering their spirituality, and keeping mentally active through the purchase of new, brain-challenging computer programs. The entire anti-aging industry might as well be called Canute Inc.

Needless to say, it is much more comfortable and comforting to think about the wellderly than about the invisible illderly in nursing homes. Corporate America has no interest in marketing its products (with the exception of nursing facilities themselves) to the illderly. Like Friedan, marketers today would never dream of using the word "old" or the phrase "old age" in any advertisement. And the media generally use images of old people who do not actually look old. Apart from the grizzled former surgeon general C. Everett Koop, who appears in a commercial for help-summoning devices recommended for old people who live alone, most actors and celebrities featured in advertisements for products designed for those over sixty-five seem to be as ageless as the Geico gecko. Nowhere is the cultural schizophrenia about old age more evident than in the proliferating television commercials for drugs designed to enhance male sexual performance. Medication to treat erectile dysfunction (impotence is another forbidden word) was intended primarily for men over sixty—or for younger men with diseases, like diabetes, that may impair potency at any age. The commercials for these drugs, however, routinely feature couples who appear no older than their forties. Thinning hair, flabby skin, jowls, skeletal-looking hands, liver spots, obvious osteoporosis—none of which, it should be emphasized, ought to prevent anyone from enjoying sex—are nowhere to be seen. Older consumers are encouraged to continue active sex lives, and to buy an expensive drug if the man needs it to function—but only if they do not have any of the obvious physical signs of old age. The spokesperson for the popular osteoporosis-prevention drug Boniva is the actress Sally Field, a slim woman in her sixties who looks twenty years younger (at least with professional makeup and a soft-focus lens) and is seen in television commercials playing with young children—

as if the real market for osteoporosis drugs consists of young mothers rather than women in menopause. In an updated version of the commercial, Field does admit that she is a grandmother—but her appearance channels Gidget. Nowhere in any commercial for any product or service is there an image of a woman crippled by osteoporosis, hunched over her walker trying to handle a bag of groceries (a scene I witness daily on the streets of New York). This woman does not exist in advertisements for medications or food, any more than she exists in ads for cosmetics—though she buys all of these products. To put someone who really looks old in an advertisement or commercial would be to draw attention to what the advertisers are trying to avoid—the fact that people are going to grow old, and visibly so, regardless of whatever drug they take, whatever they eat, and whatever "anti-aging" skin potion they buy.

What is being marketed, then, is not old age but a concept of aging that ends where the more disabling, restrictive stage of old age begins. Part of the process is the defining of middle age and old age upward, as not only average life expectancy at birth but life expectancy at sixty-five has risen. Typically, Americans in their fifties now call themselves middle-aged (although "middle-aged," like "old," is not a popular modifier). Given that few people are still walking around between ages 100 and 110, this self-definition of every age is more a state of mind than a statement of demographic reality. There is a proliferating business in Web sites, such as Livingto100.com and Eons.com, catering to boomers who want to increase their odds of living longer. The premise of all of these sites is that if you live right in midlife (or what the pro-longevity crowd insists is midlife), you will not experience old age as people have experienced it for generations and continue to experience it today. Linda Natansohn, senior vice president of strategic development for Eons in 2008, declared that "if you are a boomer, you have a gift. You are going to live 20 years or more on average than your grandparents did. If you are 50 now, you might live to be 100. . . . So you want to get some insight as to what you are doing right, and what you can do better."[6] Many of these Web sites calculate probable life expectancy based on current habits; there are actually two unrelated "death clock" sites—DeathClock.com and DeathClock.org. RealAge.com, a health media company endorsed by such celebrity doctors as Mehmet Oz, a cardiac surgeon and professor at Columbia University College of Physicians and Surgeons, does something slightly different: instead of predicting longevity, it assesses the difference between a person's chronological age and a "real age" based on lifestyle factors. The RealAge test asks some 150 questions about everything from alcohol consumption to family history and then makes "personalized" recommendations about how to achieve a younger score. Many of the recommendations, such as eating a good breakfast and brushing and flossing after every meal, are no more useful or controversial than the directives mothers give to small children. But if people who take the RealAge test sign up for its regular emails, the communications will often include advertisements from drug companies and supplement manufacturers aggressively marketing their latest products to potential customers with a supposedly elevated risk for certain diseases.

Dr. Oz himself took the injudicious step of suggesting, on *The Oprah Winfrey Show,* that people might someday take anti-aging pills to deal with everything from wrinkles to dementia. Needless to say, there is no effective, scientifically tested anti-aging pill for humans at this time—only unregulated, unproven, untested supplements. Online peddlers of resveratrol supplements quickly seized on Oz's comment to imply that he had endorsed their products. The doctor, who now has his own television talk show, expressed indignation when his image was appropriated by the supplement industry, but I think that he left himself wide open for the misappropriation by his participation in an operation like RealAge, which is selling the decidedly unrealistic idea that it is possible to "reverse" aging by clean living.[7] That a nationally respected surgeon would become a fellow traveler to this bandwagon says much about the susceptibility of doctors, as well as the medically uneducated, to hopes for the discovery of a fountain of youth. Andy Mikulak, vice president for marketing at RealAge, notes that his company's "primary product is an e-mail newsletter series focused on the undiagnosed at-risk patient, so we know the risk factors if someone is prehypertensive, or [at risk] for osteoarthritis."[8] You thought you were feeling fine? Since the chief risk factor for arthritis is age itself, it must be thrilling to receive e-mails with ads touting the benefits of prescription anti-inflammatory drugs long before you have any need for them. Are you a woman in her late thirties who is having heavy menstrual periods and dealing with them by using an extra tampon or sanitary napkin? You may be targeted by an ad for a medical company pushing a treatment that removes the lining of the uterus in menstruating women who already have all the children they want. If you change your mind and want to have another child before menopause, tough luck. "Prehypertensive" represents a particularly aggressive type of marketing; it is the equivalent of "pre-need" (meaning you're not dead yet) in the funeral business. It is undeniable that everyone with hypertension must, at one point, have been "prehypertensive." Just as all among the living are "pre-need," we are all "pre-sick." What is so meretricious about this type of marketing is that it plays on the combination of longevity worship and the misplaced conviction of so many baby boomers that there is a preventive or cure for everything—even age-related diseases that one might or might not develop at some point in the future.

Longevity enthusiasts, especially in the boomer generation, never ask whether a longer life will necessarily be a gift; most are convinced that they can bend old age to their will through their own good behavior, reinforced by a little help from Big Pharma. There is a breathtaking arrogance about this assumption, coupled with a denial of the role that accidents, of both genetics and environment, play in the health of human beings at every stage of life. Boomers can do everything right—exercise regularly and heartily, eat organic foods, cuddle warm puppies, and eliminate unnecessary stress from their lives (although that is certainly easier said than done)—and nevertheless find themselves in the unfortunate half of those over eighty-five who need a huge amount of help in their daily lives. They can strive to improve memory—through playing mentally demanding games, mastering complicated computer programs, and learning a foreign language or a new skill like playing the piano—and nevertheless descend into the inferno of irreversible dementia. As John Updike observed when Ronald Reagan was dying of Alzheimer's, the former president had become "a haze of pure existence, unencumbered by any memory of his venturesome life or even by his faithful wife's name, while his own name, thanks to his grateful party, is attached to the capital's airport and a huge downtown building of appropriately vague purpose. He haunts the national village; he warns us of what, even with salubrious amounts of brush-cutting and horseback-riding and plenty of sleep, can happen."[9] Live too long, and most of us will be carried off by heart or vascular disease, cancer or Alzheimer's—and not in an instant, a week, or a month but over a lengthy, excruciating period of time. Dr. Sherwin B. Nuland, a retired surgeon and distinguished historian of medicine, describes the "universal processes that we will all experience as we are dying." These include "stoppage of circulation, the inadequate transport of oxygen to tissues, the flickering out of brain function, the failure of organs, the destruction of vital centers . . . the weapons of every horseman of death." These paths to death, Nuland emphasizes, "are trod by everyone, no matter the rarity of the final disease."[10] At any age, the pathways may be direct or indirect, but the prevalence of chronic, degenerative, irreversible diseases in advanced old age ought to give pause to those promoting the belief that a long life, if one does everything possible to take care of oneself, is likely to be a healthy, self-sufficient life.

Ageism is a charge that will inevitably be leveled against anyone who questions the unrealistically cheery image of old age presented not only by the media but by the pharmaceutical establishment, which stands to profit from the discovery of a fountain of youth based on credible science (even if the anti-aging benefits of that fountain prove as marginal as the benefits of currently available drugs approved by the Food and Drug Administration in the vain hope that they might delay the destructive progress of Alzheimer's). One of the more nausea-inducing drug pitches of the past five years was an endlessly repeated television commercial for Aricept—a prescription medication approved by the FDA for the treatment of Alzheimer's but found, in a British study (a major research endeavor not financed by drug companies), to have no significant demonstrable effect on patients' functioning or on the length of time between diagnosis and mental deterioration so severe that it leads to a nursing home.* One commercial showed a smiling man at the dinner table surrounded by his loving family. Two equally sunny middle-aged daughters expressed their faith that Aricept was helping their father "be more like himself." Dad was never shown struggling to come up with familiar words, deciding painfully whether to butter his bread with a knife or a fork, forgetting that socks need to be put on

* A randomized study of 565 patients published in 2004 in the British medical journal *The Lancet* found that after three years Alzheimer's patients taking Aricept had exactly the same rate of mental disability and risk of being institutionalized as patients taking a placebo. The groups also showed no differences in behavioral symptoms, such as inability to speak or perform everyday tasks, and there was no difference in the reported emotional well-being of family caretakers.

before shoes, getting lost a block from his own home, or flying into a rage out of frustration at his inability to perform a multitude of everyday tasks that used to be second nature—all common characteristics of people in the middle stages of Alzheimer's. Never mind. No television commercial would want to show what, inevitably, comes next in the degenerative progress of the disease.

The media's focus on healthy, well-off sixty-somethings as models of what aging can and should be like for everyone has fostered a selective form of ageism that differs from the more universal ageism of my youth. Writing for magazines aimed at older audiences for the past twenty years, I have made my own contribution to constructing a template of old age that minimizes the plight of those who are frail, poor, or both, and one of the reasons I am writing this book is that I came to feel, especially as I saw the real, not-for-prime-time struggles of much older friends, that I was presenting a half-truth that amounted to a lie. When the *AARP Bulletin* assigned me to write an article about people over fifty who had made major improvements in their health habits (often after a life-threatening crisis), I immediately thought about a high school friend, Janet Coleman, who had beaten the odds by surviving major surgery for metastasized bladder cancer, followed by arduous and lengthy chemotherapy. Janet then proceeded to lose fifty pounds. The picture accompanying the article showed my gorgeous fifty-six-year-old friend playing golf and looking (truly) not recognizably different from the high school cheerleader she once was. Janet was the youngest person I interviewed for the article; the oldest was sixty-four. Some years later, another close friend was stricken with the same type of cancer at age seventy-five and had to undergo the same radical surgery, requiring full removal of the bladder, that Janet had endured. Unlike Janet, my seventy-five-year-old friend was never the same afterward. She did not recover her physical strength, or the vigorous quality of life she enjoyed before the operation, although she tried valiantly to do so as she went through repeated rounds of chemotherapy. There was to be no happy ending for my septuagenarian friend, who lived just another two years—even though her cancer was supposedly in a less advanced stage than Janet's at the time of diagnosis. The most obvious difference between the two stories, one with a happy ending and one with an unhappy ending, is the age of the women when they began their battles. It is simply dishonest to paint a portrait of old age in which men and women, as they move closer to their eighties and nineties, can expect the same results from medical procedures that people can expect in their forties, fifties, and sixties. And even though changes in health habits (such as weight loss and exercise) are beneficial at any age for their own sake, they will not necessarily keep us from our appointed death. AARP, arguably the most effective lobby in Washington, mirrors the conflicted attitudes of American society about old age. There is a disconnect between the organization's media strategy—which highlights the "young old" and the most fortunate among the "old old"—and its core mission of preserving and extending government entitlements for the majority that needs economic help badly. AARP succeeded mightily in riding out the anti-government waves that prevailed throughout the administrations of Ronald Reagan and George W. Bush, but it will face an even bigger challenge as the proportion of the old population expands while politicians, especially but not only on the right, tout cuts in Medicare and Social Security as the easiest way to reduce the federal deficit. The endlessly cheerful portraits of independent young old people—who don't look like they need anything from anyone—living and loving lives that do not seem diminished at all is not well suited to sensitizing Americans of all ages to the plight of those among the old who need so much that they do not have.

Just as the media tend to focus on the healthy young old, they also tend to focus on those whose race, education, and economic class have given them the best possible chance for what gerontologists and sociologists call successful aging. In an article that featured predictable examples of sixty- to eighty-year-old skydivers, mountain climbers, and rock climbers, a writer for the *Los Angeles Times* described the "new old" as a population consisting of those who "have led active and healthy lifestyles, who have benefited from recent medical advances or are simply genetically blessed with good health in advanced age. They are the cutting edge of what experts say will soon be considered the norm."[11] What the article failed to mention was that most of these blessedly healthy "new old" are financially secure white men and women who have an even greater advantage over the poor and members of minorities in old age than they did when they were younger. In 2008, several major studies showed that although overall life expectancy was still increasing, the life expectancy gap between the rich and the poor—and between those with the lowest and highest levels of education—had actually widened since the 1980s. In 180 counties in some of the poorest areas of the nation, including the Deep South and Appalachia, life expectancy declined—by 4 percent for men and a startling 19 percent for women.[12] The sharp drop for women was attributed to rising rates of obesity and smoking. Many of the diseases that create the poorest health outlook for the old—including diabetes, chronic pulmonary illnesses, and some of the most common types of cancer—are directly linked to the poor education, poor nutrition, and poor medical care that are part of the culture of poverty in this country. African Americans, for example, are twice as likely as whites to develop Type 2 diabetes, for which obesity is a major risk factor—and obesity is much more prevalent among the poor of all races than it is among those with higher incomes. Blacks with diabetes are also much more likely than whites to suffer serious complications as a result of their disease; they are twice as likely to go blind and have a limb amputated and six times as likely to develop serious kidney disease. One in four black women over fifty-five has diabetes, which may explain why black women rarely appear in features on skydiving and surfing clubs for seniors. Even if the most wildly optimistic predictions about the emergence of drugs to slow down the aging process prove true, such pharmacological innovations will do little to help a diabetic eighty-year-old African American woman who has already lost a foot or her sight to a lifetime of poor nutrition, poor education, and poor medical care. Leaving aside those who are "simply genetically blessed," old people who have benefited the most from recent medical advances tend to be those who were dealt a better economic hand at every stage of their lives. Rather than focus on the dubious benefits of increasing longevity through pharmacology or bionic body parts, we would do better to focus as a society on correcting the social inequities that begin at birth and only intensify with every decade. It is undeniably worse to be poor and sick at eighty than at fifty, but the reasons why it is worse have little to do with ageism and everything to do with more general issues of racial and economic inequality. The crowd at the panel on whether ninety would become the new fifty was almost entirely white.

There is also a vast class disparity between the thinking of relatively well-off professionals about retirement and that of people who have spent a lifetime in low-paying, often physically taxing jobs. Raising the age of eligibility for full Social Security benefits—a process that has already begun and will affect everyone born after 1943—is one of the most common solutions offered for the coming financial crunch as retirees make up an increasing proportion of the American population. Second careers and part-time work are suggested to promote not only the financial but also the emotional and psychological well-being of the old. I cannot imagine retiring unless I am forced to—which would mean being "fired" by the reading public—and I am in favor of later retirement and second careers as a general proposition. However, advocates of early retirement and/or second careers fail to take into account the vastly different life experiences of blue-collar and white-collar Americans. Consider a description in *The New York Times* of the enviable life of Dr. Peter I. Pressman, a respected breast cancer surgeon who retired from the operating room at age sixty-eight. Pressman soon discovered that full-time retirement was not for him. "I needed more structure in my life," he said. "I also missed the ongoing relationships with my patients and the intellectual and social stimulation from interacting with colleagues." When Weill Cornell Medical Center in Manhattan asked him to develop a genetic risk assessment program to help women with a strong family history of breast cancer, he jumped at the chance. "I'm in the clinic two days a week and see every patient personally," he said. "With this commitment, I find I structure my time better and get to do a lot more."[13] Such possibilities are always open to healthy people with a lifetime of professional knowledge that remains useful to others. But what if Dr. Pressman were the equally gifted medical massage therapist, now in her late sixties, who saved me from disabling back pain in my thirties? My friend is still working in a doctor's office—she was never paid much, because insurance companies do not reimburse, in most cases, for massage—even though she has severe arthritis in her hands as a result of decades of hard physical labor. No one is going to offer her a cushy office and a large salary to develop a program advising people about how to avoid back pain—although she is well qualified to do so. Her body reveals the effects of a lifetime of physically taxing work, and her vast knowledge is not valued as highly as that of a retired doctor, lawyer, or architect. There are people—many, many people—who *need* to retire because their bodies can no longer bear the strain of what they do for a living. We cannot "fix" Social Security by deciding that all people ought to work into their seventies or eighties and if they can't, well, they must have done something wrong to be in such bad shape. One wonders whether people would be so enthusiastic about extending longevity if they remembered that adults in midlife (at least in the United States) are generally expected to work more than forty hours a week.

Thus, the myth of young old age—or new old age—as the norm presents a formidable obstacle to any effort to deal pragmatically with the social, economic, and medical problems associated with real old age. The notion that all old people are capable of working longer—much longer—to earn their keep encourages procrastination about the difficult political decisions that must be made in order to preserve Social Security and Medicare for Americans living today as well as for generations yet unborn. The moralistic premise that everyone, whether a nonunion maid in a hotel or a billionaire CEO, ought to be able to save enough money to finance a thirty-year retirement is plainly ludicrous. Yet as the financial crisis deepened in 2008, nearly all of the advice about how to save more, whether dispensed online, on television, or in print, was aimed at upper-middle-class Americans with disposable income. I watched one consumer segment after another on morning television news shows (which target their "soft" lifestyle features to women presumed to be at home), and they generally suggested that the way to save for retirement was to cut frivolous spending on unnecessary items. I look at television correspondents and anchors making hundreds of thousands to millions of dollars a year, and I wonder how they can keep straight faces while delivering consumer advice based on their own ample incomes. Tell it to the half of American families whose yearly income is under $61,000. Tell it to single mothers in low-wage jobs with no employer-paid pension benefits. Tell it to people whose jobs provide no health insurance and who have maxed out their credit cards not on flat-screen televisions but on overdue medical bills (the number one cause of personal bankruptcy in the United States). The false yet widely held belief that only moral turpitude prevents Americans from saving enough also blinds us to the fact that many of the poorest old have been poor all of their lives and could not possibly have saved enough money for retirement. And many of the oldest old, regardless of how much they put aside as middle-aged adults, are bound to outlive their savings unless they possess vast wealth.

As I write, one of the financial victims of longevity has been saved by private donations, thanks to a *Washington Post* article about a 107-year-old man who was about to be evicted from his assisted living facility in Fredericksburg, Virginia. Larry "Curly" Haubner, who had worked at everything from stacking lumber to serving as a doorman in a New York apartment building, was in good health and lived alone in his own house until age 102. Then he fell off his bicycle and had to be moved to an assisted living facility, where people have their own rooms and do not require skilled nursing care. His neighbors took up a collection for him then, because his Social Security income could not begin to cover the cost of a private assisted living home. Well, no one expected that the money would run out, because, after all, Haubner was already 102. But at 107, as the *Post* reported, Haubner was faced with the prospect of applying for Medicaid, which would require him to move to a skilled nursing facility that he does not need because he is in generally good health. *Post* readers contributed more than $56,000, which will pay for Haubner to stay in his assisted living home for another two years. "It's incredibly heartwarming that during this tough economic time for everybody, these people have found it in their hearts to donate the way that they have," said the lawyer who manages Haubner's financial affairs."[14] This is indeed a heartwarming story for one old man who had the good fortune to attract extensive media attention. But many invisible people, mainly women in their eighties and nineties, face exactly the same situation as Haubner, and there is no one to help them when they fall off their bicycles—or simply run through their life savings. Not long after the Haubner story, the *Los Angeles Times* ran an article about a ninety-seven-year-old homeless woman, Bessie Mae Berger, living in a 1973 Chevrolet Suburban with her two sons in their sixties—one severely disabled and the other once employed as a full-time caregiver for his mother through a state program that no longer exists. She worked as a packer for a biscuit manufacturing company until she was in her sixties, and her lifetime wages were so low that her Social Security checks could not pay the rent for even a one-room apartment in California. She was not eligible for any housing subsidies because she and her sons were determined to stay together. She augmented her Social Security by begging, in spite of police warnings not to do so, and many passersby refused to believe that she was nearly 100—although she was born six weeks before the sinking of the *Titanic* in 1912.[15] Either Bessie Mae Berger is a less sympathetic needy old person than Larry Haubner or Los Angeles is a generally less sympathetic community to the needy—if they present themselves in person—than southern Virginia. Whatever the explanation, there is something truly askew about the priorities of a society in which researchers enthrall wealthy audiences with the possibilities of increasing longevity through science while adequate provisions are not made for the housing of old people who need help today. As long as we indulge (and exculpate) ourselves with the conviction that medicine will enable every old person to remain healthy enough to take care of himself or herself, as long as we consider individuals morally culpable for not having earned enough money to finance their ninth or tenth decade of life, we will never face up to our obligation to provide for old people as they are.

In similar fashion, the belief that a magic potion to cure serious age-related diseases is just around the corner impedes the preparations that must be made to care, in a more humane way, for growing numbers of mentally impaired old people who will be unable to take care of themselves in the next two decades. This is not an argument against cutting-edge research but in favor of realism about the complex and difficult nature of the scientific quest for a way to combat the worst diseases of the old. That embryonic stem cell research is unlikely to produce cures for diseases like Alzheimer's in time to help aging baby boomers makes it more, not less, important to invest in science today. There may be a promising pathway for researchers in new methods, including analyses of spinal fluid, to identify biological markers for Alzheimer's before any symptoms develop, but it would be foolish to count on the fruits of such research being available to delay or prevent the onset of symptoms in middle-aged or "young old" Americans whose bodies now contain the seeds of this fatal brain disease. By all means let us forge ahead with biomedical research, but let us do so with the understanding that, for the foreseeable future, an expanding population of the dependent oldest old will continue to need more help than our society currently provides.

Finally, all Americans—not only the old, but those who are on the threshold of the transition to young old age—must take an unflinching look at the consequences, for both individuals and society, of using every tool of modern medicine to extend what have already been very long lives. Not long after I began writing this book, a front-page article appeared in *The New York Times* about 104-year-old Hazel Homer, a Long Island woman who, just a month before her hundredth birthday, underwent surgery, at a cost of some $35,000 to Medicare, to install a special defibrillator and pacemaker in her failing heart. The surgeon who performed the operation, Dr. Steven M. Greenberg, said proudly that Mrs. Homer was "just a peek into the future." Greenberg acknowledged that he "wouldn't have wanted to advertise" the procedure until he knew how long Mrs. Homer would continue to live. "People pay more for their BMW," he added, "which will not save their life." In the extra four years that Mrs. Homer was granted, she shifted from living alone to requiring the full-time services of a home health care aide—all very well if one can afford a live-in aide, which Medicare does not pay for. She was confined to a wheelchair and had both failing vision and hearing—not exactly the picture of healthy aging touted by longevity enthusiasts. But just how healthy can anyone reasonably expect to be at 104? Asked by the *Times* reporter what she likes most about her life, Mrs. Homer replied: "That I'm alive, I guess. That's the big thing. That I'm alive."[16] It is reasonable, not heartless, to raise the question of whether just remaining alive, as long as expensive medical procedures make it possible, is a worthy goal. If that sounds like a harsh observation coming from someone in her early sixties, I can only say that my mother, at eighty-eight, was even more appalled by Mrs. Homer's story than I was. And my mom has lived long enough, and endured enough of the real health problems of old old age, to have a reality-based view of aging not available to younger people who actually believe that age can be defied. "You'll change your attitude if you live to be ninety" is the most common response to my skepticism about the virtues of promoting longevity. This platitude assumes that anyone who does not view extreme longevity as personally or socially desirable must be unaware that a fierce desire to continue living, even in what for many becomes a vale of tears and torment, is built into our species.

I am quite certain that if I live into my nineties, I will—like my mother and grandmother before me—make the best of things. My mother's way of making the best of things, like her mother's, involves an unsparing candor about the vicissitudes of old old age—and their views have certainly played a powerful role in shaping mine. I am horrified by Hazel Homer's story—and by the doctor who thinks that enabling a one-hundred-year-old to live four more years is a great achievement—not because I think that the old should shuffle off the stage of life for the convenience of the young but because implanting an expensive artificial device in a centenarian who is barely able to see and cannot walk epitomizes a health care system based on the premise that aggressive steps should be taken to extend life at any cost. I am referring not only to the financial cost—although it is significant—but to the psychic cost, to an individual as well as to a society, of reflexively adopting a pro-longevity posture. Longevity enthusiasts simply brush aside the reality of old old age today and base their proposals on the assumption that future generations of centenarians will *not* be confined to a life in a wheelchair as their sight grows dim and their hearing fails. The myth of young old age does not allow for the real old old age of people like Mrs. Homer—much less the worse fate of those whose bodies are shells for brains that no longer function.

I should say for the record, in view of the noxious charges initiated by the far right about universal health care as an attempt to impose euthanasia on seniors through "death panels," that as much as I disagree with Mrs. Homer's choice, I think that it was her choice to make. I am deeply concerned, however, by doctors who are not candid with patients, whatever their age, about their chances of survival after a specific treatment or procedure or about the quality of life they can expect if the operation is a "success." I think that for every old person who wants "everything done" to live just one more day, week, month, or year, there are many more old people, like my mother, who care more about the quality of their lives than about merely staying alive. The mentally competent old, like the mentally competent young, are perfectly capable (arguably more capable than the young, who do not know what being old means) of making sound decisions about their own care. But the old are frequently denied adequate information about the consequences of continuing aggressive medical intervention, because the downside is sugarcoated by doctors who are themselves reluctant to face mortality. The middle-aged, not the old, are the instigators and disseminators of most of the pop culture gibberish about the wonders of the new old age.

The current myth of young old age is the logical outgrowth of another American myth, which harks back to a time that never was—an era in which most Americans supposedly grew up in three-generation households and communities in which the wisdom of age was venerated by all. In this America, young people supposedly respected their elders and looked after them in their own homes. If only the middle-aged would live up to their traditional responsibilities, as they did in the good old days, the survival of more and more people into a stage in life where they can no longer take care of themselves would not be a problem. But, as Dr. Robert Butler notes, "the lamented family of the past had many children and was largely a two-generational family, horizontal in character with many brothers and sisters, uncles and aunts; boarders were sometimes counted as family. It was also a family routinely affected by the deaths of its younger members, as many mothers died in childbirth and young children did not live to adulthood."[17] Nearly 25 percent of nineteenth-century children had lost at least one parent. In the early decades of the twentieth century, children still had less than a 40 percent chance of having two living grandparents.

At this point in the history of longevity, a majority of American children have not just two but four living grandparents. In the past, there was no need to construct a myth about the vitality and independence of the very old because so few people lived long enough to present the obvious needs that tend to arouse guilt in the younger generation. Today, with the pain and need of the most dependent elderly staring us in the face, we ignore the evidence before our eyes and choose to believe that nearly all of our oldest elders are capable of leading fully independent lives—as we fantasize that we will be too. We cling to the hope that medical science and our own attentiveness to our bodies will keep us among the wellderly for as long as we all shall live.

CHAPTER TWO

Youth Culture: An American Tradition

In many books about aging during the past two decades, America's youth culture is described as an aberrant product of the twentieth century. Conventional wisdom assumes that there is a sharp contrast between the current American dread of growing old and a halcyon past in which Americans venerated their elders and deferred to the wisdom, experience, and authority of old age. "Until relatively recently," one psychologist argues, "the old, more than any other age group, controlled power, assumed leadership, and set the example for others. In the early centuries of American history, in nearly every aspect of community, family, and work life, old people reigned. Only during the 20th century have they temporarily been knocked to the mat, viewed largely as a social burden."[1] This statement is demonstrably false, but it fits neatly with the idea that ageism is responsible for most of the problems of the old today. As many scholars have noted, the small number of people who survived into their sixties did enjoy high status in the colonial era, especially in the Puritan colonies of New England. But there were not enough old people in the seventeenth and eighteenth centuries for anyone to view them as a major social burden. In 1790, when the first census was taken in the United States, half of Americans were under sixteen, and only about 2 percent were over sixty-five.[2] Life, at every age, was fragile and susceptible to being snuffed out at any moment.

At a 1710 funeral service for a fellow minister who died at the ripe age of seventy-eight, a Boston preacher reminded his congregation of the many fatal misfortunes that might befall a person, regardless of age.

> We don't know when we shall die, nor do we know when such and such about us shall die. Young persons don't know that they

> shall live to be old, 'tis likely many of them will never live to Old Age; for, undeniable experience shows, that death snatches away the young as well as the old. Some are still-born, born dead; some live but a few hours in the world, and then pass into eternity; some live a few months, some a very few years, and yet die Children. Some die in youth, when young, hale, strong and vigorous; death comes and frees them from time to eternity. . . . The youngest and strongest know not that they have one more day to live. . . . So the Ancient, the decrepit can infer, that it maybe expect death every day. . . . We shall therefore strive to govern well our affects, and to be in readiness to part with . . . Dearest Relatives and Friends, whenever God pleaseth.[3]

Given the very real possibility that one might, at any age, be snatched into the next world at any moment, it is hardly surprising that in the Puritan moral universe advanced old age was considered a special sign of God's favor. The fire-and-brimstone preacher Increase Mather, observing that God was the authority who conferred the "crown" of old age, went on, in a famous sermon, to argue that seniority meant superiority. "Indeed the infirmities of Old Age are the effect of Sin," Mather said, "but Age itself comes from none but God. . . . If any man is favoured with long life, it is God that has lengthened his days. . . . God has put honour upon Age. . . . If there is cause to reprove [an old man], you must consider that he is a Father, and therefore not use harsh language, but treat him with that decency that becomes his *Seniority,* and in respect of his Age, *Superiority.*"[4] Yet most Puritan ministers exalted the elderly not for their putative wisdom or accumulation of experience but simply because they were close to death—and therefore to eternal life. They were living examples of the transience and inevitable decay of the body and, consequently, of the advisability of focusing attention on one's immortal soul rather than on finite earthly pleasures.

The revolutionary era, with its political emphasis on the natural rights of all men and a philosophical bias in favor of Enlightenment deism and liberal, less hierarchical forms of Protestantism, fostered a much less reverential attitude toward the old; the idea that seniority equals superiority could not have been more antithetical to the views of the relatively young men who made the Revolution. Thomas Jefferson was thirty-four when he wrote the Declaration of Independence in 1776. George Washington was a venerable forty-four; John Adams, forty; John Hancock, thirty-nine; James Madison twenty-five; Alexander Hamilton just twenty-one. Of the men regarded today as the most august of the founding fathers, only Benjamin Franklin, at seventy, was old enough to be considered old—even by the standards of his own society—when the United States declared its independence from Great Britain. Implicitly and explicitly, the Revolution was an attack on hereditary privilege as the governing principle of society. Thomas Paine, who was thirty-nine when he wrote the revolutionary polemic *Common Sense* in 1776, would later argue in *The Rights of Man* (1791) that equality among generations was a necessary component of the more general idea that all men are endowed with certain unalienable rights. The old deserved no special authority simply because of their age, and the dead could not impose their will on the living. "Every age and generation must be as free to act for itself, *in all cases,* as the ages and generations which preceded it," Paine declared. "The vanity and presumption of governing beyond the grave, is the most ridiculous and insolent of all tyrannies. Man has no property in man; neither has any generation a property in the generations which are to follow."[5]

One of the more convincing demonstrations of the shifting American attitude toward age in the postrevolutionary era was a change in the traditional seating arrangements of New England meetinghouses, where town business was conducted. Before the mid-eighteenth century, most New England towns adhered to the practice of "seating the meeting" by giving the most prominent seats to older men, followed by wealthy men (in the order of their wealth), and, last and least, "useful men (by degrees of usefulness—however that might be measured in a particular locale). By the 1790s, towns throughout New England had reversed the order of precedence, and wealth came before age. This was not, of course, the reversal of order that the egalitarian Paine had in mind in *The Rights of Man*. The towns even auctioned off meetinghouse seats to the highest bidder.[6] The historian David Hackett Fischer, whose *Growing Old in America* (1977) offers what I consider the most astute portrait of the increasing negativism toward old age in the early republican United States, presents this change in the New England town meetinghouses as a prime piece of evidence for his views about the relationship between the Revolution and the rise of youth culture. In a review of Fischer's book, Lawrence Stone (a historian of premodern England, not of the United States) pooh-poohed the ageist implications of the New England meetinghouse shift and attributed the change largely to a more rigid economic hierarchy that emerged after the Revolution.[7] While the distribution of wealth in the early 1800s is beyond the scope of this book (although there is a strong argument to be made that Stone was confusing or conflating circumstances in America and England), there was certainly no institution in early America that reflected public views more directly than the New England town meeting. It is difficult to imagine a more revealing statement of public opinion than the approval of auctions that sold the seats of the oldest to the richest members of the community.

Although most Americans in the early 1800s did not live into what is considered old age today, there were enough old people—especially in New England, which had a higher standard of living than the Southern and most of the Middle Atlantic states—to leave a record of the isolation and economic struggles attached to living beyond age fifty, as well as the biblical three score and ten. Men and women who had not succumbed to childhood infections, and women who had survived childbirth, could often expect to live into their sixties and seventies and even into their eighties. As survivors of common diseases that could not be prevented and for which there was no treatment, old people in the late eighteenth and early nineteenth centuries must have been among the hardiest members of the species. Yet old age—then as now—often meant economic hardship. There was no state or national assistance for the elderly poor in the early republic, and some townships actually auctioned off impoverished old residents to farm owners in need of workers. This callous measure, which lasted in some areas into the 1820s, was designed to defray the cost to local taxpayers of caring for those who had no nearby relatives to take responsibility.[8] Paula A. Scott, in a groundbreaking study focusing on households in Hartford, Connecticut, from 1790 to 1830, makes a convincing case that social mobility and the breakdown of hierarchical family structures after the Revolution meant that many Americans who did live to be old were on their own when it came to making their way through the closing years of life. "Though we often think of the United States in this era as communally and family based," she argues, "evidence on the elderly's lives shows that to a large extent constructing old age was an individual responsibility."[9] Some nineteenth-century families did, of course, provide for the care of parents who could no longer take care of themselves. The rich old fared best because they were often able to maintain their own homes, even when their health failed, by hiring a companion and servants. For the middle-class elderly, life was much harder—and often depended on their continuing ability to work. The Reverend Eliphet Williams, who went on serving as a Congregationalist minister until his death at seventy-six, wrote his brother in 1804: "I take a pen to write a Line, but with a trembling hand. Such is my debility that I can scarcely make a mark." As a result of his frailty, Williams complained that he was "greatly stritened for *Cash,* in consequence of diminution of Sallary &c."[10] And Williams was lucky, because most Congregationalist ministers had lifetime tenure. Timothy Maltby of Hartford was less fortunate. At sixty-five, no longer able to perform the physical labor of farming, he took up weaving carpets to support himself. The poor and those without stable families—again, the comparison with modern American life is inescapable—often became homeless. Scott cites Revolutionary War pension applications of men whose lives consisted entirely of moving from one short-term residence to another. Timothy Stephens, a partially disabled seventy-one-year-old handyman and day laborer, explained in his application: "I have no family to take care of, but myself, and no place of residence but with those who employ me at work."[11] The early nineteenth-century equivalents of Bessie Mae Berger's Chevrolet were the stables, attics, and basements that housed old people who hired themselves out by the week or the day. (Those who would argue that Revolutionary War veterans, unlike today's old homeless people, were willing to work are ignoring the fact that now most middle-class people would not even let a homeless man or woman into their houses, much less provide food and shelter in return for chores. There used to be a polite homeless man named Bill—he appeared to be in his sixties—who constantly offered his services to people on my block on Manhattan's Upper East Side. Sometimes I would see him in a nearby park, where he used the public restroom to wash himself every day. As it happened, I was about to have my apartment painted and was in need of someone to help me take thousands of books off my shelves and put them away in boxes. Not a single teenager in my building had responded to my offer to pay $10 an hour for the help; packing books was apparently not a job that would impress a college admissions officer. I thought about hiring Bill, but my building's superintendent—who knew the man and liked him—was nevertheless horrified at the thought of my letting him into my apartment to work. I often think about this man when people say that the homeless, of whatever age, are either crazy or lazy. Bill wanted to work, but no one would give him a chance at even the most menial kind of labor. I still feel ashamed that I was one of the many people who would not hire him: I wish that I had trusted my own instincts. Like Bessie Mae Berger, he rented a post office box, where he picked up his monthly Social Security check.)

Old women—in the past and the present—have always fared worse than old men. Throughout the eighteenth and much of the nineteenth centuries, most women did not retain control of marital property; many were forced to turn over any assets, including the houses in which they had lived their entire married lives, to children. In the best-case scenario, the children cared for their mother—although in a house that was no longer hers—but it is not difficult to envisage the family tensions that could ensue when a woman accustomed to being the mistress of her own home was reduced to the status of a tenant. More commonly, children sold the old family home. Whether the mother moved in with her children or had to live out her old age in a boardinghouse was entirely up to the adult children. "Do write me," a seventy-two-year-old widow, Eunice Stone, pleaded with a friend after she moved into the home of one of her children. "I hear or no nothing of any friend I feel almost forgotten—& alone—altho' pleasantly situated with the family of my children, but the tryal of breakup & leaving [her home in East Hartford] was no small tryal."[12] Scott sums up the economic situation of the elderly poor in the early republican period: "The fact that it was impossible for a substantial number of elderly people to maintain themselves does not, in itself, prove that the aged were especially vulnerable to hardship in early national America. That proof comes when we acknowledge that once individual efforts failed, other supports were unreliable. . . . Early national society was not ruthless to its aged citizens; it simply expected them to make their own way much of the time."[13] For a significant proportion of those who lived into old age in early America, the happy three-generation household was as unattainable—and often as unwanted—as it is today. Moreover, the expectation that individuals can and should be able to provide for their own welfare, even when they reach an age when their resources are bound to run out, is a recurrent theme in American history. The description of early nineteenth-century America as a society in which "once individual efforts failed, other supports were unreliable" has been rendered less harsh by Social Security and Medicare but remains as applicable to many of the oldest old today as it was more than two hundred years ago—in large measure because Social Security was never intended to be more than a supplement to personal savings and private pensions.

Thomas Paine—ahead of his time as usual—made the first proposal for what would be considered an old-age pension in the modern sense in his *Agrarian Justice* (1795). He urged that every citizen over age fifty receive a pension of ten pounds per year. The lame and the blind, whatever their age, would receive the same sum. Although *Agrarian Justice* was written in France, where Paine had narrowly escaped being executed because of his opposition to the death sentences imposed on Louis XVI and Marie Antoinette, the author made it clear that he thought a pension system was necessary for every country. Writing in a world in which, despite expanding trade, wealth in Europe still depended heavily on the ownership of inherited land, Paine saw the breakup of hereditary estates, property taxes, and government disbursement of tax revenues as the only practical ways to create a fund for the old and the sick. "There are, in every country, some magnificent charities established by individuals," Paine wrote. "It is, however, but little that any individual can do, when the whole extent of the misery to be relieved is considered. . . . It is only by organizing civilization upon such principles as to act like a system of pulleys, that the whole weight of misery can be removed." He emphasized that "it is justice, and not charity, that is the principle of the plan. In all great cases it is necessary to have a principle more universally active than charity; and, with respect to justice, it ought not to be left to the choice of detached individuals whether they will do justice or not."[14] Such proposals did not find favor in the young United States, which owed so much to Paine's passionate writings on behalf of the American Revolution. *The Age of Reason* (1794), which had attacked orthodox religion and set forth the astonishing proposition that all "sacred" books, including the Bible, were written not by God but by men, was more important in the downgrading of Paine's reputation in the early republic than were his economic writings, but the hostility of many prominent Federalists, including George Washington and John Adams, to Paine's attacks on inherited property also played a role. Only when Paine's old friend and admirer Thomas

Jefferson was elected president in 1800 were the wheels set in motion to bring Paine back from Paris, where he never intended to spend the rest of his life, on an American ship. Paine, who had contributed to the revolutionary cause by allowing *Common Sense* and *The Crisis Papers* to be distributed free, was destitute and beholden to the charity of friends when he died in New York in 1809. His proposals for general government assistance to the old were almost entirely ignored by Americans until after the Civil War, when veterans and their widows became the first large group of U.S. citizens to receive government support in their old age. Paine's upholding of support for the poor as a matter of public justice rather than private charity is the crux of political debate over the role of government that continues to divide the American nation; one is struck by the degree to which the principles of *Agrarian Justice,* long accepted in the social democracies of Europe, remain antithetical to the "free market," anti-government philosophy espoused by the political right in the United States today. Paine's ideas about collective economic and social responsibility, coupled with his animus toward most religious institutions, may explain why Congress has never seen fit to memorialize the revolutionary firebrand among the many sculptures of important historical figures in the U.S. Capitol.

Although the poor and homeless remained largely invisible in the early republic, there were fortunate old people with sufficient means, active minds, reasonably healthy bodies, and enough energy to serve as models of what a good old age might be. Two notable examples are Thomas Jefferson and John Adams, whose correspondence in the closing decades of their lives—sprinkled with quotations from the classics in Greek and Latin and filled with lively debate on contemporary issues ranging from religious intolerance in the young republic to higher education—provides ample evidence of a well-lived old age in spite of many losses. Adams lived to age ninety and Jefferson to age eighty-three; in one of the more poignant coincidences of American history, both men died on July 4, 1826—the fiftieth anniversary of the Declaration of Independence. The two founders enjoyed relatively good health—Adams until he was nearly ninety, when his sight failed and he was no longer able to read. Jefferson, who broke his arm at age seventy-eight, found it difficult to write because of an earlier wrist injury and severe arthritis but continued to do so until the last months of his life. Throughout his final decade, Jefferson devoted most of his time to the founding of the University of Virginia, while Adams kept battling against religious bigotry in the Commonwealth of Massachusetts. (One of the greatest disappointments of his old age was that he was unable, in his role as a delegate to the state's constitutional convention in 1820, to persuade his colleagues to adopt an amendment guaranteeing religious liberty under state law. Both Jews and Roman Catholics were barred from elective office in Massachusetts until 1833.) In their letters, Adams and Jefferson made it clear that they regarded themselves as fortunate exceptions and dreaded the kind of unproductive old age experienced by many of their contemporaries. "When all our faculties have left, or are leaving us," Jefferson wrote Adams in 1822, "one by one, sight, hearing, memory, every avenue of pleasing sensation is closed . . . when the friends of our youth are all gone, and a generation is risen around us whom we know not, is death an evil? . . . I have ever dreaded a doting old age; and my health has been generally so good, and is now so good, that I dread it still." Then, sounding not at all like a man resigned to death, Jefferson described reading as his chief delight and added, "Altho' I know it is too late for me to buckle on the armour of youth, yet my indignation would not permit me passively to receive the kick from an Ass."[15] Only ten days later, Adams replied that Jefferson's letter was "the best . . . ever written by an Octogeneanarian." He agreed with Jefferson that although death was not an evil, "we ought not to wish for it till life becomes insupportable; we must wait for the pleasure and convenience of this great teacher." Then, sounding as unresigned as Jefferson, he observed that although he could no longer read, "my delight is to hear others read, and I tease all my friends most unmercifully and tyranically. . . . The Ass has kicked in vain, all men say the dull animal has missed the mark."[16] Both Adams and Jefferson, aware as they were of their physical infirmities, displayed an intensity of feeling and intellect that completely contradicted the traditional Puritan exaltation of old age as a time for dispassionate contemplation and preparation for eternal life (about which both men had serious doubts).

From the early 1800s until the Civil War, there was still a good deal of moralizing to be found in sermons on the virtues of old age and the importance of respect for one's elders, but most of these tracts emanated from conservative clerics who were psychologically and theologically oriented toward the Puritan past rather than the evangelicalism of the Second Great Awakening or the liberalizing trends within Northern

Protestantism that made Unitarianism a powerful force in New England. Most religious authors presented a picture of old age that, apart from its proximity to eternal life, was utterly dismal. The Connecticut minister Stanley Griswold, in what must be one of the most depressing collections of sermons ever published, observed in 1801 that many old people "who sleep in the dust, once tasted with a high relish the pleasures of thought, of invention, or memory . . . but live to have their mental power benumbed, memory fail, the force of mind abate, and second childhood return." These unfortunates may once have been cultural or political luminaries but then became "weak like other men, the light of their mind was put out, the strength of their genius decayed, and the last stage of life exhibited a mournful contrast of what they had once been."[17] (He apparently was unacquainted with Jefferson and Adams.) Secular observers of old age, including journalists and authors of light verse, ridiculed old men who retained an interest in love and sex. Isaac Bickerstaffe, in a piece of light verse titled "He Would If He Could; or, An Old Fool Worse Than Any," wrote:

Surely never mortal, at my age
Was such a buzzard, such a calf:
A man who years should render sage!
I know not which to cry or laugh.
In love at sixty-six!
Ouns! Infamy should fix
A brand on the crime:
Is threescore a time
For beginning boyish tricks?[18]

Even nonsexual pleasures, for both women and men, were frequently portrayed as inappropriate and ridiculous in the elderly—and, as more tolerant social observers pointed out, the old themselves were often most censorious toward contemporaries who refused to "act their age." Caroline Kirkland, whose popular essays and books held a particular appeal for women, was a nineteenth-century Miss Manners who combined observations about etiquette with broad and witty social critiques. She had little use for the dreary decorum prescribed for and by many old people. In 1852, she noted that many respected elders in American communities would like to pass "sumptuary laws which should proscribe certain colors, forms, and ornaments of dress after a certain age; and if the ordinance could be so devised as to prohibit laughing, and liveliness, and joining in youthful pleasures, from and after the same period, it would be still more gratifying."[19] Kirkland went on to observe tartly that

> in certain quarters it is thought rather impertinent if mammas or married sisters do not withdraw into the shade on all occasions of reunion for merry doings. Travellers in the United States have repeatedly recorded their astonishment at this peculiar state of things:—that the approach to maturity incapacitates—and especially ladies—for American society. This is really enough to make one paint, patch, and powder; dye one's hair and eyebrows, and wear false curls and braids, teeth, beards, and mustaches; suffer the martyrdom of tight shoes on agricultural feet, obviate every awkward deficiency or redundance of nature with whalebone and cotton batting, and, in short do all those dreadful things which draw upon desperate people, disposed to catch at straws on the ocean of Time, the reproach of *not* growing old gracefully![20]

In the two decades before the Civil War, the subject of old age was treated with attitudes ranging from ambivalence to outright disrespect by the first generation of great American writers, who were responding to the challenge posed by Ralph Waldo Emerson in his famous "American Scholar" oration at Harvard in 1837. Declaring boldly that "we have listened too long to the courtly muses of Europe," Emerson charged the young scholars and writers in his audience—which included Henry David Thoreau and James Russell Lowell—to forge a distinctive literature and culture based on their own thought and experience instead of imitating the works of their elders (thought to be their betters) across the sea. Young Americans must realize, Emerson said, "that if the single man plant himself indomitably upon his instincts, and there abide, the huge world will come round to him." This was hardly a message calculated to inspire veneration of one's elders, although Emerson became more respectful of the wisdom of age as he himself grew old. Thoreau, who was just twenty years old when he heard Emerson's oration, expressed open contempt for the idea that the elderly possess special wisdom. In *Walden* (1854), although he noted that "it is never too late to give up our prejudices," Thoreau stated his basic credo that no customs or beliefs, of however long standing, can be justified without proof—and he thought that the young were best qualified to seek out proof and truth.

> What old people say that you cannot do you try and find that you can. Old deeds for old people, and new deeds for new. Old people did not know enough once, perchance, to fetch fresh fuel to keep the fire a-going; new people put a little dry wood under a pot, and are whirled round the globe with the speed of birds. . . . Age is no better, hardly so well, qualified for an instructor as youth, for it has not profited so much as it has lost. One may almost doubt if the wisest man has learned any thing of absolute value by living. Practically, the old have no very important advice to give the young, their own experience has been so partial, and their lives have been such miserable failures, for private reasons, as they must believe; and it may be that they have some faith left which belies that experience, and they are only less young than they were. I have lived some thirty years on this planet, and I have yet to hear the first syllable of valuable or even earnest advice from my seniors. They have told me nothing, and probably cannot tell me any thing, to the purpose. Here is life, an experiment to a great extent untried by me; but it does not avail me that they have tried it. If I have any experience which I think valuable, I am sure to reflect that this my Mentors said nothing about.[21]

Thoreau, who was only twenty-eight when he moved to Walden Pond and began the journal that would be published seven years later, represented an extreme among American philosophers and writers in his disdain for old age. Nevertheless, his views were well within the tolerable range of American opinion in the mid-nineteenth century, and it is hardly surprising that his writings would acquire a new popularity more than a century later, with the generation that sparked the youthful rebellions of the 1960s. Even Emerson, who was much more of a philosophical centrist than Thoreau and who, unlike Thoreau, lived to be an old man, regarded old age more as a necessary evil than as a desirable state of being. "Nature abhors the old," he wrote, "and old age seems the only disease; all others run into this one." He added that it was necessary to "face the facts and see the result. Tobacco, coffee, alcohol, hashish, prussic acid, strychnine are weak dilutions: the surest poison is time."[22] Yet Emerson also deplored prejudice against individual old people and professed that it was possible to grow younger in spirit even as the body disintegrated. Writing in an era when no one was under any illusions about the capacity of medicine to ameliorate the physical deterioration of old age, Emerson, like Jefferson and Adams, drew a sharp distinction between mental and physical deterioration. One of the most striking aspects of nineteenth-century American literature (Nathaniel Hawthorne is a notable exception) is how little the best writers had to say about old age at all and how rarely they created fully rounded older characters. Almost nothing in nineteenth-century American literature compares with the complex portrait of a middle-aged man and his old father in Dickens's *Great Expectations* (1861), or the painful description of dying—although the character is not old but middle-aged—in Tolstoy's *The Death of Ivan Ilyich* (1886). The obvious exception is Captain Ahab, who is old by the standards of his day when *Moby-Dick* (1851) opens. Ahab, however, is a portrait not of old age but of the effect of an unending quest for revenge on the psyche—although his fate certainly can be seen as a parable about the effects of obsession over time. Only in the twentieth century, and later rather than sooner, would some of the best American writers, among them John Updike and Philip Roth, begin to focus on old age as a subject worthy of attention in itself.

Some scholars are so committed to the idea that the American youth culture is a twentieth-century (or at least a post–Industrial Revolution) phenomenon that they ignore countervailing evidence from public life as well as literature. W. Andrew Achenbaum, in his study *Old Age in the New Land* (1978), states flatly that the American electorate before the Civil War "clearly considered older men fit and even uniquely qualified for the presidency."[23] That conclusion is not borne out by the ages of presidents who followed those of the revolutionary generation. The first presidential candidate born in the nineteenth century, Franklin Pierce, was forty-eight when he was elected in 1852. Abraham Lincoln, the second candidate born after the turn of the century, was nearly fifty-one when he became president, in 1861, of a nation about to be torn apart. In fact, only two presidents between 1800 and 1860—William

Henry Harrison and James Buchanan—were over sixty-five when they took office. Harrison, known as Old Tippecanoe for his role in a famous battle against the Shawnee chief Tecumseh (which gave rise to the 1840 campaign slogan "Tippecanoe and Tyler Too"), won more than 53 percent of the popular vote even though he was attacked because of his age and previous illnesses. When Harrison died of pneumonia a month after his inauguration (which would seem to bear out the charge that his age and health ought to have been an issue), he was succeeded by the fifty-one-year-old John Tyler. Only twice again in the antebellum era would Americans elect men anywhere near Harrison's age—the sixty-four-year old Zachary Taylor in 1848 and the sixty-five-year-old Buchanan in 1856. Yet Achenbaum claims that in spite of Harrison's death, "Americans continued to nominate and elect elderly men to the presidency. Old age often seemed to enhance rather than to reduce a candidate's attractiveness."[24] If that were true, even though average life expectancy was shorter in the nineteenth century than in our own, most presidential candidates would have been in their late sixties rather than their early fifties. Lincoln was certainly not considered elderly when he ran for the presidency; indeed, he was seen in the North as the representative of a younger generation, less bound by old convictions about slavery and states' rights than his predecessor, Buchanan, who was born in 1791.

Another factor—arguably the most important one—affecting intergenerational relations in nineteenth-century America was the mobility encouraged by the endless supply of fertile land west of the more heavily populated areas of the original thirteen states. Sons did not have to wait for their fathers to die to come into their inheritance; they could and did strike out on their own, frequently taking their wives with them (or sending for them after they were established). The westward push across the continent would not have been possible if most Americans had remained in close enough proximity to their parents to care for them until death. The reality of generational estrangement and mobility, as opposed to the myth of generational closeness, is well conveyed in Laura Ingalls Wilder's beloved *Little House on the Prairie* series, which describes the life of the restless, westward-moving Ingalls clan in the 1870s and 1880s. Laura was born in Wisconsin in 1867, and Ma and Pa Ingalls did not take their own parents with them when they moved westward through Kansas and Minnesota, finally settling in the Dakota

Territory. There is no suggestion in these books that the young adult generation was financially responsible for the older generation—or vice versa. The popular 1970s television series based on the *Little House* books, by contrast, featured many sentimental reunion scenes between adult generations—another reflection of the myth about previous American generations' benevolent treatment of the elderly that had taken hold in late twentieth-century mass culture. (The *Little House* television series took liberties with more than its depiction of the Ingalls family relationships. In one memorable episode, the married, adult Laura goes to hear a lecture by Ralph Waldo Emerson, who actually died in 1882, when the real Laura Ingalls was only fifteen.)

After the Civil War, the status of old people was negatively affected by a wide variety of economic and social changes that had considerably more influence than the brash musings of the young Thoreau. The rise of industrial capitalism changed American views about the usefulness of the old for pragmatic reasons having little to do with the philosophical questions about the wisdom of old age raised by scholars and writers in the early republic. Between 1860 and 1910, although more than six hundred thousand men had been killed in the Civil War, the American population nearly tripled—from some thirty-one million to more than ninety-two million. The new immigrants were mainly young, and they provided the muscle for the steel mills, railroads, power plants, and construction projects that were transforming the economic life of the nation. This continuing influx of young immigrants skewed the U.S. population in favor of the young, even though more Americans were living longer. According to the 1870 census, only 3 percent of Americans were over sixty-five, compared with 4.7 percent in England—and the over-sixty-five population rose only another percentage point between 1870 and 1900. In the mines and the factories that turned raw materials wrested from the earth into the finished products of the Gilded Age, young working men and women aged quickly, and older workers were seen not as repositories of much needed knowledge and experience but as liabilities on a sped-up factory floor. A sixty-year-old farmer who had survived many droughts in his lifetime might have a good deal of useful advice to impart to a grandson on a family farm, but no sixty-year-old factory worker knew more about producing an incandescent lightbulb than the twenty-year-old laboring beside him. By the turn of the century, older workers were described as "superannuated" by social Darwinists, who considered it obvious that the old could not meet the demands of contemporary industrial society. "The things that most promote the welfare of the wage-earning class militate most against old age employment," wrote one social observer in the popular magazine *McClure's*. "The old man today . . . slow, hesitating, frequently half-blind and deaf, is sadly misplaced amid the death dealing machinery of a modern factory."[25]

The lasting influence of late nineteenth-century social Darwinism on American views about old age has been greatly underestimated by those who view the youth culture as a relatively recent social construct. The most prominent figures in American industrial capitalism—including Andrew Carnegie, Thomas Edison, and John D. Rockefeller—all believed that Darwin's theory of evolution by means of natural selection should be applied, and did apply, to man in a state of civilization. These titans of the Gilded Age embraced the idea of "survival of the fittest"—a phrase coined not by Darwin but by Herbert Spencer, a British philosopher whose works are little read today but who was enormously influential in late nineteenth-century America. Darwin had stated explicitly that as soon as man moves from a state of nature to a state of civilization, natural selection becomes subordinate to both environmental factors and human morality. He pointedly observed that "the aid which we feel impelled to give to the helpless is mainly an incidental result of the instinct of sympathy, which was originally acquired as part of the social instincts, but subsequently rendered . . . more tender and widely diffused. Nor could we check our sympathy, even at the urging of hard reason, without deterioration in the noblest part of our nature. . . . If we were intentionally to neglect the weak and helpless, it could only be for a contingent benefit, with an overwhelming present evil."[26]

It is undoubtedly true that workers in their sixties (regardless of whether they were half blind and deaf) had more physical limitations than younger men and were therefore not as well equipped to cope with the demands of an industrial workplace less safe and more demanding than most workplaces are today. But the social Darwinists of the Gilded Age were equally convinced that white-collar workers, professionals of all kinds, and scholars lost their mental vigor as they aged. Needless to say, men like Carnegie, Edison, and Rockefeller, all of whom lived into their eighties, did not apply this evaluation to themselves. Carnegie did retire from active management of his businesses at age sixty-six, but his activities as a philanthropist—which had a greater impact on the nation than his acquisition of a fortune as a steel magnate—continued until his death at ninety-one.

The most notorious example of ageism combined with social Darwinism is Dr. William Osler's valedictory address upon his departure from Johns Hopkins University in 1905, when he left for England to take up a new post as Regius Professor of Medicine at Oxford. Osler, a brilliant researcher, teacher, and medical administrator, remains one of the most famous figures in the history of medicine on both sides of the Atlantic. At Johns Hopkins, he was the key leader in building a world-class medical institution from the ground up, and any of his speeches would have drawn immense interest from scholars and doctors. However, his farewell address, delivered in Baltimore, achieved broad notoriety and became front-page news across the nation because Osler's main theme was the diminution of creativity over age forty and the uselessness of men over sixty. He even titled his speech "The Fixed Period," after an 1882 Anthony Trollope novel with a plot centered around the chloroforming of sexagenarians. Osler, who was fifty-six at the time, went on to further distinction at Oxford, did not chloroform himself, and died of natural causes at seventy. His audience at Johns Hopkins included a good many venerable faculty members, who may have been somewhat taken aback to hear their esteemed colleague say that it was a bad thing for an institution of higher education to "have all the professors growing old at the same time." Osler expounded on his theories about the relationship between age and declining creativity at length.

> In some places only an epidemic, a time limit, or an age limit can save the situation. I have two fixed ideas well known to my friends, harmless obsessions with which I sometimes bore them, but which have a direct bearing on this important problem. The first is the comparative uselessness of men over forty years of age. This may seem shocking, and yet . . . the world's history bears out the statement. Take the sum of human achievement in action, in science, in art, in literature—subtract the work of the men above forty, and while we should miss great treasures, even priceless treasures, we would practically be where we are to-day. It is difficult to name a great and far-reaching conquest of the mind which has not been

given to the world by a man on whose back the sun was still shining. The effective, moving, vitalizing work of the world is done between the ages of twenty-five and forty—these fifteen golden years of plenty, the anabolic or constructive period, in which there is always a balance in the mental bank and the credit is still good. In the science and art of medicine young or comparatively young men have made every advance of the first rank. Vesalius, Harvey, Hunter, Bichat, Laennec, Virchow, Lister, Koch—the green years were yet upon their heads, when their epochmaking studies were made. To modify an old saying, a man is sane morally at thirty, rich mentally at forty, and wise spiritually at fifty—or never. . . .

My second fixed idea is the uselessness of men above sixty years of age, and the incalculable benefit it would be in commercial, political and in professional life if, as a matter of course, men stopped work at this age. . . . In that charming novel, *The Fixed Period,* Anthony Trollope discusses the practical advantages in modern life of a return to this ancient usage, and the plot hinges upon the admirable scheme of a college into which at sixty men retired for a year of contemplation before a peaceful departure by chloroform. That incalculable benefits might follow such a scheme is apparent to any one who, like myself, is nearing the limit, and who has made a careful study of the calamities which may befall men during the seventh and eighth decades. Still more when he contemplates the many evils which they perpetuate unconsciously, and with impunity.[27]

News reports on Osler's speech, quoting the text at length, were published on February 24, 1905. The next day, with harsh and unexpected criticism descending upon him, Osler clarified his remarks and explained that he had only been joking about the chloroform. "I meant just what I said," he acknowledged. "But it's disgraceful, the fuss that the newspapers are making about it. I know there are exceptions, but they only serve to illustrate the rule. I have spent some time writing an essay entitled '*La Crise De Quarante Ans,*' which will prove what I say. I have not yet finished the essay, and I have been years in accumulating the facts it contains. As to chloroforming men at sixty, that was only a pleasantry." *The New York Times* reported that the doctor "laughed heartily" after he had explained the joke.[28] The papers, predictably, would not let go of the story. The very next day, the *Times* published a front-page article about the suicide of one Captain William S. Winder, a seventy-one-year-old Confederate veteran, who shot and killed himself at his home in Baltimore. Among his papers was a clipping of the address by Osler (which had, of course, been prominently reported in the Baltimore newspapers because it was delivered at Johns Hopkins). The *Times* reported that "Capt. Winder, who was a bachelor, had led a retired and lonely life for some years. His sight had practically failed, and he recently suffered from insomnia."[29] For some weeks, the press continued to publish reports of suicides supposedly related to Osler's speech. Osler's critics were particularly angered by his pessimistic views about the prospects for intellectual creativity for men over forty. No one, it should be noted, even bothered to mention women, whose prospects outside the home were of no interest to male scholars. Osler himself allowed that older women were still useful to their families and presumably should not be chloroformed. He might have been influenced by ruminations such as *The Elderly Lady,* published in 1906. "But lately I have come to believe that the people who live in the Land of Old Age have their own particular part to play," the female (supposedly) author wrote, "and that they help to make up the sum of life; after all one need not dust and sweep and make pies and cake to be of service to those we love. We would not wish to see our little children fetch and carry, and yet they are the dearest things in the world to us. And so we older people, I believe, do more than we know for those we love when we sit in our own quiet country, as I found out a little while ago when I started to make an excursion into the world that works."[30] This vision of an old woman sitting as a contemplative Buddha in her peaceful environment, untroubled by and untroubling to younger people who live in the world of hustle and bustle, offers a particularly constricted view—no need even to bake!—of the possibilities of female old age. One can only imagine what energetic nineteenth-century women in the ninth decade of their lives, like the indomitable suffragists Susan B. Anthony and Elizabeth Cady Stanton, would have had to say about little old ladies making a contribution by providing dear little children with an opportunity to fetch and carry.

In response to Osler's speech, newspaper and magazine articles invariably mentioned the most notable achievements of men over forty, including Benjamin Franklin, Abraham Lincoln, Benjamin Disraeli, and

William Gladstone. Osler would (and did) reply that those were the exceptions that proved the rule, but his real mistake was in extending his remarks about the youthfulness of those who made breakthroughs in science and medicine to encompass the arts and politics. If Osler had limited his remarks to the dominance of the young in groundbreaking scientific research, he would not have aroused such controversy: for whatever reason, much of the history of science supports the contention that researchers under forty are more creative than their elders. But accomplishment and creativity over forty, even in an era when the average life span was shorter, were more the rule than the exception in nonscientific fields. It is impossible to resist the temptation to do exactly what the newspapers did in response to Osler's speech. What if Beethoven had stopped composing at age forty? No late quartets, no *Missa Solemnis,* no *Hammerklavier* Sonata, no Ninth Symphony (completed in 1824, just two years before his death). Or imagine Tolstoy's body of work without *War and Peace* and *Anna Karenina*. Or Brunelleschi without his dome. . . . The list is endless, and these men were not exceptions among their contemporaries. They were exceptional in their genius, but there is no indication that people of more ordinary capabilities, if they were fortunate enough to escape early death by infectious disease, were any less useful in their forties and fifties than they had been at an earlier stage in life.

But Osler was speaking with the characteristic arrogance of his profession (at a time when medicine was finally making genuine progress in understanding the causes of common life-threatening diseases). He also represented a social Darwinist perspective that appealed to many physicians, whose profession gave them almost daily exposure to the literal meaning of "survival of the fittest." Furthermore, as William Graebner points out in *A History of Retirement* (1980), Osler regarded medicine itself as "a proto-Darwinian contest" in which new, science-based ideas and treatments fought for supremacy with outmoded practices based on tradition and superstition rather than evidence. In this contest, age—and older physicians—were seen as the enemy of medical progress.[31]

The reason why Osler's speech aroused such widespread interest and controversy outside the medical community was that the rise of industrial capitalism and the application of new managerial techniques (often and not always accurately described as "scientific") to many businesses had given not only old but middle-aged workers good reason, for the first time in American history, to fear for their jobs simply because of their age. Newspapers were filled with articles about men as young as their early forties, in fields as varied as typesetting and insurance sales, who were turned away by potential employers explicitly because of age. In Chicago, a group calling itself the Anti-Age Limit League was formed in 1905—a few months after Osler's speech—for the specific purpose of lobbying Congress to enact laws prohibiting discrimination in hiring against men over forty-five. The employment of women, once again, was not considered at all in the league's proposals—probably because it was assumed that no man would want the jobs for which women were being hired. "The league announces that it does not intend to antagonize the employment of women within the sphere of her sex or actual necessities," the *Chicago Daily Tribune* reported, "but holds that man possesses the inherent right to be considered first as the head and bread winner of the family."[32] So much for women who had no man to serve as the breadwinner for them or their children. The following day, the *Tribune* reported on the experiences of James F. Downey, the league's president, who was a former printer and newspaper editor. Downey, then in his sixties, recounted his arrival at a publishing office in Chicago. The potential employer looked him over and said, "Oh, you won't do at all. You're too old. We want young blood here." Ordinarily, Downey explained, "the refusal is couched in gentler terms. Lots of times I have had employers look me over sharply and then say, 'Sorry, sir, but we have just filled that vacancy.' And then you go home, and in looking over the want ads the next day you find them still advertising for the position you were told had been filled already."[33]

The New York Times published an editorial on the newly formed Anti-Age Limit League that reflected the ambivalence of American society about not only the old but the middle-aged. The editorial noted that "the average of all native whites at death is 36, so that those who are working at 45 appear to be working on another man's time." This analysis is exceedingly peculiar for more than one reason. First, the idea that anyone who has the temerity to exceed average life expectancy is somehow stealing work from younger people was especially ludicrous a century ago, when those who did not die in childhood or childbirth had a fairly good chance of achieving a modern life expectancy. The average life expectancy of thirty-six was largely a reflection of high mortality from infectious diseases in early childhood. Economic class, then as now, played a decisive role in one's prospect of reaching old age. The Ochs family, which bought the *Times* in 1896, was known for the longevity of its members. Second, longevity was already increasing as a result of improved sanitation and nutrition. Between 1880 and 1890, average life expectancy increased by four years, from thirty-six to forty. That was a much greater leap than it appears to a twenty-first-century reader, precisely because the "average" was lowered by the still-high rate of infant and early childhood mortality. Presumably, what really concerned the owners of the *Times* about the Anti-Age Limit League was the possibility that federal legislation might interfere with their own hiring practices. The real explanation for the furor over Osler's speech was the dissonance between the growing desire of many business owners to lower the age of their workforce and the absence of social arrangements for pensions that would provide even a minimum standard of living for forcibly retired workers.

All pre-twentieth-century statistics on retirement should be viewed with caution, given that census takers did not even begin asking relevant questions about age and employment status until after the Civil War. However, all available data suggest that the percentage of employed men over age sixty-five dropped steadily after 1870. According to one estimate, 80.6 percent of men over sixty-five were gainfully employed in 1870, but only 63.7 percent were employed by 1910.[34] The U.S. Census found that participation in the labor force by men over sixty-five dropped by more than 7 percent between 1890 and 1900 alone.[35]

The rise in unemployment of older workers during the Gilded Age—also the age of mass immigration—reflects both the existence of a much larger pool of available workers in the last quarter of the nineteenth century and the demands of mechanization, which made it harder for older men to keep up with younger ones in the industrial workplace. Before the Civil War, mandatory retirement had been almost unknown in the private sector of the economy, in part because of the relatively small number of old people and in part because, as one scholar notes, the smaller scale of businesses before industrialization did not produce "a large, concentrated working class on which to apply mandatory retirement."[36] The very existence of the Anti-Age Limit League, and the negative responses from business owners like the publisher of the *Times,* attest to the fact that many older men who wanted to continue working were being retired against their will. The printing industry is a classic example of the effect of mechanization and industrialization on older workers. The Linotype machine, invented in 1884, had become the industry norm by the mid-1890s and required younger workers with better eyesight, more nimble fingers, and greater endurance. Age limits for the hiring of new workers became common, and employers became increasingly willing to impose retirement on older workers who had been with their companies for decades. A poignant verse published in 1911 in *The Inland Printer,* the official publication of the long-established printers' union, captured the impact of the Linotype on older workers during the decades bracketing the turn of the century.

The typo's old pick from the case
Has changed to machine's rapid pace—
To iron and steel,
To shafting and wheel,
And the keyboard has taken his place. . . .

Adieu to the "strings" and the paste,
To the longest we often have raced;
Old-timers are "out,"
But the young comp.'s about
And filling up columns with haste.[37]

Ironically, both age limits in hiring and compulsory retirement were linked with the successes of labor between the late 1880s and the early 1900s in persuading or forcing employers to institute a shorter workday. For workers ranging from printers to silk weavers, what was once a standard ten-hour workday moved between 1887 and 1902 toward a nine-and-a-half-hour day and then a nine-hour day. But, in a stellar example of the law of unintended consequences, the shorter workday—because it required people to work faster—greatly increased the impetus of employers to get rid of the old in favor of the young. "No matter how benign the intent of the labor organizations," writes Graebner in his history of retirement, "the major impact of the shorter work day was to intensify the pressure on older workers. . . . Employers who could neither pass their costs on to consumers nor reduce wages sought to lower operating expenditures by eliminating less efficient older employees."[38]

The desire of ownership to phase out older workers was, of course, at odds with an economic system in which private pensions were almost nonexistent. In 1875, American Express became the first business to introduce a limited pension plan, but few other private companies followed suit. Only around 1910, when the need to increase worker productivity became a more urgent concern for management, did significant numbers of businesses begin to sponsor some pension coverage. According to one scholar, twenty-one major businesses a year inaugurated pension plans between 1910 and 1920. Still, when the New Deal began in 1933, only 15 percent of American workers were eligible in theory for pensions provided by their employers—and only 5 percent of retired workers were actually receiving benefits.[39] One of the most critical deficiencies of the private pensions inaugurated at the end of the nineteenth and the beginning of the twentieth centuries was their failure to pay benefits to the widows of workers. The last quarter of the nineteenth century did, however, produce one piece of social legislation that proved a precedent for the more progressive attitude toward old-age pensions that would be enacted into law more than four decades later, as Social Security became the signature achievement of the New Deal. When pensions for Civil War veterans were first authorized by Congress in 1862, the subsidies had been limited to men who had been injured in battle and were unable to perform manual labor. But in 1890, Congress took the important, pioneering step of changing the law to permit any disabled veteran—whether he had a war injury or not—to receive a pension. By 1906, old age alone was enough to qualify a veteran for a pension. Unlike private pensions, the government's veterans' pensions were also paid to widows. While these measures did nothing for retired workers who had not fought in the war, they came much closer to the modern concept of what government ought to do for the elderly than any of the early private attempts to provide some cushion for forcibly retired workers.

Like so many economic hardships incurred by the elderly poor from the end of the eighteenth century through the beginning of the twenty-first, the change in the status of older workers during the Gilded Age had a much greater impact on blue-collar and low-level white-collar employees than on members of the upper classes. The median age of presidential cabinet members, under forty-seven in the period from 1789 to 1824, rose to nearly sixty during the period from 1875 to 1899.[40] Moreover, social Darwinism provided a foolproof rationale for privileged and accomplished older men to exempt themselves from their beliefs about the general unfitness of older workers. As the British philosopher Spencer wrote of the poor, "If they are sufficiently complete to live, they *do* live, and it is well they should live. If they are not sufficiently complete to live, they die, and it is best that they should die."[41] For Spencer's followers, the converse was also true: if men were able to amass a fortune and live and work to a ripe old age, they were by definition the fittest of their species. According to newspaper accents, dignitaries with stage seats for Osler's address included Ira Remsen, fifty-eight, president of Johns Hopkins; Daniel Coit Gilman, seventy-three, head of the Carnegie Institution; Alpheus W. Wilson, seventy, presiding bishop of the Southern Methodist Episcopal Church; and Mendes Cohen, seventy-three, a civil engineer and railroad executive. There were no reports that any of these men rushed off to retire (or to chloroform themselves) after Osler's address.

The debate about Osler's remarks was conducted almost entirely on secular, utilitarian grounds: Were men in their forties, fifties, and sixties useful or were they not? America's Puritan heritage might as well have been nonexistent for purposes of this discussion; there was almost no talk about the value of the old as moral exemplars or as those whose minds were fixed on spiritual verities because of their position at the head of the line awaiting eternal life—*nearer my God to thee*. One of the few public figures who came forward to defend the intrinsic value of the aged, on humanistic grounds, was Felix Adler, the founder of the New York Society for Ethical Culture. Adler observed that the shakiness of belief in immortality, particularly common among those who had accepted Darwin's theory of evolution, had likely created even greater anxiety about death and aging. "Science has great authority," he observed in *The Spiritual Attitude Toward Old Age,* "and if a scientist says that there are only twenty years of the three score and ten that are really flooded with sunshine, people listen attentively to him."[42] The materialist's conception of life, embodied by Osler, was that of a hill, where a period of ascent toward the peak was ultimately followed by a period of mental and physical descent and decline. Adler, however, saw life as a "series of terraces, each higher than the last. From age to age, through ascent following on ascent, rising from power to power, from glory to glory, at last we do not stumble into a hole, but pass as it were into the open heaven."[43] Osler's error lay in his refusal to acknowledge the enormous individual variations in the age at which a decline might manifest itself, while Adler simply refused to talk about the reality of declining capabilities at any age. That his plateaus, or terraces, might just as easily mark the beginning of a falling-off as the takeoff point for further ascent seems obvious. In a sense, Adler was attempting to summon up the special wisdom of contemplative old age as an answer to social Darwinists, who assessed the value of the old in strictly utilitarian terms and naturally found them wanting. His thinking also ran counter to the strong earlier strain in American culture, articulated by Thoreau, in which one might doubt that the aged had learned anything by living. Both Adler and Osler, in very different ways, were exemplars of the nineteenth-century intellectual attraction to vast theoretical systems that did not address exceptions and contradictions. Adler's concept of the old moving "from glory to glory" had as little universal applicability as Osler's sweeping portrait of intellectually decrepit men over sixty.

In spite of the opposition to Osler by men his own age—men who occupied positions of influence and had no intention of stepping down or acknowledging any diminution of their intellects—the idea of superannuation did creep into white-collar professions of every kind. Even religious institutions—particularly those representing liberal Protestant denominations whose members had been most strongly influenced by Darwin's theory of evolution and by social Darwinist misinterpretations of that theory—were convinced that only a younger clergy could respond effectively to the new doubts generated not only by contemporary science but by industrial capitalism. The Puritan idea that nearness to the afterlife conferred exemplary virtue on the old was becoming as alien to late nineteenth-century Americans as it is today. God's representatives on earth, it seemed, could no longer be sure of keeping their jobs until they were ready to exchange temporal for eternal life. If an old man who had devoted his life to the service of God could not be sure of employment, how could an elderly professor of history or an American Express clerk make a case that he was indispensable to his employer?

For upper-middle-class Americans, whose longevity was increasing much more rapidly than that of manual laborers, the first two decades of the twentieth century could not fail to produce a rising awareness of the gap between life expectancy and the possibilities of a dignified, socially valued life for the oldest Americans. This gap, which first became evident as attitudes toward older workers grew more negative in the 1890s, had turned into a chasm by the end of World War I. The first major study of the closing decades of adult life, *Senescence,* was published in 1922 and reflects a strong sense of the social and individual, external and internal, conflicts associated with increasing longevity. The book's seventy-eight-year-old author was G. Stanley Hall, the first president of the American Psychological Association. Hall, best known for his work on adolescent development, was decidedly angry about his retirement as president of Clark University, even though he was said to have mandated his own departure. Then and now, many who embrace "voluntary" retirement have actually been pushed, and many more have second thoughts afterward regardless of whether they originally considered retirement a good idea. Hall challenged Osler's conviction that most men do their best work before forty, and he was in the anomalous position of having decided to break with the world of work but advocating that old people with vigorous minds have something special to offer as national and international leaders. Hall never used the term "ageism," which did not emerge for another half century, but he did refer to the old as a marginalized minority. His ambivalence about the "wisdom" of the old ran deep, for he recognized that in order to be thought wise, the old are expected to detach themselves from earlier passions and ambitions—exactly what a man (like all professional men of his generation, Hall did not consider the lives of women) cannot do if he is to retain an active presence in public affairs. Hall presented the dilemma in the first person, although most of the book was written in a dry, academic third-person voice.

> They say our emotional life is damped. True, we are more immune from certain great passions and our affectivity is very differently distributed. But what lessons of repression we have had to learn! If the fires of youth are banked and smoldering they are in no wise extinguished and perhaps burn only the more fiercely because they cannot vent themselves. . . . If we break out, it is ascribed not to its true cause of outer circumstance but to the irritability thought characteristic of our years. Age has the same right to

> emotional perturbations as youth and is no whit less exposed and disposed to them. Here, as everywhere, we are misunderstood and are in such a feeble minority that we have to incessantly renounce our impulsions.[44]

This *cri de coeur* sounds absolutely modern, although it was made at a time when, according to American folklore, everyone respected the old. Yet here is Hall, born before Thoreau started mocking the old in print, sounding like an indignant, aging baby boomer and insisting on the right of the old to emotional expressiveness. He is caught, like twenty-first-century Americans, between a vision of what a different kind of old age might be and a reality that, in spite of his keen mind and energy, does not offer him what he wants or needs. It is a dilemma that now confronts the boomer generation, whose oldest members are just beginning to step across the threshold between middle age and "young old" age. The significance of this threshold is not diminished—indeed, it may be magnified—by the realization that retirement at the marker age of sixty-five now seems undesirable to many and may be economically impossible for all but a few.

CHAPTER THREE

Boomer Beginnings and Age-Defying Denial

In 1965, when I began working for *The Washington Post,* there came a day, sometime in midyear, celebrated by all of the younger, poorly paid reporters. This was the date in the fiscal year when our income reached the maximum amount subject to Social Security deductions and, to our delight, we found an extra $25 or so—a real fortune for people making $105 to $175 a week—in our paychecks. Not that any of us resented paying Social Security taxes. Most of us believed that the money was due our grandparents for a lifetime of hard work, and we assumed (although the possibility of our reaching Social Security age was about as real to us as Armageddon) that those who came after us would view the deductions from their paychecks with equal equanimity. Somewhere in the country—we liberals knew not where—there were right-wing children of the Other Sixties, destined to become junior players in the Reagan revolution of the 1980s and then, moving upward in the conservative ranks, senior advisers in the administration of George W. Bush. These young troglodytes already regarded Social Security and its brand-new companion, Medicare, with deep suspicion—as one more piece of evidence of the pernicious, lasting influence of the pinkos who had sneaked into mainstream American politics during the New Deal. But most members of the baby boom generation, like our parents, took the heritage of the New Deal for granted. Part of that inheritance was the belief that the nation, as a whole, owed something to people who had worked all of their lives and were no longer able to take care of themselves. The concept of "greedy geezers," living high on the hog at the expense of productive younger workers paying Social Security taxes on an ever-increasing proportion of their income, was at least two decades away. The prosperity of the boomers' childhood and young adulthood instilled a fundamental belief that there would always be enough to go around for every generation, and this assumption bred a careless confidence about the long-term future that has influenced our approach to every stage of our lives and has been shaken only in recent years. The material progress of our youth provided the foundation for two other psychological characteristics that have shaped the boomer generation's battle against aging—faith in the possibility of repeated self-transformation and a quasi-religious reliance on the capacity of medicine and technology to transform the process of growing old when self-help efforts fall short.

I technically missed being a boomer, since I was born in June 1945—six months before demographers date the beginning of the official baby boom. My father, who was blind in one eye, was deemed unfit for combat and stationed in Chicago during the war, so he and my mother made an early contribution to the baby production line that geared up in earnest nine months after combat veterans began returning from overseas. Anyone born near the end rather than the beginning of the war, however, belongs psychologically to the boomer generation, because we grew up in an era defined by rising expectations. The Depression and the war were stories told to us by our parents; the spectacular advances in the living standards of our parents' generation were the air we breathed as children.

The "greatest generation," it is now repeated ad nauseam, was much thriftier than its improvident baby boom progeny, and this piece of received opinion is based on the Depression-era childhoods of Americans now in their eighties. But it is equally important to recall that the largest proportion of the greatest generation did not enter adult life until the early 1940s. The end of the war, which coincided with our parents' coming-of-age, was followed by such a long period of economic expansion (albeit punctuated by recessions) that many adult Americans whose own parents had lived on the edge of poverty were propelled into the middle class. The GI Bill moved millions of young adults out of a blue-collar family past into white-collar jobs. In America during the 1950s and 1960s, it was easy for the greatest generation to save *and* spend in ways that those who were already adults during the Depression could not have imagined. After veterans received a higher education subsidized by the GI Bill, our parents—many already married—bought their houses at mortgage rates of 4 percent. My father was making about $10,000 a year when he and my mother bought their first house for just $22,000 in 1956—an income-to-mortgage ratio that almost no middle-class American buying a house today can hope to enjoy. When it came time for children born in the late 1940s to go to college, tuition at all but the nation's most expensive private universities was affordable for middle-class parents: they did not have to go into debt and forgo saving for their own retirement as so many middle-class parents have been forced to do during the past twenty years. The idea of an affordable retirement with winters spent in some warm climate seemed entirely plausible to those who had made it into the upper-middle income bracket by the 1960s. To save for the future, they did not have to deprive themselves of luxuries, whether in the form of a weekly T-bone steak or the American Express tours to Europe that were becoming increasingly popular in the dawn of mass airplane travel. The only miscalculation of the greatest generation's middle class was that it did not foresee how many of its members, especially women, would live so long that their substantial retirement savings, even supplemented by Social Security, would prove totally inadequate.

When members of my generation came of age in the 1960s, we shared the largely unexamined conviction that, however different our lives might be from those of our parents, many of the same economic privileges would accrue to us. This conviction profoundly influenced many of our decisions in young adulthood. Economic security made it much easier psychologically for college students to discard the fears of the McCarthy era and to join in protest movements on behalf of civil rights and against the Vietnam War and, later, sex discrimination. In the expanding job market of the 1960s, we were sure that regardless of how we spent our youth, plenty of jobs would await us when we were ready to take on the mantle of adulthood. It scarcely occurred to any college student my age that he or she would not be able to find a job when it was wanted and needed—even allowing for time off at the countercultural bazaar. And we were right. We had no reason to think that the affluence of the greatest generation represented a unique moment in American history, when the nation had both the resources and the will to lavish all kinds of benefits on those who had fought the Second World War. We did not anticipate that the nation would be much less eager to extend the same benefits to those who had fought the unpopular Vietnam War, much less to those in the boomer generation who avoided military service by receiving college deferments. There was a strong assumption—based on what George Orwell once identified as the "major mental disease" of foreseeing only "a continuation of the thing that is happening"—that the favorable economic conditions of our youth would remain the norm.[1]

The 1960s and early 1970s were times of serious generational conflict, but the conflict was mainly between my generation and that of our middle-aged parents—not between the young and the genuinely old. We thought of our parents' generation as old, but our concept of age was psychological rather than biological. Genuinely old people who seemed to share our values—Dr. Spock, for instance—seemed closer to us in many ways than our parents, who were in their forties and fifties and always seemed to be on the opposite side of the sexual revolution, the antiwar movement, and, a few years later, the women's movement. Our parents still held power in society; for the most part, people in their sixties and seventies did not. Lyndon Johnson was just fifty-six when he announced that he was returning to his Texas ranch and would not run for a second full term as president in 1968—a fact that seems utterly incredible to me when I recall the vast remove at which Johnson seemed to stand from my own generation. Richard Nixon was just fifty-five when he took the oath of office in 1969. He was, after all, only four years older than his 1960 opponent John F. Kennedy; Nixon had only seemed to belong to an older generation because of his fuddy-duddy floorwalker aura and his unease with the new medium of television. People beyond their mid-sixties with high public profiles and the influence to make their voices heard were the exceptions rather than the rule, and exceptions like Dr. Spock did not affect the general invisibility of most older Americans. They were seen as retired in every social sense of the word—meaning not only that they were no longer drawing a regular paycheck but that they had retired from active participation in public life, in the sense that political leaders were said to "retire" from public roles in the late eighteenth and early nineteenth centuries. Although William Osler's tongue-in-cheek suggestion that men over sixty ought to be chloroformed would undoubtedly have aroused just as much outrage in 1965 as it had in 1905, the idea that retirement was the inevitable and suitable state of life for those approaching three score and ten had gained widespread acceptance among young and old. It probably would have surprised most young Americans—I know I would have been astonished—to learn that many supposedly retired adults in the 1960s were still working and that earnings from employment accounted for nearly 30 percent of their income.[2]

Between the beginning of the twentieth century and the baby boom after the Second World War, the distress and disdain expressed by social Darwinists about the unproductivity of the old had been transformed into a widespread conviction that the "unproductive" years were really "golden years"—and that society was at least partly responsible for making them so. This transformation had begun with the 1935 passage of the Social Security Act. As Arthur Schlesinger Jr. notes, Social Security "meant a tremendous break with the inhibitions of the past. The federal government was at last charged with the obligation to provide its citizens a measure of protection from the hazards and vicissitudes of life. . . . The constitutional dedication of federal power to the general welfare began a new stage of national history."[3] Private employer pension plans were still rare in the 1930s but would expand considerably in the two decades of rising affluence following the war—the heyday of American manufacturing and generous benefits negotiated with powerful unions. By the late 1960s, a new class of elderly snowbirds—the boomer generation's grandparents—established a middle-class ideal of retirement not as a time of pinched dependency on children or charity but as an opportunity for relaxation and leisure activities that they could not have imagined when they were raising children during the Depression. My own maternal grandparents, who both came from working-class backgrounds, were able to escape the bitter Chicago winters and begin spending part of each year in Florida in the early 1960s with what they had saved during the flush postwar years from my grandfather's bar and bowling alley and small real estate business. My parents certainly expected to do even better by the time they reached their sixties. Thus, the views of middle-class boomers about the economic prospects for old age—to the extent that we thought about old age at all—were strongly shaped by the stories of our upwardly mobile grandparents and by the even greater advantages enjoyed by our parents.

To this point, I have been talking about the economic expectations of the older boomers, who came of age in the second half of the 1960s and the early 1970s. It has often been said that the boomers really should be divided into two generations—those born from 1946 to 1957, which demographers mark as the height of the postwar boom, and those born from 1958 through 1964, the demographic terminus of the boomer population bulge. (It is no coincidence that the end of the baby boom coincided with the widespread availability of the birth control pill, the first easily obtainable, almost totally reliable contraceptive over which women had complete control.) But prosperity in youth was experienced by younger as well as older boomers. Barack Obama tries to position himself as America's first "postboomer" president, but he is well within the margins of the younger sector of the baby boom population. Younger baby boomers raised in upwardly mobile middle-class families, like the older boomers, grew up in an environment in which their parents were able to save as well as spend. Even those raised in more straitened economic circumstances, like Barack and Michelle Obama, were able to enjoy the benefits of scholarships and loans in a society that was investing more in higher education. (And they did not have to fight a war to receive those benefits.) The younger baby boomers also managed to get through college before the steep tuition hikes that would affect Gen X children born in the 1970s and 1980s. Anyone who thinks that the recessions of the mid-1970s or the early 1980s had the same profoundly unnerving effect on the psychic security of young adult boomers that today's economic downturn is having on Americans now in the same age group is suffering from historical amnesia. When times grew tough from, roughly, 1973 to 1975 and again in the early years of the Reagan administration, boomers simply acquired more credit cards, whether they were in their twenties or thirties at the time of their greatest financial stress. I never gave a second thought, at thirty-six, to taking out a mortgage at a 16.5 percent interest rate—a historic high—when I had the unexpected chance to buy the apartment that I had rented for years in Manhattan. I assumed, buoyed, like my contemporaries, by the expectations of my youth, that times would get better and I would be able to refinance at a more reasonable rate. And I was right. At roughly the same time, Obama, in his early twenties, took what his parents' generation would have considered a totally unacceptable risk—spending several years at a variety of jobs between college and law school while trying to figure out what to do with the rest of his life. As is well known, Obama worked as a community organizer, among other jobs, in New York and Chicago between his graduation from Columbia University in 1983 and his entrance into Harvard Law School in 1988. This was classic boomer behavior, influenced by the cultural path paved by older boomers in the 1960s, when departing from a rigid linear progression from college to professional school to a lifelong career became socially acceptable. Like my purchase of an apartment—which my parents considered risky but I did not—Obama's experimentation after college was rooted in the economic optimism shared by both halves of the boomer generation. Just two decades earlier, putting off the chance to turn a bachelor's degree into a law degree would have been seen as rash for a young white man and almost unhinged for a young black man.

(There was also a small, fortunate cohort—those born in the late 1930s and early 1940s—wedged between the greatest generation and the older baby boomers. The men in this demi-generation were too young to fight in Korea and too old to fight in Vietnam, but like the boomers who followed them, the "baby bust" generation grew up with the economic advantages of being raised by parents who enjoyed all of the financial rewards of having seen the war through to the end. Furthermore, this small group of late-Depression and early-war babies entered the job market under even more favorable conditions than the boomers, because the economy was expanding but there was less competition from their contemporaries.)

It is important to note, however, that expectations of continuing stability and prosperity—notwithstanding the characteristic boomer optimism displayed by superachievers like Obama—were held much more strongly by middle-class and upper-middle-class white boomers than by African Americans or poor whites. (Hispanics, apart from the cartoonish Ricky Ricardo on *I Love Lucy,* had not even figured in the perceived cultural mix of the 1950s, the formative decade for older boomers.) Black Americans of the boomer generation were much more likely to have grown up in three-generation households, out of economic necessity as well as cultural tradition, than whites.* The postwar migra-

* Today, black and Hispanic Americans are still twice as likely as whites to live in a household with their grandchildren. Approximately 8 percent of African Americans and Hispanics over thirty, compared with 4 percent of Americans as a whole, live in three-generation homes.

tion of whites to the suburbs, which were still almost entirely closed to blacks, increased generational as well as class segregation and misled many middle-class white boomers about the economic problems of growing old in the richest nation on earth. The only old people most of us knew when we were growing up were our own grandparents, with whom we had limited direct contact if we did not live in the same town. If our grandparents were able to take care of themselves, as mine were when they were in their sixties and I was in my twenties, we assumed that other people's grandparents were in the same position. As for the old old, they were largely invisible. I did not have any occasion to see the face of old-age poverty until I finished college and went to work as a reporter for the *Post*. There, on the streets of Washington, I saw poor old people who had been completely nonexistent, or at least out of sight, on the suburban streets of my childhood.

In the mid-1960s, before the country and Lyndon Johnson's presidency were consumed by the Vietnam War, LBJ's War on Poverty was highlighting the plight of poor people, particularly the young, in cities. Ironically, the poor old were growing poorer at a time when the number of Americans living below the poverty line in other age groups was declining. The poverty that mattered most was the poverty of the young, and while that makes sense as future-oriented social policy, it ignores the fact that the old must eat too and that, as Franklin D. Roosevelt's aide Harry Hopkins observed during the Depression, "people don't eat in the long run." In the second half of the sixties, old-age poverty increased as poverty in other groups declined. The Senate Special Committee on Aging found that between 1968 and 1969, the number of Americans over sixty-five living in poverty grew by more than two hundred thousand, to a total of 4.8 million. During the same period, the number of the poor in all other age groups declined by 1.2 million.[4] There were two reasons for the expansion of the poor elderly population during the sixties—increasing longevity and the fact that many new retirees had entered the labor force during the Depression and therefore had relatively low lifetime earnings upon which their Social Security benefits were calculated. (In the early 1970s, Congress passed a significant increase in Social Security benefits, and the proportion of old people living in poverty began to fall slowly in spite of inflation.) Members of my parents' generation, still middle-aged, would reap the benefit of these adjustments, but their already old parents were much poorer than the World War II generation would be after retirement. My grandparents, I began to realize, had been much luckier than most of their contemporaries from equally modest working-class backgrounds. (I eventually learned that their economic good fortune was the result not only of the respectable postwar bowling alley and real estate business but of Gramps's having earned quite a good living as a bookie during the 1930s.)

In the nation's capital, most of the poor old people I met on my rounds as a reporter were black. They were not only the wrong race but, as the incisive social critic Michael Harrington wrote in *The Other America,* "the wrong age to be seen. . . . [The aged poor] are often sick, and they cannot move. Another group of them live out their lives in loneliness and frustration: they sit in rented rooms, or else they stay close to a house in a neighborhood that has completely changed from the old days. Indeed, one of the worst aspects of poverty among the aged is that these people are out of sight and out of mind, and alone."[5] In the 1960s, in Washington and around the country, growing numbers of poor old people were losing many of the public and private spaces where they had once belonged, where they could be seen and see one another. Their daily lives were affected negatively not only by the chronic poverty Harrington described but by one of the unintended consequences of the spreading youth culture of the sixties—the demise of many commercial establishments that had once welcomed old people on fixed incomes. In 1970, a report prepared by the National Council on Aging described the reluctance of many businesses to accommodate older customers:

> If too many of them frequented a cafeteria where food was low in cost and where it was possible to sit for a long time over a cup of coffee and a roll, younger people began to go elsewhere to eat, repelled by the sight of arthritic hands carefully counting out coins, dragging feet, and clothes unkempt or clumsily restyled. All too often even a friendly proprietor was obliged to change the rule [allowing people to linger over one cup of coffee] or close his restaurant. Then the [older] customers disappeared, to hot dog stands or to the hot plate in a furnished room.[6]

This sad process, which unfolded before my eyes as a young reporter, was not simply a bit of vanishing Americana but a harbinger of what was to come for old Americans without the resources to take care of themselves in a sunny climate. At the time, Washington was home to a small chain of cafeterias called Scholl's, which served much the same function (albeit on a smaller scale) as Horn & Hardhart did in New York City. When I first went to work for the *Post* and, like most cub reporters, was on the late shift, I used to eat dinner in a nearby Scholl's because it offered the best value on my skimpy salary. I was always aware of the old age of most of the other customers, and I remember carrying cafeteria trays for people who could not manage them and their canes at the same time. People did linger for an hour over coffee; no alcohol was served, and the atmosphere was one of deadly propriety. As soon as pay raises allowed, I moved on to bars that served a younger crowd and worse food at higher prices. The National Council on Aging was quite right: I hadn't much enjoyed eating my meals surrounded by people who held up the cafeteria line by carefully counting out their change and who shouted at one another across the table because so many of them had impaired hearing. The last Scholl's took a few decades to go out of business—although when the end arrived, it wasn't for lack of customers but because of rising rents. (The Scholl's where I used to eat, at the corner of Vermont Avenue and K Street—just a few blocks from the White House—was transformed into a Citibank branch. There is certainly a good case to be made that a steady supply of cheap meat loaf, mashed potatoes, and Parker House rolls would have provided much more long-term benefit than another bank branch to the residents, young and old, of the nation's capital. The same process played out with the Horn & Hardhart cafeterias in New York; when the last Automat closed in my neighborhood in the 1980s, the old people who used to sit for hours over a cup of coffee and a piece of pie were forced to move on to McDonald's—the only other affordable establishment where customers were allowed to sit as long as they liked.)

The disappearance of restaurants that had once welcomed the old, the poor, and in many cases the infirm was not a cause but a symptom of the generational segregation that—in spite of the people of Dr. Spock's age who marched with the young against the war—became more widespread during the sixties. And I believe that the sixties also marked the beginning of the division between the relatively healthy young old and the less visible, more frail old old that defines American attitudes toward aging today. Maggie Kuhn and the Gray Panthers were the face of the feisty, newly empowered young old in the 1960s; the hunched-over women trying to balance their canes and trays while carefully counting out the nickels and pennies to pay for their supper at Scholl's were the face of the powerless old old. You had to be fit enough and healthy enough to march in demonstrations in order to be embraced with the patronizing "young at heart" designation. If your heart was literally too weak for you to march and be seen marching, who in the outside world could perceive you as young in spirit? But if you were strong enough to keep up and embraced the values of the truly young people around you, age could be seen as just a number rather than a physical reality. That is the way many of the more privileged members of my generation have chosen to look at age, aging, and the old for most of our adult lives. We did not envisage the power of "just a number" when the number had not yet come to claim us.

The cultural milieu of the late 1960s and early 1970s—inseparable from but outlasting the prosperity of that time—has been equally important in shaping the conviction that age can be defied. A vital part of that culture, for the oldest and the youngest boomers, was a belief in the possibility of repeated self-reinventions—through therapy, through religious conversion, through self-help, through determined efforts to change the very shape of our flesh—without regard to chronological age.

It was not only Obama's time-out between college and law school that followed a classic pattern set by older boomers while "Barry" was growing up in Indonesia and Hawaii. He was over thirty and his wife, Michelle, was twenty-eight when they married, and they delayed having children for several more years. The extension of a young adulthood unencumbered by a permanent job or personal commitments (whether you consider that extension a good or bad development) has proved to be one of the lasting imprints of the boomer generation. It is more or less taken for granted today that the choices people make in their early twenties are provisional and reversible, but even during the first half of the 1960s, there was a considerable stigma attached to a woman who graduated from college without an engagement ring on her finger and to a male graduate (unless he was going on to law or medical school) who had not landed what seemed like a job with a future. Taking time off to travel around the world, acquiring sexual experience with people whom one was not necessarily intent on marrying, and changing career plans laid out in college were choices that began to seem socially acceptable only in the late 1960s. This sense of entitlement to change course was not the least of the cultural divisions between the boomers and their parents—as well as those born in the 1930s and early 1940s. The boomers did not belong to the generation in which, as Philip Roth (born in 1933) observed, "everyone *wanted* to be thirty." Above all, adulthood for those who came of age before the 1960s had always meant that there was no getting off this train. In the late 1960s and 1970s, by contrast, the cultural message was, "You don't have to get on this train at all. And if you do climb on board, you can get off at the next stop." This message had its good and its bad points. The provisional nature of young adulthood made it possible to alter a clearly wrong course without being paralyzed by shame or the accusation that a desire for change was a clear sign of immaturity. On the negative side, the sense that it was possible to endlessly re-create oneself blurred the distinction between malleable social influences and intractable biological imperatives. It was easy to be fooled by appearances—especially one's own.

In no area of life was this more evident than in the decision of so many highly educated, professional boomer women in the 1970s to delay childbearing until the last possible moment, thereby creating emotional havoc when a woman or a couple was forced to face the fact that getting pregnant and carrying a baby to term become vastly and progressively more difficult after age thirty-five. An entire high-tech fertility industry developed in response to the self-deluded refusal of this demographic group to acknowledge the connection between childbearing and age. Fortunately, younger boomers and Gen X women learned from the mistakes of their elders. Most women today know that if children are essential to their vision of a fulfilling adult life, they must start dealing with the issue in their early thirties and not assume that they are going to be among a group of lucky forty-year-olds who conceive a healthy last-chance baby. More than two decades ago, I interviewed a number of women in their late thirties and early forties—from the older boomer cohort—on the subject of infertility for *Glamour* magazine. A few had simply remained unmarried until their late thirties, but most had been married for many years before trying to conceive. They all offered variants of the same story, which amounted to, "I just didn't know I was going to have trouble getting pregnant because of my age. . . . I've always taken good care of myself. . . . I look and feel much younger than my mother did at the same age." It didn't occur to these women that however young they may have looked and felt, appearances have nothing to do with the age-related deterioration and loss of healthy eggs in a woman's reproductive system. Today, I see a disturbing symmetry between the failure of many boomers to pay attention to the ticking of their biological clocks in their thirties and the conviction that they can actually make time stand still as they enter their sixties. That the Obamas are invariably described as "young" by the media (still run by boomers but increasingly shaped by younger adults) is itself a reflection of the somewhat distorted view of aging that boomers have disseminated throughout the culture. Young in relation to whom? By any realistic demographic standard, the Obamas are middle-aged—a description that boomers dislike almost as much as the word "old."

Although I do not possess a scintilla of nostalgia for the rigid, age-related expectations that defined my parents' adult lives, there is a huge difference between working on what can and should be changed (to paraphrase the Serenity Prayer of Alcoholics Anonymous) and refusing to accept what cannot be changed. The ubiquitous inner-directed self-help ethos of the 1970s, which defined the coming-of-age of many boomers as much as the outer-directed social protest movements of the 1960s, has proved to be one of the most durable legacies of that time. Movements asserting that ninety can become the new fifty *if we only try hard enough* are the direct descendants of movements that assured us, just four decades ago, that we might remake outer reality by laboring at self-driven inner change through everything from psychotherapy to embracing a new religion. Part of the power of self-help is its transcendence of political divisions. Today's Christian right groups aiming to "change" homosexuals into heterosexuals are as committed to remaking reality, and as doomed to failure, as the 1970s couples who had open marriages in the hope of eliminating sexual jealousy. Self-help, of course, is a philosophy and a marketable business as old as America, from Benjamin

Franklin's autobiography through Norman Vincent Peale's *The Power of Positive Thinking* (which was published in the 1930s and has never gone out of print) and Gail Sheehy's *Passages* in the 1970s to Oprah (who will surely be replaced as an entertainment icon by someone else, unimaginable as that may seem at the moment, now that she has said her last goodbye to her weeping studio audience). What distinguished the self-help culture of the 1970s from earlier American self-help incarnations—and remains with us today—was the shift from the useful and traditional message "You can change your life" to the less salutary, often antirational message that we are capable of changing anything about our lives if only we don't "sabotage" ourselves. The latter message is bound to lead to grief when aimed at that most intractable of realities, old age.

In some respects, the inner-directed decade of the seventies represented a reaction, motivated by sheer exhaustion, to the social upheavals and movements of the sixties that had promised so much and, from a decidedly short-term perspective, delivered so little. In 1970, with the recent memory of cities burning after Martin Luther King's assassination, almost no one (with the interesting exception of New York's liberal Republican senator Jacob Javits) could see forty years down the road to President Barack Obama.* Veterans of the antiwar movement were also tired and thoroughly frustrated by the drawn-out ending of the Vietnam War during the years of Richard Nixon's presidency. Many experienced a profound sense of futility when the fighting did not end until 1975—and only after the American invasion of Cambodia had been responsible for the rise of the Khmer Rouge, who went on to murder millions more of their countrymen. In retrospect, it is not surprising that many young (and not-so-young) people turned in the following decade to groups and to psychological and religious gurus

* Actually, the year was 1958 when Javits predicted the election of a black president by the year 2000. In a startlingly prescient essay for *Esquire* magazine, titled "Integration from the Top Down," Javits asked, "What manner of man will this be, this possible Negro Presidential candidate of 2000? Undoubtedly, he will be well-educated. He will be well-traveled and have a keen grasp of his country's role in the world and its relationships. He will be a dedicated internationalist with working comprehension of the intricacies of foreign aid, technical assistance and reciprocal trade. . . . Assuredly, though, despite his other characteristics, he will have developed the fortitude to withstand the vicious smear attacks that came his way as he fought to the top in government and politics. . . . Those in the vanguard may not expect to be the targets for scurrilous attacks, as the hate mongers, in their last-ditch efforts, spew their verbal and written poison."

promising transformation from within in the era that some have sentimentalized as "the golden age of self-help."[7]

It was as easy in the 1970s as it is today to satirize even the more reasonable manifestations of the self-help movement. The psychiatrist Thomas A. Harris's *I'm OK, You're OK,* a title that permeated popular culture so thoroughly that people soon forgot its origins, was first published in 1969 as a popularization of an earlier best seller, *Games People Play* (1964), by the psychiatrist Eric Berne. But Harris, who had been Berne's protégé, had an even more receptive audience for his how-to book, which evangelized on behalf of the more authentic, joyous lives that could be attained through a therapeutic method known as transactional analysis, or, more affectionately, TA.* Harris's book did not actually make it to the *Times* best-seller list until 1972, but it remained there for nearly two years and became one of the best selling self-help books of all time. In his introduction, Harris bluntly states the self-help credo of the decade: "If the relationship between two people can be made creative, fulfilling, and free of fear, then it follows that this can work for two relationships, or three or one hundred or, we are convinced, for relationships that affect entire social groups, even nations. The problems of the world . . . essentially are the problems of individuals. If individuals can change, the course of the world can change."[8] On a superficial level, this statement sounds very much like the feminist slogan "The personal is political." In fact, Harris's self-help mantra ran directly counter to the feminist movement (though feminism did include a self-help component in the form of consciousness raising). But what feminists meant when they asserted that the personal is political was that many difficulties women had viewed as isolated, individual problems were the result of sex discrimination built into social, economic, and political institutions. While it might be necessary, in the interest of personal happiness, to change one's own relationship with men or with an employer, individual change was no substitute for institutional changes that, say, imposed meaningful legal penalties for domestic violence or that outlawed sex discrimination in employment. Individual change, or consciousness raising, might be necessary but it was far from sufficient.

It is also important that TA was a form of therapy practiced in groups

* TA, as it was known to every sentient being in the 1970s, was the name given to the therapy by Berne.

and that *I'm OK, You're OK* was published at a time when even the relatively small number of people who had been willing to invest their time and money in interminable one-on-one psychoanalysis were beginning to think that their resources might be better devoted to something that promised results in, say, less than five to ten years. Group therapy was a lot cheaper than psychoanalysis, and it appealed to people who had come of age in the more open emotional and sexual atmosphere of the 1960s, when the fact that a man had potency problems or a women had trouble reaching orgasm no longer seemed like dark secrets that could only be confided while prone on a couch to a silent, authoritative father figure (or, more rarely, mother figure). Easy as it is to make fun of a philosophy highly unsuited to resolving dilemmas in which no one is OK, one need only reread this book (I read it in the 1970s too) to realize that the therapeutic and self-help ideas expounded by Harris have about as much relationship to the staged "therapy" dispensed by twenty-first-century TV psychologists like Phil McGraw as Dante's *Inferno* (the book) has to do with the infernal *Inferno* video game released in 2010. Consider this passage from Harris, following a description of TA sessions for parents who wanted to learn how to discipline their children without violence:

> I believe people who have capitalized on violence have taken comfort from the point of view certain psychologists have held that watching violence is a safety valve which helps persons drain off violence rather than act it out. There is no way to validate this point of view. I believe there is mounting evidence, in fact, to invalidate it. These psychologists hold the view that feelings accumulate as if in a pail that every so often must be emptied. It is more accurate to think of feelings as a replay of old recordings which can be turned off at will. We do not have to go around dumping our feelings; we can simply turn them off, keep them from flooding our computer, and can, instead, fill that computer with something else. Emerson said, "A man is what he thinks about all day long."[9]

What a sensible (in the nearly archaic sense of being fully aware as well as the modern sense of reasonable) passage this is! Yet Harris never explains, for example, exactly how you get from a therapy session that helps an abusive parent change his or her ways—which would seem to be difficult enough—to a culture that does not glorify violence. He mentions gun violence as a major social problem in his book, but he never addresses the question of how a great many perfectly nice people, who would doubtless never dream of beating up their children, can support political candidates who are responsible for laws that allow deranged Americans easy access to guns. What was missing from the golden age of self-help—even in its most helpful incarnations—was a firm sense of the distinction between outer realities that can be affected by inner change and those, like age itself, that cannot.

The self-help spectrum ranged from ideas like TA, which were reasonable whether you accepted their basic premises or not, to secular and religious cults that functioned as if the objective outer world did not exist. I define a cult as a group that not only regards outsiders with fear and disdain but tries to prevent its members from pursuing any goals that conflict with the group's ideology. By this standard, cults included both sui generis movements like the Moonies (followers of the Reverend Sun Myung Moon, a Korean entrepreneur-guru) and ultra-Orthodox Hasidic sects that took in many young people who had rejected their modern Orthodox, Conservative, or Reform Jewish backgrounds. (I am well aware that some will object to my use of the term "cult" to describe the Hasidim, whose historical roots go back several centuries, but I do not know what else you would call a religious sect that essentially requires its adherents to live as Jews did in seventeenth-century Poland. It is sometimes said that the only difference between a cult and a mainstream religion is time, but attempting to maintain isolation from the era in which one lives is also a feature of cults.) All of these insular groups attracted confused young people looking for more structure in their lives, including many who had overdosed on drugs and promiscuous sex during the 1960s. Communities of Christian "Jesus freaks" offered the same kind of structure to young people who wanted strict rules to govern themselves. On the surface, many of the historically rooted religious movements of the seventies could not have been more different from secular, commercial self-help programs like EST. (EST stands for Erhard Seminars Training, named for a California hustler, a former car salesman who—after changing his name to Werner Erhard from John Rosenberg in the early 1960s—got rich in the 1970s by persuading Americans looking for nirvana to shell out $250 for sixty-hour training "seminars" in which they were told that everything, from cancer to the death of a child, was basically all in their heads. EST seminar leaders called participants assholes if they claimed that their problems had anything to do with an outer, objective reality. Restriction of bathroom privileges and food intake was a basic feature of the EST sessions, which were compared to brainwashing by many investigative reporters at the time.)* What the religious cults of the 1970s had in common with EST's secular psychological gobbledygook was their hostility to rationality and their ability to separate people from their money.

From the psychological standpoint of the recipient of an authoritarian message, there was little difference between hearing an EST seminar leader tell a disciple that she was responsible for her own cancer and hearing a Satmar rebbe tell a refugee from a wicked secular Jewish home that she must not see her sister because her sister wore short skirts and did not shave her head and cover it with a *sheitel*. Furthermore, both religious and secular cults were rooted in the belief that it is possible to wipe out the past. Change your name from Eric to Elijah and you can shuck off an upbringing in a home in which being a devoutly observant Jew, according to a model laid out centuries ago, was not the single most important fact of your life.

Of course, most members of the boomer generation never found themselves in thrall to EST, Jesus freaks, or Jews who chose to live in modern ghettos, but the connections between the fringes, whether secular or religious, and mainstream self-help ideologies was the idea that changing one's own attitude could change everything. Long after the EST suckers had written off their losses ($250 was, after all, a considerable sum in the early 1970s), long after pilgrims had returned from trips to India after failing to find definitive bliss with Baba Ram Dass,

* Mark Brewer, in a lengthy, much reprinted analysis published in 1975 in *Psychology Today,* described the technique used by Tony Freedley, one of Erhard's original followers and a senior EST trainer. "He goes for the throat," Brewer wrote. "They [the particpants] were present because their lives did not work. Their lives were shit. Hopeless. They did not know what they were doing, they did not know how to live, were struggling, desperate, confused. They were ASSHOLES! Tony savored the word a moment, used it again, and thenceforth, as is a matter of course in the training, the recruits were always referred to as assholes . . . until they 'got it.'" Barbara Grizzuti Harrison, in an essay titled "Invasion of the Mind-Stealers" published in the long-defunct seventies magazine *Viva,* described her experience at an EST seminar in this fashion: "It's as if the Wizard of Oz had set up business in Dachau and invited victims to pay $250 a marked head for the privilege of being stripped naked and dynamited. Or, it's like being on a tour of a minefield with an insane guide who, speaking in tongues, leads his passive charges to exactly those mines that will explode in their beseeching faces."

long after some of the new Hasidim had decided that the seventeenth century wasn't such a great time to live after all, there remained a strong residue of conviction among many boomers that personal change is the answer to most problems. The lasting impact of the golden age of self-help on those who were young in that time is the belief that if only one can find the *right* new path, it might be possible to overcome some of the more intractable and distressing realities of the human condition and life cycle. If the particular form of self-help you chose had failed to transform your life in the desired fashion, the proper response was not to accept the immutability of certain realities but to find a new answer in a new medium of transformation.

For many boomers now in their fifties and early sixties, the narcissistic component of the self-help movements that flourished in our young adulthood has fused with a faith in science and medicine (the latter consisting of both modern high-tech and alternative treatments) to reinforce our determination to "defy" age. "Thinking young" and "being open to change" are seen as the most important manifestations of successful aging, and even our generally worshipful attitude toward medicine coexists, not always easily, with a self-help ethos insisting that clean and virtuous living (including an apple and several servings of dark greens a day) will indeed keep the doctor away. One of the most frequent, predictable comments made by my contemporaries and near contemporaries, ranging from their mid-fifties to mid-sixties, is, "We've lived much healthier lives than our parents, and that's why we look and feel so much better than our parents did at the same age." As a group (especially in the upper middle class), aging boomers have lived in a healthier way than their parents—if only because more of us never smoked, or gave up smoking at a relatively early stage in our adult lives. But as for looking and feeling better, I'm not so sure. I recently came across a faded snapshot of my parents on a trip to the Caribbean in the 1970s. My mother was in her mid-fifties, and my dad in his early sixties; they are both trim, tan, and wearing shorts, and they look terrific. If there was any significant difference between their level of health and activity thirty years ago and mine today, I don't remember it and I can't see it in the visual record of their lives. For my father, there was an invisible difference; a heavy smoker for most of his adult life, he would be dead of lung cancer within ten years. My mother now lives in her own apartment in a retirement facility with several levels of care. She is no longer fit because she suffers from the severe pain of advanced osteoporosis. Even though she exercised regularly in her sixties and seventies, her activities are increasingly circumscribed by her physical limitations. We do not talk much about this, about how she feels about these limitations, about how she views her own longevity. I suspect the main reason I do not raise these questions is that I am afraid to hear her answers. But I know one thing: my mother's mental grit cannot change the physical realities of her life, and there are no "medical miracles" on the horizon that will make her life better.

The health gurus, online and offline, who suggest that lifestyle changes can somehow produce a "real age" that is more real than one's biological age are really selling snake oil. The lifestyle changes themselves are not the snake oil; anyone is going to feel better generally and have a more satisfying life if she doesn't smoke, drinks alcohol only in moderation, exercises regularly, and maintains meaningful relationships with friends and family. But that tells us little about whether an individual will actually live longer or remain healthy during that long life. Studies do show that the average life expectancy of a group of people with good health habits is higher when compared with a group that drinks heavily, smokes, and exercises only by clicking the remote. That group generalization, however, tells us nothing about the ticking clock within an individual. A fifty-year-old who is told that her "real age" is forty (thanks to exercise and a dog) may already be incubating a form of cancer that will end her life in only ten years. Or she may die in a nursing home at age ninety-five, after years of Alzheimer's. The dog and the exercise are good things *in themselves,* but they really tell us nothing about what fate awaits an individual in the final decades of his or her life. One's real age is one's real age. In his fifties, a dear friend of mine would submit once a year to the uncomfortable male ritual of a manual prostate examination, and he would always report, with a mixture of pleasure and skepticism, that the doctor told him he had "the prostate of a thirty-year-old." That is, until he didn't—and he was affected by the benign prostate enlargement that eventually comes to nearly all men, producing symptoms that can generally be controlled by drugs. "What happened to the prostate of a thirty-year-old?" my friend asked his urologist, who, once symptoms appeared, dropped his reassuring line about youthful prostates. He replied, "You haven't been thirty for thirty years." Denial is not necessarily a bad thing—as long as one never loses sight of the reality that is being denied. The growing number of Americans who turn to cosmetic surgery and chemical fixes like Botox attests not only to the desire to turn back the clock but to the belief that it is possible to do so. There is no doubt that a sixty-year-old woman may look better after surgery to minimize her jowls and smooth out the chicken neck that is one of the telltale signs of physical aging, but she will still be (and look like) a sixty-year-old who has had a "successful" face-lift and chin-lift. The desire of baby boomers to remain physically fit—fitter than their parents were at the same age—benefits their physical and mental health only if the pursuit of fitness is not accompanied by the delusion that a combination of exercise and endless high-tech surgeries will restore not only the general well-being but the athletic capacities and/or appearance of youth.

Joint replacement surgery, for example, used to be performed mainly on those over sixty-five and on people whose joints were so painful that they interfered with everyday activities. During the past decade, the percentage of hip and knee replacements performed on men and women from forty-five to sixty-four increased rapidly, according to the American Academy of Orthopaedic Surgeons—an increase due largely to the determination of athletic baby boomers to continue to engage in the challenging, high-impact sports that they have played since their teens. One such patient, profiled in *The New York Times,* is fifty-two-year-old Jay MacDonald, an investment banker who has already had one knee replacement, arthroscopic surgery for torn cartilage on both knees, and rotator cuff surgery on his right shoulder. He had to beg his surgeon, Dr. Stephen J. O'Brien, at New York's Hospital for Special Surgery, to perform the rotator cuff surgery even though O'Brien thought the chances of success were extremely low. "You have to," MacDonald told his surgeon. "I want my life back. I want to surf—I've been surfing since I was 8. I do big waves, 16-footers. I can't stop just because of a rotator cuff."[10] Not only does this investment banker want to enjoy sports and live his life pain-free, *he wants to be able to do what he did when he was a kid*. O'Brien repeatedly counsels middle-aged patients with replaced knees and shoulders to moderate their exercise—to run twenty miles a week instead of forty, or take easier skiing trails—but he repeatedly runs up against the expectations of patients who believe that aging means never having to give up anything. Many of these repeat orthopedic surgery candidates sound like cosmetic surgery addicts: they never consider what their refusal to make any compromises with aging might mean over a long period. Harry Packman, a fifty-year-old lawyer and another patient of O'Brien's, has had sixteen surgeries on his knees and shoulders since his mid-twenties and plays in three softball leagues. "He's spent a lot of time in physical therapy," the *Times* reported. "That's where he met his third wife, who was working as an athletic trainer at a rehab center while he was rebuilding a back muscle torn playing touch football."[11] Perhaps the first two wives got tired of having a husband who spent most of his time playing baseball and football, having one surgery after another to repair the injuries to his aging body, and spending time in rehab so that he could return to the field and injure himself again. Repeated injuries surely ought to be a red flag to anyone that his or her body is saying no to a continuation of activities that came naturally at ages fifteen, twenty-five, and thirty-five. Consider the difference between these Peter Pans and the great pitcher Sandy Koufax, who retired from baseball at age thirty-one, after a 27–9 season in 1966, because he was pitching with constant, acute pain in his elbow and did not want to risk crippling his arm for life. Of course, Koufax was a professional athlete, and professionals tend to have a more accurate estimation than weekend warriors of what their bodies can do. And if Koufax were pitching today, he could take advantage of arthroscopic surgeries that were not available to his generation of athletes. The point is not that boomers should adopt a sedentary way of life at the first twinge in their muscles and the first ache in their joints (indeed, inactivity accelerates such problems) but that a refusal to adapt to the inevitable changes of aging—manifested by a demand for endless surgeries that only demonstrate the extent of the violence that seekers after the fountain of youth are inflicting on their bodies—bodes ill for a future in which somewhere, someday, a conscientious surgeon will have to say, "No more." Charley Lau, a former hitting coach who exerted an enormous influence on baseball players in the 1970s and 1980s, once observed that "the player who ages poorly is the one who lets his vanity get in the way of his judgment. Making 'adjustments' is another word for having the good sense to know that you're getting older."[12] As an example, Lau cited Reggie Jackson, the slugger and Hall of Famer who, in his mid-thirties, manifested a weakness—an inability to get around on high fastballs—characteristic of aging home run hitters. Jackson, who might have been out of baseball before he reached the 500 home run mark that (in the era before steroids) guaranteed election to the Hall of Fame, altered his stance and worked with a lighter bat until he started hitting home runs on that pesky pitch to the opposite field. He retired at age forty-one, with 563 homers. Nonprofessional fitness obsessives who refuse to recognize and adjust to physical limitations in their fifties and sixties are in precisely the same position, psychologically and physically, as middle-aged professional athletes who delude themselves about being able to succeed by performing exactly as they did in their younger days. In effect, the driven amateurs among the boomers are saying, "I not only want to ski, but I want to ski the most difficult slopes the way I used to. I not only want to continue running, but I want to continue running marathons. And I'm willing to do anything—pay any price, bear any burden, have myself cut open dozens of times—to make that happen."

The question is how the boomers will react when they discover, as those who live long enough inevitably will, that age is not just a number and that the desire to look younger or push one's body to the edge athletically is much more easily satisfied by modern medicine than the desire to remain free of life-threatening, age-linked diseases. At some point, nearly every boomer will have to cope with the shattering of vanity and self-delusion about the capacity to remain, as the song goes, forever young. Just before Christmas, I was standing in line at a frigid bus stop when an old woman, who appeared to be in her eighties and was hunched over and crippled by osteoporosis, wheeled her chair onto the bus lift and told the driver, "Let me off at the stop closest to Bloomingdale's." A woman next to me, who appeared to be in her fifties, whispered under her breath in a voice that could be heard by everyone at the bus stop, "I'd rather be dead than live like that." My thought had been that anyone willing to venture into Bloomingdale's, with or without a wheelchair, during the week before Christmas must still be strongly engaged with life. But the fifty-something's inability to empathize with a woman in a wheelchair—or even to imagine an old age in which pain and difficulty are constant companions—is consistent with the denial of aging that has always been characteristic of my generation. Most people who live into their eighties are not confined to wheelchairs, but some are. If people live into their nineties, their chances of incurring severe disability go up even more sharply. In the nursing home where my grandmother ended her life, only a handful of the residents were *not* wheelchair bound. That severe disability in advanced old age is a real possibility does not mean that it is a certainty. Nor does it mean that boomers should fail, in middle and early old age, to maintain habits and activities that will make life better today and may stave off some of the worst afflictions of old age, should they live into their ninth and tenth decades, for a few extra years. But the operative word is "may." It is a failure of both imagination and reason to assume that some generational magic based on self-help and self-discipline, or future advances in medicine and technology, will ensure that we will never be one of those unfortunates in a wheelchair.

CHAPTER FOUR

Miracles of Modern Medicine and Other Half-truths

Who would deny that we live in an age of medical miracles? The boomer generation has had a ringside seat for the unveiling of each new marvel, from the polio shots we received as kids to the stents that are now keeping Dick Cheney and Bill Clinton alive. Ours was the first generation for whom antibiotics were always available and the last to spend any part of its childhood fearing the scourge of polio. The first medical memory of many of the oldest boomers, born in 1946, is standing in line to receive the Salk polio vaccine in 1955. Because major polio outbreaks had struck during nearly every summer after World War II—averaging twenty thousand cases a year—we were used to being kept indoors and forbidden by anxious parents from going near public swimming pools or beaches.[1] Late at night, after our mothers and fathers thought we were asleep, we would hear them whispering about a girl on the next block who would never be able to walk again without braces, about a boy who was confined to an iron lung and whose parents had "lost hope." Only a year before the success of the nationwide Salk vaccine trials was announced by researchers, both my brother and I had come down with severe headaches, muscle pain, high fevers, and vomiting—all known to be early symptoms of polio. When our fevers broke and it became clear that the sore muscles were not going to be followed by paralysis, our usually stoic mother dropped her head into her hands and wept for an hour. Only then did we understand how much danger she thought we were in. Astoundingly—we were still too young to understand how astounding it was—just two years would pass before the grown-ups stopped talking about polio altogether. We stood in those long lines in 1955, and by the summer of 1957, the number of new polio cases in the United States had fallen by nearly 75 percent.

By itself, victory over polio would probably have been enough to produce a profound optimism about the capacities of medicine among members of the boomer generation. But the miracles continued throughout our young adulthood and into middle age. When I was a child, the diagnosis of most forms of cancer meant a proximate, not a distant, death sentence. That is why the word "cancer" was so frequently avoided in the 1950s by patients themselves, their friends and relatives, and doctors who had to deliver the bad news. Today, countless Americans have lived for years with forms of cancer that would, only a few decades ago, have killed people within months. I have a close friend who received a kidney transplant nine years ago when he was only weeks away from death, and many other friends whose damaged hearts are beating steadily with the aid of defibrillators, stents, and pacemakers.

When we were already young adults, after all, both organ transplants and artificial joint replacements still belonged to the realm of science fiction. And while we certainly were not dwelling on old age while in our twenties, it did not occur to us—or, for that matter, to our grandparents—that much could be done about even the most mundane, non-life-threatening conditions of the aging body. Benign prostate enlargement, joints stiff and aching from arthritis, even the dreaded "dowager's hump" for unlucky old women (and a few men) with severe osteoporosis: these were simply taken for granted. Whatever practical difficulties and pain might be caused by these common changes associated with aging, they had to be endured because they could not be reversed or, in most instances, alleviated. Effective medications to lower blood pressure, reduce the pain of arthritis, relieve the frequent urination that is one of the most aggravating symptoms of a growing prostate, or slow the rate of bone loss among the elderly were experimental or nonexistent in the 1960s. There were no instruments, apart from the X-ray (which could only detect broken bones and certain tumors), enabling a doctor to view the intricate inner workings of the human body without cutting it open. In 1960, it would have seemed like voodoo for a cardiologist to tell a patient, if he had no obvious symptoms of heart disease, that his coronary arteries were largely blocked and an operation was needed *now* to prevent a heart attack. A heart attack—often a fatal one—was frequently the first and last piece of evidence that too little blood was reaching the vital organ. Today we take for granted the existence of drugs and surgical procedures to treat age-related conditions that were—not in the distant past but in our own adult lifetimes—swift and sure routes to death. So I suppose it is not surprising that many boomers are confident that they will live to witness other medical miracles in old age, in the form of better treatments or cures for the killers that still await everyone—the diseases that have, to this point, proved stubbornly resistant to both pharmacological and surgical intervention.

Unfortunately, this optimistic mind-set often fails to make a distinction between treatment and cure. There seems to be something approaching genuine public indignation at the fact that we have not yet found a way to cure cancer, still the most feared of diseases (followed by Alzheimer's). Richard M. Nixon, the first president to promise a "cure" for cancer, pledged in 1971 that the dreaded disease would be conquered in time for the celebration of the nation's bicentennial. According to this line of thinking, if we could put a man on the moon, we could certainly perform the feat of putting an end to a complex disease with intertwined genetic and environmental components. Barack Obama is only the latest in a long line of political leaders to commit himself to finding a cure for cancer—and his 2008 economic stimulus package, at a time of financial crisis, promised a one-third increase in federal money for cancer research. The phrase "war on cancer" is used frequently, by politicians, spokesmen for fund-raising groups, and prominent researchers. There have been significant advances in cancer treatments, many of which have fewer debilitating side effects than they did only a decade ago, and in early detection, which, in the case of some (but by no means all) cancers, means that the rogue cells are less likely to have spread at the time of diagnosis. And more people are living with cancer for more years. But the death rate from metastatic cancer (meaning that cancer cells have already spread through the lymph nodes and bloodstream when the disease is first identified) dropped only 5 percent between 1950 and 2005.[2] There is no cure for most serious forms of cancer—with the exception of certain childhood cancers—if what is meant by a cure is a procedure or a medication regimen that puts an end to the original condition, with little possibility of recurrence during a normal life span. In this sense, peritonitis from a burst appendix is curable, while most forms of cancer are not. To talk about winning a war on cancer is to talk about winning a war on death and aging—the latter being an increased risk factor for cancer just as it is for heart disease, Alzheimer's, and all of the other horsemen of death.

One of the most frequently made arguments by those who believe that age can be vanquished is that the disability rate has dropped substantially in the over-sixty-five population since the early 1980s. In March 2006, the U.S. Census Bureau issued a report indicating that the rate of self-reported disability—defined as "a substantial limitation in major life activity"—by Americans over sixty-five decreased from more than 26 percent in 1982 to just under 20 percent in 1999—a decline of about 1 percent per year.[3] That's good news, but it comes with a vital caveat that was left out of most of the optimistic media reports. Unfortunately, there is almost no evidence of a reduction in the rate of the severest disabilities among Americans over eighty-five—those who make up the bulk of the institutionalized population. In an exhaustive review that included many of the studies on which the reports of disability decline are based, *The Journal of the American Medical Association* gave a rating of "good" to only two out of eight major disability surveys. Four of the studies were rated "fair," one "poor," and another was given a mixed rating of "fair to poor."[4] Two of the widely quoted studies were based entirely on the noninstitutionalized over-sixty-five population. That people living in their own homes have a lower disability rate than those who are institutionalized seems so obvious that it is close to a journalistic felony to have reported the data from these studies without a huge warning flag. In the language of gerontological research, the most significant forms of impairment are called ADL (activities of daily living) disabilities, meaning that physical or mental decline—generally both—prevents people from managing important aspects of their lives. These include everything from going to the toilet to walking short distances without help. ADL disabilities produced by dementia are most strongly associated with the need for institutional care. Of all the surveys evaluated in the *JAMA* report, only one found any decline in the severest disabilities. The other surveys showed either no change or an increase. The authors state clearly that the much ballyhooed disability decline "did not hold across all specific measures of disability." The decline manifested itself mainly among old people with less severe limitations, usually physical, that interfered with such activities as doing household chores, shopping, lifting, climbing stairs, and walking.[5] Another recent analysis by the same authors, funded by the National Institute on Aging, concluded that much of the great decline in disability had been reported by those who had cardiovascular disease, musculoskeletal diseases (such as arthritis), and vision problems (such as cataracts).[6] This is a significant finding, because the everyday impact of all of these conditions—in contrast to a disease like Alzheimer's, which always ends in total disability—has been eased by much more effective surgical treatments and drugs developed during the pasty forty years. Arthritis is not curable, but its pain can be eased by anti-inflammatory drugs, and destroyed joints can be replaced. Joint replacement surgery was not even a possibility for our grandparents, and almost everyone my age can remember older relatives who became housebound as the pain grew intolerable. The great French writer Colette (1873–1954), who was wheelchair bound and largely confined to her apartment in the Palais Royal as a result of the severe arthritis that began to cripple her in the early 1940s, would, if she were alive today, probably have had hip replacement surgery and be walking jauntily along the Seine. In similar fashion, more sophisticated forms of cataract surgery have preserved the vision of millions who, as recently as the 1960s, would simply have gone blind. But these essentially technological advances should not be confused with cures or treatments for diseases—from cancer to Alzheimer's—that are not yet fully understood and that strike more frequently and more harshly when an aging immune system is already compromised. Such diseases account for most of the functional disabilities associated with advanced old age. One of the more startling findings of the recent NIH-funded study was that lifestyle changes in those over sixty-five—even among those in their sixties and seventies—had little to do with the overall decline in disability. Ordinary household devices, such as microwave ovens and cordless phones, and technologically driven changes like direct deposit banking were said to have more to do with enabling older Americans to go about their everyday lives. This strikes me as a highly suspect measure of reduced disability, since the fact that Grandma no longer has to get up to answer the phone does not mean that she is healthier; it simply means that she can remain sedentary and accomplish tasks that required physical effort fifty years ago. The University of Michigan economist Robert F. Schoeni, a coauthor of the analysis, said that "understanding what led to these improvements [in disability] is much more than an academic exercise" because, as the first baby boomers turn sixty-five, "it is imperative that policymakers and clinicians have a clear sense of what led to declining disability rates so that they can have the best chance of achieving future reductions that will allow millions of Americans to function independently well into old age."[7] It occurs to me that if laborsaving devices like microwaves and services like direct deposit banking are as important to old people as the study claims, these energy-conserving tools might actually be encouraging physical deterioration. I have an indelible image of my grandmother, in her early nineties, standing over her kitchen counter rolling out piecrust and putting pies in the oven. If her back hurt too much, she would sit down on a stool to avoid bending over when she used the oven—but she always managed to get the job done. Surely this level of activity kept her in better physical shape than putting a frozen entrée in a microwave night after night, and the food she made herself certainly had more nutritional value than precooked dinners from a supermarket freezer.

But even if reductions in minor functional disability over the past four decades—regardless of the cause—have improved the quality of life for the old, marketers of the new old age assume that the future will be much better for the boomer generation because of its longtime focus on a healthy lifestyle. Think again. There is certainly an educated, upper-middle-class segment among the boomers—the kind of people who obsess about their "real age" versus their chronological age—that does focus on healthy behavior as the key to a healthy old age. But a new and depressing study of Americans ages forty to seventy-four—a group that includes both the boomers and the young old—shows that boomers have developed poorer, not better, health habits as they have aged. The study, comparing the health habits of adults from 1988 to 2006, focused on five behaviors that have a positive impact on health—consumption of fruits and vegetables, regular exercise, moderating alcohol intake, abstaining from smoking, and maintaining a healthy weight. During the period of the study, adherence to all five healthy habits dropped from 15 percent of the population to 8 percent. Obesity in this group jumped from 28 percent to 36 percent—an unsurprising trend since the consumption of fatty fast food is up and the proportion of those eating five fruits or vegetables a day dropped from 42 percent to 26 percent.[8] One of the most depressing results of the study: middle-aged Americans at an elevated risk for heart disease because of diabetes, high blood pressure, or high cholesterol were no more likely than others to stick to a healthy diet or exercise regimen. Dr. Dana E. King, the study's lead author and a professor of family medicine at the Medical University of South Carolina, called the results of the research project "disappointing and disturbing." One of the ironies of the situation, he suggested, was that people may be counting on medical advances to offset the effects of their own behavior. "I worry that some people are taking medication instead of following a healthy lifestyle," he said. "You take a pill and say, 'I'll eat whatever I want, and my doctor says my cholesterol is fine.' Your pill may be lowering your cholesterol, but it's not doing the other 100 things that proper eating and exercise do for you."[9] The report also raises the question of whether laborsaving devices—those microwaves, portable phones, and computers that give us so much more time for lounging on our posteriors—may be an important factor in promoting the obesity linked to so many serious diseases. One of the greatest fears of many experts on aging is that the epidemic of obesity among young and middle-aged adults will wipe out recent gains in life expectancy and that overall disability rates will begin to rise again. "Obesity is really the joker in the pack," says Dr. Robert Butler. "It's terrible to think that because many of the middle-aged are fatter than Americans were in the previous generation, life expectancy could begin to go in the other direction unless people change their ways."[10]

The possibility that boomers are counting on drugs and other medical interventions to save them from their own bad habits is only one likely explanation for the contradiction between the results of this important study and boomers' image of themselves as much more youthful-acting, fit, and healthy than their parents were at the same age. Another explanation is the huge class disparity between the rich and the poor and between the best- and worst-educated Americans. Whether in youth, midlife, or old age, poor Americans have the worst health habits, in areas ranging from smoking to diet, and are least likely, because of financial constraints and a lack of the medical awareness that education provides, to receive high-quality health care. Another explanation is that the media, whose correspondents (especially those covering medical issues) are members of the hyper-health-conscious upper middle class, tend to focus on people like themselves. If you are writing an article about the benefits to be derived from improving health habits in midlife, you choose examples that illustrate your point. I picked my athletic high school friend who had lost fifty pounds after surviving cancer as the ideal person to be featured in the *AARP Bulletin;* it would hardly have served my purpose to interview the former football stars and cheerleaders at my high school reunion whose main leisure activity, judging from their overweight bodies, was sitting on the couch in front of the television. It is entirely possible that the healthy lifestyle of boomers has always been exaggerated by the media and that no one should have been surprised by a study showing that the health habits of boomers are growing worse as they age. Our expectation of what our own old old age will look like twenty or thirty years from now is based as much on our own illusions about how much more attention we pay to fitness than our parents did as it is on the overselling of the capacity of modern medicine to conquer disease rather than to treat its symptoms.

Most Americans, unless they are already old, tend to think about serious diseases, with the exception of dementia, as afflictions entirely separate from the aging process. Marketing and media hype (the latter created by the former and vice versa) have misled the public in two fundamental ways—by suggesting that cures for mankind's most serious and frightening diseases are imminent and that the medical reversal or significant retardation of aging itself may not be far behind. In a fundamental sense, most lethal diseases are age related. They are the result of everyday damage to the human organism; the damage that is countered in youth by the body's astonishing capacity to repair itself becomes in old age too overwhelming for the repairing agents—themselves damaged by the work they have performed so long and so nobly—to handle. That is why ordinary wounds in children heal with a rapidity that can only elicit envy and gratitude from parents, and why what would be a simple bruise, hardly worth noting, in a twelve-year-old might be a source of agonizing pain to a frail ninety-two-year-old. The increasing inefficiency of an aging body trying to repair itself is also the reason why falls by those in their eighties and nineties so often mark the beginning of irreversible physical decline: when it takes a very long time for a fracture or tissue tear to heal, other things often go wrong in the meantime as a result of the inactivity imposed by the original injury. I have never read a more lucid explanation of the relationship between aging and disease than the one supplied in an essay, published in 2002 by *Scientific American,* by three distinguished researchers on aging—S. Jay Olshansky, professor of public health at the University of Illinois at Chicago; Leonard Hayflick, professor of anatomy at the University of California, San Francisco; and Bruce A. Carnes, senior research scientist at the National Opinion Research Center. The authors assert that "any discussion of aging should first clarify its terms."

> Various definitions have been proposed, but we think of aging as the accumulation of random damage to the building blocks of life—especially to DNA, certain proteins, carbohydrates and lipids (fats)—that begins early in life and eventually exceeds the body's self-repair capabilities. This damage gradually impairs the functioning of cells, tissues, organs and organ systems, thereby increasing vulnerability to disease and giving rise to the characteristic manifestations of aging, such as a loss of muscle and bone mass, a decline in reaction time, compromised hearing and vision, and reduced elasticity of the skin.
>
> This accretion of molecular damage comes from many sources, including, ironically, the life-sustaining processes involved in converting the food we eat into usable energy. As the energy generators of cells (mitochondria) operate, they omit destructive, oxiding molecules known as free radicals. Most of the damage caused by these reactive molecules gets repaired, but not all. Biologists suspect that the oxidative assaults ultimately cause irreparable injury to the mitochondria, thereby impeding the cell's ability to maintain the integrity of the countless molecules needed to keep the body operating properly. . . .
>
> *Aging, in our view, makes us ever more susceptible to such ills as heart disease, Alzheimer's disease, stroke and cancer, but these age-related conditions are superimposed on aging, not equivalent to it. Therefore, even if science could eliminate today's leading killers of older individuals, aging would continue to occur, ensuring that different maladies would take their place. In addition, it would guarantee that one crucial body component or*

> *another—say, the cardiovascular system—would eventually experience a catastrophic failure. It is an inescapable biological reality that once the engine of life switches on, the body inevitably sows the seeds of its own destruction.* (italics mine)[11]

The statement, signed by sixty-one distinguished scientists, asserts, in essence, that the body's clock will continue to move toward midnight even if the last ten or fifteen minutes can be made more agreeable than they are today. Most Americans understandably don't want to hear this news. Some scientists strongly disagree with the statement that biological aging will always ensure that "one crucial body component or another" will eventually fail—even if diseases now among the leading killers of the elderly were to be eliminated. They believe that anti-aging research has the potential to vastly extend the current human life span in a fashion that may not only make 90 the new 50 but 115 the new 90. Richard A. Miller, a pathologist and gerontological researcher at the University of Michigan, suggests that "an effective anti-aging intervention might increase the mean and maximal human life span by about forty percent, which is a mean [average] age at death of about 112 years for Caucasian American or Japanese women, with an occasional winner topping out at about 140 years."[12]

Exactly what the winners will have won by living to 140 is a separate question, one belonging to the realm of ethics as much as medicine. The theory behind real anti-aging (or, if you will, pro-longevity) science—as distinct from fountain of youth hoaxes that have persisted throughout human history and have no scientific basis—is that by identifying and somehow switching off a gene that controls the aging process, it will be possible to defeat common age-related killers without yielding the field to new agents of bodily destruction. All developed nations, including the United States, are accustomed to and respectful of medical research directed at specific diseases—even if, as is the case with Alzheimer's, the research may not pay off for this generation or for the next. Anti-aging research is something else; it is based on the concept that aging itself is the ur-disease containing the secrets of susceptibility to all of the other diseases that kill old people. Immortality is not the stated objective of such research; putting off mortality as long as possible—much longer than anyone today can currently imagine—is.

But would these very old people be healthy and vigorous enough to make life worth living? The Long Life Family Study, an international inquiry into the factors that enable some families to produce many members who not only live into their eighties and nineties and beyond but also manage to retain much of their mental and physical vigor, suggests that these exceptional people may have a very different genetic makeup from those who, though they may be living longer thanks to medical advances, are not well enough to enjoy their extra years. While it is often said that heredity accounts for 30 percent of how well or how poorly people age and environmental factors 70 percent, LLFS investigators have found that the ratio is reversed in families with vigorous nonagenarians and even centenarians—with their healthy longevity 70 percent attributable to a fortunate combination of genes and 30 percent to environment. The much greater importance of heredity in families that, generation after generation, produce people who not only live far beyond the average life expectancy but are basically healthy was, typically, buried deep in an optimistic *Time* cover story titled "How to Live 100 Years."[13] After skipping over the lead investigator's observation about the importance of genes in such families, the article went on to talk about how we might all benefit from emulating a New England family, the Hurlburts, who have eight surviving brothers and sisters between ages seventy-nine and ninety-six. "Agnes was mentally nimble enough as she aged that she learned to drive when she was 63 . . . ; Walter, 84, is an accomplished painter; Muriel, 89, writes poetry and sews quilts; James, 91, is also a poet; Peter, 80, taught himself to play the piano and ice-skate after midlife; Millie, 93, burns through a half a dozen books every few weeks . . . ; and Peggy, the baby at 79, loves to cook and read."[14] That is all wonderful, just as centenarian composers and nonagenarian skydivers are wonderful, but surely the family members' ability to engage in all of these activities is as much a product of their genetically based good luck as a cause of their current good health. It must be said once more that stretching one's mind and body to the limit is a good thing at any age, but that does not guarantee either an exceptionally long life or, more important, a long life as healthy as the lives of the Hurlburt siblings.

It is not always easy, certainly from a nonscientist's perspective, to distinguish between real anti-aging science and the vast array of products, from unproven and untested supplements to self-help books by those who believe that age is just a number and a state of mind, that already appeal to a gullible public. Americans now spend more than $6 billion a year on these products, and the last thing marketers want is for the public to make a clear-sighted, evidence-based assessment of whether such potions do anything more than enable denial of the physiological reality and inevitability of aging. Even when serious researchers are involved, however, careful distinctions are frequently lost. David Sinclair, the Harvard researcher whose description of the impact of the chemical resveratrol on aging mice so impressed the audience at the World Science Festival, is always careful to say that he is trying to find a way to develop drugs that target the diseases of aging, not to stop aging itself. Yet listen to his business partner, Dr. Christoph Westphal, a venture capitalist who has both an M.D. and a Ph.D. in biology from Harvard, talk about the implications of the research. "I figured if there's going to be one chance that I'd take an 80 percent pay cut to be the C.E.O. of a company rather than general partner in a venture firm, then this was it," says Westphal, who co-founded Sirtris Pharmaceuticals. "If we're right on this one, everyone's going to want to take these drugs and they're going to treat many of the major diseases of Western society."[15] Between 2004, when the company was founded, and 2007, Westphal and Sinclair raised more than $103 million in venture capital. In 2008, the company was bought by GlaxoSmithKline, the world's largest pharmaceutical company, for $720 million. "We can control our destiny," Westphal says. "We can actually go for this crazy idea that you can target genes that control the aging process."[16] Such statements go far beyond the search for ways to ameliorate the diseases of aging. The inescapable implication of statements like Westphal's is that Americans in their forties, fifties, and sixties can reasonably hope for a magic potion that will turn us into a generation of 120-year-olds who can take a pill to prevent Alzheimer's just as we now take a pill to stop a headache. One problem, always noted far down in news reports about future medical miracles, is that many substances that seem to work in tests on animals (like mice) with short life spans are poisonous if taken in therapeutic doses by humans. Sinclair has declared that his resveratrol compound is unlikely to be toxic to humans because it regulates enzymes "that naturally go up and down according to diet." But Phillip A. Sharp, a Nobel laureate in medicine and physiology and director of the McGovern Institute for Brain Research at the Massachusetts Institute of Technology, has strong reservations. "Mice are not men," he says, "and even if you treat a mouse he can't tell you if there's something wrong with his paw. Until you go into long-term human studies, there will always be unknown risks." Sharp's caveat was quoted near the end of a long, enthusiastic article in *The New York Times* about resveratrol and Sirtris.[17] That is always how stories about potential anti-aging "breakthroughs" are presented—hopeful hype first, cautionary voices last.

Ironically, the long, unconscionable controversy over embryonic stem cell research, in which this crucial and promising area of scientific endeavor became entangled in American abortion politics, has contributed to public misperceptions about the rapidity with which basic scientific research can produce real-life cures. President George W. Bush, in deference to the Christian right's belief that using spare embryos from fertility clinics for scientific research is the equivalent of abortion, imposed severe limits on embryonic stem cell studies in 2001 and placed American research at a great disadvantage relative to other countries. Barack Obama campaigned in 2008 on a pledge to end the Bush restrictions, and he has made good on his promise. During Obama's first year in office, the National Institutes of Health—its new head is a scientist and evangelical Christian who supports embryonic stem cell research—made dozens of new cell lines available to researchers.

Bush had established a bizarre policy that allowed research only on stem cell lines that had been established, with embryos discarded by fertility clinics, before August 2001. The thinking behind the policy—if it can be called thinking—was that since the pre-2001 embryos had already been destroyed to produce the cell lines, it was ethically valid to use the old lines for research but not to use any more embryos slated to be discarded by clinics. The trouble was that cell lines do not remain scientifically useful forever, so Bush was essentially barring all future publicly financed research. Moreover, many couples who have undergone successful in vitro fertilization procedures wish to donate their spare embryos for research. Under Obama's policies, they will be able to do so. Long before Obama's election, however, it had become clear that the majority of Americans were much more interested in the hope that embryonic stem cell research might offer to sufferers from Alzheimer's, Parkinson's, cancer, and spinal cord injuries than in preserving the "rights" of embryos soon to be thrown out by fertility clinics. Stem cell research has been an issue in many state elections, and opponents of the research have generally been defeated, including in conservative areas of the country. Even hard-core religious fundamentalists, it seems, would rather avoid Alzheimer's or Parkinson's while they are waiting for the Rapture to whisk them off to heaven.*

The problem with the good news that embryonic stem cell research will now go forward is that the public relations campaign against right-wing religious restrictions on the research has, understandably and probably inevitably, oversold the possibility of immediate practical results to conquer such diseases as Alzheimer's and Parkinson's. It is impossible to overstate the importance of basic cellular research (on both embryonic and adult stem cells) for the future of medicine, and of science in general, and for a basic understanding of the processes of life and death. But Americans, who have never been particularly supportive of basic science unless it offers a quick payoff, really got on board the embryonic stem cell research bandwagon because they expect the basic science to produce miracle cures in their own lifetime. The grieving Nancy Reagan became the face of the stem cell lobby for millions who have watched their loved ones descend into irreversible dementia. Michael J. Fox became the symbol for Parkinson's sufferers, and the late Christopher Reeve for people of every age affected by spinal cord injuries. The message was always implicit and sometimes explicit: *this new science will prevent you—you who are alive today—from suffering as we have suffered*. Lobbying groups for older Americans, with the mighty AARP in the lead, are among the strongest supporters of embryonic stem cell research. AARP, which has attempted to recast its image as a representative of golden-agers by attracting new members between ages fifty and sixty-five, has run numerous optimistic articles about stem cell research during the past fifteen years. I wrote a number of those articles, and I

* Not so fast. At this writing, a federal district judge appointed in 1987 by Ronald Reagan has issued a temporary injunction against Obama's order expanding embryonic stem cell research. The Obama administration announced immediately that it would appeal the decision, and the lower court's injunction is now stayed while the case likely makes its slow way to the Supreme Court. This anti-science lawsuit is being financed by the Alliance Defense Fund, the most important legal arm of the Christian right, and the plaintiffs are two adult stem cell researchers asserting that government funding for embryonic stem cell studies will hurt their work (even though ten times as much money is now being spent on adult stem cell as on embryonic stem cell research). It is as if a court had said to Drs. Jonas Salk and Albert Sabin in the late 1940s "You can't go ahead with your research on a polio vaccine because it will provide unfair competition for people trying to develop better braces."

fully agree that this basic research may one day produce, if not cures, new treatments for the most serious age-related diseases. But in the interviews I conducted with leading research scientists for these articles, I was struck by their caveats as well as their dedication; most of them suggested that embryonic stem cell research was more likely to produce practical benefits for the grandchildren of today's baby boom generation than for its children—much less the boomers themselves. They would not always talk on the record, because many were fearful that their sensible caution about the time lapse between basic research and usable treatment would be seized on by the religious right as yet another argument against embryonic stem cell studies. Sinclair promised his audience at the 2008 World Science Festival panel that treatments could be only a few years or a decade away and that such breakthroughs are "really close . . . it's not something for the next generation." Other scientists, however, are wary about overselling Americans by promising that they will benefit in their own lifetimes from today's research. David A. Shaywitz, an endocrinologist and stem cell researcher at Harvard, speaks about treatments derived from such research in terms of generations rather than years. He told me, while I was working on a long article on stem cell research for the *AARP Bulletin,* that health advocacy groups and the media, as well as spokesmen for many new biotech companies, had underemphasized the importance of patience in trying to sell stem cell research to the public. "In contrast to the tidy tableau of television's *CSI,*" Shaywitz cautioned, "science in the real world is often slower and messier than we'd like. Ultimately, however, I suspect that embryonic stem cells will evolve into a therapeutic tool even more useful than anything we can now envision. By developing this technology today, we can hopefully establish therapies that will benefit our children and grandchildren in the years to come."[18] Barry Gumbiner, chairman of the Department of Cell Biology at the University of Virginia, takes great pains to explain why the public is mistaken to assume that cures will swiftly follow great advances in basic research that allow scientists to comprehend diseases at the cellular level. "We have understood for a long time why a volcano erupts," he notes, "but that understanding hasn't enabled us to make the volcano stop erupting." Basic research in cellular medicine and biology now reinforce each other, in that researchers understand how genes operate in certain diseases (colorectal familial cancer is one example) and can identify the crucial protein in the process. "But that understanding doesn't lead directly to the ability to create tissues and artificial organs," Gumbiner says. "That's going to be very, very difficult, because at this point, we don't even understand the process by which cells originally of the same type assume different structures, in different organs, within the body."[19] (That process is called morphogenesis.) The hope is that as scientists acquire a better understanding of morphogenesis, they will be able to use the new knowledge to culture embryonic stem cells in a laboratory and program them to turn into specific tissues and even organs. Alzheimer's, for example, wipes out the neural connections, called synapses, which enable brain cells to function cooperatively as the master organizer of all human actions—and as the keeper of memories. If embryonic stem cells could be programmed, in a laboratory, to turn into the kind of brain tissue eradicated by Alzheimer's, the potential implications for treatment are obvious. At this point, however, scientists do not even know how the process of cell and tissue differentiation works in nature.

Research on both embryonic and adult stem cells falls under a broad classification known as regenerative medicine, a term coined by William A. Haseltine, chairman and CEO of Human Genome Sciences. "Unlike most medicines today," Haseltine explained in an article in *The Brookings Review,* "regenerative medicine uses human cells and substances to regrow tissue."[20] Human proteins and genes, produced in purified form in laboratories, are used to treat a variety of diseases. One already familiar form of regenerative medicine is the use by diabetics of insulin produced with recombinant DNA technology; a second type employs cells and tissues themselves for treatments. For example, artificial skin now made in laboratories with human cells is available for the treatment of severe burns. Bone marrow transplants have been performed for decades. But just as patients receiving organ transplants are dependent on immunosuppressive drugs to mute the body's reaction against any alien DNA, so too would future patients have to take drugs to prevent rejection of alien cells that would form the basis of genetically engineered medicines. Finally, scientists hope to find synthetic materials that will actually meld with human cells. Today's artificial plastic and steel joint replacements do not fuse with the body—they exist within it, providing functional replacement for human tissues and bones—and artificial joints do not last forever. The future of which Haseltine speaks is one where worn-out tissues and organs might not only be replaced by artificial materials but also regrown and rejuvenated. But the timeline for these scientific hopes—and which of them will prove to be attainable for the treatment of human beings—is the great unknown.

The media—especially television and the Internet—have played a significant role in promoting exaggerated public expectations about the imminence of cutting-edge, breakthrough genetic treatments for fatal diseases. One of the most notorious examples of the genre occurred in 2001 when CNN interrupted its regular Sunday morning programming on November 25 with "breaking news from the world of science." CNN's Martin Savidge reported: "A U.S. laboratory says that it has successfully cloned the first human embryo. The Advanced Cell Technology (ACT) scientists have been reportedly working on the project for the past several months. They describe their results in the *Journal of Regenerative Medicine*. . . . These findings could mean breakthroughs in treatments for deadly diseases." (The significance of cloned embryos for therapeutic purposes lies in the possibility that the genetic material could be used to treat someone with cells containing his or her own DNA, thus avoiding the need for immunosuppressive drugs to prevent rejection.) By 10 a.m. on the morning of the "breakthrough" story, Tim Russert of *Meet the Press* was on the case, joined by the president and CEO of Advanced Cell Technology; a writer from *U.S. News & World Report* (which had an exclusive agreement with the company to cover the story and had just issued an advance release of its own story about the "breakthrough"); and NBC science correspondent Robert Bazell. Describing the interviews as "an historic moment here on *Meet the Press,*" Russert promised, "We'll be covering [the] battle with the U.S. Congress over the coming weeks. A new world is upon us."[21] Not exactly. The regenerative medicine journal certainly had published a story, written entirely by scientists employed by ACT, claiming that it had cloned a human embryo. At the same time, *U.S. News* had released an advance copy of a story titled "The First Clone." The article breathlessly noted that for the past eighteen months "*U.S. News* has reported from inside the ACT laboratory, with exclusive access to the cloning scientists and their laboratory work."[22] Bully for *U.S. News*. As it turned out, the cloned "embryos" had died before they even had eight cells. By Monday, serious science writers for publications like *The New York Times* and *The Washington Post* were on the case. It was undoubtedly not a coincidence that the publicity blitz by a biotech company with money at stake began on the weekend, when most knowledgeable science writers are off duty.* The downside of the stealth announcement was that by the time most people heard about the dubious "breakthrough," a corps of justifiably skeptical professional science writers was uncovering the misleading hype at the heart of the story. Gina Kolata was the reporter who wrote in the *Times* that despite the biotech company's announcement, "the embryos died before they had even eight cells, and most died long before that. Cloning experts outside the company said the experiment was a failure."[23] Rick Weiss of *The Washington Post* described the cell clusters as "still so unformed that some ethicists and scientists remain divided over whether they should be called embryos." National Public Radio interviewed John Eppig, a senior staff scientist at the Jackson Laboratory, who said that the work described by the ACT scientists was of minimal importance and added that most scientists would not have reported such preliminary results. But the debunking of the "embryo cloning" claim, which proceeded throughout the week, did not stop leaders of the political and religious right from expressing outrage. Anti-abortion politicians demanded new legislation to ban embryo cloning, even for therapeutic purposes.† German leaders and physicians, Japanese scientists, and the Vatican all chimed in. In fact, human cloning has proved to be a continuing minefield not only for the general media but for the scientific press—and scientists. Less than three years after the ACT debacle, the press once again proclaimed that human cloning had been accomplished—this time in South Korea. At first, science writers for mainstream publications had no reservations, because the work of the researchers was published in the highly regarded journal *Science*. Kolata's front-page story in the *Times* ran under the uncompromising headline "Cloning Creates Human Embryos."[24] Dr. Robert Lanza, medical director of ACT, took his hat off to his colleagues in South Korea and declared, "You now have the cookbook, a methodology that's publicly available." No, they didn't. In 2006, an investigating committee at Seoul National University told the world that the researchers had faked their data; they had not succeeded in cloning embryos

* This entire episode is explored at length in a splendid article, by Jon D. Miller, in the Fall 2002 issue of *Nieman Reports*.

† Many experts favor the "therapeutic cloning" of embryos, designed to culture stem cells to be used only to develop treatments for disease. But cloning could, in theory, be used to create duplicates of existing human beings.

at all. Unlike ACT, they had not merely exaggerated the significance of producing a collection of cells that soon died but had actually cooked the books and claimed that nonexistent embryos had survived.[25] The South Korean exposé was a testament to the integrity of peer review and the scientific method; the faked data published in *Science* could not stand up to the educated scrutiny of the researchers' scientific peers. And the science writers were not to blame for taking research published in a reputable scientific journal at face value. *U.S. News & World Report,* CNN, and NBC News, by contrast, were very much to blame for taking the earlier embryo cloning story at face value, because one does not need to be a scientist to understand that if cells do not survive in a laboratory, they are useless for research, must less for therapeutic purposes. However, all of the false claims about human cloning underline the reasons why the public and the media should be much more skeptical about extraordinary research and medical claims that tap into the ancient human hope and fantasy of eternal life. The media and the public should be listening to the voices of scientists like Gumbiner and Shaywitz, who emphasize the complexity of what stem cell researchers are trying to do and who do not promise cures in the near future. The news media should be particularly wary of claims by scientists who are trying to raise private capital for their own projects. And it is unethical, in my view, for any news organization to enter into agreements with private biotech companies that, implicitly or explicitly, trade access to the researchers for a splashy, overly optimistic news story. Unfortunately, media credulity on these subjects is only likely to expand as the number of publications and traditional media outlets that fund serious investigative reporting in all fields, including science and medicine, decreases. Online news, with its inherent preference for speed over accuracy, can only worsen the problem. These stories have enormous reader appeal, because they tell people what they want to hear. That treatments may be a generation or two, rather than five or ten years, away is not an argument against basic scientific research. The difficulty of the science makes it more, not less, important for researchers to move full speed ahead now in all areas that offer promise for the alleviation of the most serious age-related diseases.

It is dangerous, though, for individuals to delude themselves about the long and difficult road that likely lies between the laboratory and effective treatment for dreaded diseases. Belief in magic pills and the imminence of magic cures has adverse social as well as personal consequences. As Dr. Muriel Gillick notes, "If we assume that Alzheimer's disease will be cured and disability abolished in the near term, we will have no incentive to develop long-term care facilities that focus on enabling residents to lead satisfying lives despite their disabilities."[26] If those of us now in our forties, fifties, and sixties truly believe that most of us are going to be in excellent health as octogenarians and nonagenarians, then there is no reason to develop strategies—either social or personal—to prepare for a less optimal and optimistic future. We're going to be just like the actress Betty White, hosting *Saturday Night Live* at age eighty-eight. We'll be paying our own way, overwhelmed with job offers, and in good enough health to work as hard as we always did. We'll be perfectly able to take care of ourselves. Won't we?

CHAPTER FIVE

A Mind Is a Terrible Thing to Lose

Age-related dementia, of which Alzheimer's disease is the most common form, leaves its victims defenseless and is the slayer of all wisdom, all memory, all that makes the human mind human. Note that I do not say "all that makes a human being human." That is essentially a theological and philosophical question, which I leave to those who wish to find some meaning or purpose in dementia, in either a religious or a more secular social dimension. As far as I am concerned, dementia has no more moral meaning than plague, smallpox, or cancer. All of these, as Susan Sontag points out forcefully in *Illness As Metaphor* (1978), were long attributed—by a succession of witch doctors dispensing bad faith, bad medicine, or bad psychotherapy—to character failures on the part of the sufferers rather than biological bad luck. "Illness is the night-side of life, a more onerous citizenship," Sontag observes. "Everyone who is born holds dual citizenship, in the kingdom of the well and in the kingdom of the sick. Although we all prefer to use only the good passport, sooner or later each of us is obliged, at least for a spell, to identify ourselves as citizens of that other place."[1] That statement applies to dementia even more strongly than it does to the other scourges in the kingdom of the sick, because Alzheimer's imposes not "a spell" of suffering but a life sentence—or, rather, a death-in-life sentence. And it is a death that must be endured bit by bit, as the person is slowly deprived of everything she has cherished throughout life—unless she is fortunate enough to be carried off by another, more merciful disease before she descends into the last stages of unknowing helplessness. And those who live in the kingdom of the well cannot even be certain about the unawareness of a terminal Alzheimer's patient. "At least she doesn't know" is the conventional salve applied to those grieving for someone who has lost all powers of communication but is still technically alive. It is indeed terrible to suspect that, in the broken synapses of a broken mind, there might still be seconds or moments of reconnection in which the person is aware of helplessness—rather like those rare patients who become conscious in the middle of surgery but are unable to move or cry for help. This worst-case scenario has not been ruled out by scientific research. I do not believe in an immortal soul independent of the human body, because I do not believe in God or any form of supernaturalism. Nor do I argue, as some psychologists and philosophers do, that there is a mind or consciousness independent of the intractable material mass of gray matter that is the human brain. To contend that consciousness (like spirituality) is a phenomenon separate from or greater than the brain itself strikes me as just another refusal to acknowledge that *Homo sapiens,* with the most sophisticated brain of all species on earth, nevertheless belongs to the animal kingdom. What others call the mind or the spirit is the literally marvelous result of what the brain, a physical organ, has made of its encounters with stimuli over a lifetime. We do know—a knowledge based on evidence rather than belief—that the human animal, like all animals, is capable of responding to pain even in extremis, and that seems more important to me than religion's definition of humans as beings possessing souls or certain secular philosophers' view of humans as beings with a consciousness independent of the corpus. One of the most horrible manifestations of advancing dementia is that its sufferers have increasing difficulty in their attempts to describe the physical pain they may be experiencing. In an editorial in *The New England Journal of Medicine,* Dr. Greg A. Sachs, a geriatrician and medical ethicist with the Indiana University Center for Aging Research, observes that mute dementia patients may, ironically, undergo pointless aggressive medical interventions while receiving insufficient palliative care for pain. "Since individuals with advanced dementia cannot report their symptoms," he writes, "these symptoms are often untreated, leaving them vulnerable o pain, difficulty breathing, and various other conditions."[2] The only meaningful question about Alzheimer's is how, as individuals and as a society, we care for people with this merciless and currently unconquerable disease in the absence of the holy grail of a cure. But this question addresses the humanity of the well, not the humanity of the sick.

The most important thing Americans need to know about dementia is how many of the old—nearly half of those over eighty-five—are affected. The prevalence of Alzheimer's doubles in every five-year period over age sixty-five.[3] These statistics cannot be cited often enough. I provide reference notes, from impeccable sources such as the National Institute on Aging, the Alzheimer's Association, and the Alzheimer's Foundation of America, because many people refuse to believe me when I first cite the figures. In spite of the publicity surrounding many high-profile cases of Alzheimer's in recent years, our society is in a massive state of denial about the commonness of the disease among the old old.* Yes, we know that President Ronald Reagan, the composer Aaron Copland, the New York Metropolitan Opera impresario Rudolf Bing, the philanthropist Brooke Astor, and the essayist E. B. White—to name only a few diverse luminaries—all died of Alzheimer's, but we look at these cases as dreadful exceptions. Live beyond your early eighties, and whether you are a criminal, a butcher, a baker, a candlestick maker, a musical genius, or a nuclear physicist, you are increasingly vulnerable to the disease. There are several reasons why many people initially reject these statistics, even though Alzheimer's is the second-most feared disease in America (after cancer). The first, most obvious reason is that the prospect of losing one's mind is so horrible to contemplate that no one wishes to do so—especially as he or she moves closer to the age of greatest risk for cognitive disaster. If Alzheimer's were not so strongly age related, I believe that it would be more feared than cancer. But because most of us, by the time we reach our forties, know someone who is struggling with and living with cancer, we are aware that the disease could touch us—and not necessarily in the distant future. Alzheimer's, by contrast, is a disease with which only a minority of middle-aged Americans have had direct contact—unless their parents are already among the old old. Thus, the middle-aged fear cancer more than Alzheimer's because more of them have seen its ravages personally.

The second factor in the denial of Alzheimer's risk is media coverage, which continues to focus relentlessly on the misleading "10 percent

* One study of 856 men and women, released at the end of 2007 by the Fisher Center for Alzheimer's Research Foundation, suggested that the proportion of the old old with dementia might be somewhat less—about 37 percent—than the more widely accepted figure of 50 percent. However, the study was limited to people living at home and questions were asked of their caretakers and family members. Any estimate that does not include those living in institutions is bound to be an underestimate because dementia is the leading reason for admission of older patients to nursing homes.

over sixty-five" statistic. Even the wrenching 2009 HBO documentary *The Alzheimer's Project* (with a segment produced by Maria Shriver, whose father has the disease) avoided forthrightly stating the real statistics for the old old and instead kept repeating the 10 percent risk figure. This documentary, with both its strengths and its weaknesses, was important because it was the first major attempt by the media to present a comprehensive picture of Alzheimer's for a mass audience. In the past, timorous infotainment forays into Alzheimer's—like the 1989 made-for-television movie *Do You Remember Love?* starring Joanne Woodward—never ventured into the dark regions of late Alzheimer's. Instead, audiences were presented with a sentimental pastiche emphasizing family devotion and the indomitability of the human spirit—a particularly dishonest portrait of a disease that directly attacks and ultimately vanquishes the spirit and mind contained within the brain. The movie was Alzheimer's Lite—confusion and memory lapses on the part of a brilliant college professor, but no despair, muteness, or incontinence. Those would begin where the movie ended, with the character played by Woodward looking as if she considered herself the luckiest woman on the face of the earth because she still does remember love.

There is also a great deal of social shame and stigma surrounding Alzheimer's, as there once was surrounding cancer. Only forty years ago, cancer was almost never cited as a cause of death in obituaries; the common newspaper formulation was that so-and-so died "after a long illness." Today, Alzheimer's is occasionally cited in obituaries, but not nearly as frequently as it should be, given the prevalence of the disease in the old old. Brooke Astor's obituary was a conspicuous exception—probably because her mental competence in her final years was already the subject of a legal battle. Alzheimer's patients are often suffering from more than one illness, and families generally choose the cause of death that conveys the least stigma. Many Alzheimer's patients die of pneumonia, as the part of the brain that affects the basic function of breathing, as well as the ability to cough up phlegm, shuts down. The question is why there is a greater stigma attached to a failing brain than to a failing heart or lungs.

I could not have ventured an explanation ten years ago, before I had witnessed the long mental deterioration of the person I loved most in the world, a man who, until he was stricken by the curse of Alzheimer's, possessed a great, subtle, witty, and disciplined mind. *He* was ashamed of his condition; he never used the word "Alzheimer's," even though he knew perfectly well that he was losing his memory, his spatial skills, and his command of language. I don't know whether I absorbed some of his sense of humiliation, or whether I simply felt it would be a betrayal to name what he would not name himself. I do know that until I saw what happened to him, I had—although, as someone who has written frequently about science, I know better—subconsciously told myself that highly intelligent people don't get Alzheimer's. I suspect that most people who know better delude themselves in this indefensible, if not inexplicable, fashion. Even a scientist like Elkhonon Goldberg, in *The Wisdom Paradox: How Your Mind Can Grow Stronger As Your Brain Grows Older* (2005), talks on the one hand about Isaac Newton's dramatic mental and memory decline near the end of his life and asserts, on the other hand, that a lifetime of hard intellectual work can armor us against brain malfunctions in old age. The wishful and illogical subtext is, *Though a life of the highest intellectual endeavor didn't protect Newton, it will surely protect me*. Humans are the only species capable of lying—to ourselves even more effectively than to others. An inability to lie is, in fact, one more loss that manifests itself in the middle stages of the degenerative Alzheimer's process. Just as attempts to deceive (however transparent at first) are a sign of mental maturation in children, so too is the loss of the power to deceive a sign of mental deterioration in old age. Reported cases of Alzheimer's are less prevalent—especially before age eighty-five—among those with the highest levels of education, but it is possible that education simply allows people to disguise their failing memories for a longer period by enabling them to draw on a larger "cognitive reserve" than their less educated contemporaries. Old memories, including memories of learning, are the last to fade away: if someone with Alzheimer's read *The Origin of Species* and *War and Peace* in college, he is more likely to remember them than he is to recall yesterday's top news stories. Rereading the classics is one way for Alzheimer's victims who have been readers all their lives to prolong the period when they can still derive pleasure from books: someone in the middle stages of Alzheimer's may forget what he read in a new novel earlier in the day, but he will remember the contents of a novel that left a deep imprint in his young adulthood.

A revealing portrait of the stigma that society still attaches to Alzheimer's appeared in a *New York Times* account of the trial of Brooke Astor's son, Anthony Marshall, who was accused and ultimately convicted of stealing from his mother. But, the reporter wrote, "it is Mrs. Astor's dignity that seems to be on trial in the courtroom. For weeks now, the prosecution, trying to make the case that Mr. Marshall took advantage of his mother's mental frailty, has compelled witness after witness, dear friend after dear friend, to say for the public record the things that we all hope, should we end up in a state of mental decline, would go unsaid to anyone but the doctors, and only if they really must know." The reporter was horrified by the fact that Mrs. Astor's longtime physician, Rees Pritchett, testified on the stand that she had described herself to him as "gaga." The doctor went on to reveal details about Mrs. Astor's mental state "and, yes, gastrointestinal problems (details of the latter evoked audible discomfort even from the reporters in the room)."[4] If Brooke Astor's dignity seemed, to those journalists, to be on trial, it is only because they are as unwilling as the rest of American society to face the truth about what Alzheimer's does to its victims, whether they come from the highest or the lowest economic and social class. Indeed, the shame and lying that so often surround Alzheimer's helped make it possible for Marshall to do what he did to his mother.

Yet there is no doubt that the stigma attached to Alzheimer's has declined significantly in recent years, and much of the credit goes to former first lady Nancy Reagan, who not only allowed her husband's diagnosis to be announced publicly in 1994 but also has spoken out strongly on behalf of embryonic stem cell research, in the hope that it will lead to treatments or cures for future victims of Alzheimer's. Mrs. Reagan's candor has helped destigmatize Alzheimer's in much the same fashion as Betty Ford's frank acknowledgment of her battles with breast cancer and prescription drug addiction helped to destigmatize both cancer and drug rehabilitation a generation ago. This destigmatization has been accompanied, not surprisingly, by the availability of more public information about Alzheimer's. At the same time, new brain imaging tools are providing a picture, for the first time in the living brain, of the initial changes that may one day herald the onset of Alzheimer's. And basic research at the molecular level is steadily mapping the human genome and identifying more of the genes that play a role in this extremely complicated disease. The ultimate hope offered by this research is that by identifying the many genetic pathways to the full-blown development of Alzheimer's, researchers may be able to develop targeted drugs that narrow or cut off the pathways and inhibit the degenerative process *before* a patient suffers from life-altering changes in mental functioning. Significantly, nearly all of the high-level researchers interviewed for *The Alzheimer's Project* spoke not of cures but of drugs to inhibit the progress of the disease. And none of them offered a timeline. One researcher studying families who have an extremely rare form of the disease—early-onset Alzheimer's, which can strike even in the thirties and forties and accounts for only 5 percent of all cases—thanked the families for having agreed to undergo brain scans each year and said bluntly that while the research would probably not help family members who are alive today, it would bear fruit for their children and grandchildren. The part about treatments being developed for future generations, not our own, is what baby boomers don't want to hear and what boomer journalists don't want to say. None of the scientists interviewed for the documentary talked about the number of drugs that have already been tested and failed in clinical trials. Only fourteen months after the HBO movie aired, for example, the drug company Eli Lilly halted late-stage clinical trials of an experimental drug involving more than 2,600 Alzheimer's patients in thirty-one countries, because those who took the drug actually showed worse cognitive functioning than those who had taken a placebo. That disappointment followed two other failed results in clinical trials sponsored by new biotech as well as long-established drug companies. Of course, repeated failures of untested drugs and procedures are the only way to progress in medicine. Most drugs, whatever disease they are targeting, do fail to pass muster in clinical trials: those missteps are forgotten by the public when a breakthrough is finally made, and dead-end approaches are an integral part of ultimate research success stories. But when every experimental drug, long before its efficacy is demonstrated, is hailed in the general press as a potential miracle for sufferers from a dreaded disease, unjustified hope for immediate progress is stimulated in the public.

Alzheimer's poses a special problem: once symptoms appear, any attempt at treatment to reverse brain damage—even if one were available—may already be too little, too late. Lennart Mucke, of the Gladstone Institute of Neurological Disease at the University of California, San Francisco, noted, in a generally bleak roundup of treatment prospects published in *Nature* magazine just before the television documentary aired, that Alzheimer's disease "probably develops insidiously over many years, if not decades. Some of my colleagues believe that even so-called early clinical stages of AD reflect advanced-stage brain failure that may be impossible to reverse."[5] The gap between the general optimism of the scientists quoted in the television documentary and the lack of specifics did not go unnoticed by reviewers of *The Alzheimer's Project*. *The New York Times* noted that the filmmakers ignored "many caveats about the long, bumpy road from clinical trial to prescription pad" and suggested that a "likely reason the project's creators were so intent on a sunny view of Alzheimer's in the future is that the portraits of the disease as it is lived now are so harrowing." The review concluded, "The zeal and dedication of researchers is inspiring, and so are the patients and caregivers who struggle with the disease every day, but over all, 'The Alzheimer's Project' celebrates hope at the expense of caution."[6]

Unlike scientists, most people are understandably interested mainly in what Alzheimer's does, not what it *is* in either a physiological or a neurological sense. Yet it is important to understand some basic medical facts, because comprehension of the disease's complexity is a necessary prophylactic against the false hope that deludes Americans about the imminence of a cure. In a normal brain, neurons communicate with one another in ways that enable them to solve new problems and complete complicated tasks that involve many different aspects of mental functioning. The skills required to drive, for example, are stored in long-term memory—the brain's elaborate system for filing and retrieving information over extended periods of time, even an entire life. Since most Americans learn how to operate an automobile and drive in adolescence, they need only add new information upon encountering digital-age gadgets not seen in the past (which happens to me every time I rent a car). By contrast, the directions needed to drive to a new destination are unlikely to enter long-term memory unless the journey is repeated several times. The normal adult brain, that marvel of internal communication, enables us to process new directions at the same time that we continue to exercise our basic driving skills on the autopilot of long-term memory—in this case reinforced by repetition. In Alzheimer's, over time, this awesome process of interaction between brain cells, which we take for granted throughout most of our lives, is disrupted, and the cells themselves eventually die.

Communication between cells in the Alzheimer's brain is impeded by the development of amyloid plaques, which consist mainly of a protein called beta-amyloid. In Alzheimer's victims, the amyloid protein forms sticky plaques instead of being flushed out of the brain in normal fashion, and the plaques can insert themselves into the cell. (The failed Eli Lilly drug attempted to reduce the number of amyloid beta plaques in the brain, and company spokesmen theorized that too little of the protein might be even more harmful than too much. Other scientists said it was also possible that the amyloid plaques visible on brain scans are symptoms rather than a basic cause of Alzheimer's.) Also evident in the Alzheimer's brain are neurofibrillary tangles, composed largely of a substance called the tau protein, and these tangles eventually kill the neurons. In brain scans, it looks almost as if the tau tangles are strangling the brain cells. Both tangles and plaques can be found on scans of normal brains, but Alzheimer's brains have many more of these cell-disrupting formations. In Alzheimer's and other forms of irreversible dementia, the cerebral cortex—the outer surface of the brain responsible for all intellectual functioning—shrinks dramatically. Again, shrinkage is often detectable in the normal aging brain but is not significant enough to cause major changes in functioning. In the past, such physiological changes in the brain could be detected only in an autopsy, but scanning devices can identify them in the living today. Since there is no cure for Alzheimer's, and no treatments that significantly slow the course of the disease, such cans are useful primarily for research purposes. The same is true of an even newer and surer way of diagnosing patients with some signs of memory loss who are certain to develop Alzheimer's—spinal taps, in which the spinal fluid is analyzed and amyloid beta protein is found. Again, the hope of researchers is that by identifying biomarkers like the amyloid protein and intervening early with an as-yet-undiscovered drug that works, they will be able to prevent or delay the development of full-blown Alzheimer's. While early identification tests are undeniably useful to researchers, it is difficult to see how they could be useful, in a practical sense, to anyone but families who carry the specific mutated gene that causes early-onset Alzheimer's. Such information might well influence decisions, ranging from career planning to childbearing, by young members of the families. But it is hard to see how definitive early identification could be anything but a heavy emotional burden to most people destined to develop Alzheimer's in their seventies or eighties. I imagine only two kinds of people who might benefit, if that is the right word for the acquisition of such terrible knowledge, from these tests. The first are those who have no moral objections to suicide and would wish to take their fate into their own hands while they are still competent enough to act. The second are people with substantial assets who might avoid losing their entire estates to long-term care by transferring their money to their children. But even the latter financial benefit is somewhat problematic, given that the Internal Revenue Service might not look kindly on those who transfer assets after receiving definite news that they are on their way to Alzheimer's.

In late-onset Alzheimer's there is no clear pattern of inheritance. About two-thirds of Alzheimer's victims have no close relative with the disease; thus, age itself is the main risk factor. There is no single known gene, or gene mutation, that inevitably leads to Alzheimer's in those over sixty, although there is one identified gene that raises risk.* Scientists have now concluded that many "susceptibility genes" play a role in who gets the disease and who doesn't in the late stages of life. A concerted research effort to identify more of these genes is under way, because each new susceptibility gene might offer a target for drug intervention. Gerard D. Schellenberg of the University of Pennsylvania, one of the leading scientists in the field, explained in *The Alzheimer's Project* that identifying as many susceptibility genes as possible will be crucial in deciding how to target drug research money. But the number of genes involved, and the commonness of the disease among the old, mean that identifying the most fruitful pathways for pharmacological intervention will be highly complicated. Furthermore, scientific understanding of the interaction between genes and environmental factors, including health habits and education, is in its infancy. The truth, which was downplayed in the section of *The Alzheimer's Project* focusing on

* That gene is called the apolipoprotein 4 allele, or Apo E4. But experts view the gene as useful only for research and do not urge anyone to undergo genetic testing for the marker, because many individuals with the gene will never develop Alzheimer's.

advances in basic laboratory research, is that science has a long way to go before researchers even know where to begin looking for drug treatments that might have any practical effect. One of the most fascinating aspects of the interviews with top-level researchers was their own susceptibility to denial about the real-life risk (including their own) of developing the disease. Schellenberg mentioned, almost as an aside, that his father had developed Alzheimer's in his early eighties. But, the scientist said, he wasn't particularly worried about his own risk because his father had developed Alzheimer's "that late." Schellenberg concluded hopefully that he might not possess many "susceptibility genes" because his father had manifested symptoms of Alzheimer's in his eighties rather than his sixties or seventies. Like Goldberg in *The Wisdom Paradox,* Schellenberg was looking for a way to tell himself, "It can't happen to me." I found this a particularly compelling example of denial, because Schellenberg had already said that age itself—regardless of whether one has a close relative with Alzheimer's—is the chief risk factor. That his father developed Alzheimer's doesn't mean that his son will do so, but the fact that he did not develop the disease until his eighties certainly doesn't mean that the younger Schellenberg has little need to worry. One could only suspect that Schellenberg the man was simply denying what Schellenberg the scientist knows better than most people about the chances of developing Alzheimer's in old age.

Unlike the patients featured in *The Alzheimer's Project,* many of whom had agreed to participate in ongoing research, the average Alzheimer's victim will be diagnosed not by any high-tech brain scan or spinal tap but by behavioral symptoms that vary among individuals but usually include an obvious loss of language skills, a difficulty in recalling recent events, and an inability to learn anything new—something as simple as the location of a building one has never visited before, even if the building is located on a familiar block. The importance of seeing a doctor for a diagnosis lies in the need to rule out causes of *reversible* dementia, which include treatable conditions such as a thyroid imbalance or kidney failure and can produce the same symptoms as early Alzheimer's. Severe depression, which can be treated with drugs, should also be ruled out because many of its most common symptoms—inability to concentrate and withdrawal from ordinary activities—are also symptoms of Alzheimer's. For most of us, it is enough to know—more than we can bear, actually—that if we are diagnosed with Alzheimer's, we will eventually, in an unpredictable period of time, lose our memories of everything we hold dear and our ability to function. On average, according to the Alzheimer's Foundation, people live for eight to ten years from the time Alzheimer's is diagnosed. If some other illness does not end our lives before we descend into advanced Alzheimer's, we will be incontinent, dependent entirely on others, and (for the most part) unable to recognize our caregivers or anyone we love. If someone we love has Alzheimer's, that is the fate awaiting him or her.

So what about all of those ads for Alzheimer's drugs promising to help Dad be "more like himself"? In a companion book to the television series on Alzheimer's, no less an authority than Dr. Richard J. Hodes, director of the National Institute on Aging, said flatly in the introduction that "research has yet to achieve success, as defined by the ability to prevent Alzheimer's disease, *or, if it develops, to slow its progression*" (italics mine).[7] This quote did not appear in the television segment on science, and nowhere did any scientists—or any caregivers—question the effectiveness of the "memory pills" (as both doctors and caregivers frequently call them) being constantly advertised on television. Yet such questions are raised by tough-minded doctors every day. Dr. Thomas Finucane, a geriatrician and professor at Johns Hopkins University, said in 2004 that "in 10 years we'll be embarrassed by how much of this stuff we prescribed" and told a conference of health professionals at Johns Hopkins that he thought hundreds of millions of dollars were being wasted on the drugs, which cost approximately $150 to $200 a month.[8] Most drugs approved by the FDA for mild to moderate Alzheimer's—the best known are Aricept and Exelon—raise levels of acetylcholine, a chemical that transmits nerve signals to the brain. Clinical trials financed by drug companies showed a slight improvement in cognitive test scores, and that's enough to gain FDA approval. But none of these trials showed a significant improvement in everyday functioning. Indeed, television ads for such products now carry a legally mandated acknowledgment that the drugs "cannot alter the course of the disease." One can only wonder why anyone mindful of this caution would bother to take such nostrums. *Consumer Reports* states that "it is the rare person who has a significant delay in the worsening of their symptoms over time."[9]

A 2004 study financed by the British National Health Service and published in the medical journal *The Lancet*—one of the few clinical trials not financed by drug manufacturers—found no difference at all, after three years of taking either Aricept or a placebo, in the rate of admission to nursing homes and the development of total disability. There was also no difference in the emotional well-being of caretakers for the two groups. If these drugs worked well enough to truly improve the daily functioning of people with Alzheimer's, their caregivers would know. At the time, the Alzheimer's Association issued a statement suggesting that nursing home placement might not be the most appropriate way to measure the effectiveness of a drug. I could not disagree more; I think that the ability of caregivers to keep Alzheimer's victims at home is by far the best way to measure the effectiveness of a drug marketed to give dubious hope to the hopeless. Anyone who loves someone with Alzheimer's begins with an absolute determination to keep him or her at home as long as possible. One of the most frequent promises husbands and wives make to each other is that neither will put the other in a nursing home. I don't think that anyone who cares deeply about an Alzheimer's victim turns to a nursing home unless there is no way out—unless the burden of physical care has become impossible to bear and there is no money for aides to ease the strain. Thus, it seems perfectly reasonable to judge these drugs by their ability, or inability, to keep people out of institutions. The Alzheimer's Foundation is extremely cautious in its description of the drugs on its Web site, noting only that "some of these medications can be used alone or in combination, and can provide some relief of symptoms and may slow the decline in mental function to some extent."[10] *Can. May. To some extent.* What ringing endorsements! The real question is why, given that these drugs are incapable of reversing brain degeneration or of keeping people from deteriorating enough to need a nursing home, doctors prescribe them. And yet doctors continue to dispense unfounded hope with these prescriptions and caregivers continue to administer the pills—as long as the person is able to swallow (another function eventually knocked out by the degeneration of the Alzheimer's brain). In one segment of the television series, a doctor tells a woman newly diagnosed with the disease, "We're not going to just sit here. We're going to be proactive." What he undoubtedly means is that he is going to write a prescription for one of the drugs that have marginal, largely imperceptible benefits—even according to the most optimistic studies financed by the drug companies. The obvious answer is that everyone—doctors, caregivers, patients in the early stages—wants to hope.

The most horrible part of this disease for any caregiver is the knowledge that the only thing to be done is to give aid that is essentially palliative in nature, in an attempt to help the person maintain his dignity and sense of self as long as possible. What do you say when someone with a once sparkling mind and quick tongue turns to you on the crosstown bus and haltingly searches for the words to describe his frustration? "I feel that somewhere inside me is the person I really am," he explains, "the person I used to be, I mean . . . before . . . but I can't find him. I can't talk to him." More important, what can you do to help? You try to provide experiences, from watching baseball games to attending concerts, to stimulate the part of the brain that it still functioning. You bring out photo albums of things you have done, places you have gone, in the past. He says, "I'm so stupid" as he turns the pages of the album and asks, repeatedly, for the names of the places where the pictures were taken. And you know, beyond doubt, that whether he uses the word "Alzheimer's" or not, he knows perfectly well what is happening to him. You feel a pain in your gut as you try to accept the limitations of your capacity to make things better for him. And when you fail to resign yourself to your own impotence, you find, like Job, that you curse the day you were born. So if there's a memory pill prescribed by a doctor, even if you have read enough of the medical literature to strongly suspect that the drug has little or no value, you make sure that this man, who has just told you that he can no longer talk to himself, takes the drug. He took the pills docilely, but I am quite sure that—while he could still think things through—he had no faith in them. Once he said in Yiddish, after taking the pill on a glorious summer day, "*Gornish helfen*" (Beyond help). This had been the punch line of a number of old Jewish jokes he used to tell, in the days when he could still tell jokes.

During the past twenty-five years, as a result of the establishment of the National Institute on Aging and private efforts of the Alzheimer's Foundation and prominent individuals like Nancy Reagan, the image of dementia as an inevitable part of old age has been replaced by what is called a "biomedical model" of Alzheimer's as a disease. Not only has the biomedical model, despite giving rise to unfounded expectations of an imminent cure, been useful in destigmatizing Alzheimer's—to the degree that it has been destigmatized—but it is the only model that offers rational hope of figuring out this disease. If biomedical reality dictates that nearly half of those over eighty-five will develop Alzheimer's, it also tells us that half of the old old will *not* suffer from severe dementia. Thus, biomedical research provides the only realistic possibility of finding out why half of us will develop Alzheimer's if we live long enough and half of us won't—and solving the puzzle is the only way to prevent millions of new cases. This statement will be disputed by those who believe, on the basis of no solid scientific evidence, that they can prevent Alzheimer's by healthy living in midlife. I am in no way suggesting that *unhealthy* living has nothing to do with the overall risk of Alzheimer's. We know, for example, that obesity raises the risk of diabetes, and that both diabetes and obesity are associated with a higher risk of Alzheimer's in old age. It stands to reason, therefore, that if cases of preventable diabetes could be reduced through nutrition and exercise programs (and experts believe that nearly half of all Type 2 cases are preventable), the prevalence of diabetes might drop in both the over-sixty-five and the over-eighty-five population. While it makes sense to try to deal with obvious, identified risk factors like diabetes (which can wreck middle-aged bodies long before patients reach the age at which Alzheimer's is most common), it is a very different matter to suggest or conclude that being slim, fit, and healthy in middle age and young old age will provide immunity to Alzheimer's—a proposition promoted in media accounts of every new lifestyle study. There was a good deal of publicity, for example, about an "interventional study" designed by researchers at the University of Illinois in which sedentary adults between ages sixty and seventy-five were recruited for a test of the cognitive effect of exercise. Those who walked, as opposed to doing exercises limited to stretching, improved on cognitive tests after a six-month trial. But the study was conducted on normal adults with normal mental functioning, and there have never been studies of the effect of exercise on a brain already under attack from Alzheimer's. A longitudinal Swedish study showed that adults who reported having exercised in midlife had a lower incidence of Alzheimer's than those who had led sedentary lives. But observational studies, which rely on people's memories and accounts of their own behavior, are notoriously unreliable. "The only thing we can say unequivocally is that exercise is good for you, at every age; that it increases blood flow to the heart, and a healthy heart means a healthier brain in a person who's already healthy," said Dr. Robert Butler. "But that doesn't mean it's going to prevent a pathology like Alzheimer's, which is such a common disease with so many contributing factors. Good health habits are good, period. But there just isn't any solid evidence that exercise, or anything else, for that matter, is a guarantee against this disease."[11] The uncompromising realism of this assessment (Dr. Butler, who was a personal friend of mine, was a visionary but not a dreamer) was underscored last spring when a "science court" convened by the National Institutes of Health did a thorough analysis of all of the "lifestyle studies" designed to show whether a variety of good health habits—ranging from exercise to eating lots of green vegetables—could prevent or delay the onset of Alzheimer's. The court consisted of fifteen scientists with no vested stake in Alzheimer's research, and their verdict contradicted all of the optimistic forecasts that healthy living will preserve our brains. "Currently," the panel concluded, "no evidence of even moderate scientific quality exists to support the association of any modifiable factor (such as nutritional supplements, herbal preparations, dietary factors, prescription or nonprescription drugs, social or economic factors, medical conditions, toxins, or environmental exposures) with reduced risk of Alzheimer's disease." Dr. Martha L. Davigius, the panel chairwoman and professor of medicine at Northwestern University, said sadly, "This is something that that could happen to any of us, and yet we are at such a primitive state of research . . . the evidence is the evidence and we have to say what it is." Yes, we do. Except for those of us who are making money by selling an endless array of products designed to convince the public that there is something we can buy or do to protect ourselves from the unthinkable.[12]

One of the virtues of the identification of Alzheimer's as a pathological process is that the biomedical model offers a powerful counterargument to stereotypes of aging as an inevitable gateway to senility. Yet—wouldn't you know it?—there is an anti-biomedical school of thought that objects to labeling Alzheimer's as a disease and views dementia as a social construct rather than a physiological reality. Psychologists and sociologists make up most of the advocates for what is called the social constructivist model of dementia, in which the loss of the mind is viewed as the product of a society with distorted social relations and market-oriented values. What society calls dementia, in this view, is really only another form of normalcy—and the demented are demented, at least in part, because they are treated as demented by their caregivers. With proper, focused care, the course of Alzheimer's patients may be arrested or even reversed "by interacting with them in a way that evokes positive emotions."[13] These people are right about just one thing—that focus on research should not be used as an excuse for failing to devote money and thought to improving the care of people suffering from irreversible dementia and providing support (now non-existent) for exhausted caregivers. But just about everything else that antagonists of the biomedical model within the "helping professions" have to say is a perfect example of what I call junk thought in *The Age of American Unreason* (2008). The British psychologist Tom Kitwood argues that even—or especially—the demented have important lessons to teach the rest of society. One of those lessons: "Reason is taken off the pedestal that it has occupied so unjustifiably, and for so long; we reclaim our nature as sentient and social beings. Thus from what might have seemed the most unlikely quarter, there may yet emerge a well-spring of energy and compassion."[14] The idea that reason and compassion are at odds is a stellar example of junk thought, most frequently articulated by exponents of the most antirational forms of religion in an effort to bolster their conviction that religious believers treat their fellow human beings in a much more kindly manner than do reason-obsessed atheists and agnostics. Kitwood does not explain exactly who is reclaiming his or her sentient social beingness through the unsought gift of dementia. In an article coauthored with Kathleen Bredin, Kitwood speaks about a "pathology of normality." The authors insist that "the general pattern of everyday life, with its hypocrisy, competitiveness, and pursuit of crass materialism is, from a human standpoint, deeply pathological; those whose way of being dovetails smoothly into the pattern are the most 'normal' and well-adjusted. . . . Thus, when the interpersonal field surrounding the beginnings of 'dementia' is looked at in this way, the problem is by no means focused on a single person whose brain is failing. Those others who have face-to-face contact are also involved; and in the background, so also is the prevailing pattern of social relations."[15] Translation: when you think about it, we are all demented in some way, and even the concept of dementia is demented. All of this is reminiscent of the psychiatric view, widely held in the 1950s and 1960s, that cold, ungiving mothers were responsible for childhood autism. The shrinks did not stop adding their own junk thought to the anguish of mothers seeking help for autistic children until research, beginning in the 1980s and continuing to this day, established genetic and biochemical bases for autism.[16]

Now a new generation of junk thinkers suggests that caregivers, given the right attitude, might be able to stop or even reverse the degenerative course of Alzheimer's in their loved ones. Jesse F. Ballenger, an American scholar, quotes many of these theorists with great approval in *Self, Senility, and Alzheimer's Disease in Modern America,* a historical study published in 2006. The book purports to address "the dread surrounding dementia as a historical problem"—and a fairly recent one at that. Ballenger asks, "When did this fearful line . . . dividing people with dementia from the rest of us appear in American culture? Was it simply the product of the attention given to Alzheimer's disease, or does it have deeper historical roots?" He then proceeds, in completely ahistorical fashion, to argue that "it was only in the late nineteenth century that the fear and anxiety we feel about dementia today clearly emerged in American culture."[17] This assertion is simply untrue, and anyone who has read correspondence from the eighteenth and early nineteenth centuries between old and eminent Americans cannot escape fearful references to senility. Dread of mental deterioration in old age, even at a time when so few people lived to grow old, was a major concern for old people in the early American republic. And although the pathological nature of the disease that now bears his name was not identified by Alois Alzheimer until 1906, Enlightenment thinkers were fully aware that the normal vicissitudes of aging were quite different from dementia. "Dying at the top" was the expression used by John Adams in discussing the rumor that the Scottish philosopher Dugald Stewart had, like Isaac Newton and Jonathan Swift, descended into dementia. (The rumor proved untrue; Stewart had been stricken by a mysterious paralysis and recovered sufficiently to publish major works in the last years before his death, at age seventy-four, in 1828.) Adams and Jefferson wrote each other frequently about how fortunate they were to suffer from physical illnesses instead of mental decrepitude. "Crippled wrists and fingers make writing slow and laborious," Jefferson observed. "But, while writing to you, I lose the sense of these things, in the recollection of ancient times, when youth and health made happiness out of every thing."[18] Six months before both men died, Jefferson wrote Adams about the deterioration of both men's physical condition, including Adams's loss of sight. "The account I receive of your physical situation afflicts me sincerely. But if body or mind was one of them to give way, it is a great comfort that it is the mind which remains whole, and that its vigor, and that of memory, continues firm."[19] Both men made frequent allusions to what they considered the horrendous fate of contemporaries who had lost their mental faculties and were unable to recognize their closest relatives and friends. It is simply a misreading of history for anyone to suggest that old-age dementia was ever regarded by Americans as anything but a tragedy—or, as Jefferson put it, "the life of a cabbage."[20]

Perhaps the most painful documentation of old-age dementia in previous centuries is provided by those who recognized that they were losing their mental competence while they were still able to express themselves in writing. Frederick Law Olmsted, the founder of American landscape architecture, realized in 1895, at age seventy-three, that he could no longer trust his short-term memory to rise to the demands of overseeing his business. "It has today for the first time become evident to me that my memory as to recent occurrences is no longer to be trusted," he wrote his nephew and adopted son, John Charles Olmsted, in the spring of 1895. The great shaper of public landscapes had apparently been saved by his other son from a serious business error that would have revealed his failing memory to an important client. "I try to look at the situation from an outside and impersonal point of view," Olmsted wrote, "and so looking at it I see that I ought no longer to be trusted to carry on important business for the firm alone." He added hopefully, "I have no reason to think I have lost capacity in respect to invention, design or reasoning powers in any respect, only that my memory (or presence of mind) in regard to recent occurrences is less trustworthy than it has been." Between the spring and fall of 1895, Olmsted's condition, which was likely Alzheimer's, worsened dramatically. In a letter to his other son, Frederick Law Olmsted Jr., the great architect implies that he may soon be unable to communicate by letter. "I write only in yielding to a constant impulse, vain tho' I feel it to be, to be doing something for you," he tells his son. "My time for that has past. I can only pray, and I am a poor hand for that. I try in vain to think of something that I can yet do. . . . You can still write me for some time I hope. As long as I have interest in anything earthy [*sic*] it will be in what interests you."[21] The repetition in this short note, and the frustration of being unable to help loved ones, are characteristic of those who, in the middle stages of Alzheimer's, lose their ability to communicate effectively. Olmsted was soon moved to the McLean Asylum in Massachusetts, and he spent the last five years of his life there—cut off from everything except the landscape he had designed himself when his creative mind was at the height of its powers. If one wishes to see old-age dementia as the fault of someone or something wrong with modern society (selfish or untrained caregivers, hypercompetitive capitalism, indifference to the fate of unproductive humans) rather than as a neurobiological catastrophe, one must ignore the ample historical evidence that not only the young but the old of sound mind have always regarded loss of memory as the worst fate that can befall anyone in old old age.

Another argument advanced by those who assign a moral meaning—whether in a social or a religious sense—to Alzheimer's is that the biomedical model omits the perspectives of the demented themselves. This seems to me the most specious argument of all, because it ignores the fact that loss of perspective is the essence of degenerative brain disease. Ask those in the early stages of Alzheimer's what they want—and many people in the early stages, even though they have obvious difficulties with short-term memory, are as sound in their judgment as anyone else—and what they want is for their memory problems to stop. In the middle stages of Alzheimer's, when judgment is impaired, what I have observed is men and women struggling valiantly, against odds that they no longer quite understand, to hang on to whatever capabilities and perceptions they can. A loving caregiver, for his or her own sake as much as that of the Alzheimer's sufferer, tries to help the person hang on to that self as long as possible. This stage of the disease often gives rise to delusions (on the part of caregivers and social critics of caregivers) that it is somehow possible, with sufficiently devoted one-on-one interaction, to "reverse" the course of Alzheimer's. The person you love has a "good day," sometimes engendered by a happy event that may have given a temporary boost to the neural connections being inexorably severed by plaques and tangles. The good day can be anything from a day on which he talks more fluently than usual to a day on which he remembers what happened in the news the day before. And you allow yourself irrational hope. Perhaps the deterioration is stopping. Perhaps this is as far as it goes. But the good day is never followed by another good day, and it is an insult to caregivers to suggest that if only they knew how to give the right support, perhaps the sufferer would improve. Or at least not get worse. This is pure junk thought, and it is very cruel junk thought.

The sociologist Karen Lyman, in a paper so influential that it is still widely quoted in the literature of dementia even though it was written twenty years ago, argues that "power relationships," in both family and institutional settings, play a crucial role in the progression of dementia. "The literature on family caregivers presents a one-sided view of the caregiving relationship and illustrates the 'medicalization of deviance,'" Lyman writes. "Caregiver strain is explained by the deterioration of the demented care recipient. The source of trouble in caregiving is located in the misbehavior of the demented person, which is explained by the progression of the dementing illness."[22] Lyman seems not to understand that only the biomedical model makes it possible to distinguish between deterioration and "misbehavior." I don't know anyone—and I admit that most of my personal experience with Alzheimer's caregivers involves the devoted family members of the man I loved—who could even conceive of "misbehavior" in someone with a disease defined by an increasing lack of control over every aspect of one's life. Faced with the progression of a dementing illness, caregivers are strained not by what they regard as bad conduct but by the constant, ever-changing line between promoting as much dignity and autonomy as possible for the person with Alzheimer's and not endangering his physical safety. When someone no longer remembers how a stove works or that the burner needs to be turned off, he cannot be allowed to heat up his own soup. When he stops remembering to look for stoplights or stop signs at corners, he can no longer be permitted to drive. When he begins to get lost in familiar surroundings, he must be accompanied, or watched unobtrusively, to make sure that he finds his way home. Anyone who thinks that caregivers take pleasure in these restrictions either is a fool or is acquainted with some of the most mean-spirited people in the world. Yet Lyman and other social constructivist theorists consistently, implicitly, and explicitly attempt to shift some of the responsibility for deterioration from the disease to the caregiver. Reviewing the literature of caregiving, Lyman objects to the idea of caregivers as the "hidden victims" of Alzheimer's.

Changes in the caregiving relationship are traced to disease progression, rather than examining disease progression as a consequence of changes in the caregiving relationship. The demented person is viewed as burdensome but not burdened by the illness or by changes in relationships. The demented one is viewed as a stressor, not as one who is experiencing stress. As a result, people with dementia are largely invisible in most of the literature; they are merely disease entities, independent variables. . . . From a review of this research, it becomes clear that it is those suffering from the impairment, not their caregivers, are still "hidden victims" of dementia.

In the caregiver strain literature, one consistent finding is that it is not cognitive decline that is most burdensome, resulting in a decision to institutionalize the demented family member; it is troublesome behavior. A poignant irony is that many of the "behavior problems" associated with dementia may be traced to problems in the caregiving relationship, which are overlooked if the behavior is attributed to the disease. The medicalization of senility shifts attention from problems in the social situation of caregiving to locate problems in the pathology and misbehavior of the demented person. The focus overlooks the impact of the treatment context and caregiving relationship on the experience of dementing illness.[23]

What this sociologist calls "behavior problems" *are* the result of cognitive decline. They are not the result of old marital or relationship problems, which presumably the parties either resolved or resigned themselves to during the years before Alzheimer's. Fortunately, I know nothing about what finally forces a caregiver to consider institutionalization, because my companion died of another disease before entering the last stages of Alzheimer's. He was one of the lucky ones, and so was everyone who cared about and for him.

Everything one knows about the human capacity for evil surely indicates that there must be some caregivers—like abusive parents who believe that crying babies are bad and must be punished—who use the helplessness of an elderly Alzheimer's victim to make the person pay for real or imaginary crimes. In a recent British study of 220 family caregivers, 1.4 percent reported that they had physically abused the person in their care. The real rate of physical abuse within Alzheimer's families must be higher, because participation in the University College of London study—one of the few to ask directly about family abuse—was voluntary. Perhaps more significant was the fact that half of the family members admitted to having occasionally screamed at the person in their care.[24] But that, I would argue, is the fault not of the biomedical model of dementia but of social systems that provide no support for family members responsible for the day-in, day-out care of a person who is increasingly unable to care for himself. Moreover, everything one knows about the human capacity for good suggests that the majority of caregivers regard their commitment to care for the person they love as one of the most serious and meaningful endeavors of their lives. It is sad, but all too human, that seriousness and sense of duty, as well as love, do not act as absolute barriers to anger and impatience—and such outbursts wound and shame both the care receiver and the caregiver. The evidence-based biomedical model of Alzheimer's—unlike the junk thought model, which suggests that the right kind of caregiving can roll back the tide—is precisely what makes a caregiver cringe if she hears herself saying "Hurry up" or "Listen to me" in a sharp tone to someone who, as the caregiver knows perfectly well, can no longer hurry up or retain what he hears. I would never be so presumptuous as to suggest that the pain of caregivers is worse than the pain of people with Alzheimer's—especially during the period when the latter begin to recognize that they are losing their minds and understand that they are helpless to do anything about it. I can only say that watching darkness visible envelop the bright mind of someone I loved is the worst pain *I* have ever experienced. I would have saved him if I could.

There is certainly a real crisis in caregiving that our society is failing to address, as opposed to an irremediable power imbalance between caregivers and care receivers. The true villain, especially in the United States, is not biomedicine but inhumane and just plain stupid social and health policies that amount to "It's your lookout" when faced with chronic, incurable age-related diseases. More than two-thirds of Alzheimer's patients are cared for at home, usually by a spouse—and usually, in view of the gender gap in life expectancy, by a woman. Most of those at home are in the early and middle stages of the disease, and institutionalization usually occurs in the last stages of Alzheimer's, when the spouse is no longer physically capable of bearing the burden of daily care. As the government's Medicare Web site says clearly, "Medicare . . . doesn't pay for help with activities of daily living or other care that most people can do themselves. Some examples of activities of daily living include eating, bathing, dressing, and using the bathroom." In other words, Medicare doesn't pay for any of the help that home caretakers of Alzheimer's patients need. If you don't have enough money to pay for home health care aides, you're on your own. Nor does Medicare pay for long-term care. If people do not have long-term care insurance (and most Americans don't, because it is simply too expensive), they will have to exhaust their savings in order to qualify for Medicaid, the government program that does pay for long-term care of disabled low-income Americans. Private long-term care insurance, which generally does pay some of the costs of home health aides, is an unaffordable joke for the vast majority of older Americans. That is why such policies pay for only about 7 percent of long-term care costs. In 2005 (the last year for which figures are available), the typical buyer of long-term care insurance policies had over $100,000 in liquid assets (a financial position enjoyed by fewer than a third of Americans over fifty).[25] I toss out all of the long-term care propositions from insurance companies that I have been receiving since I turned sixty, since the annual premiums, depending on the amount of coverage, generally range from $2,000 to $3,500. I simply don't have the money, and I would be even less inclined to spend my money on long-term care insurance if I had children in their early twenties (as some of my contemporaries do) who had not yet finished their college or professional education. What I would buy, if it were available, is a much less expensive policy that would pay for extended care by aides in my own home. But most long-term care policies are a combination deal: they cover both institutional and home care, and the premiums are calculated accordingly. That's good business for the insurance companies, because many people now shelling out thousands of dollars a year for this insurance will not live long enough to need a nursing home. But it's bad news for Alzheimer's families, who need home health care aides long before an institutional solution is even contemplated.

For institutionalized patients with terminal dementia, Medicare's procedure-based reimbursement system often leads to pointless and painful medical intervention in the last months of life. A rigorous study by Harvard University researchers of deaths from dementia in nursing homes found that 41 percent of patients who died during the study had been subjected to at least one aggressive intervention—from being admitted to a hospital for elaborate tests to tube feeding—during their last three months of life.[26] Dr. Susan L. Mitchell, lead author of the study, told the press that many relatives making medical decisions had not been advised by doctors that their relatives were nearing death and therefore agreed to procedures without understanding that they had no real health benefits—including the prolongation of life. Yet 96 percent of the people empowered to make medical decisions for a relative believed that comfort was and should be the primary factor in care of terminal dementia patients. Only a third of the responsible relatives had been counseled by a doctor about physical complications that generally accompany the end of life for dementia patients. At the same time, as Dr. Greg Sachs noted in his accompanying editorial, pain was undertreated.

That it would be much cheaper, not to mention more humane, for the government to pay for palliative care or aides to help keep as many Alzheimer's patients as possible in familiar surroundings—as opposed to forcing couples to spend down their assets so that Medicaid can take over and pay for an expensive nursing home—is part of the madness of a health care system still based on the idea that individuals and nuclear families ought to be able to pay any price and bear any burden to care for loved ones who need round-the-clock supervision. Medicare does offer a hospice benefit for those who are expected to die within six months, but it offers nothing to help pay for the open-ended care of those who may live for years with Alzheimer's. Apart from federal budget considerations, the general resistance to thinking about or providing public financing for long-term care is encouraged by the still-prevalent assumption that women will always be available as caretakers for dependent family members. In *The Alzheimer's Project,* the devoted stay-at-home wife (or an available daughter) was the implicit assumption upon which most of the filmed stories were based. All of the homes in which couples lived were spacious and attractive, and it was clear that there was money for aides. The nursing homes, too, were attractive, housing patients in private rooms (which are not even a possibility for Medicaid patients). There was one daughter who had quit her job in Minneapolis and moved home to take care of her mother on their family farm. The documentary never explained how the daughter managed financially after quitting her job, and it never explored the daughter's thoughts about her own economic future if her mother lived, say, another decade with the disease.

What will happen when there are many more old people without a longtime partner or spouse to help them through the middle stages of Alzheimer's—a time when those with dementia can still function with help but cannot be left unsupervised and alone for any length of time? That is exactly what Americans will face in the next forty years, when ten million baby boomers are expected to develop Alzheimer's at some point in their lifetimes. Today, about 5.2 million Americans suffer from the disease, but 2010 saw the beginning of the onset of five hundred thousand new cases annually, as predicted by the Alzheimer's Association sometime ago. The number of new cases is expected to rise to 1 million a year by 2050. What then? We aren't doing a very good job of caring for a much smaller population of Alzheimer's sufferers today. Boomers have had smaller families than the members of the greatest generation, who now make up the bulk of the Alzheimer's population, and there will be fewer middle-aged adults to share the responsibility for taking care of their boomer parents. Furthermore, women who are able to function as caretakers for their parents will become increasingly scarce during the next two decades. Divorced women—and the World War II generation had a much lower divorce rate than today's caretakers—are much more likely to be employed full time, in both middle age and young old age, than their mothers were. Finally, the financial collapse of 2008, which slashed not only the value of real estate assets but the retirement savings accounts of boomers with jobs, will continue to keep boomers of both sexes in the workforce at a time when their parents were retiring—and were therefore available, at least in theory, to help out with the needs of older family members. Many boomer couples in their sixties are composed of a husband and a wife who are still working and whose two incomes are very much needed. If one of them develops Alzheimer's, the entire economic foundation of their household collapses. What if the salary of one partner cannot pay for health care aides to look after the sick partner at home—much less pay regular bills? The crisis is upon us now, but public policy makers have done nothing to address the fearful reality that several million more Americans are about to lose their minds in the coming decade. I never gave much thought to Alzheimer's until it touched my life directly, because no member of my family was ever stricken by the disease. But if I should one day find myself among the unlucky ranks of those with old-age dementia, I will, like many women of my generation, have no children and probably no partner to care for me (in the absence of an unpredictable late-in-life *coup de foudre,* which no one should ever rule out but no one should ever count on). The possibility is terrifying, because I now have a good idea of what it would mean to lose one's mental powers without being sheltered by the love of people who care enough to help. Yes, we can hope that science will come to our rescue sooner rather than later—but hope is not a plan of action.

CHAPTER SIX

WOMEN: EVENTUALLY THE ONLY SEX

I AM HAVING DINNER with a friend, a distinguished physician belonging to the pioneering generation of women who broke the gender barrier in medical schools in the early 1960s, and I tell her I am writing a book about old old age. "Oh, you mean you're writing a book about women," she says. She is right: old age is primarily a women's issue. Females, as is well known, are the survivors of our species. Except in the poorest countries in the world—cultures in which female infanticide is still a common practice and the risk of dying in childbirth remains high—women outlive men by a substantial number of years. In the United States, two-thirds of those over eighty-five and 85 percent of centenarians are women.[1] Gender differences in life expectancy do not disappear until age 105. So if you are a married 105-year-old woman whose husband has also lived to 105, he may have derived enough out of still being alive to be capable of taking care of you. But if you have a living husband under 105, you will almost certainly be the one doing the caretaking. Lesbians in long-term relationships are about the only women as likely to have a partner to look after them as to be the caretaker. And if you did not have children—whether you are widowed, divorced, or never married—you will have to rely mainly on your own resources.

Live into your nineties, and your surviving female friends, however much they care about you, won't be able to give you much help. They won't be able to lift you if you fall. They won't be able to drive you to the emergency room in a crisis or bring you home from the hospital after surgery. And they won't be able to help you out with the numerous everyday tasks, from stepping safely into and out of the shower to bending over to empty a garbage can, which are as difficult for the frail elderly as they are easy for the healthy young. When I was in my thirties—a decade coinciding with the high-water mark of the feminist movement—my friends and I used to talk about starting a retirement home for elderly women writers, who would provide one another with companionship and intellectual stimulation in the true spirit of sisterhood. It never really occurred to us that being old might mean needing help with basic physical activities and that our ability to supply intellectual stimulation, to ourselves as well as others, might not remain a given. For any woman realistic enough to contemplate the possibility of physical and mental decline preceding a death that does not take place until she is in her nineties, the idea of having no backup is frightening—and it should be. If there are cuts in Social Security and Medicare, women will be disproportionately affected, given that most men will already have been transported to That Great Entitlement Program In The Sky.

The cruelest paradox of all is that while women outlive men, they are two-and-a-half times more likely than men to suffer from serious disabilities in old age. Crippling arthritis, diabetes, Alzheimer's, and other forms of dementia are all more common in women than in men. Part of the explanation is simply female longevity; women are much less likely than men to die in their sixties and seventies of heart attacks or strokes. Because the risk of Alzheimer's doubles every five years after age sixty-five, a woman who lives to ninety is obviously in greater danger of contracting the disease than a seventy-five-year-old.[2] But a study released in 2009 by Duke University Medical Center found that 48 percent of the gender gap in disability rates is attributable to two common and chronic conditions—obesity and arthritis. (The obesity cited so frequently as a risk factor for some of the worst age-related diseases should not be confused with being—or feeling—overweight in an ordinary sense, which means simply that a person weighs more than some cultural ideal of slimness. Obesity, according to the National Institutes of Health, begins with a body mass index of over thirty. A woman five feet, five inches tall would have to weigh more than 180 pounds to be considered clinically obese. Morbid obesity does not begin until she weighs 240 pounds. One out of five Americans is obese, and one in fifty is morbidly obese. This represents a genuine public health crisis that should not be confused with unrealistic, culturally imposed standards of thinness and attractiveness.)

The Duke study, presented at the annual scientific meeting of the American Geriatrics Society, was the first attempt to isolate the impact of specific health conditions on the overall gender gap in disability. The researchers measured disability by asking people about their capacity to perform ordinary daily tasks, such as dressing themselves, walking, climbing stairs, and reaching for objects. Dr. Heather Whitson, assistant professor of medicine at Duke and lead investigator of the study, said, "This is important because it suggests that women's tendency to pack on extra pounds in their childbearing and perimenopausal years translates into loss of independence in old age."[3] The painful, mobility-reducing impact of arthritis is compounded by obesity, for the obvious reason that every additional pound places an extra burden on damaged joints. For women, one of the most disturbing aspects of the Duke findings about the contribution of obesity to the gender gap in old-age disability is that smoking-related cardiovascular disease, stroke, and emphysema—once associated mainly with men—are now becoming more common in women. Lung cancer has replaced breast cancer as the leading cause of cancer deaths in women. If the trend continues, the outcome could be an even wider gender gap in disability. It is impossible to predict, in the absence of long-term research about the effects of major changes in health habits, the extent to which the disability rate would drop among old women if they monitored their weight more carefully in their earlier adult lives. The more scientists learn about the most dreaded diseases, cancer and Alzheimer's, the more complicated the conditions appear to be, with strong genetic as well as potentially modifiable environmental components—including poor health habits. What can be said with certainty is that if women ignore what is already known about the long-term as well as the short-term hazards of obesity and smoking, they are setting themselves up for the worst possible health outcomes in old age. (Given the undeniable, scientifically documented health hazards of true obesity, "pro-fat" and "size acceptance" groups are doing women a disservice by suggesting that it is not only possible but easy to be obese and perfectly healthy and that medical warnings in this regard are in some way connected with the exaltation of thinness fostered by the fashion and beauty industries. It is certainly possible to weigh more than models—most of us do—and be in perfect health, but it is much tougher to maintain good health while weighing 50 to 150 pounds over already generous government guidelines. The connection between obesity and diabetes, even if there were no other medical risks attached to extra poundage, should give women pause about accepting any message that says fat equals healthy.) That millions of women will still die of cancer and Alzheimer's in old age even if they cultivate healthy bodies in their younger adult lives is no excuse for not doing everything possible to mimimize known risk factors. Disability is a women's issue.

Old-age poverty is also a women's issue—and poverty itself plays a role in the higher disability rate among women. Obesity and diabetes, in particular, are much more prevalent among the poor in all age groups than among those with higher incomes and more education. "Thus, when politicians talk about cutting old-age entitlements," Dr. Robert Butler observed, "they are mainly talking about denying health care and social security to poor old women." More than 75 percent of old people living below the official U.S. poverty level are women. Four out of ten of these women fall into the category of the "near poor" (meaning that their incomes range from 25 to 50 percent over the official poverty level).[4] Old women of all races are poorer than old men, and old Hispanic and African American women are the poorest of all. Half of black and Hispanic women who live alone—double the number for white women—are existing below the official poverty line. Nearly half of minority women depend exclusively on Social Security, because so many of them spent their lives trapped in low-wage jobs with no employee pension benefits.[5]

White women who live into their eighties and nineties are also at a great disadvantage in comparison to men, although they are better off than minority women. Conventional wisdom assumes that the expanding presence of women in the workforce since the 1970s will cushion boomer women against the poverty that became the lot of so many of their grandmothers after widowhood. That assumption will probably hold true for women now in their late forties, fifties, and early sixties who have worked full time for their entire lives before retirement. But it will not necessarily apply to the large number of boomer women who interrupted their careers for some years to care for children or aging parents, who never had a partner to share their living expenses, who never enjoyed the enormous economic advantage that accrues to both men and women who make up one-half of a two-income couple. But a woman derives the full economic advantage conferred by marriage only if two conditions are met: she manages to stay married to the same man, and she never takes a significant amount of time off from work to devote herself to full-time motherhood. In 1948, only about 17 percent of married mothers were in the labor force. By 1995, 70 percent were working.[6] That percentage remained stable throughout the first decade of the twenty-first century. These statistics do provide some support for the premise that boomer women are likely to be better off financially in old age than previous generations. Certainly any work history is better than none when it comes to both Social Security benefits and private pension plans. But a number of factors, apart from longevity itself, point to severe economic problems for a large proportion of boomer women in old age. First, full-time female workers still earn only eighty cents for every dollar that full-time male workers earn. Second, all women—not only minorities—are much more likely than men to work at part-time jobs without pension and health benefits. Ironically, the fact that men accounted for four-fifths of layoffs during the severe job losses of 2008 and 2009 provided even more evidence of the lower economic rewards attached to "women's work." A company saves much more by laying off a high-salaried man with excellent health and pension benefits than it does by getting rid of a woman who is already making less money than a man and may have no benefits at all. Finally, the much greater prevalence of divorce in the boomer generation means big economic trouble for many women. In the 1990s, divorced and never-married women made up only 10 percent of the over-seventy-five population. Fast-forward to the 2020s, and divorced or never-married women will make up 25 percent of that population. The poverty rate among this all-female group is double that of the elderly population as a whole.[7] Under current law, a divorced woman cannot claim any portion of a spouse's Social Security benefits unless she was married for a decade. The majority of divorces, however, take place after seven years. Let us consider the plight of a hypothetical divorced eighty-year-old woman in 2040 and say that she married late, at age thirty, in 1990. She and her husband wanted to have children right away (she was already thirty, remember), and she gladly or not so gladly gave up her job to care for her children until they reached school age. Let us suppose further that she and her husband split up seven years into the marriage, when their children were ages two and six. This woman, under present law, will receive nothing from Social Security for her seven years of contributing to a marital partnership. True, she would almost certainly have gone back to work full time after her divorce, but those seven lost years would have a huge impact on her independent Social Security benefits, her lifetime earnings, and her own ability to save for the future. If her husband was rich, she might have received a hefty divorce settlement, thereby avoiding the adverse economic consequences of divorce experienced by most women. But let us assume that our hypothetical eighty-year-old raised her children and worked in the real world—the world in which nearly all women become poorer, not richer, after divorce.

In the world as it is, women—whatever their marital status—pay a high price for dropping out of the workforce to provide full-time child care, even for a period of under three years. It is not surprising that women with husbands in the top fifth of income earners are most likely to take a time-out from full-time jobs. What is surprising is how much earning power these women have already lost when they do move back into the workforce. In 2006, the Hidden Brain Drain Task Force, founded by the economist Sylvia Ann Hewlett, commissioned a national survey, conducted by Harris Interactive, to study the impact of women's interrupted career patterns. The study focused on the most qualified and credentialed professional women, with advanced degrees or summa cum laude undergraduate degrees—those who had held high-level jobs before they left to care for children. The results ought to give pause to all women. When women try to return to work after only 2.2 years off, they find that they have lost 18 percent of their earning power. In business and finance, women lose 28 percent.[8] Furthermore, many women who have "off-ramped," as Hewlett puts it, cannot find jobs at all. Only 40 percent of women who have off-ramped—again, for just over two years—return to full-time jobs. Approximately 24 percent take part-time jobs. Overall, while more than nine out of ten women surveyed wanted to rejoin the labor force, only three-quarters actually did so.[9] In 2040, an eighty-year-old woman will feel the full economic impact of the time-out she took in her thirties—and the longer time-out she took, the poorer she will be.

Few people in their thirties—male or female—base major life decisions on preparing for life in their eighties. The inability of most thirty-year-olds to imagine what it might feel like to be eighty is a major factor in promoting the myth of young old age. When most people have children, for example, they do not do so because they expect their offspring to be a comfort to them in old age (and if they do, they are as likely as not to be bitterly disappointed) but because there is a powerful biological and emotional imperative to reproduce and to imprint one's unique genetic legacy on the future. Few thirty-five-year-olds think, *Gee, maybe I shouldn't have a baby because I might have to quit my job and I'll be in the poorhouse at ninety.* And few of us would want to base every major decision on worry about what might or might not happen sixty years in the future. It is important, though, for young adults to be aware of the long-term implications of their decisions. One economic fact can easily be understood: we will need more money to finance longer lives. And since women have the longest life expectancy, it would behoove them to take a hard-eyed look at the economic consequences not of childbearing itself but of allowing childbearing to become the decisive factor in a rationalization for a broken work history. I am suggesting not that all women choose paid work over being stay-at-home moms but that they make their decision only after thinking seriously about what it might mean over the full arc of their lives.

In the 1990s, however, many professional women did reduce their participation in the workforce. By 2005, the labor force participation rate of married mothers with preschoolers had dropped about 4 percent, from a peak of 54 percent in 1997. For mothers of children from ages six to seventeen, labor force participation also dropped two percentage points, from 77 percent in 1997 to about 75 percent in 2005.[10] This was the decade in which "choice feminism," as the writer Linda Hirshman put it, became fashionable as a description for women who saw nothing wrong with giving up work in order to care full time for their children for a considerable number of years. Choice feminism was supposedly an improvement on "no-choice feminism," under which women felt obliged to have it all. Having-it-all feminism was perfectly embodied by a popular commercial in the 1970s for a perfume called Enjoli, in which a sexy woman sang, "I can bring home the bacon, fry it up in a pan, and never let you forget you're a man, 'cause I'm a woman, W-O-M-A-N." By the 1990s, it was said, women had become fed up with doing it all, and choice feminism—the choice to opt out of the workplace—was seen as a desirable alternative to bringing home the bacon and frying it up in a pan.

The choice of working or not working, it should be emphasized, does not exist for the majority of poor and middle-income women, who take paying jobs because their families could not survive without their economic contribution. But this choice did exist in the high-flying 1990s for the kind of women portrayed in the Brain Drain study. A third of the women who quit their jobs after they had children told researchers they did so because their husbands made enough to support the family. In other words, they quit because they could. But there seems to have been more at work psychologically in the decision of many highly qualified women to opt out of paid work for a significant period of time. Perhaps the most unsettling recent portrait of these psychological and emotional factors is provided not by sociologists but by a novelist, Meg Wolitzer, in *The Ten-Year Nap* (2008). One of her characters, Amy Lamb, originally intends to take a twelve-week maternity leave from her job as a trust and estates lawyer but winds up staying at home until her son and only child is ten years old. Amy and her husband have "occasional, circular conversations about the possibility of Amy going to another law firm. It would be tough, she knew. Work wasn't like a trolley; you couldn't just jump on and off. Lawyers did their own word processing now, and she would have to learn how. . . . The longer she was away, the more difficult it seemed to go back."[11] At a dinner for corporate lawyers and their spouses, Amy concludes that "work did not make you interesting; interesting work made you interesting."[12] The financial consequences of not working outside her home do not occur to Amy until her husband tells her how deeply in debt they are and suggests that they really cannot afford to live on just one income. When Amy finally does go back to work, at a job with few of the prospects for advancement that she enjoyed when she left the workforce eleven years earlier, she seems to have little sense of what the ten-year nap cost her, not only in lost earnings but in future benefits—the benefits that might come in so handy at age eighty, in the unimaginable year 2040. I found this book, written by a novelist born near the end of the baby boom, highly disturbing because its female characters all seemed to exist in a state of submission to fate, to unwilled and uncontrollable ideas about the claims of both maternity and work. The idea that interesting work makes interesting people is a classic feminine, not feminist, fantasy—the work equivalent of Prince Charming. Interested people look for interesting work, though they may not always find it. And even if they don't find it, they work because they know that not only their present but their future standard of living depends on earning money over a long period of time. Hewlett's Brain Drain study uncovered a number of differences between women's and men's attitudes toward work that support Wolitzer's novelistic observations. "When asked what motivates them at work," Hewlett observes, "male executives highlight power and money, while female executives highlight connection and quality." Women listed high-quality colleagues, the ability to "be myself," flexibility, and teamwork as their top motivators at work; money and power were at the bottom of their list.[13] I do not know whether these findings fully reflect women's real values, or whether there is still a strong stigma against women who openly express their ambition. The answers likely reflect a combination of both factors; certainly the 2008 campaigns of Hillary Clinton for the Democratic presidential nomination and Sarah Palin on the Republican vice-presidential ticket—in spite of their very different political values—revealed the existence of a deep reservoir of hostility toward female ambition. It is beyond the scope of this book to discuss the changes in society, and in a workplace culture whose rules are determined largely by a linear male career pattern, that would make it easier for mothers of young children (and daughters of aging parents who require care) to stay in the workforce instead of abandoning it for a considerable period of time or downsizing their ambitions and settling for part-time jobs that fit into their domestic responsibilities.

Although control freaks obsessed with vanquishing old age would disagree, there is very little—apart from commonsense measures such as quitting smoking, exercising regularly, and maintaining a healthy weight—that any of us can do to improve our chances of a successful old age, with maximum ability to enjoy life and a minimum of age-related constraints. Working steadily, in order to increase both public and private economic benefits in old age, is one of the few certain midlife contributions that we can make to our own welfare in later life. A woman is likely to have lower lifetime earnings than her husband even if she does work full time for most of her life, but it is better, even if the husband's pension is larger and a woman has stayed married to one man, for her to have her own 401(k). This is true now, and it will remain true regardless of changes in the Social Security system and the economy as a whole. The economic insecurity and unemployment of the past few years only underline the dangers for any woman who chooses to depend entirely on the income of her partner. For women who divorce in midlife (unless they are married to a generous serial divorcer like the financier Ron Perelman, noted for conferring lavish settlements on each of his ex-wives), the economic consequences of depending on a man become apparent in the short term. But for women who do remain married, the price tag will not reveal itself until long into widowhood. The money a college-educated woman did not earn in her thirties may metamorphose into every "extra" she cannot afford in her eighties—the household help, the vacation, the college graduation check for grandchildren, the occasional restaurant meal. For low-income women, those lost earnings may translate into unaffordable necessities—from much needed prescription drugs to nutritious but expensive fruits and vegetables. One of the many reforms long advocated by feminists is that women receive Social Security credit for their unpaid child care and housework. But if you think that's going to happen as the huge boomer generation ages, and as the consequences of the nation's private indebtedness and increasing public deficit remain a major force in government policy decisions, I have a bridge to Brooklyn I want to sell you. Each young adult woman must ask herself Rabbi Hillel's question: "If I am not for myself, who will be for me?" It may well be that the economic downturn and turbulence of the past few years have administered a salutary dose of reality to relatively well-off married women who apparently have total confidence in their ability to hang on to their husbands and have dismissed the potential long-term economic consequences of taking ten-year (or two-year) breaks from paying work. If so, that will be an unintended positive consequence of the scare that the American middle class has been living through.

Taking care of business is particularly important for young and middle-aged women because there are many unquantifiable emotional hardships associated with female longevity that cannot be changed by anything a woman does earlier in her life. Chief among these are loneliness and a sexual invisibility that, in the absence of a longtime partner, become the lot of most old women. In 1995, when I had just turned fifty, I wrote a short essay about loneliness and old women. I knew full well that the subject would be considered a "downer" by most of the magazines that had published my work in the past, but I did not anticipate that I would fail to find a single taker for the article. "We don't feel that this depressing portrait represents our reader's active lifestyle," wrote one editor who had enthusiastically accepted every other article I had ever written for her. Here is the depressing portrait:

The Loneliness of the Long-Distance Woman

A white-haired, well-dressed woman, who appears to be in her seventies, addresses a man who is trying to dissuade his two preschool-age sons from throwing plastic bottles at each other on the subway. "If my grandsons are any guide, your children will stop doing that about two years from now," the woman says gently but authoritatively. The father looks at her, nods politely, and sidles away when she tries to engage him in further talk about child rearing. On a park bench, there would have been nothing unusual about such a conversational overture. But this was the New York subway, where the cardinal rule of etiquette is that you rarely initiate verbal or eye contact with your fellow passengers.

Throughout the fifteen-minute ride to my destination, I watched this woman break the contact taboo several more times. She asked a teenage girl what time it was and then tried to talk to her about the heat. She offered a pregnant woman her seat (the woman declined), and recalled that when she was pregnant with her last child, the subway cars weren't air-conditioned. She even read a man's newspaper over his shoulder (a supertaboo) and asked whether he'd seen the previous night's Mets game. In each instance, the other person evaded her with a subtle body shift that, to any veteran New Yorker, signals a clear no.

I grew literally sick to my stomach with pity, for I have never seen a countenance so etched with loneliness—a loneliness so profound that this woman was willing to risk one small rejection after another for even the briefest moments of human contact. As luck would have it, we got off at the same subway stop and headed for the city's busiest weekend farmers' market. Of course—recognizing me from the subway car—she struck up a conversation. (Talking with strangers at farmers' markets, by the way, is not a violation of New York decorum.) Rachel—she told me her first name while we picked out corn—was a seventy-seven-year-old retired high school English teacher whose husband died three years ago. Her daughters and grandchildren lived in California, and although they visited her and she visited them at least twice a year, that was it. And it was not enough for Rachel. Some of her closest friends moved to Florida or Arizona after retiring, but Rachel, a born-and-bred New Yorker, couldn't bear to leave the city. My shopping bag filled with vegetables, I took my leave and said, "It's been nice talking to you." And it had been. If I were a better person, I would have asked for Rachel's phone number and made a date for dinner or a concert (she told me she loved classical music). But I didn't do it.

At fifty, my days and nights are crowded with personal and professional duties and pleasures. The man in my life has had some medical problems during the past year–nothing life threatening, but scary enough to require more of my time and attention and to underline how much we mean to each other. As a writer, I've never been busier, juggling a book and a dozen short-term projects. I don't see enough of my closest friends, my two nieces, my brother, or my mother. In short, I'm spread too thin in relationships with people who already have a significant claim on my life, and I don't have time for a lonely new acquaintance.

But I can't stop thinking about Rachel. While loneliness is hardly the exclusive province of women or of people in their sixties, seventies, eighties, and beyond, it is an issue with a particularly unsettling resonance for a woman my age–young enough to be almost too busy juggling multiple demands, old enough to imagine what it might be like to be cast adrift from my social moorings. "Social loneliness" (a phrase that, at first glance, looks like an oxymoron) is the term psychologists have invented to describe a dearth of friendships and family networks. "Personal loneliness," by contrast, is the lack of one person who means more to you than anyone else in the world–and to whom you mean more than anyone else. Because the harsh demographics of aging dictate that most women will outlive the men they love, older heterosexual women will, almost inevitably, face a crisis of personal loneliness. It is generally assumed, however, that women–because they tend to cultivate friendships with other women throughout their lives–are much less vulnerable to social loneliness than men. I'm not so sure.

The upbeat glossy women's magazines–even the new crop trying to reach readers over forty–ignore this subject. A lonely woman approaching strangers doesn't fit the cheerful, in-control image being marketed to advertisers. In truth, it doesn't fit the image women my age have of ourselves. Loneliness is considered somewhat shameful–one of the last social taboos in a country where people are willing to appear on television and talk about nearly every other form of intimate unhappiness. Like debt—one of the few other personal misfortunes Americans still try to keep to themselves—loneliness is presumed to be entirely one's own fault.*

While it is understood that personal loneliness is unavoidable if a woman lives long enough, social loneliness is regarded almost as a sign of moral turpitude. When I tell friends my Rachel story, their near-universal reaction is that she must have been a bad mother or a bad teacher or a bad friend to suffer from social isolation in her late seventies. *If I'm a good girl, that won't ever happen to me.* What this self-protective reaction ignores is the degree to which aging itself, as well as the loss of a spouse, may erode social networks. Anyone who has ever retired or been fired knows how little contact she is likely to have with her former co-workers after the farewell lunch. Old friends move away. And for a woman, the loss of a spouse or long-term partner inevitably alters her relationships with coupled friends.

This is still, in spite of the prevalence of divorce, a coupled society. The personal loneliness of men and women who have lost beloved partners is surely equal, but there is one major difference: unattached men over sixty are a scarce commodity, and women—the organizers of social life—generally step in to make sure that a widower is never left alone unless he wants to be (and sometimes not even then). Unless they are misanthropists and misogynists, aging men do not have to suffer from social loneliness. Married women don't abandon women friends who have been widowed, but they do tend to relegate them to a smaller corner of their lives. "You become the lunchtime friend, not the prime-time friend," says one acquaintance, a widowed sixty-eight-year-old who went through the same thing twenty years ago after a divorce. I asked whether she couldn't just call up one of these "couple" friends and say, "I'm going to that new movie near you, I'd love to see you, and I thought we might meet for Chinese afterward." She replied, "That would be like putting up a sign saying, 'I'm lonely.' It makes people avoid you."

The sad thing is that she's right. I see those subway passengers turning away, ever so slightly, from Rachel. I see myself walking away from her in the greenmarket. Scared.

—August 17, 1995

* As a result of the economic crisis that began in 2008, the taboo against talking publicly about debt no longer applies as strongly as it did when I wrote this article. The linkage between debt and moral turpitude remains.

When I wrote this essay, I was still too young to be thinking about old old women in their eighties and nineties. Although it may be true that few women in their sixties and seventies are afflicted by the extreme social loneliness that Rachel displayed, female friends cannot provide the same bulwark against isolation for women who survive decades longer—for the obvious reason that the longest survivors must endure the death of their dearest friends just as they endured the deaths of their lifetime partners. In the age group from sixty-five through seventy-four, 78 percent of men—but only 57 percent of women—are married. From ages seventy-five through eighty-four, the percentage of married men drops by only three points, to 74 percent. Among women, however, only 38 percent in the same age group have living husbands. Over eighty-five, only 15 percent of women—but 60 percent of men—are married.[14] When one considers old age from a purely demographic standpoint, it is not only a women's issue but an issue of how women are to survive alone—economically, physically, and emotionally.

As a feminist, I have been greatly disappointed by the failure of women's movement leaders from the 1960s and 1970s to face old old age as a women's issue with the same fierce determination they once employed in the battles for reproductive choice and equal rights for women in education and the workplace. Older feminist figures like Gloria Steinem and the late Betty Friedan have had plenty to say about middle-aged women, but they have generally avoided the subject of old age—especially advanced old age. Limiting the discussion of old age primarily to the young old, as Friedan did in *The Fountain of Age,* is just another way of avoiding the subject. Leave out the ninth and tenth decades of life, and you can pretend that aging men and women have essentially the same needs and challenges. In a chapter that purports to be about sex, titled "Intimacy Beyond the Dreams of Youth," Friedan writes:

> Woman or man, we begin to know, before it is too late, that we can *choose* to tear down the walls we have built up against that joyous, painful intimacy, *choose* to take the risks of it, *choose* to create the experiences, reunions, that will keep it alive, over the distances of time and space. But space itself, and time too, must be created anew; we have to use it differently, move maybe to a different space, for the bonds of intimacy to continue to grow and nourish us in age.[15]

This windy, opaque passage (how exactly can time and space be created anew?) seems to suggest that old age offers the possibility of equal sexual opportunities to men and women. Let us momentarily leave aside, for purposes of argument, the inescapable fact that there are not nearly enough men within a reasonable age range to go around for every heterosexual woman over sixty-five. Are we talking about cuddling and cooking together? Where is sex in this new intimacy that both women and men are supposed to be able to choose? What about the crucial role of sheer physicality in erotic attraction? How many seventy-five-year-old men feel a stirring in their groins at the sight of a seventy-five-year-old woman? How do old women feel about their own bodies? Writing in her early seventies, Friedan claimed the older women had managed to "transcend" fear of the loss of youthful beauty and the diminishment of their sexual attractiveness to men.[16] The authority quoted by Friedan was none other than Susan Jacoby. *That* Susan Jacoby, however, was an author writing at age forty-three, decrying the increasing popularity of cosmetic surgery among women her own age and the rush to erase wrinkles with a new product called Retin-A. (Botox hadn't yet been born.) She advised women to stop wasting money and energy in the futile quest for a more youthful appearance and instead "to cultivate the kind of unconditional self-acceptance embodied in the zestful marriage proposal that concludes Shakespeare's *Henry V.*"[17] Henry tells his intended bride, "But, in faith, Kate, the elder I wax, the better I shall appear: my comfort is, that old age, that ill layer-up of beauty, can do no more spoil upon my face: thou has me, if thou hast me, at the worst; and thou shalt wear me, if thou wear me, better and better." But Henry was a man. And when I inspect photographs of myself in my forties, I look very, very good—as good as anyone not afflicted by an incurable case of vanity could expect to look. It is difficult to understand why Friedan, in a book about old age, would use a forty-something woman's satisfaction with her looks as "proof" that old women aren't troubled by the loss of their physical allure. One might as well quote an essay by a twenty-year-old who has never been pregnant on the physical changes associated with childbearing. At sixty-five, I am entering that perilous zone in which I run into a female contemporary I haven't seen for twenty years and we assure each other, "You look great." The "for your age" is unspoken by friends of the same generation, but it is frequently spoken by young people to their elders.

I do not mean to suggest that men are unconcerned about changes in their physical appearance or that most women are obsessed by changes in their looks—only that the surface changes associated with moving from middle age to young old age and from young old age to old old age are more distressing to women than to men. Women, particularly feminists, are apt to deny this publicly—although a few courageous female souls have written honestly about this subject. Nora Ephron, in her late sixties, has dissected the unhappy trajectory of the aging neck, just as she described her insecurities about having small breasts when she was in her thirties.[18] (Small breasts, by the way, may be liabilities in youth but are a great advantage in later life, because there is less tissue to succumb to gravity.) Letty Cottin Pogrebin, a dedicated feminist, summed up the whole process when she was in her mid-fifties.

> Experts say that women live eight years longer than men but look old ten years sooner because we lack men's thicker skin and the hair follicles that hold their skin in place. That must explain why the cheerful parentheses at the corners of my smile have started looking downtrodden and my top lip is beginning to produce those spidery vertical creases that soak up lipstick.
>
> Just this year, my jaw, the Maginot Line of facial structure, surrendered to the force of gravity. On each side of my chin the muscles have pulled loose from the bone. Once I had a right-angle profile; now there's a hypotenuse between my chin and neck. . . .
>
> My "perky" bosom is a thing of the past. The breasts long ago flunked Bette Midler's test: "Put a quarter under each tit; if the coins drop, you're young enough to go braless." My twenty-three-inch waist is ancient history. . . . My belly, round even when I'm slim, is flabby, bisected top to bottom with an uneven cesarean scar and limned with pregnancy stretch marks courtesy of my full-term twins. . . .
>
> What I've described here is not a maimed or disfigured human being but a *normal* female body in its fifty-fifth year of life. If this inventory conjures up a grotesque image, it's because most of us are not used to confronting the ordinary aesthetic of aging. . . . Even in the ladies' locker room or the communal dressing rooms at Loehmann's, older women drape their towels and maneuver their underwear so deftly as to keep the body under wraps.[19]

In spite of the visible evidence that nature is having its way with our once prized physical attributes, most older women devote a good deal of time and thought to avoiding the dreaded pejorative "She's let herself go." My grandmother said, more than once, that the worst thing about living in a nursing home was that she was surrounded by other women who had let themselves go. Gran was one of the few residents who bothered to put on lipstick before she went to eat in the communal dining room. An endless checklist is required to avoid letting oneself go. First, makeup. Because the natural look was de rigueur when we were young, many boomer women never wore any makeup, other than lipstick, until we entered our forties. Regardless of their age, our mothers and grandmothers almost never left the house without makeup; my grandmother called it "putting on my face." But the fact is that makeup, properly and subtly applied, does even more for women in their sixties and seventies than it does for middle-aged women. Take a look at Speaker of the House Nancy Pelosi (b. March 26, 1940), Secretary of State Hillary Clinton (b. October 26, 1947), and Jane Fonda (b. December 21, 1937). They all look very good for their ages, and each of these women knows how foolish it would be to expose herself to the public's gaze without putting on her face. In the retirement community where my mother lives, all of the women in their eighties and nineties are carefully made up when they appear in public. Unlike the women in my grandmother's nursing home—most of whom suffered from some form of dementia—my mother's neighbors have not let themselves go. As Gran noted, it is a nearly infallible sign of a failing brain when an old woman stops wearing makeup.

Maintaining a youthful-looking head of hair, either by coloring or the selection of appropriate wigs, is another essential element in the battle against letting ourselves go. No one under age fifty can remember a time when altering the color of hair was seen as a sign of moral laxness in women. That prejudice began to disappear with the famous 1956 Clairol advertising campaign, developed by Shirley Polykoff, featuring the tagline "Does she . . . or doesn't she?" The answer: "Only her hairdresser knows for sure." At the time, only 7 percent of American women used artificial coloring on their hair. Within a decade, nearly half of all American women would be dyeing or bleaching their hair.[20] Polykoff, the only female copywriter at the renowned Foote, Cone & Belding advertising agency, eventually became the firm's only female vice president on the strength of her Clairol campaign. (Her career could easily have been the inspiration for the character of Peggy in the American Movie Channel's critically acclaimed series *Mad Men,* about the days when men ruled the advertising—and every other—business.) By the 1970s, the unprecedented entry of large numbers of middle-class women into the workforce put an end to any lingering notions that women who used artificial hair coloring were morally loose; as the older boomer women moved into their forties, they realized that concealing gray hair was not only an expression of personal vanity but a smart career move. Today, only a small number of women in powerful positions are willing to risk gray hair. Secretary of Health and Human Services Kathleen Sebelius, in her early sixties, is one, and I am hard put to think of many others. It's unlikely that Pelosi's chestnut-highlighted brown hair is the work of nature. Ditto for Clinton's blond streaks. I doubt that she would have dared to run for the presidency while sporting a head of white hair, even if her crowning glory were as fluffy as her husband's.

Clothes are the third rail for women in their sixties and seventies if they remain determined not to let themselves go. The problem is that unless a woman is rich enough to buy custom-made clothes, like Clinton's pantsuits, which minimize the aesthetic liabilities of an aging body, most fashionable clothes are cruelly designed to expose what older women would like to conceal. The NPD Group, a leading market research firm, found that women over sixty-five spent almost as much on clothes as the twenty-five- to thirty-four-year-olds who are the target readers of glossy fashion magazines. But older women (with "old" beginning at forty in this context) are virtually invisible in those magazines. Once a year, *Vogue* publishes a special edition that does highlight older women—and nearly all of them are women who look unusually young for their age and who are very, very thin. In this regard, they are the equivalent of the forty-something couples featured in Viagra commercials. When *Vogue* published its first issue focusing on older women in August 2001, the magazine featured spreads on Sigourney Weaver, fifty-one, wearing a black cashmere backless halter (a garment that no woman with sagging breasts could ever put on, because it has to be worn without a bra); Mica Ertegun, seventy-one, in an all-enveloping satin cloak with her face covered by what looks like Kabuki makeup (there's a great idea for female politicians and executives); and Charlotte Rampling, sixty-five, whose face was partly concealed by a cloud of hair. (Rampling, another almost ghoulishly thin woman, gave up nudity onscreen at age sixty-one.) There were also soft-focus shots obscuring the wrinkles on socialites like Anne Bass and Annette de la Renta. The message: it's great to be an older woman if you are as thin as a thirty-year-old model and can devise some way to hide your face. One problem for aging boomer women is the contradiction between the ideals of fleshly freedom acquired in our youth and the need to rein in today's flesh in order to remain, if not material for a spread in *Vogue,* someone to be taken seriously at a job interview. *Rocking the Ages,* the 1997 report on generational marketing prepared by Yankelovich Partners, tells a revealing story about a phone call received in 1968 by Florence Skelly, one of the firm's founders, from the president of the company that made Playtex girdles. It seemed that the middle-aged wife of the Playtex president had thrown away her own girdle. "What does this mean for my business?" the flummoxed executive asked Skelly. What Skelly concluded, after considerable research, was that Playtex could forget about selling girdles not only to the daughters but to many of their mothers.

> The new generation had some distinct ideas: Girdles were not comfortable. They were confining. Stodgy. Old-fashioned. Boomers just coming into their own as a power in the marketplace didn't want to wear them. When their mothers tried to pass on esoteric girdle knowledge to their daughters, the daughters weren't listening. And in a seismic shift, the new freedoms demanded by the daughters were beginning to influence the buying habits of the mothers.[21]

Today, however, the girdle has been reinvented in the form of Spanx, a lighter, more flexible approximation of the torture instruments once called long-line bras and girdles. Women under forty, if they are of normal weight, don't need Spanx, but many women over forty, whatever their weight, feel that they look much better with the "smooth" line provided by squeezing themselves into these new foundation garments. The problem is that squeezing oneself into body-shaping garments made of the new flexible synthetic fabrics may be more comfortable than wearing a whalebone corset, but it is certainly not as comfortable as the next-to-nothing undergarments we wore in our youth. Then there is the question of whether these stifling "minimizers" (how endless are the euphemisms for garments designed to control flesh!) really make a fifty- or sixty-something woman look better or younger or whether, like cosmetic surgery, they make her look like a fifty- or sixty-something woman who is really, really uncomfortable.

The conventional wisdom among women's magazine editors, advertisers, and marketers in the fashion industry is that women themselves don't want to look at pictures of clothes modeled by their contemporaries. Sam Shahid, who designed advertising campaigns for Calvin Klein and Abercrombie and Fitch, told a fashion reporter that clothing companies and designers avoid gray-haired models because they believe "it will ruin my image to have an older woman wear my clothes."[22] Shahid, who was creative director in the early 1990s of *Mirabella,* the now-defunct magazine aimed at women over forty, was convinced that a magazine directed toward that age group—not to mention women over sixty—couldn't work because "fashion photographers don't want to work for a magazine like that. Even the reader—she may be 60—doesn't want to look at another 60-year-old wearing the clothes." Only ten years ago, with the economy booming, one of the comical anachronisms influencing marketers' views about older women and fashion was the conviction that women over sixty were likely to be retired. "For women of retirement age, going on a browsing spree is a major pastime," Candace Corlett, a market researcher who specialized in the over-fifty women's market, told *The New York Times*. "They have money to spend, but they spend it mainly on travel and gifts for their grandchildren. They would shop for themselves, but the big shopping venues, the department stores and the malls, don't present a lot of impulse opportunities for older women."[23] This portrait of sixty-something ladies of leisure whose chief pleasure in life is a "browsing spree" was already antiquated thirty years ago, but in today's economic climate, with people still reeling from the losses of their pension plans, the idea of retired women with time on their hands seems downright ridiculous. Letting oneself go (or having spare time to browse for clothes) will not even be an option if the retirement age for collecting full Social Security benefits continues to rise. Only occasionally is this expression used about older men—usually in regard to recent widowers, who are presumed (often by women who want to take them in hand) to be incapable of figuring out when they need a haircut or how to find matching socks without the assistance of a wife. In most instances, though, men are allowed to look their age without suffering adverse personal or professional consequences. There are exceptions, especially in the entertainment business, but there is no comparison between the shoring-up efforts required of a woman and a man who want to stay on camera after age sixty. Consider the contrast between Barbara Walters and Mike Wallace, both of whom appeared on television regularly into their eighties. Walters, who continues to appear on special interview programs, has had so much cosmetic surgery (unless she is a wrinkle-free freak of nature) that it would be impossible to tell how old she is if there weren't so many Americans who remember her from the 1950s as the *Today* weather girl. Wallace's craggy face and liver spots, by contrast, reveal his age as clearly, if not as precisely, as the rings of a redwood.

This is not a rant about the unfairness of the double standard of aging but a straightforward commentary on what it takes for women to be perceived to have aged gracefully even during their sixties and seventies—the young phase of old age. And keeping up appearances is not only a matter of professional and social survival for women who are still working: it is also a necessity for survival as a sexual being. When Maggie Kuhn told the General Assembly of the United Presbyterian Church that sex was one of the essential ingredients of successful aging, she was simply ignoring (much like Friedan) the fact that, lesbians excepted, a majority of women over seventy—much less eighty and ninety—have no access to a sexual partner. Let us concede that masturbation is a form of sex, but it seems to me an emotionally unrewarding activity for those who remember two-way passion. In adolescence, even (or perhaps especially) for those encumbered by religious guilt, masturbation can be emotionally as well as physically intoxicating because it is greatly enhanced by the dream of a future Other. In old age, especially for those who have lost a cherished partner, masturbation is little more than a release of physical tension, accompanied by a painful reminder that there is no Other, and may never be again. Here is where anxiety about appearance, and the undeniable diminution of the physical charms associated not only with youth but with middle age, challenge the female half of the rosy portrait of aging sexuality portrayed in those Viagra commercials. Women over seventy—however fit, however thin, however fashionably dressed—have as much chance of looking like the sexy wives in those Viagra commercials as most women in their twenties have of looking like the models in *Cosmopolitan, Glamour,* and *Vogue.* If a woman is involved with a man who has loved and desired her for many years, it doesn't matter so much. In a miracle of nature and human imagination—a miracle that may, sadly, elude many older couples who have fallen out of sympathy—each sexual act between aging bodies encompasses the memory of the same act performed at an age when the bodies were beautiful in both an objective and a subjective sense. It is unrealistic, and in many instances cruelly so, to suggest that it requires only an outgoing personality and a "young at heart" attitude for an old woman to find another man, a new man who, lacking the compassionate lens of a passionate history, is nevertheless capable of seeing her flawed body as a pleasure-giving instrument. It does happen, and publications aimed at people over sixty-five love to feature stories about men and women who have found new mates almost as much as they love to give space to articles about ninety-five-year-old skydivers. But the exceptional love/sex story rarely happens for very old women.

I would not dream of making any generalizations about how important sex is to old women or men—whether they fall among the young old or the old old—but one thing can be said with certainty: without a sexual partner, the easiest thing to do is pretend that sex doesn't matter. An old man who still wants sex, whether he needs potency-enhancing drugs or not, can find a partner—whether she is many decades younger or closer to his own age. If a seventy-year-old man wants sex, he can marry or live with a woman twenty years younger without incurring the slightest bit of social disapproval. If he can be aroused only by a much younger woman, he can, if he has sufficient money and/or prestige, find a partner in her twenties, thirties, or forties. Women do not have the same options if they want a man in their lives. A seventy-year-old woman is unlikely to arouse the erotic interest of a man ten years, much less thirty years, her junior. And most men of her own generation are dead, taken, or gay. This, again, is a fact—not a diatribe against dirty old men. When I was in my forties and many men mistakenly concluded that because I was not wearing a wedding band I was unattached, I was astonished at the number of much older widowers and divorced men—one was already over eighty—who asked me out. I simply had no sexual interest in men thirty years older than I was, and I also felt a sisterly sense of indignation on behalf of the many smart, accomplished, attractive, unmarried women in their sixties and seventies who were being ignored as potential sex objects by their male contemporaries. I fumed at the arrogance of these men. Who did they think they were, that they were entitled to their pick of women from every generation? Some of them, for God's sake, were too old to have been eligible for combat in the Second World War—when I was, as the saying goes, barely a gleam in my father's eye. They were older than my father! Now I see things somewhat differently and somewhat more charitably. Darwin's theory of evolution by means of natural selection may not explain everything in the universe, but it certainly explains human sexual behavior better than any of the lofty antirationalist notions, from theistic religions to Freudianism, that attempt to prescribe "mature" sex (and proscribe a great deal of the sex that people actually desire) for both men and women. The natural age-related waning of potency in healthy males, and the many age-related diseases (such as diabetes), as well as the medication needed to treat them, must inevitably require a more powerful sexual stimulant for an old man. Men are biologically hardwired to be aroused by women whose appearance announces their fertility. The rare uncoupled man in his sixties, seventies, or eighties is apt to find a more powerful aphrodisiac in a young, estrogen-rich woman in her reproductive years than in a female contemporary—however attractive she may be "for her age." The yearning for a surge of youthful potency cannot easily be reconciled with the image of a woman whose body is also ravaged by time. I have heard women of my generation speak in enraged tones about the involvements of their male contemporaries with much younger women, and this bitterness disturbs me. These women are furious not only at married men who cheat on their wives with young women but with widowers who prefer a younger woman to an older wife who has died. It seems to me that one might as well dispute the famous "I accept the universe!" statement by the early nineteenth-century feminist Margaret Fuller as rail against the desire of men for younger women. It is certainly true that most of us (however considerable our accomplishments, however youthful our appearance) do not have the same opportunity to impress young men with our prowess in bed. I find it difficult not to feel a pained sense of recognition when an aging male writer takes on this subject not with braggadocio but with an inescapable awareness of the temporal nature of everything. Philip

Roth, in *The Dying Animal* (2001),* describes the affair of a professor in his sixties with a former student in her twenties.

> Don't misunderstand me. It isn't that, through a Consuela, you can delude yourself into thinking that you have a last shot at your youth. You never feel the difference from youth more. In her energy, in her enthusiasm, in her youthful unknowing, in her youthful *knowing,* the difference is dramatized every moment. There's never any mistaking that it's she and not you who is twenty-four. You'd have to be a clod to feel you're young again. If you felt youthful, it would be a snap. Far from feeling youthful, you feel the poignancy of her limitless future as opposed to your own limited one, you feel even more than you ordinarily do the poignancy of every last grace that's been lost. It's like playing baseball with a bunch of twenty-year-olds. It isn't that you feel twenty because you're playing with them. You note the difference every second of the game. But at least you're not sitting on the sidelines.[24]

It is pointless for a woman beyond middle age to argue with hard-wired biological drive and the ungovernability of desire, to take an aggrieved stance toward every one of the small number of healthy widowers and divorced men over sixty-five who turn to a younger woman instead of to a life-seasoned woman of their own generation. There is considerable evidence that women, too, would rather be in the game (though perhaps not with a man so young that he reminds them every second of how old they really are) than on the sidelines. For women beyond their childbearing years, what matters sexually is not a man's fertility, or his physical appearance, but his skills as a lover (including his ability to maintain an erection). When AARP conducted a major survey in 2005 of the sexual attitudes and preferences of Americans over forty-five—with the oldest respondents in their nineties—potency-enhancing drugs had been available for only seven years. More than 20 percent of men over fifty had tried these drugs, and 68 percent said their sexual satisfaction had been greatly enhanced. But the big surprise—to those who assumed that men were using these drugs only with much

* In 2008, the book was made into an affecting movie, titled *Elegy* and starring Ben Kingsley and Penelope Cruz.

younger partners and that many older wives had no interest in sex—was that women in all age groups reported that their own sexual pleasure had increased as a result of their partners' use of drugs like Viagra and Cialis. They may not be typical, but there really are married men over sixty-five who do want to have sex with their wives, and there are some unattached men over sixty-five who want to have sex with women somewhere near their own age. There just aren't enough of them. Dr. Jennifer Berman, a leading sex researcher and one of the few female urologists in the United States, said the notion that "older women are just happy to be done with sex" is based on cultural stereotypes that equate women's sexual desire with a youthful body. "Certainly I see women of all ages who've lost desire," says Berman. "But for every woman who says to me, 'My husband wants sex and I'm not interested,' there's a woman who says, 'I want sex and my husband isn't interested.' This woman can be thirty or she can be seventy.' "[25]

I have been speaking, primarily, of sex among young old women, at an age when the possibility (if not the probability) of finding a new partner is still alive. For nearly all heterosexual women who live into their eighties and nineties, the end of sex is a certainty long before the end of life. It is difficult to determine how much this matters to women, given the greater day-to-day importance of economic and health problems. Most older women I know downplay the importance of sex and claim that they do not feel any real sense of deprivation. I must say that I think they are doing a con job on themselves. What is irretrievably lost, one must learn to do without. This is arguably the last lesson of a long life—a lesson that the young, middle-aged, and young old are understandably reluctant to learn. But only in the realm of sex do I hear older people claiming that they do not miss what they have lost. I have never heard a hearing-impaired classical music lover, forced to use a hearing aid that distorts the sound of music, claim that music was no longer important to her. I have never heard a person in a wheelchair claim that she no longer has any regrets about not being able to stand on her own feet. I have never heard anyone with severe osteoporotic pain insist that she never thinks about what it was like to spring out of bed in the morning and feel a rush of energy and well-being course through her body and brain. But I have heard plenty of women claim that they don't miss sex. This might well be true if a woman never enjoyed sex in her younger years, but many of my older friends are passionate women to whom sex was once extremely important. What is going on here, I suspect, is not so much denial as shame. Yes, dirty old men are figures of fun, but dirty old women are figures of contempt. For women, there seems something shameful about longing for the passion that was always closely connected to their sense of physical desirability. To whom, apart from a partner who has loved her many years, is a ninety-year-old woman apt to be desirable? No one wants to think or talk about this, least of all the marketers promoting the fiction that "age is just a number" and the boomers in their fifties and sixties who prefer to talk about how much younger they look and feel than their parents did at the same age. Old women may have to do without, but that is no reason to pretend that there is anything good, or virtuous, or pleasurable about being forced to give up what was once a vital part of your womanhood and your humanity—and that men are beasts because they have more choices.

To some, it may seem frivolous to talk about loneliness, the loss of sex, and a diminished sense of physical attractiveness in the same breath as the more fundamental, life-and-death question of whether old old women can afford to pay for both food and medicine or whether they are sick and in pain. The salient point, however, is that women are much more likely than men to experience all of the most severe quality-of-life problems—emotional and physical—associated with longevity.

I am the daughter and granddaughter of women who lived very long lives with intact minds. I watched my grandmother fade into the shadows of a nursing home populated mainly by those who could no longer comprehend anything about the world around them—whether proximate or distant. I watch my mother live with osteoporotic pain about which she rarely complains, but I see her wince whenever she has to exert the slightest pressure on any object or when she brushes her arm, ever so lightly, against a door frame or a piece of furniture. I remember my grandmother's sad years of confinement, I see my mother's pain, and I feel a rage at those who believe that extending the boundaries of longevity is a great advance for humankind. I am certain that living with an intact mind and a ruined body is better than living with a ruined mind and reasonably intact body, but too many women are destined to suffer both fates. My mother, on her most pain-filled days, sometimes says she might be better off if she didn't understand what was going on around her. And yet Mom—who, like everyone else in my family, has always been passionately interested in politics—seemed to gain a new lease on life with the 2008 presidential campaign and the election of Barack Obama. The night of Obama's election was the first time I ever heard her say that she was glad to have lived long enough to see something. For my mother, Obama's presidency was a surprise that kept her completely engaged with what was happening around her in the America of 2008. The French writer and sensualist Colette, who was confined to bed by severe arthritic pain for years before her death, at age eighty-one, in 1954, spoke and wrote precisely and poignantly about the importance of surprise even, or perhaps especially, in a life that is coming to an end. "So, as luck will have it, I am fated to suffer pain," she wrote, "which I reconcile with a gambler's spirit, my ultra-feminine gambler's spirit, my instinct for the game of life, if you prefer it; the Last Cat, toward the end of her life, gave every indication by the movement of a paw, by the smile on her face, that a trailing piece of string was still for her a plaything, food for feline thought and illusion. Those who surround me will never let me want for pieces of string."[26] At a luncheon not long before her death, she remarked to her friends, "With a little pride, I can endure my pain. But I do need to be surprised. So take the trouble, please: astonish me. I do not know how to go on without these last bursts of laugher."[27] Colette's final years (apart from her pain) were a glorious exception to the fate that awaits most old women, then and now, in many Western countries. But then, her entire life had been a glorious exception. She died with her brilliant mind intact and remained productive as a writer until the end. She also had a devoted younger husband, whom she had married in 1935, and received a constant stream of visitors, France's leading intellectuals, in her apartment in the Palais Royal. Colette was, in her own way, the equivalent of all of those nonagenarian skydivers that American magazines love to feature. What woman, whatever the state of her health, would not like to end her time on this earth in possession of her talents, her clarity of thought, her female charm, her friends, a husband to watch over her, and, last but not least, a very nice home. Many women in their eighties and nineties do not possess any of these blessings and would be satisfied just to finish their lives in domestic surroundings of their own choosing. Middle-class assisted living communities in the United States, however hard they try to provide a homelike atmosphere, are about as far as one can get not only from the Palais Royal but from a simple room of one's own choice. With the exception of visits from adult children and grandchildren, most assisted living facilities are as segregated by generation, economic status, and social class as the postwar suburbs in which a huge proportion of the greatest generation raised its families. And assisted living facilities, like nursing homes, are inhabited almost entirely by women. They are the last homes of the last survivors.

CHAPTER SEVEN

GREEDY GEEZERS AND OTHER HALF-TRUTHS

IN 1988, the cover of the venerable, much-respected liberal Washington magazine *The New Republic* featured a cartoon depicting a mob of affluent, corpulent, golf-club-carrying old people labeled "Greedy Geezers." The characters on the cover, who resembled nothing so much as the overstuffed American capitalist plutocrats of Soviet propaganda of the 1930s, were intended to illustrate a long article by Henry Fairlie, a prominent British journalist based in Washington, attacking U.S. old-age entitlement programs and the World War II generation, which was just beginning to collect its Social Security benefits and whose members had, in Fairlie's view, been the beneficiaries of "an understandable if increasingly misdirected sympathy." These lazy, acquisitive old people considered themselves "entitled to be rewarded for no more than performing the accepted tasks of life, or fighting in the Second World War" and believed that if they had raised a family and contributed to society by working, "then when they cease to be productive they have a right to live off the still-producing like the grasshopper in the fable; that because their needs diminish, their expectations are entitled to rise."[1] Fairlie called for a redefinition of old age and its entitlements, "with the majority of benefits going only to the needy." He also predicted, in the absence of a reduction of benefits to the so-called greedy geezers, "a revolt of the working members of society when the huge baby-boom generation reaches retirement age."[2] The time was not yet ripe for politicians to take such warnings seriously. In the last year of Ronald Reagan's administration, even though there was still much lip service paid to cutting the budget and the size of government, no one in the White House was about to take on the sacred cows of either Social Security or Medicare.

Fairlie, then sixty-four, was a premature curmudgeon, even taking a swipe in his article at psychotherapy for the elderly ("If one needs a psychiatrist by the time one is 65, one should take the quick way out—make a swallow dive from a high bridge to the tarmac").* But he was prescient in his suggestion that the retirement of the boomers, coupled with increasing longevity, would pose a serious problem for the boomers themselves and for the much smaller cohort of younger workers who would be expected to support them.

Nevertheless, few Americans in the 1980s would have dared to be curmudgeonly enough to describe Social Security, as the former Republican senator Alan Simpson did in August 2010, as "a milk cow with 310 million tits." Simpson's unfortunate metaphor was rendered even more unfortunate by the fact that he was responding to an article by the head of the Older Women's League (OWL), who attacked his record on women's rights and pointed out that the majority of Social Security recipients are old women. As a retired senator, the seventy-nine-year-old Simpson receives a hefty government pension, so he does not need Social Security. Inexplicably selected by President Obama to serve as co-chairman of the federal deficit reduction commission, Simpson is a classic example of a geezer who has all the money he needs, because he spent much of his adult life feeding at the government trough, and is therefore free to bash his contemporary fellow citizens who do need Social Security. Thirty years ago, however, the presence of the entire huge boomer generation in the labor force, grumbling but not exactly revolting about their ever-increasing Social Security taxes, made it easy to put off any serious discussion of how the system was going to be financed in the future. After all, this was my *mother* who was being called a greedy geezer. Did I really want anyone to cut her Social Security benefits? Even if she was not destitute, she was far from rich. It had of course begun to occur to some of us in the boomer generation that

* This piece ought to be anthologized, along with William Osler's 1905 speech on chloroforming men over sixty, in some sort of special volume of ageist rants by Englishmen. I wonder what has made sixty-something Brits of the male sex so cranky over so many generations. Perhaps they have been unhinged over the past two centuries by the spectacle of too many long-lived members of the royal family—true examples of greedy geezerdom—extending their exercise of inherited economic and social privilege into their nineties. Fairlie's generation may also have been overexposed to crotchety roles performed by the aging Rex Harrison.

Social Security would probably not turn out to be nearly as good a deal for us as it had been for our parents, who entered the labor force at a time when deductions were low because they were based on projections of a relatively small elderly population. Throughout the 1960s and 1970s, my father had made four to eight times as much money as I did—but we paid roughly the same amount of Social Security tax because of the income ceiling for deductions. In 1965, when I began working full time, the taxable income maximum for Social Security deductions was $4,800. By 1975, that had more than tripled—to $14,800—and by 1995 the taxable base would rise to $61,200. In 2010, the maximum was $106,800. I point this out not because I object to paying these taxes or ever objected to paying them; indeed, I think that all income should be subject to Social Security deductions. It is simply a fact that the World War II generation has received much more in Social Security benefits than it ever paid into the system, but unless I live to be one hundred (something I have no wish to do), I will never collect anything in benefits comparable to the taxes I have paid.

But now, since the oldest boomers have reached the symbolic age of sixty-five, the demographic pieces for a genuine generational clash are falling into place. In the summer of 2009, the fierce opposition of many over sixty-five to the Democrats' push for broader access to health care for younger Americans suggested that the coming generational clash, as the ranks of both the young old and the old old increase in relation to the rest of the population, could be worse than any turmoil that might have been anticipated twenty-five years ago. Throughout the summer of fury over health care, belligerent, hard-core Obama haters disrupted town hall meetings, packed loaded guns near events where the president was speaking, and carried posters calling health care reform a communist and a socialist plot on the one hand and a descendant of fascism on the other. On some posters, Obama's image (often altered to make his complexion appear darker than it is) was Photoshopped with a Hitler mustache. The old weren't packing pistols, but no group was more agitated and more opposed to change of any kind in health care. More than sixty thousand members resigned from AARP, the mighty lobby on behalf of the interests of older Americans, simply because it endorsed health care reform in general. The explanation for the stance of those among the old who opposed health care reform was pure self-interest:

they feared that any reform plan for the young would be financed by cuts in Medicare. It was a classic example—like Alan Simpson's denigration of Social Security recipients themselves—of "I've got mine and you've got yours to get" psychology. The old make up the only large group of Americans who do have government-financed health care—which vitiates any claim that they were motivated by opposition to "socialized medicine." None of the angry senior citizens at town hall meetings were rushing to Washington to make a bonfire out of their Medicare cards.

In 1965, when Lyndon Johnson shepherded Medicare through Congress on the wave of enthusiasm following his defeat of the conservative Republican standard-bearer Barry Goldwater, there was no generational clash over the new program. The cost of health care (and health insurance) was not prohibitive for the young and middle-aged, and extending health benefits to seniors living on fixed incomes seemed a simple matter of economic and social justice—a win-win situation. I doubt that Medicare could be passed today, in view of the major burden that health insurance premiums and co-pays impose on anyone under sixty-five who does not work for a large corporation or government agency with generous health benefits. It is probably unreasonable to expect that the angry faction among the old, who are well cared for under the current system, would see and accept the clear connection between access to health care for the young and the ability—and willingness—of young workers to finance both Medicare and Social Security at their current levels. The question is whether the grasshopper boomers, the oldest of whom are just reaching the traditional retirement age of sixty-five, will adopt the attitude of blind entitlement displayed by some of their parents in the health care war. The angry old people are right in one respect: new limits to Medicare *are* eventually going to come. The only question is whether they will evolve as part of rational cost cutting—which will involve reining in private insurance companies and involve Americans of all ages—or whether they will be imposed, willy-nilly, because the social insurance system is running out of money. It is highly unlikely, however, that the fiercest opposition to health care reform is coming from America's richest "geezers." My guess, although there is no research on the question, is that most of those AARP resignations came not from the very rich or the very poor but from old people who, while not poor by official government standards, have only a small financial cushion and are scared of losing what little they have.

Between the early 1960s and the turn of the millennium, the proportion of Americans over sixty-five living below the official federal poverty line dropped from one in three to one in ten. That was a substantial achievement, due in part to the legacy of Johnson's Great Society, and in part to the fact that adults who came of age during World War II, and began retiring in the late 1970s and early 1980s, were the first generation of Americans who had spent their entire working lives contributing to the Social Security system. The members of the greatest generation also saw their highest earning years at a time of continuing and dramatic economic growth and prosperity. The post-World War II executives portrayed in *Mad Men* may have been dark and troubled characters, but their financial prospects were spectacular. The older boomers, however, are moving through their late fifties and early sixties not under the relatively and retrospectively benign economic conditions of the late 1980s and 1990s but in the middle of a global economic crisis that will surely define the first decade of the twenty-first century for future historians.

Even though people now in their late seventies, eighties, and nineties have received a high return in Social Security and Medicare benefits for relatively low contributions during their working lives, most older Americans could not be considered affluent by any stretch of the imagination. Consider this: according to the most recent figures of the nonpartisan Congressional Research Service, only one-fourth of Americans over sixty-five have incomes of more than $33,677 a year.* Another quarter have incomes under $11,139.[3] Household income drops precipitously with every decade, mainly because the older the "household," the more likely it is to consist of a woman living alone. The median household income for sixty-five to sixty-nine-year-olds is nearly 35 percent higher than the annual income of seventy- to seventy-nine-year-olds—clearly indicating the large drop in financial resources when a husband dies. Although some expenses (such as outlays for food) obviously decrease in a one-person household, others (such as property taxes and car maintenance costs) remain exactly the same. The loss of a hus-

* The Congressional Research Service is a special division of the Library of Congress established to aid lawmakers in the House and Senate in financial calculations for legislation. All figures cited from this report are drawn from financial data updated in March 2008. They do not, therefore, include data after the housing and economic crash that spiraled out of control in the fall of 2008. But the basic distribution of income was not significantly affected for those over sixty-five.

band—unless he leaves a huge estate to his wife—almost automatically makes women poorer, because their Social Security payments are cut and women may lose private pension income altogether. Furthermore, many lower-middle-income women slip below the poverty line almost as soon as they are widowed as a result of leftover medical bills and funeral expenses.[4] Yes, there are greedy geezers—multimillionaires who, in spite of their wealth, don't have an ounce of shame about collecting their Social Security checks. "I paid my Social Security taxes, I'm entitled" is their mantra. That's technically true, but there is no good reason it should be true. There is no justification for Warren Buffett receiving any Social Security payments (as I suspect he would be the first to agree, given that he has designated most of his estate for philanthropic purposes). There is every reason why government money that now goes to rich seniors should be redistributed not only to the one-fourth of elderly Americans who are poor by technical federal guidelines but to those who fall in the middle of the income curve. Social Security payments account for more than 80 percent of the income of the half of Americans over sixty-five who live on less than $19,000 a year.[5] And when one considers the Congressional Research Service's finding that three-fourths of Americans over sixty-five have annual incomes under $34,000, it is obvious that Social Security is desperately needed by everyone but the small minority of the truly rich. An annual income of around $34,000 does not go very far, even if one accepts the proposition that old people need less than younger adults and ought to be able to get by on less money.

To say that the old "need" less is true on one level: old people do not have to pay for their children's education, because they have already done so; many are through with mortgage payments; and they receive tax breaks and discounts on everything from movie admission to public transportation. But for the sickest of the old, expenses for prescription drugs—only partially covered by Medicare—can amount to thousands of dollars each year. Rents rise regularly, and the one-third of seniors who rent are also the most likely to be poor. And old people must often pay for a wide variety of services—from having groceries delivered to housecleaning—that, when they were younger and healthier, they used to perform for themselves. Finally, the idea that old people have inherently fewer "needs" than younger adults is suspect and smacks more of social prescription than description. It seems highly questionable (and bad for the economy) to conclude that today's retiring boomers will not need new computers twenty years from now because they will be in their eighties—and that old computers ought to be good enough for old people. Or that aging boomers will not need new clothes because, after all, they have closets full of serviceable garments from the 1980s and 1990s. Why should old people want to dress stylishly, anyway? As for new books, well, the old can just reread the books they have been acquiring since their twenties. Heh-heh, they will have forgotten the plots, and fifty-year-old novels will be new again. The conviction that old people need less is also very much a self-satisfied upper-middle-class posture, easily adopted by those who have spent a comfortable lifetime getting and spending. The sixty-somethings who talk about simplifying their lives by ridding themselves of surplus possessions are those who have a surplus to get rid of. They are people who need to toss old clothes because their closets are stuffed. They already own more than one television and they get cable. They are not the sort of people who had to worry about how they would pay for a converter box to enable their one ancient, rabbit-eared set to continue operating when television switched to digital. Like everything else about old age, there is a class dimension to concepts of what people do and do not need. The statement that old people have fewer needs might easily be translated as "You'd damn well better learn how to get by with less if you can't pay for it yourself."

The stereotype of the greedy geezer is based, in large measure, on the oft-repeated statistic that Americans over sixty-five own 75 percent of all assets. But this is a misleading figure, because the largest proportion of assets is owned by a very small proportion of the elderly. Nearly half of Americans over sixty-five receive no income at all from assets. Of individuals who do derive income from assets (such as interest on savings and dividends from stocks), half receive less than $2,000.[6] This figure would be lower if it reflected the decline over the past two years in interest rates on the conservative investment vehicles favored by the old. And although about three-quarters of those over sixty-five own their own homes, the use of real estate to generate income (even for those with no mortgages) has become problematic to impossible since the housing bust of 2008. Many widows in their eighties who had counted on the sale of their homes to finance long-term care found that their property was, at least temporarily, worthless. With the need for long-term care staring them in the face, they discovered that they could not sell their houses or condominiums at any price.

The baby boom generation, however, took the biggest hit. The full impact of what will surely, at some point in the future, be called the Crash of '08 on the boomers will not be felt for many years, perhaps decades. But it is certain that for many of us, old age is going to be tougher financially than we anticipated. The collapse of the housing bubble is an important element in the cloudy financial outlook for boomers (especially those closest to retirement), but several long-term trends and underlying social factors predated the crash. These included a low rate of personal savings; the rush of companies to abandon traditional defined-benefit pension plans in favor of 401(k)s, which—as Americans saw in the most dramatic possible way in 2008—are exposed to downturns in the stock market; and the growth of income inequality since the 1980s. Income inequality is arguably the most important factor of all, because the poorer people are, the less likely they are to have any assets other than their houses. Only half of working Americans today—the more prosperous half with better jobs—even have 401(k)s, according to the Society of Professional Asset-Managers and Record Keepers.[7] Most of the lamentation in the media about the decline in value of 401(k) assets was done by, and on behalf of, the 50 percent of Americans prosperous enough to have made an income that allowed them to contribute to the retirement savings accounts. Most waiters, retail sales clerks, receptionists—people whose jobs place them among the working poor and the just-getting-by—do not make enough to contribute to such accounts. In a devastating analysis issued by the Center for Economic and Policy Research (CEPR), a liberal think tank, Dean Baker and David Rosnick conclude that boomers—particularly those in lower-income groups—"are likely to be hugely dependent on Social Security as a source of retirement income" and "are much less well prepared for retirement than the cohorts that preceded them."[8] This was not the way things were supposed to be. But in spite of the baby boom generation's needs—and however well or poorly the economy recovers—there will surely be substantial political pressure for cuts in benefits. Both the size of the federal deficit and the long-term economic difficulties of younger voters (including younger boomers) in the past three years are likely to make young working Americans much less quiescent about ever-increasing Social Security and Medicare deductions than my generation was. Like most Americans who graduated from college in the 1960s, I was debt-free when I began my working life. I wonder whether I would have been so sanguine about the Social Security deductions from a cub reporter's meager paychecks had I owed, as so many young people do today, tens of thousands of dollars in student loans.

The collapse of the housing bubble was front and center when the CEPR issued the original version of its report, and the statistics did not receive a great deal of publicity in the general media—perhaps because they were genuinely frightening. The net worth of households in the forty-five-to-fifty-four age group fell by 45 percent between 2004 and 2009. The older baby boomers were in even worse shape. Households in the fifty-five-to-sixty-four group lost almost half of their wealth—down from $315,400 to $159,800. The boomers had invested their money in their own houses, and even when real estate prices recover, many boomers (unlike their parents) will reach age sixty-five without even being close to paying off their mortgages. The proud tradition of "burning the mortgage"—an occasion celebrated in the United States for many generations—represented the attainment of an important middle-class goal that will continue to elude many boomers well into their putative golden years. "As a result of the plunge in house prices," the CEPR report states forthrightly and grimly, "many boomers now have little or no equity in their home . . . even if they have been home-owners for several decades. These households will be in the same situation as first-time homebuyers, forced to struggle to find the money needed to put down a down payment for a new home. This will make it especially difficult for many baby boomers to leave their current homes and buy housing that might be more suitable for their retirement."[9] In other words, if a sixty-year-old boomer owes $200,000 on the house he inhabits—which he could only hope to sell for $175,000 today—the house is useless as a financial tool. And even if real estate prices rebound significantly in the next ten years, the house will probably not produce the profit that the owner was counting on to finance his retirement. Reliance on the house as retirement nest egg was based on the presumption that property values would continue to rise as dramatically throughout the boomers' early old age as they did during the late 1990s and the early 2000s.

Lest one be tempted to dismiss the authors of the CEPR study as lefty doomsayers, Baker outlined the dangers of the inflated housing market as early as 2002. In 2004, he acted on his convictions as an economist, sold his condominium in Washington, D.C., at a significant profit, and moved into a rental apartment with his wife. This story is told by the *New York Times* economic reporter Edmund L. Andrews in *Busted* (2009), a stunning tale describing the ways in which Andrews, a respected financial journalist, fell prey to the lure of easy mortgage money that he could not afford to pay back. "Baker's friends told him he was throwing away money [by selling his condo]," Andrews recalls. "But Baker, a bearded and bearish man, had been warning so loudly about the housing bubble that he couldn't stand the thought of being hammered by the very bust he had been predicting." Andrews remorsefully reflects upon his 2004 conversation with Baker.

> When Baker told me his news, he sounded more elated than I had ever heard him before. I listened, feeling chagrin and foreboding. I congratulated Baker on his willingness to buck the crowd, and I meant it. But I didn't have the nerve to admit that I was doing exactly the opposite of what he had done. Not only was I buying a house near the peak of the market; I was doing it with an interest-only loan and taking the biggest gamble of my life.[10]

Andrews's story is a cautionary tale that does not entirely explain the compulsions that drove someone who really did know better to the verge of bankruptcy and foreclosure. But people like Andrews (who makes more than $130,000 a year at the *Times* and whose book, if it sells enough copies, may yet pull him back from the brink) were not in the group hardest hit by their own stupidity and the collapse of the housing market. As the CEPR report indicates, the greatest life-shattering losses have been sustained by low- and lower-middle-income boomers. In 2004, the bottom fifth of American households in the forty-five-to-fifty-four age group had only an average of $3,500 in net wealth; by 2009, their net wealth had dropped into a negative zone, at –$2,300: these families lost more than they had possessed in the first place. In the middle fifth of Americans between ages forty-five and fifty-four, net wealth dropped by 42 percent, while in the top fifth—those with a net worth averaging $2.5 million in 2004—wealth dropped by just 35 percent. To sum up, if an American household was already poor in 2004, its assets were wiped out by the Crash of '08. The middle group, measured by net worth, was in bad financial trouble. And if an American household was worth more than $2.5 million before the crash, it was down to $1.6 million afterward.[11] No doubt the latter group of Americans, whose net worth dropped by $900,000, is feeling poor, but such families still have money left. It is hard to see how the two-fifths of boomers at the bottom will ever recover fully. The reason why poor and middle-income boomers lost a much larger percentage of their wealth is that the poorer people are, the more likely it is that their house is their only asset.

It is certainly possible to be too pessimistic about the long-term impact of the housing collapse, but—once again—the importance of economic class cannot be overestimated. There are many older boomers with good jobs who bought their first houses in the late 1970s, long before the escalation of property values. If they made their mortgage payments and did not borrow against their home equity, they are in good shape even if the value of their houses on paper is much less than it was four years ago. Many economists are as prone as the public to making the error, noted by George Orwell, of being unable to imagine that current conditions will ever change. Just as deluded homeowners assumed that the housing bubble would continue to expand indefinitely, many of the most bearish economists are now assuming that housing prices will never recover in time to help those who put all of their eggs in the real estate basket. However bad things look now, boomers with jobs should not necessarily assume that they are condemned to an old age eating cat food (if they can afford it) until the next Social Security check arrives (if it arrives). This is true even for boomers who bought their houses long after the 1970s. Consider a hypothetical older boomer couple, around age fifty-eight, with an $80,000 mortgage on a condominium that might have sold for $150,000 in 2006 but would sell now for only $80,000. Yes, the condo is worthless to the couple today, but if both husband and wife work another eight to ten years and pay down their mortgage—and real estate values rise again—they will wind up with at least part of their longed-for retirement nest egg. There are, unquestionably, a great many ifs in this scenario—the biggest one being that both partners keep their jobs and are able to work throughout their sixties. Nevertheless, this is certainly a plausible outcome for boomers who own houses in areas of the country where people want to live and will continue to want to live—however impossible it is for them to buy a house right now. And the same scenario is even more plausible for younger boomers—including those whose retirement savings accounts have lost a third of their value during the past few years.

A decrease in the value of assets is a catastrophe only if one needs the money immediately—as I and many older boomers have good reason to understand from personal experience. I own and live in a cooperative apartment in Manhattan, and, if the real estate section of the *Times* is to be believed, my home would sell for about 30 percent less today than it would have five years ago. But I don't want or need to sell my apartment, which, as it happens, is still worth much more than I paid for it. (Lest anyone think I am taking credit for financial acumen, I should mention that I happened to be in the right place at the right time, as a sitting tenant in a rental building that the landlord wanted to convert to a cooperative. In the early 1980s, under New York State law, owners had to obtain the agreement of 51 percent of sitting tenants to turn a rental building into a co-op. The landlord bought the tenants' consent by offering ridiculously low prices—called inside buyers' prices—enabling them to buy the apartments they were renting. It worked for both the owner and tenant, because tenants who could not afford to stay were able to sell their apartments at the market rate, thereby turning the insider's price into a fine profit. If a tenant could afford to stay on, so much the better for her: she was the lucky recipient of a once-in-a-lifetime bargain. Et voilà, a financially insecure writer who expected to be a renter for life was turned into a homeowner.) But although I owe my house to the peculiarities of one state's law, there are many older boomers around the nation in exactly the same situation—having bought when prices were low and having stayed right where they were instead of leveraging their houses to buy grander properties. Many boomers like their longtime homes just fine, thank you very much, and wouldn't be selling them even if the housing bubble were still expanding. By the time boomers want or need to sell their homes in order to pay for old age, the housing deflation of the past few years may have receded into a nasty historical memory—albeit a relatively recent one.

The housing bubble collapse deepened and reinforced the impact of two other factors—the boomers' notoriously low rate of personal savings and the decline of traditional fixed-benefit pension plans in favor of more volatile (and less costly to employers) 401(k)s. A large proportion of my generation—boomers who came of age in the 1960s—did not save, period. They belong to the half of the population—those retail clerks and other low-level service workers—who don't make enough to put money away, who don't receive pensions from their employers, and who are either ineligible for or too poorly paid to contribute to tax-deferred retirement savings accounts. Few Americans now remember that 401(k)s, established by Congress in the 1970s, were originally intended as a perk—and a way of lowering taxes—for high-level executives. The idea seemed to make perfect sense: your employer would match your annual contributions, and the money would be socked away, not subject to taxation, until you started withdrawing from the accounts at or around retirement—when you would presumably be in a lower tax bracket than you were in the prime of your working years. Workers at the low end of the pay scale were not expected to take advantage of 401(k)s, because they needed every bit of their paycheck to live month to month. They would have to be content with traditional pensions—which the new accounts were never intended to replace. Unfortunately, many companies used the existence of the 401(k) as an excuse to dump their traditional pension plans. Today, though, only about 20 percent of American workers are covered by old-fashioned fixed-benefit plans—and many companies that went bankrupt have already broken their promises to older workers. Thus, many boomers who are five to ten years away from retirement have no traditional pension and no 401(k). While the average 401(k) lost about a third of its value during the Crash of '08, most of these accounts were not large enough to provide retirement security even before the stock market took a nosedive; their far-from-impressive average balance was roughly $45,500. The employees with the highest salaries, of course, have much larger retirement accounts because they can afford to make larger contributions. Alicia Munnell, director of the Center for Retirement Research at Boston College, crunched the numbers and found that only 5 percent of Americans earning between $80,0000 and $100,000 made the maximum allowable contribution of $16,000 a year. Among those making more than $100,000, one-third contributed the maximum.[12] And we are talking about people, again, whose incomes far exceed the $61,000 family median.

One thing is certain: older baby boomers who are lucky enough to have remained employed throughout the job-shedding recession are not going to retire anytime soon. They will have to be dragged out of their offices, because they simply cannot afford to retire one minute before poor health, or further layoffs, make it impossible for them to go on. For the minority of older boomers who *did* save in midlife, every additional working year is a year in which the stock market and the housing market may recover and restore at least some of the value of their assets. For those who do not have any assets other than their houses, hanging on to a job as long as possible is a necessity. It may not be a bad thing that the boomer dream of early retirement—which was always at odds with boomer life expectancy—has been one of the first casualties of the 2008 crash. Joe Mancini, who is fifty-eight and works for an electronics distributor, told the *Times* that he had hoped to retire at sixty but, because his retirement savings account had been devastated, he "can't even put a date on it now."[13] I don't have much sympathy for the Joe Mancinis of the boomer generation, because I see no reason why anyone who hopes to live well into his eighties should feel entitled to retire at sixty. Nowhere is it written—certainly nowhere in American history—that a thirty-year retirement is part of "life, liberty, and the pursuit of happiness."

Even before the meltdown, old people were already working—both full time and part time—in growing numbers. According to the Bureau of Labor Statistics, the number of workers ages sixty-five to sixty-nine rose by 25 percent between 2000 and 2008. In older age groups, the percentage increase was even higher—32 percent for those ages seventy to seventy-four, 38 percent for those seventy-five to seventy-nine, and 67 percent for those over eighty. The AARP reports that more than five hundred thousand people over eighty—a figure I find startling—were working to supplement their Social Security income in 2008.[14] Many of these people are former full-time retirees who were victimized by conservative-backed federal policies that enabled companies to break their pension and health care promises to retired workers. Eighty-nine-year-old Frank Wilkinson was an airline pilot who lost his pension when his former employer went bankrupt more than twenty years ago. He works twenty-five hours a week at a program funded by the AARP Foundation, which helps other seniors find jobs. "They're really desperate to supplement their Social Security income," Wilkinson says. "It's rewarding to be able to help people worse off than I am."[15] For older boomers whose homes and retirement savings accounts have plummeted in value, the need for work will be even more urgent in old age. The real question, in a society that cannot provide anything like full employment for young adults, is where the jobs are going to come from for the growing population that cannot afford retirement. Consider the plight of those who are, say, ten years from the traditional age of retirement and are employed in troubled industries like newspaper and magazine publishing, auto manufacturing, or housing construction. Where does a fifty-something employee go to find work if he or she is laid off from a job at a magazine or at an automobile company—whether as a midlevel executive or as a worker on an assembly line? A few months ago, when I was preparing a list of contacts at newspapers, magazines, and online publications to send advance copies of this book, I found that 25 percent of those on my last contact list—only three years ago—had been fired. Many are in their mid-fifties—a time of life when, in a better economy in healthy industries, they would have been at the height of their influence and looking forward to many more years of productive work. Their jobs have simply disappeared. Even those who received buyouts or what passes for generous severance settlements these days cannot hope to equal the income they have lost by being forcibly retired.

Given their financial situation, it is hard for most boomers over fifty-five not to shudder when liberal Democrats, as well as far-right Republicans, begin talking about the need to cut elder entitlement programs in the same tone as one might say the sun rises in the east and sets in the west. If many millions more boomers live into their eighties and nineties, and if their aging is accompanied by significant cuts in Social Security, younger Americans will have to step up and contribute to the care of Granny and Gramps. We do not know whether middle-aged children will take pity on the boomers. We surely do not know whether today's teenagers will be prepared in their middle age to foot the long-term-care bills for the growing number of octogenarians, nonagenarians, and centenarians. Will younger Americans decide, in the end, that civilized societies do not let old women and old men sleep on the streets, regardless of their past financial errors? Stay tuned.

The prospects for younger boomers—those now in their late forties and early fifties—are brighter than for older boomers, if only because they have more time left to pay off those mortgages and save more. But much of the fate of the younger boomers depends on whether the job market ever really recovers or whether an American economy with something close to double-digit unemployment—not to mention additional underemployment—becomes the norm rather than a temporary, solvable crisis. Even if the economy does recover robustly, many economists believe that younger boomers who lost their jobs in the recession—even if they find new employment—are bound to enter retirement at a severe disadvantage. Till von Wachter, an economics professor at Columbia University, says that most workers will not find new jobs that pay as much as their old jobs—and that their lifetime earnings will inevitably be lower as a result of a midlife employment interruption.[16] In a study of job losses incurred during the recession of 1982, Wachter and his colleagues found that even fifteen or twenty years later, those laid off had not returned to their former wage levels. Such findings have especially grave implications for baby boomers in their mid-forties who were laid off in the massive white- and blue-collar job cuts of 2008 and 2009, because older workers always have a tougher time finding new jobs than those laid off in their twenties and thirties.[17] Also, workers who have lost their jobs in one recession are more likely to be laid off again. "What tends to happen is the worker has to start over with a new employer, sometimes in a new industry," points out Ann Huff Stevens, a professor of economics at the University of California, Davis. "You're at the bottom of the totem pole again."[18]

But even the best-case scenario will only help upper-middle- and high-income boomers who had enough to ride out the losses in the first place. There is no scenario, however pessimistic or optimistic, that would counteract the tendency of the struggling middle class to become poorer in old age and still poorer in old old age. Economic class, along with gender, and marital history are the most powerful predictors of financial status in old age. The annual Congressional Research Office analysis of elderly income shows how few older Americans today actually have income-producing assets, and how dependency on Social Security increases with age. The Center for Economic and Policy Research report presents a worst-case but quite realistic scenario detailing exactly how the Crash of '08 has blighted financial prospects for many boomers who will be reaching retirement age during the next two decades. And the UCLA analysis of the long-term effects of layoffs during the 1982 recession gives us insight into the permanent impact of job losses in any given period of history. The last study is especially significant, because it suggests that Americans now in their twenties and thirties—the very people who will be expected to foot the bill for boomers' Social Security and Medicare—will be under considerable financial stress their entire adult lives if they have lost jobs in the recent recession.

It is difficult to conceive of a scenario in which the increasing numbers of the old old are to be supported except through higher taxes on just about everyone—something that no one in either political party has the courage to say. Although many economic and political analysts have long anticipated a rebellion by younger American workers as the baby boom generation begins to retire, they did not take into account the possibility that the largest single generation in American history, primed by medical advances to live longer than any previous generation, would suffer severe financial reverses just as its oldest members entered their sixties. There is already a loud and angry chorus of boomer bashing that portrays an entire generation as a group of selfish, profligate babies who bankrupted themselves—and, potentially, the nation—through their eagerness to snap up easy credit and their unwillingness to save money. But, as numerous experts have pointed out, the boomers were only doing what many Americans of all ages were doing by taking the money offered them. And Depression babies, as well as some greedy members of the revered greatest generation, made a lot of money by providing free-lunch credit to the boomers. As the advanced age of many of Bernard Madoff's clients clearly demonstrates, no generation has a monopoly on greed and stupidity. Many of Madoff's clients were in their sixties, seventies, and eighties, and it evidently did not occur to them that there might be something fishy about an investment fund that, year in, year out, in good times and bad, provided larger returns than anyone else was getting from other investment vehicles. The much ballyhooed "wisdom of old age" apparently had not taught them the fundamental lesson that if something seems too good to be true, it probably is. In any case, the particular generational self-absorption of boomers seems to have played less of a role in this bubble-and-bust cycle than a fatal combination of greed and the financial ignorance among many Americans in every generation.*

Even if younger Americans now draw appropriate lessons from their parents' financial mistakes, the numbers do not add up to a decent standard of living in retirement if the proportion of the old old continues to increase dramatically. The urgent question that must be faced today is whether it is reasonable to expect ordinary middle-class Americans to save enough money to support themselves for two or three decades after they stop working. Throughout recorded history, no society has ever had to face the prospect of huge numbers of its citizens living three decades beyond the age where, regardless of the particular economic system, it becomes more difficult—and finally impossible—to hold down a full-time job. And even if every American over sixty-five could work at least part time until he or she died—and even if fantasies about ninety becoming the new fifty were fulfilled—there is no evidence that the U.S. economy can generate millions more jobs for old people. Rising unemployment among Americans now in their late sixties and early seventies who are actively looking for jobs provides a foretaste of what is to come in an economy where more and more people must work after what they thought would be the beginning of their retirement. Between 2007 and the beginning of 2010, according to the Bureau of Labor Statistics, unemployment nearly doubled, to 6.7 percent, among those over sixty-five who were looking for a job. In 2000, reported unemployment in the same age group of job seekers was only 1.9 percent. And unemployment among the young old who

* In *The Ascent of Money* (2008), Niall Ferguson provides a catalog of Americans' financial illiteracy. A third of Americans have no idea what the interest rate on their credit cards is—or, indeed, what interest rates mean in dollars and cents. Two-thirds of Americans do not understand how compound interest works. Fully 59 percent of high school seniors do not even know what Social Security is. See pp. 10–13.

want and need work is undoubtedly understated, because, at a time when so many younger Americans are unemployed, people in their sixties are fighting steeper odds than they would be if employers did not have their pick of younger applicants. David Certner, legislative policy director for AARP, says the fact that so many job seekers over sixty-five are still looking for work, and are counted in official unemployment statistics, "shows how bad the economic situation is. A lot of people normally give up at that age."[19] An article in *The New York Times* quoted a sixty-seven-year-old woman laid off a year earlier from her job as an interpreter for a law firm who had sent out more than one hundred job applications in a month and received not a single reply. There is almost nothing left over from her combined Social Security and pension benefits of approximately $2,000 a month after she makes her mortgage and car payments, and her mother, who is in her nineties, sometimes sends her an extra $100 to tide her over until the next Social Security check.[20] The growing need for employment among those only five to ten years older than the boomers, and the extra difficulties that the old encounter when they try to remain in the job market, do not bode well for the future of a more heavily indebted boomer generation.

It is often pointed out that Social Security was never designed to be more than an income floor for retired citizens—a supplement to their personal savings. But average life expectancy in 1935, when President Franklin D. Roosevelt signed the Social Security Act, was only sixty-two. Even then, the New Dealers who designed Social Security were well aware that longevity would increase throughout the twentieth century, as indicated by a conversation in 1935 between Treasury Secretary Henry Morgenthau Jr. and Roosevelt's aide Harry Hopkins:

HOPKINS: Well there are going to be twice as many old people thirty years from now, Henry, than there are now.

MORGENTHAU: Well I've gotten a very good analysis of this thing and I'm going to lay it in her [Secretary of Labor Frances Perkins] lap this afternoon. I'm simply going to point out the danger spots and it's up to somebody else to say whether they want to do it. I'm not trying to say what they should do—I want to show them the bad curves. . . .

HOPKINS: That old age thing is a bad curve.[21]

FDR's aides, prescient as they were, probably could never have envisaged a curve as bad as the one now predicted by the U.S. Census Bureau for 2030, when Americans over sixty-five are expected to make up a fifth of the population. Those future retirees are now middle-aged parents bringing up families, and it is hard to see how they can save enough money, even through the most stringent economizing, to finance a long retirement in which they will enjoy a decent middle-class standard of living into their late eighties and nineties. Yet the premise that individuals ought to be able to save enough for old age is a tenet of American received opinion. The primary disseminators of this cliché—consumer advisers who write how-to books (think *Retirement for Dummies*) and admonish the public on television shows—imply that moral turpitude, greed, and carelessness are the real obstacles to saving enough for the future. There is rarely any acknowledgment of the fact that many Americans do not make enough money to save money. Most days when I wake up to the *Today* show, some perky woman (nearly all of the savings experts touted on TV are both perky-looking and female) is talking, as one was this morning, about saving more money by such capital-accumulating strategies as denying one's children the latest doll or video game or using a cheaper brand of makeup. I am wholeheartedly in favor of dispensing with video games in favor of library books (I'll admit to reservations about cheap makeup), but the consumer maven did not have any ideas about what parents should do to save for retirement if one or both of them are unemployed and toys and makeup have already been eliminated from the household budget in the effort to buy enough groceries at the supermarket for a week.

Moreover, I am not at all certain that any saving plan except mandatory taxation works for the average person living on an average salary. When I look over my statement of contributions to Social Security for the past forty years of my working life, I know (as the political right maintains) that I could have done better financially had I saved the money and invested it—even in conservative bonds and savings accounts. But here's the catch: there is no way, in my twenties and thirties, that I would ever have saved even a small percentage of the money that federal law required me to contribute to Social Security. Anyone who expects young adults, most of whom cannot even imagine illness, much less death, to forgo today's pleasures so that they can pay for long-term care in their nineties does not have a realistic view of human, or at least of American, nature. And by the time people do begin to develop some awareness of their own mortality—let us say, for the sake of argument, in their forties—there is often a stark choice between paying for as much of their children's higher education as possible or saving for their own retirement. Do we really want a society in which instead of writing a check to the college registrar, people in their forties and fifties write out checks for their own long-term care insurance?

Americans are often criticized for having the lowest rate of personal savings in the developed world, and that is true. By March 2009, U.S. personal savings had risen from subzero (meaning that we were spending more than we were earning) to a munificent 4.2 percent. In the same month, savings in the European Union (which also rose after the 2008 financial collapse) reached 12.2 percent.* In Asia, people save even more. I do not pretend to know why Americans save so much less than Europeans, who generally pay much higher personal income taxes to support a much broader social welfare safety net, including universal health coverage. But I do know that the American penchant for instant gratification, coupled with opposition to higher taxes that would create a larger government-financed social safety net, spells huge long-term economic trouble for the old—particularly the oldest old—in our society. As a nation, our dominant ideology has been that individual responsibility, not collective social responsibility, is the key to a free and prosperous society. Conservatives take a hard line on eschewing collective responsibility, even in extraordinary circumstances like the Great Depression of the 1930s or the housing collapse of 2008. Liberals are much more willing to assert a collective, public responsibility for economic well-being when financial circumstances become dire for large numbers of people. But both liberals and conservatives find it almost impossible to separate the ideology of the primacy of individual responsibility from the nonideological question of what to do about problems that cannot be dispelled through any amount of individual financial effort, however earnest the effort may have been.

To cite just one example, parents with ordinary incomes cannot provide a level of education and health care that will help severely disabled children make the most of their abilities. Only public support can do that. We can say that saving the severely disabled is not worth the

* Figures supplied by the U.S. Bureau of Economic Analysis and Eurostat, March 2009.

money (I can't wait to hear a politician make that speech on the floor of the House or Senate), but we cannot pretend that an American parent with an average salary can do it alone. In similar fashion, a decent life for the old old cannot, in most cases, be financed by individuals. If we are not going to kill Granny, we are going to have to support Granny. During the past few years, the hope has often been expressed that Americans now in their twenties and thirties will learn from the mistakes of the grasshopper boomers and put nearly all of their disposable income in retirement savings accounts instead of going clubbing in their twenties and buying home entertainment centers in their thirties. Maybe so, maybe not. History certainly does not support the idea that once the immediate aftermath of a catastrophe is over, people draw the appropriate lessons to avoid future catastrophes. But even if twenty-five-year-olds—unless they already have high-paying jobs—were to start putting aside 10 percent of their income every month, that does not mean they would accumulate enough to live comfortably into their nineties and beyond.

Nor does a higher savings rate, even if younger Americans go along with the fantasy and turn it into reality for themselves, offer any answer to the question of how American society is going to look after the boomers who are running out of time to finance their old age. Let us concede that some of the higher-income boomers were feckless with their money, but they are, after all, the parents and grandparents of today's young adults. Didn't they try to give their children the best of everything? Don't grown-up Generation Xers owe their parents something for buying that new computer and springing for that summer class trip to China instead of making the kids get a job at the local McDonald's? Didn't boomer parents do the best they could, even if it wasn't good enough? Don't boomers now deserve their Social Security and Medicare? Excepting the richest Americans over sixty-five, there are only two possible economic outcomes if life expectancy continues to increase. Either taxes must be raised on everyone to provide more benefits for the elderly poor and near poor—especially for the oldest old—or we must sit by while the rate of poverty among the old rises significantly and undoes a half century of social progress. There is another possibility—that rising rates of obesity, and an accompanying increase in diabetes, will bring an end to the increase in life expectancy that, throughout much of the twentieth century, was considered a birthright. But hoping for worse health and shorter lives hardly seems consistent with the American dream. The economic problems posed by increasing longevity are frequently, and mistakenly, presented strictly as a matter of medical costs—the disproportionate amount of money spent on health care in the final years and even weeks of life. The real problem is what people are going to live on if they outlive their savings.

In my mid-twenties, in the late 1960s and early 1970s, I lived and worked as a journalist in Moscow, and my closest non-Russian friends were other journalists from European countries. Many of us have kept in touch with one another over the past four decades, because the bonds formed between press colleagues in a hostile environment—where we were constantly being harassed by the Soviet secret police—proved unusually strong. We are now in our sixties or early seventies and have had similar careers in journalism and scholarship—writing books, contributing to magazines and newspapers, teaching, and lecturing in our own countries and around the world. We have not grown rich from a lifetime spent in the media and scholarship, but we are not poor either. By the standards of our far-flung countries, most of us have done well professionally and reasonably well economically. All of us are still working—one of the rewards of a writer's life—but there is a striking difference between the European and American friends of my youth. The Europeans are approaching the next decades of their lives without any serious economic fears. The Americans are scared. The difference does not lie in our comparative rate of personal savings but in the fact that my European friends have been taxed throughout their lives to support a social safety net that now embraces them—and that will allow them to keep what they have saved (in spite of the high taxes) regardless of whether they ever fall ill and need long-term care. Across Scandinavia—its countries so often used by right-wingers here as a horrible example of what Americans should never, ever want—people do not have to exhaust their assets, leaving their spouses at risk, if they are unfortunate enough to need nursing home care for Alzheimer's disease. The government pays—just as it pays for the home health care aides that American families must cover themselves if they want to keep a relative at home. A Norwegian friend writes, in response to my inquiry about long-term care:

> My aunt died just before Christmas last year. At 87, she suffered from senile dementia and was unable to take care of herself, and she spent the last two years of her life in a local nursing home in central Norway. She had no children and left about 600,000 kroner ($85,000) to her only surviving sister, and her nieces and nephews. . . . None of those assets had been touched while she was in the home. The situation was similar for my father and mother, who died in 1996 and 2001 respectively. All my father's assets went to my mother, who survived him, and she had the wits (in accordance with the wishes of my sister and me) to share what she had with her seven grandchildren about six months before she passed away.

My European friends did not enjoy paying high taxes; indeed, they used to envy their American colleagues for having so much more of their paychecks left every month, thanks to the lower U.S. tax rate. But most of my friends say today that they probably would not have saved any more money than America's boomers if the government had taken less of their wages. The American political right considers European tax rates a violation of individual liberty—and that is the reason why the right opposed Social Security from the outset and has always resisted increases in Social Security taxes. And the right is not entirely wrong; any tax for programs that will provide future benefits amounts to a statement that a great many people must be legally forced to do what is in their long-term best interest. Another reason for my European friends' peace of mind about their future is that they cannot lose their private pensions, as so many Americans have, as a result of employer bankruptcy or criminality (as in the Enron case here). The social safety net in most of Europe is designed to prevent such breaches of contract between employers and their former employees. There is a trade-off between liberty and security in almost every action of government, and that is certainly true of taxation to finance the lives of those who are too old to work and of government regulation that prevents failing companies from making their employees pay the price while top executives give themselves a send-off with a golden parachute. Since we do not euthanize the old when they become too expensive (Tea Party fantasies notwithstanding), society winds up paying in the end if government does not require young adults to contribute to the maintenance of a strong public safety net. As the bitter health care debate demonstrated, America now lacks any social consensus about how to pay the bills for health and welfare today—not to mention the much larger bill, soon to be presented, for the old age of a generation that is entering retirement in hard times. It speaks volumes that it was so difficult for the Obama administration to obtain sufficient congressional support to pass a bill without the kind of single-payer system that exists in every other industrialized Western country—a law that contains only what other nations would consider the sensible "baby steps" of preventing insurance companies from dropping customers who get sick and prohibiting the companies from discriminating against people with preexisting conditions. The anger over a rise in the Medicare payroll tax (but only for Americans making over $200,000 a year) to pay for subsidies for those who cannot afford insurance is one small part of the larger controversy about whether medical care really is a human right that any modern society ought to guarantee.

The myth of young old age, which simultaneously overestimates the earning potential and underestimates the needs of the dependent old old, also poses a major impediment to any serious, reality-based discussion of social justice for both old and young. Healthy old old age is costly, and unhealthy old old age is even costlier. If, as a society, we see longevity as a good thing, then we're going to have to pay for it. But all we are hearing from public officials, now that the brief period when conservatives could use the health care debate to prey on the fears of the elderly has passed, is how to pay less to support longer lives. If there really were such a thing as a radically new brand of old age in which everyone can take care of himself or herself, there would be no reason to worry. Society would be off the hook. The boomers—healthy beneficiaries of this wonderful new old age—would surely be able to tote that barge and lift that bale until the very end.

CHAPTER EIGHT

The "Wisdom of Old Age"

Even when longevity enthusiasts concede that many of the old old often have serious health and financial problems and that their lives do not exactly consist of one round of skydiving after another, there is always one concept—the "wisdom of old age"—that can be and is used to justify the proposition that living longer is an intrinsic good for individuals and society. "The death of an old person is like the burning of a library" is a frequently quoted aphorism, attributed to many cultures,* that ignores not only the ordinary vicissitudes of extraordinary longevity but the extraordinary horror of dementia. Even if we are talking about old people with healthy brains, however, the "wisdom of old age" is more of a faith-based than a reality-based proposition. The death of an old person may just as easily resemble the destruction of a YouTube video as the burning of a library. The so-called wisdom of old age is an a priori assumption for those who believe or wish to believe in Robert Browning's vision of "the last of life, for which the first was made." Wisdom, in this view, somehow cancels out all of the indignities and sorrows of old old age: the unique and supe-

* This saying is described most frequently as an old African proverb—a strange attribution in view of the fact that for most of recorded history, most African languages were not written. So where were these libraries to invite comparison to the death of an elder? Nubian is the only modern African language with written records extending as far back as the eighth century CE. It would have made more sense, in sub-Saharan Africa, to compare the death of an old person to the silencing of oral storytelling. Perhaps this was originally an Egyptian simile, emerging after the destruction of the Alexandria libraries that began with the Roman occupation in 30 CE. I have also seen this proverb attributed to the Irish, Russians, and Chinese—any of which makes more sense than attributing it to Africans. Usually, the crediting of the proverb to Africa is followed by descriptions of elder councils initiating younger members of the tribe into the revered status of "elder adviser."

rior insight of age is supposed to trump any reservations about the poor quality of life that often accompanies great longevity. In *Childhood and Society* (1950), Erik H. Erikson, the psychoanalyst who popularized the idea of viewing life tasks in terms of age-related developmental stages, described the final stage of adult life as a working out of ego integrity versus despair. The reward for those who had accumulated enough ego integrity to overcome their despair at the imminence of old age and death was wisdom—which Erikson wisely left undefined. Several decades later, researchers at the Max Planck Institute in Berlin defined wisdom as "expert knowledge about the nature of human development and the human condition" and asserted that "the acquisition and maintenance of wisdom is facilitated by living longer." Although the researchers acknowledge that not all of the old are wise, they conclude that the percentage of wise old people is higher than the percentage of wise younger adults.[1] Just as Erikson did not define *wisdom,* the Plank scholars do not define *longer.* Even if one concedes that a mentally sound seventy-year-old is likely to possess more wisdom than a forty-year-old, that does not support the idea that a ninety-year-old is wiser than a seventy-year-old.

As neuropsychiatric research has become more neurologically and less psychologically oriented in recent years, a gloss of what sounds like hard science has been added to earlier psychological and sociological assertions of the wisdom of old age. In *The Wisdom Paradox,* the neuropsychologist Elkhonon Goldberg suggests that while some cognitive abilities, like the capacity to solve new problems, may and usually do diminish with age, the old become better at "decision-making that takes the form of pattern recognition rather than problem-solving." Pattern recognition depends on "generic" memories acquired from—what else?—one's own experience. Thus, the old are often able to "tackle a wide range of new situations, problems, and challenges, as if they were familiar ones."[2] Goldberg, who uses, among other world leaders, Joseph Stalin as an example of someone who was able to use "pattern recognition" to continue running his country after a series of strokes that certainly sapped his mental powers, does not address the harm that can result from dealing with new situations as if they were familiar—especially if the aging decision maker has made a great many bad choices in the past. Most historians, as well as those who knew Stalin, agree that he was losing his mind in his last years. Brain impairment, coupled with

Stalin's lifelong ruthlessness, produced a deranged pattern recognition that led to a new set of purges focusing on Jews. Had Stalin not died (it is now generally thought that he was murdered by his political cronies at the highest level of the Soviet government) in 1953 at seventy-four, he would have continued to follow the only pattern he knew—the melding of personal paranoia with the maintenance of political power by terror. Goldberg (who, having grown up in the Soviet Union, is under no illusions about the disasters visited upon the Soviet people under Stalin) nevertheless asserts that the main point of his accounts of cognitively impaired world leaders is that because of their rich experience and their ability to employ pattern recognition, in spite of "their often significant mental infirmities, most of these leaders remained in control . . . on top of their respective games almost until the very end."[3] But Stalin was *not* on top of his game in the closing years of his life—by his own ruthless standards and those of his colleagues. And there was no legal process for getting rid of a tyrant who, because of his mental infirmities coupled with his long-standing brutality, was becoming too great a threat to his own people, even by the admittedly low expectations of a totalitarian society. The only way to stop him was to kill him.

There are few examples in modern history of the constructive exercise of political power by people beyond their early seventies. Winston Churchill was only sixty-five—definitely not among the old old—when he assumed the leadership of the British government at the beginning of the Second World War. (To those who insist that sixty-five was older in 1939 than it is today, I would argue that the minority of those in Churchill's generation who lived into their sixties, unaided by childhood vaccines or antibiotics in adulthood, were probably the most immunologically hardy members of their cohort.) Ronald Reagan, who was seventy-seven when he left office in 1989, probably does present a significant example of the role of pattern recognition in the ability of some old people to carry on outwardly in spite of the inner decline of their mental faculties. Given the usual slow progression of Alzheimer's from its undiagnosed earliest stages to total dementia, it seems likely that Reagan, who was officially diagnosed in 1994, was already in the disease's early stages during his first and certainly his second term of office. Reagan's well-known confusion of his film roles as a World War II soldier and his real wartime life, which involved no glimpse of combat, was usually attributed to a former actor's vanity, as well as a tendency on the part of some actors and politicians to conflate their stage and platform personae with their real personalities. As a consummate actor and politician in the early stages of Alzheimer's, Reagan may simply have been using pattern recognition (and what psychologists call cognitive reserve) to play the role of a president and master of the grand "as if." But that is a very different phenomenon from wisdom—and hardly a desirable trait in someone responsible for decisions affecting war and peace. Many people in their late seventies are surely capable of carrying out the duties of high office, but there is an inherent danger, given that the risk of dementia doubles every five years after age sixty-five, in electing someone who will be closer to eighty than seventy when he or she leaves the presidency. (I think that John McCain's age was a factor, and properly so, in the 2008 election—though that sentiment was not often articulated because it has become socially incorrect. McCain's choice of Sarah Palin as his running mate surely intensified voters' concerns, whether overt or subliminal, about his age. If a vice-presidential candidate is manifestly unqualified to be president, the presidential candidate's age becomes, and should become, a much more important issue.)

It is hard to mount a socially acceptable argument against the sentimental trump card of the wisdom of old age. So what if an old person's life is so circumscribed that he or she feels little motivation to get out of bed in the morning? That's just depression talking. Bring on the mood-altering drugs, and old people will realize how lucky they are to be . . . well, alive. Just think about the compensatory hard-won wisdom acquired from having lived a long time. See the Hallmark greeting card image of great-grandparents having cozy chats with their great-grandchildren about what life was like before cars and airplanes. Think about what the boomer generation will have to tell its own great-grandchildren about growing up in a world in which you couldn't fill your ears with music twenty-four hours a day. Oh, the places we've been and the changes we've seen! How fortunate the world will be to benefit from the astuteness and experience of so many more nonagenarians and centenarians in the coming decades! The problem with this cheery mantra is that there is about as much proof of the wisdom of old age as there is of the medical efficacy of holy water from Lourdes.

And I emphasize that I am speaking not of people who have lost their memory to dementia but of the fortunate half of those over eighty-five who have retained most of their mental faculties. Since both profound wisdom and common sense are in short supply at any age, it seems illogical that these desirable qualities should manifest themselves more frequently among those of advanced age.

It is understandable that the pro-longevity movement has come to depend heavily on the wisdom of old age as a rationale for the idea that there is no point at which medicine and science ought to say "Enough" in the effort to extend the average life span. Like love, wisdom is a powerful argument for anything because it is basically unquantifiable and undefinable. There are three basic elements in the canon of old-age wisdom. The first is the assertion that the longer people live, the more reflective and perceptive they become. This belief is dependent on, but not identical to, the second article of faith set forth by the Planck researchers—the conviction that personal experience is the best teacher. The third argument for old-age wisdom, which simultaneously overvalues and patronizes the old, is the conviction that older means wiser because the old (certainly the oldest old) have risen above the ambitions and passions of their youth and middle age. They're wiser because, God love 'em, they have no choice: the old old have been ruled out of the race.

All of the new conventional thinking about old-age wisdom is embodied in an "Eldertopia" envisioned by the geriatrician William H. Thomas. This is a magical land in which old people "intervene at critical points to ensure that the [younger] adults take into account perspectives that are too easily ignored by those gripped by the fever of rank and wealth." Note the dubious assumption that the old are somehow less concerned about money than are the young. That the old do not possess the same earning capacity as the young does not mean that they are less fixated on wealth. Thomas goes on to explain how Eldertopia would work:

> Elder councils could provide a balancing perspective that considers the long-term consequences of any proposed action. The topics addressed might well include matters that the conventional political system would rather sweep under the rug.

> Elders have long spoken for Earth, its living creatures, and the children who are yet to be born. Eldertopia would have an Elder Conservation Corps that would tackle projects that strengthen the health and vitality of the natural world.
>
> Any honest accounting of the potential influence of elders and elderhood must address the contributions not only of fit and energetic elders. It must recognize the contributions that people who are weak, ill, infirm, dependent, demented, disabled, and dying can make to this struggle. The old and frail are able to surmount the dizzy bustle that clings to the young—to enter a time and place in which the spiritual and emotional dimensions of human life take precedence over the humdrum workings (and failings) of organs, tissues, and systems. This is among the most admirable of all human endeavors. What the old and frail do is show us the way. They provide us with greater insight into and a clearer perspective on the human condition.[4]

I don't know whether this passage is more insulting to the young or to the old, since it stereotypes both groups. Let us consider those elders who have "long spoken for Earth." I guess Thomas isn't talking about old men who made their fortunes from strip mining, logging, or dumping industrial waste into rivers and who are trying to hang on to every dollar they have acquired from despoiling the natural world. Presumably, elders who made money wrenching raw materials from Mother Earth and giving nothing back would be excluded from the Eldertopia councils, and only elderly conservationists would be allowed to serve. Something about this stereotype of elders as wise conservators resembles the sentimentalization of children as innocents, in that both groups are implicitly excluded from the full range of human possibilities. But the most patronizing and morally troubling aspect of Thomas's view is the idea that old people suffering from physical and mental diseases are capable of surmounting the "dizzy bustle" of the young and offering "greater insight into and a clearer perspective on the human condition." If the old could choose, it seems probable that they would trade their failing organs for the multiple demands of younger adult life. There is something repugnant about the idea that demented and suffering old people exist to provide an example for the rest of us. That suffering has some intrinsic, exemplary value, bringing humans closer to eternal verities, is a very Christian idea; it lay at the heart of the Puritan reverence for the small number of people who lived to a great old age in the seventeenth and eighteenth centuries. I found this notion disgusting when it was propounded by nuns in the parochial schools I attended, and the more suffering I have seen, the more repugnant I find the platitude that pain brings wisdom. My mother recently remarked, "The most degrading thing in the world is to wake up and have your first thought be, What's going to go wrong with my body today?" Nothing takes precedence over the failings of organs and tissues that once worked perfectly, and there is nothing mundane about this heart-wrenching and gut-wrenching process. Preoccupation with bodily functions whose efficiency used to be taken for granted is not only exhausting but also a source of deep shame for many old people, and they rarely talk about the subject because they know that most young people—not to mention their still-healthy contemporaries—are repelled by such conversations. It is admirable when the infirm, in spite of their pain and dismay at the loss of their powers, do manage to transcend their preoccupation with the body, but everyone fails in this superhuman effort in the end. It is incomprehensible to me that a geriatrician would hold such a sentimentalized view of suffering and dying. To be sure, it is comforting to believe that pain and suffering, undergone at any age, enlarge compassionate and empathetic capacities, thereby giving some meaning to events over which people have no control. But pain, at whatever point it invades a life, is just as likely to narrow perspective and reduce one's scope of concern to one's own suffering self. Anyone (that is, anyone except a saint) who has been responsible for the long-term care of a sick person has experienced the guilt-ridden exasperation attendant on trying to anticipate the person's every need and being met with yet another complaint. The exasperation is entwined with shame for the caregiver, who knows very well that she is not entitled to whine, "What about *me*?" A person who wakes up feeling as bad as or worse than he or she did the day before—and that is the case with most of the old old as well as with those who are near death—is not well placed to seriously consider the needs of others. Nor is he or she in the best position to reflect deeply and wisely on the past, given the intrusive physicality of the present. That is the reality of old old age, as opposed to Eldertopia.

Most paeans to the wisdom of old age are written by people who are nowhere near the threshold of old old age. Henry Fairlie was only sixty-four when he wrote his article about greedy geezers in 1988, but he claimed to be absolutely convinced of the richness of the contemplative stage of life that lay ahead. (He never had a chance to test his theories, because he died only two years later.) "My own age gives me some standing in this matter," he asserted. "As I approach the arbitrary line of 65, which of course I do not consider aged, my first savoring of growing old seems to promise a time of great richness, contemplation, and absorbing interest. One not only has the years ahead, but begins to recapture the whole of one's life, in ways for which even one's middle years are unequipped. . . . One is more content with simple fare in everything. It is less urgent to look for friends; one already has them, and new ones, often young, keep turning up. In growing old one has a stocked attic in which to rummage, and the still passing show and pageant of human life to observe, not only at a more leisurely pace, but with the convincing satisfaction and interest of having lived through many of the changes, even from their beginnings, that have brought us from there to here."[5] How very nice it must be to regard one's life as a "stocked attic" rather than the Augean stables; to me, growing older seems to require explorations of both habitats. *AARP: The Magazine,* in a boosterish article titled "50 Reasons to Love Being 50+," presents some of the same self-congratulatory, anticipatory thinking about the forthcoming wisdom of old age from middle-aged writers and editors. Reason 9: "Because you're more compassionate." One writer, still young enough to use the word "boyfriend" in reference to her partner, claims, "What we've learned is that all of us are inherently flawed and very, very vulnerable; that this, in part, is what it means to be human; and that—most important—we really are all in this together. It's the reason we treat our fellow humans with a heavy dose of compassion and respect."[6] I will not bother to name names and cite examples of the beastly behavior of old people, including old government leaders, whose actions show that they are just as indifferent to the welfare of their fellow men and women as they were at earlier stages of their lives. Since evidence has nothing to do with the belief that the old are any more compassionate, or generous, or open-minded, or wise than the middle-aged or the young, there is no point in trying to convince anyone of the error of their faith in geriatric goodness.

Still, it is easy to attribute wisdom to the old because wisdom can mean anything to anyone. This is true if one uses the primary *Oxford English Dictionary* definition—"capacity of judging rightly in matters relating to life and conduct; soundness of judgement in the choice of means and ends; sometimes, less strictly, sound sense, esp, in practical affairs: opp. To *folly*." It is equally true if one uses sociological jargon, as a University of Florida researcher did in a widely publicized 1997 study concluding that wisdom was even more important than health as an indicator of life satisfaction in old age. Wisdom, the author writes sagely, is "an integration of cognitive, reflective, and affective qualities."[7] In English, this means knowing what is going on in the present, being able to integrate the present with the past, and possessing empathy.

The capacity to learn from life experience—the second article of the old-age wisdom canon—is the most frequently cited explanation for the sagacity of the old. The conservative writer John Kekes observes that wisdom does not necessarily involve gaining new knowledge but understanding the significance of already known truths. Oh, what danger lurks in one's storehouse of already known truths! Life experience can lead people of all ages to unwise conclusions. I was sixty-two when Barack Obama began his campaign for the presidency, and he was my candidate almost from the beginning, but I never thought that an African American had a chance of being elected until the final weeks of the 2008 electoral contest. Neither did nearly anyone else I knew over age sixty—including fervid Obama supporters as well as blacks who were veterans of the civil rights movement. The mistake we all made was that we interpreted the current level of racism in the United States in terms of our own childhoods and coming-of-age experiences during the civil rights era. Andrew Young and Julian Bond, as they said explicitly in postelection interviews, initially held the same pessimistic view of Obama's prospects that I did. We all thought that in the privacy of the voting booth, too few whites would be willing to cast their ballots for a black man. And we were all wrong, because we were viewing the political situation from the powerful memories of our pasts. It is significant, in this context, that Americans over sixty-five were the only age group to vote against Obama; if the young and middle-aged had been as closely tied to historic racial stereotypes as the old, Obama would not have been elected. Even those of us who fought in our youth to create this new era were inclined to judge the young by the standards and behavior of our contemporaries. In fact, this misjudgment is a perfect example of the shortcomings of "pattern recognition"—a striking reminder that our own experience can mislead us. I happened to be in London promoting the British edition of my book *The Age of American Unreason* the weekend before the election. The enthusiasm of Londoners for Obama was palpable, and they simply assumed that he would be elected by an overwhelming margin. At a forum on American politics, I cautioned the audience against making this assumption. I said that I thought Obama would win, but I expected the election to be extremely close. I also said, "I'd like nothing better than for you all to wake up Wednesday morning and say, 'That foolish woman didn't know what she was talking about.'" Having asked for it, I did receive a number of e-mails on my author Web site the day after the election, and they all began, "You foolish woman. . . ." The point is that my age was a barrier, not an aid, to understanding: I couldn't see beyond my own experience to the immense generational change taking place around me. My nieces told me I was misjudging and underestimating the support for Obama among the young, but I thought I knew better. I do hope that this misjudgment will make me wiser should I live into my eighties or nineties—wise enough, at least, to know that my experience may prove insufficient as an explanation of the present or a guide to the future. In a sense, personal experience is to wisdom as witnessing a crime is to correct identification of the perpetrator: eyewitness testimony, which juries consider the most reliable form of evidence, is in fact the least reliable. That I know what I know about racial attitudes and practices in the 1950s and 1960s, when I was growing up and coming of age, does not give me any special authority on questions involving race today. It will certainly not give me any special claim to wisdom concerning this matter should I live another thirty years.

There are different ways of giving undue weight to one's own experience. I didn't think my country had changed enough to elect Obama, while James W. von Brunn, a white supremacist and lifelong anti-Semite, concluded from his version of experience that Obama had been elected because of his ties to the "international Jewish conspiracy." On June 10, 2009, the eighty-eight-year-old von Brunn walked up to the entrance of the United States Holocaust Memorial Museum in Washington, D.C., and shot and killed a thirty-nine-year-old security guard,

Stephen Tyrone Johns, who saved countless lives that day by spotting the shooter before he entered the building. It turned out that the fanatical right-wing octogenarian hated the government, immigrants, Jews, and blacks (not necessarily in that order) and had for many years maintained a Web site promulgating his conspiracy theories. When von Brunn was a young whippersnapper of sixty-one, he was sent to federal prison after walking into the headquarters of the Federal Reserve with a bag containing a sawed-off shotgun, a revolver, and a hunting knife. He told police that he wanted to take members of the Federal Reserve Board hostage because they were responsible for the nation's high interest rates. Von Brunn, like most people, was guided in old age by the prejudices and behavior patterns that he had long displayed. His act was a classic demonstration of the difference between knowledge and wisdom. As a matter of fact, von Brunn had learned a great deal between his early sixties and his late eighties; he mastered the technology of the Internet, which did not exist when he was convicted of his first crime. Those who maintain that old dogs cannot learn new tricks are wrong, but the new tricks may be used in service to an unchanged view of the world. By definition, every year of life (absent dementia) offers more experience, but the fundamental question is how that experience is interpreted. But I guess von Brunn isn't the sort of wise elder who would sit on advisory councils in Eldertopia.

One of the most scathing American literary views about the lessons acquired from experience appears in Nathaniel Hawthorne's "Dr. Heidegger's Experiment," an uncompromising gem of a short story, written in a post-Puritan, postrevolutionary society that was beginning to question the wisdom of old age attributed to its seventeenth- and eighteenth-century ancestors. The story is a grim fairy tale based on the premise that the fabled fountain of youth, sought by Ponce de León, really existed in Florida. One of the most cherished conceits of the old—in every generation—is that if our bodies could magically be made young again, while our minds retained the knowledge acquired over a lifetime, we would surely not repeat the mistakes of our youth. Dr. Heidegger puts this notion to the test by viewing the effect of an elixir of youth on four contemporaries with disreputable pasts—"all melancholy old creatures, who had been unfortunate in life, and whose greatest misfortune it was that they were not long ago in their graves."* His male guests are a Mr. Medbourne, who "had been a prosperous merchant, but had lost his all by a frantic speculation, and was now little better than a mendicant"; Colonel Killigrew, who "had wasted his best years, and his health and substance, in the pursuit of sinful pleasures, which had given birth to a brood of pains, such as the gout, and divers other torments of soul and body"; and Mr. Gascoigne, "a ruined politician, a man of evil fame, or at least had been so, till time had buried him from the knowledge of the present generation, and made him obscure instead of infamous." His lone woman guest, the Widow Wycherly, had once been a famous beauty but "for a long while past, she had lived in deep seclusion, on account of certain scandalous stories, which had prejudiced the gentry of the town against her." Hawthorne tells us that all three men had been lovers of the Widow Wycherly and "had once been on the point of cutting each other's throats for her sake." Before serving the sparkling water—which he does not drink himself—Dr. Heidegger alludes to the mistakes of his acquaintances' youth, and they laugh at him—"so very ridiculous was the idea, that, knowing how closely repentance treads behind the steps of error, they should ever go astray again." After several glasses of the elixir, the disgraced politician begins to bloviate about political topics "whether relating to the past, present, or future, could not easily be determined, since the same ideas and phrases have been in vogue these fifty years." The failed businessman develops another scam, a "calculation of dollars and cents, with which was strangely intermingled a project for supplying the East Indies with ice, by harnessing a team of whales to the polar icebergs." The Widow Wycherly, now restored to the beauty of her youth, plays one man off against the others. The men soon start to compete for her attention, and Dr. Heidegger watches a "picture of youthful rivalship, with bewitching beauty for the prize." At the same time, a mirror reflects "the figures of the three old, gray, withered grandsires, ridiculously contending for the skinny ugliness of a shrivelled grandam." The rivalry becomes so physically contentious that the vase containing the

* The quoted text appears in a 1906 edition of Hawthorne's short stories, *Little Masterpieces,* edited by Perry Bliss and published by Doubleday, Page.

remaining precious elixir is broken in the scuffle. The youthful bloom of the four reprobates fades once again, and Dr. Heidegger decides that he would never drink the elixir—even if its effects lasted years instead of minutes. "But the doctor's four friends had taught no such lesson to themselves," the story concludes. "They resolved forthwith to make a pilgrimage to Florida, and quaff at morning, noon, and night from the Fountain of Youth." Unlike Thoreau, Hawthorne did not have any great enthusiasm for youth, but he shared Thoreau's view that experience does not necessarily produce wisdom.

The moral of Hawthorne's story is not that people are incapable of learning from experience but that, as Heraclitus is said to have written, character, at any age, is fate. The crucial role of lifelong character and temperament is the most powerful argument against the third article of the old-age wisdom canon—that a magisterial transcendence of competitive drives and selfish passions qualifies the old old for guiding roles in Eldertopia. It is fully evident that change and growth can occur at any stage in life—but that does not mean they are likely to occur in people whose resistance to change, and to any challenge to their fixed views, is one of their enduring personal traits. In his study *The Seasons of a Man's Life* (1978), which builds on and extends Erik Erikson's work, the psychologist Daniel J. Levinson speculates about the nature of a "late adult transition" that occurs after retirement from a formal job. At this stage of life, a man "can engage in valued work, but it now stems more from his own creative energies than from external pressure and financial need. Having paid his dues to society, he has earned the right to be and do what is most important to himself. He is beyond the distinction between work and play. He can devote himself in a serious-playful way to the interests that flow most directly from the depths of the self."[8] Levinson's work reflects a more truncated view of adult life than the one prevailing today; he sees age sixty as the beginning of "late adulthood"—a demarcation strongly rejected by many baby boomers. (In the 1990s, Levinson collaborated with his wife, Judy, on a companion volume, *The Seasons of a Woman's Life,* which examines the differences and similarities between men's and women's life transitions. One obvious difference: many women, having taken a hiatus from paid work for child care, begin to invest more of their ego in work at a time when men are tiring of the rat race.) For both sexes, however, Levinson sees the inner-directed melding of work and play as the key to wisdom in old age. But such a union could come about only if, in old age, a man or woman allowed freer rein to desires and impulses that already existed on a conscious level but had been suppressed in the interest of more urgent midlife tasks—from putting a child through college to achieving professional goals. If an adult life has always been defined by rigidity and subservience to narrow goals defined by others, it seems unlikely that old age will suddenly free up the playful impulses of an inner child.

For better or worse, aging generally intensifies the traits of character and temperament that have informed the other stages of life. Cruelty and kindness, stinginess and generosity, self-centeredness and empathy, intellectual laziness and intellectual curiosity, parochialism and public-spiritedness: all of the qualities that define us are a combination of DNA, the environment in which we exist, and what we have made of both throughout a lifetime. And personality traits are certainly modifiable, by everything from early upbringing to formal education to the often inexplicable choices of compatible or incompatible life partners. But it is foolish to suggest that such traits are as easily modifiable in what Levinson calls the late life transition as they are at earlier stages. A man or woman who continues to engage in valued and gratifying work into his or her seventies, eighties, and beyond is surely a person who cared about work at every other stage of adult life (whether it was paid work or not). A grandparent who has tender relations with his or her grandchildren must surely have been a loving parent (although many people do find it easier to shower open, uncritical love on grandchildren for whom they do not bear ultimate responsibility). Furthermore, many changes viewed by adult children as a mellowing associated with old age are really changes of perception on the part of the younger generation. Adam Hochschild, in his moving memoir *Half the Way Home,* makes this point in an account of his ambivalent relationship with his father, Harold Hochschild, who was approaching fifty when Adam was born. Adam was intimidated by his formidable father, an international business leader whom he perceived as stiff, judgmental, and ungiving throughout his childhood. As an adult and a father himself, Adam muses about the very different nature of Harold's relationship with his grandchildren. "He wrote for Gabriel, our younger son, a long, beautiful story about two horses who talked to each other about what they saw," Adam recalls. "He waded into a brook . . . with David and helped him float a homemade boat downstream. And sometimes, riding in a car with both of them, he would burst spontaneously into song, 'California, here I come . . .' None of these things, none at all, do I remember his ever doing with me. Was all this love there for me as a child and had I just not seen it? Was this—and not the other side—the real Father? Or perhaps the two of them were wound together, as intertwined as colored swirls in a candy cane."[9] Of course the two men were one. A domestic tyrant does not turn into a tender paterfamilias simply by virtue of having lived into his ninth decade. A racist does not turn into a believer in the essential humanity of all because he has been granted extra time to consider and reconsider his passionate hatreds. A lifelong infotainment consumer devoted to celebrity gossip and reality TV does not suddenly decide to start exploring *War and Peace* and *The Iliad* to find fulfillment in old age. Wisdom does not flow from any special fountain of age any more than it does from a fountain of youth.

Of particular interest in the annals of any gerontocracy's inability to rise above old ambitions, passions, and biases are many memoirs by former government officials. These people almost never second-guess themselves, even when history has already rendered a decisive verdict against the decisions they made while in power. The exceptions, like former president Jimmy Carter's introspective memoirs, only prove the rule that if people are open to new ideas and continue to acquire wisdom with age, those traits are a continuation of, not a break with, their behavior over the course of a lifetime. Carter's life has been packed with dramatic turning points—some desired and others, like his loss of the presidency, very much unwelcome. From each of these turning points, whether or not they involved his own mistakes, Carter learned something—and the chief lesson is that there is always another way to contribute to the greater good, even if one path has closed. Carter is an intelligent, reflective man who has embraced two new careers since the voters retired him from the presidency—as a writer and as a developer of innovative humanitarian aid projects. He writes candidly about the bitterness that almost consumed him and his wife, Rosalynn, after the electoral defeat in 1980 by Ronald Reagan. (His 2010 memoir, *White House Diary,* indicates that Carter is still somewhat bitter about Sen. Edward M. Kennedy's challenge to his nomination.) What is most remarkable about the twelve books he has written in the last three decades is that he focuses not on justifying the past but on one life transition after another. In a short book titled *The Virtues of Aging,* written at age seventy-four, Carter notes that ageism is compounded by the negative stereotypes that many old people hold about themselves. "When I mentioned the title of this book to a few people," he writes, "most of them responded, 'Virtues? What could possibly be good about growing old?' "[10]

Carter's reflections, however, contrast sharply with most memoirs by those who have occupied highly visible public positions. World leaders, whether they have stepped off or been forced off the stage, generally have only one objective—justifying their past actions—when they reflect on their lives in print. Former secretary of state Henry A. Kissinger, whose extension of the Vietnam War into Cambodia in 1970 is widely regarded (except by the far right) as one of the major American foreign policy disasters of the second half of the twentieth century, is a prime example. Kissinger still considers himself one of the wisest men on the planet, and there is no evidence at all, in his ninth decade, that he has an iota of regret for, or has acquired any new wisdom about, decisions he made in the 1960s and early 1970s. In 2003, at eighty, Kissinger published a memoir that included transcripts of his phone conversations with other high government officials in the months just before the fall of Saigon and the beginning of the Khmer Rouge's slaughter of millions in neighboring Cambodia. Here is Dr. K., speaking with Senator Edward M. Kennedy, on April 29, 1975, about the evacuation of the last Americans from Saigon. He is talking to Kennedy—again, on the day the last Americans left for good—as if some sort of non Communist government is still a possibility in Vietnam. In passing, he mentions that "we could continue [fighting] in Cambodia, but right now in Cambodia, they seem to be engaging in mass executions—they don't respond to any approaches. . . . You know, the U.N. have approached [the Khmer Rouge] and we informally told the U.N. that we would be sympathetic, but they are even kicking out the French. In Cambodia, it is pretty bloody right now."[11] Yes, it was pretty bloody back then. As Kissinger knew perfectly well, Phnom Penh, the Cambodian capital, had fallen to the Khmer Rouge; President Lon Nol, whose government had been totally dependent on the United States, was done; and the Khmer Rouge had come to power largely because American planes had dropped 442,735 tons of bombs on the formerly peaceful country between March 1970 and August 1973.[12] When Richard Nixon sent the first American troops to Cambodia in March 1970, following a policy developed by Kissinger, he claimed that the United States intended only to pursue Vietnamese Communists—not to extend the war into Cambodia. Kissinger also knew that Cambodia, once such a rich agricultural country that even its poorest peasants rarely went hungry, was riddled by famine as a result of those three years of war. About the only thing Kissinger didn't know in 1975, at the time of the phone calls, was that the Khmer Rouge, which fed on public hatred of the American bombing, would soon turn on its own people, empty out the cities, and send everyone to work, starve, and die in the countryside and would eventually be responsible for the murder of more than two million. By the time Kissinger published his memoir in 2003, he obviously did know how it all turned out—but he presented the past, and his past, as inscrutable. "For the sake of our long-term peace of mind," he concluded, "we must someday undertake an assessment of why good men on all sides found no way to avoid this disaster and why our domestic drama [Watergate] first paralyzed and then overwhelmed us."[13] It does not even occur to Kissinger that the "good men" he cites (among whom he presumably considers himself) were neither very good nor very wise. And Kissinger was no wiser at eighty than he was when, as a forty-seven-year-old national security adviser, he urged another unwise man, Richard Nixon, to extend the human destruction of war to millions more people. To judge by most memoirs of old people who once ran the world, intelligence (as measured by conventional standards like advanced degrees) has nothing to do with wisdom—and neither has anything to do with age. A perfectly legitimate objection to my choices of Carter and Kissinger as examples of wisdom and arrogant folly in old age is that my judgment of their relative levels of wisdom is highly subjective and intertwined with my own political views. But that is precisely the point: there is every reason for deep suspicion of all claims to an objective standard by which wisdom may be assessed at any age.

All of the wise and witty old people whom I have known personally were absolutely recognizable later-life versions of the men and women they had been when they were younger. My dear friend Philip Vellacott, a great British translator of Euripides and Aeschylus, died at age ninety in 1997 and was active as a teacher as well as a scholar until his late eighties, when he was no longer able to travel. Philip, a premature feminist who had lectured for decades about the injustice toward women depicted in classical Greek drama (especially in Euripides), had been thought of as something of a gadfly by other classicists until the 1970s—when he entered his eighth decade. By the time I met Philip in 1984, he was deemed a wise man and a grand old man who had been ahead of his era, and he divided his time between his home in Wales and stints as a visiting professor of classics at the University of California, Santa Cruz, a hotbed of feminism. "You can be sure that when someone is considered a 'wise old man,'" he once wrote me, "all it means is that conventional wisdom has come around to the man's way of thinking. That makes me a bit nervous, actually—and it should. But I am saying the same basic things today that I was saying thirty years ago, when there was no audience for my views. Whatever is wise in what I say, or foolish in what I say, was the wisdom and folly of my middle age as well as my old age." Ay, there's the rub. If one has lived one's earlier adult life by going along to get along, by latching on to the intellectual and social fashions of the moment, there is little cause to believe that old age will magically reverse the habits of a lifetime. The greatest autobiographies and memoirs by old men and women—most written before the advent of old old age—all attest to the continuities, rather than the discontinuities, of an examined life. One of my favorite autobiographies, written when the author was in her late seventies, is *In Praise of Imperfection* (1988), by Rita Levi-Montalcini, a cell biologist who shared the 1986 Nobel Prize in Medicine with Stanley Cohen for their discovery of nerve growth factor. (NGF is a protein responsible for the differentiation of nerve cells—the process by which stem cells turn into one kind of tissue rather than another.) She writes:

> Without pre-established plan and guided at every turn rather by my inclinations and by chance, I have tried—as will be clear from a reading of this sort of balance-sheet or final account of my life—to reconcile two aspirations that the Irish poet William Butler Yeats deemed to be irreconcilable: perfection of the life and perfection of the work. By so doing, and in accordance with his predictions, I have achieved what might be termed "imperfection of the life and of the work." The fact that the activities that I have

> carried out in such imperfect ways have been and still are for me a source of inexhaustible joy, leads me to believe that imperfection, rather than perfection, in the execution of our assigned or elected tasks is more in keeping with human nature.[14]

One of the most striking features of this memoir is the consistency of the author's character, which alone accounts for the journey of a girl born into a highly patriarchal Italian Jewish family in 1909—a girl initially discouraged by her beloved father from pursuing higher education—to the highest levels of international science. When she told her father that she wanted to enter medical school, he "objected that it was a long and difficult course of study, unsuitable for a woman. Since I had finished [secondary] school three years previously, it would not be easy to take it up again. I assured him that I was not afraid of that. With the help of a tutor, I would study privately. 'If this is really what you want,' he replied, 'then I won't stand in your way, even if I'm very doubtful about your choice.'"[15] Levi-Montalcini's book might be cited as a perfect example of the wisdom of old age, but one would expect no less of a woman who had displayed a brilliant intellect, curiosity, and empathy at every stage of her life. One of her most trenchant observations—about science as a way of understanding the world rather than as a pursuit based on ambition and control—directly contradicts the idea that only in old age can people rise above gross, self-centered passions. At the conclusion of her book, she describes her last conversation with the dying ninety-two-year-old teacher who had been her mentor as a medical student and young scientist. In this moving passage, she emphasizes not the differences between old age and young adulthood but the continuities; to Levi-Montalcini, her mentor was the same man on his deathbed that he had been in his role as a teacher throughout his life.

> Our farewell—in that small hospital room whose bareness reminded me of a Franciscan's cell—could not have taken place in surroundings or under conditions more apt to bring out his qualities as a man and a scientist, consumed neither by old age, nor suffering, nor by the knowledge he had of his approaching end. He accepted the latter with a stoic serenity while maintaining till the very last an interest in research as an instrument for the understand-

> ing of nature and not as an object of competition and an instrument of power. In an era when the latter conception of scientific activity prevails, that last conversations of ours, the vivid interest he took in what he knew must be his last "briefing" on the state of my research, revealed to me the secret of the great influence he exerted on the young. It derived from the passion with which he pursued his studies and later directed those of his pupils, while remaining indifferent to the honors and plaudits that are granted old Masters. At the age of ninety-two, Giuseppe Levi was still too young and full of interests to be pleased by such fatuities—as, with supreme disdain, he was wont to call them.[16]

People who live with ardor, integrity, and wisdom continue to do so as long as their brains remain intact. Those whose lives have been defined by boredom, dishonesty, and intellectual laziness also continue their earlier course.

If the main claim of the old to wisdom is acceptance of mortality, as the Puritans thought, the best to be said about such acceptance is that nonacceptance of mortality, as in the case of Dr. Heidegger's guests, is the sure sign of a fool. If only the old truly acknowledge and accept the fact that they are going to die (and I am not at all sure that reasonably fit eighty-year-olds are any more resigned to their own mortality than a forty-year-old man who hopes to avoid awareness of his aging by bedding an eighteen-year-old), I am not sure that acceptance of mortality is a sign of any special wisdom. Such realizations are not born of an advanced spiritual, emotional, or intellectual awareness but are biologically forced on the old.

Recent books touting the wisdom of old age are devoted entirely to exceptional, and exceptionally interesting, old people—and most of the writers and researchers responsible for the touting are middle-aged. This makes sense in our culture, which offers the prospect of more years of life—at least to middle-class people—than have ever been available in the past, while simultaneously erecting considerable obstacles to those who wish to change course after their mid-forties. The midlife transition is never easy; even at the height of one's mental (if not physical) powers, there is a sense that time is running out and that some dreams may never be fulfilled. Elkhonon Goldberg's book provides a clear demonstration of the role of midlife anxiety in the need to believe that wisdom compensates for the other losses of old age. What makes Goldberg's work particularly interesting is that he, unlike many of the pop psychologists and sociologists arguing on behalf of old-age wisdom, is strongly influenced by "hard" science. So he begins his book by undergoing an MRI of his fifty-six-year-old brain to see if any gross physiological abnormalities are detectable. The scan doesn't turn up anything truly disturbing, and Goldberg notes that most doctors oppose such tests because they believe that even if there are early indications of future dementia, nothing can be done about it anyway. But Goldberg disagrees, and he and his research team at New York University have designed an elaborate computer program of exercises to boost mental functioning in older patients worried about their memory. The basis of Goldberg's argument that the aging mind can acquire wisdom to compensate for moderate memory loss and difficulties in tackling new problems is the "right-brain, left-brain" duality accepted in varying degrees (though they do not agree fully on its implications) by most neuroscientists. Goldberg presents what he calls a "radically new" concept of the roles played by the right and left hemispheres of the brain. "The right hemisphere is the 'novelty' hemisphere," he asserts, "and the left hemisphere is the repository of well-developed patterns. This means that as we age and accumulate more patterns, a gradual change in the hemisphere 'balance of power' takes place: The role of the right hemisphere diminishes and the role of the left hemisphere grows." Positive emotions are linked with the left hemisphere, he adds, and negative emotions with the right.[17] With age, Goldberg argues, "the balance shifts in favor of positive emotions, and as we age the affective tone of the left hemisphere becomes the norm. Our intuitive cultural perceptions agree with these findings. A restless octogenarian is often perceived, fairly or not, as the epitome of life unfulfilled, of a life cycle not completed, of striving for 'too little too late.' Being at peace with oneself in old age is the cultural stereotype to which most of us aspire."[18] Driving home this dubious and highly unscientific point, the author adds, "Being at peace with oneself is the attribute of normal aging. Geriatric depression is not."[19]

This insistence that depression is not a part of "normal" aging—like the assertion that dementia is not a part of normal aging—is a ubiquitous feature of the happy talk promoting the myth of a new old age. The clinical literature about depression in the old is highly contradictory, because it suggests that depression among the elderly is both common and undertreated while at the same time insisting that it has nothing to do with age. "Depression is not age-related," states a prominent British clinician, who goes on to note that depression is more common among physically ill people in hospitals than in the general elderly population. Surprise, surprise. About 25 percent of the hospitalized elderly are clinically depressed, the article states, and clinical depression affects between 30 and 40 percent of people in old-age institutions. Those with dementia and other neurological disorders, such as stroke and Parkinson's, are more likely to be depressed than other old people.[20] There is certainly an argument to be made that depression in a hospital or an institution is a perfectly reasonable, sane response to finding oneself trapped in circumstances over which one has no control and that dealing with such depression—either by surmounting it or by learning to live with it—is definitely part of the experience of normal aging. I have no doubt that depression in the old is in some cases undertreated and in some cases overtreated—the latter situation being particularly common in institutions that use drugs as a means of pacifying their residents. Doctors for whom I have the highest respect have told me that depression is often mistaken for dementia in old people who have no history of clinical depression. Muriel Gillick, an experienced geriatrician, notes that many symptoms of depression and early dementia are similar—including loss of interest in once pleasurable everyday activities, feelings of overwhelming grief and despair, disturbed sleep patterns, and a sudden spike in forgetfulness. "I'm on the side of trying antidepressants to see if the person responds," she says, "because only when the depression lifts can people deal more effectively with the losses that may have initiated the process."[21] I am certain that Gillick is right, especially when depression appears after an obvious blow like the death of a spouse or the diagnosis of a serious physical illness. What I strongly object to, however, is the idea that depression in the old is always abnormal and requires treatment—or that being at peace with oneself is necessarily the healthiest state of mind for anyone at any age.

If I were a scientist, I would be very careful about giving too much weight to what Goldberg calls "intuitive cultural perceptions." For the old old, the stereotype of the peaceful elder imposes a horrible burden: be wise, but not restless (whatever "restless" means). If you're depressed or angry (assuming you're not demented), it's because you're not exercising your brain enough—not because of objective circumstances. In conclusion, Goldberg describes the computer exercises that he and his colleagues are using as a form of mental gymnastics to boost the functioning of the aging brain. These include "an exercise designed to . . . challenge you by 'wearing you down' with a long sequence of stimuli on the screen, each requiring a different response" and "an exercise designed to train divided attention [to] have you respond to different events happening at the same time in different parts of the screen."[22] Goldberg claims that many of those who sign on for this program have seen great improvements in their concentration and memory, though he offers nothing but anecdotal accounts to support his assertions. I have no doubt that computer exercises can serve as a mental workout (many are being marketed by for-profit companies), but there is not the slightest evidence that they are any more effective than, say, learning a foreign language or taking music lessons. It's important to use one's mind actively (as opposed, say, to passively watching television) at any age. I have experimented with many computerized mental gymnastics programs, and certainly they provide new challenges for the brains of those who are concerned about normal memory and concentration lapses. But nothing Goldberg says in his excellent descriptions of brain functioning and physiognomy convinces me that mastering brain gymnastics has anything to do with wisdom. The ability not to be driven crazy when forced to deal with competing stimuli on a computer screen is extremely useful in modern life, but it seems to me the antithesis of reflection. Yet Goldberg insists that these sorts of exercises promote the successful aging that leads to wisdom:

> The image of the sage is among the most revered in every culture. After a long infatuation with youth, aging is respected and admired again even in our impatient, conceited culture. Given the massive demographic trends, it better be! One is not born to be a sage—one becomes a sage as the reward for a long journey. The journey I speak of is a journey of the mind. It is the ascendancy to wisdom. Aging is the price of wisdom, but wisdom itself is priceless. To those to whom it comes, it comes as the golden age of the mind.[23]

As a credit card commercial might say, "Denial—priceless." One of the most obvious manifestations of denial in this book by a middle-aged scientist anxious enough about his aging brain to go looking for trouble with an MRI is that he acknowledges, in an early chapter, that learnedness, intelligence, and even genius cannot protect anyone against developing irreversible dementia in old age. As he notes, "History is replete with instances of individuals endowed with great intellectual powers succumbing to dementia toward the end of their lives for reasons of genetics, or for some yet-to-be-understood environmental reasons. Contrary to our wishful thinking, an exalted social status does not offer protection in these matters, nor, as it turns out, does great intellectual power."[24] That is a scientist speaking. Yet in conclusion, he says the first message of his book is that "those of us whose mental lives have been both vigorous and rigorous approach their advanced years with a mighty coat of mental armor." This armor, he says, "is not an entitlement and its attainment in old age is not a foregone conclusion. It is a reward for the vigorous life of the mind in younger years."[25] Except when it isn't. Except when the light of the mind is extinguished, as it was for Isaac Newton, Jonathan Swift, Immanuel Kant, Frederick Law Olmsted, Sargent Shriver, and Brooke Astor. That a scientist can make such contradictory statements powerfully demonstrates the lengths to which we will go to cry, "Not me."

A great deal of the puffery on behalf of the wisdom of old age is motivated by a desire to identify some purpose, either in an evolutionary or social sense, for the longer lives that people are living today. For the growing number of American adults who have not only living parents but living grandparents (as I did until my mid-fifties), the prospect of living longer is both exciting and terrifying. We know on some level, in spite of the myth of young old age, that most people in their late eighties and nineties exert little influence in society and are forced to cope with intensifying physical disabilities, financial problems, and the fear, if not always the fact, of losing their minds. In *How to Live: A Search for Wisdom from Old People,* forty-something writer Henry Alford asserts that "humans are one of the few species with an average life span that extends beyond the age at which we can procreate. Why is this? Maybe it's because old folks have something else to offer."[26] In fact, there has never been any upper age limit for procreation in men (although there is now accumulating medical evidence that old men's sperm is more likely to produce babies with birth defects). Women are the ones who used to die around the time their eggs ran out. It would be more accurate to say, at this point in history, that we are the only species with many members who routinely live beyond the point where they can contribute productively to the community. The old do wish to be productive—if productivity is defined not merely as earning money but as contributing to others—but at some point of ill health, most of them lose the physical or mental capacity for effort that requires concentration and sustained energy. Until age eighty-eight, my mother was an active volunteer in the critical care unit at her local hospital; because she is an organizationally gifted woman who can figure out how almost any system works, she was able to be especially helpful to families caught in a health care bureaucracy they did not understand. She was productive. Now her bones are so thin that she cannot turn over in bed at night without incurring the danger of cracking a rib, and she cannot manage the physical duties of a volunteer. I know that my mother's volunteering not only helped others but gave new meaning to two decades of her life, and I know that nothing can replace the role of that work for her. So what does an old person have to offer, once he or she is physically unable to offer what was once a supreme talent? "Wisdom" is the one-word response offered by middle-aged visitors to a country in which they have no wish to live but might one day find themselves imprisoned. And so a visitor like Alford decides "to interview and spend time with as many fascinating senior citizens as I can." If you interview old people like Harold Bloom, Edward Albee, and Setsuko Nishi, a pioneering Asian American sociologist who, like most other Japanese Americans on the West Coast during World War II, was sent to an internment camp by her own government, you will take away a lot of interesting—though not necessarily wisdom-filled—stories. Alford's mother, who divorced her husband of more than twenty-five years in her late seventies, is another fascinating old person, coming up with clever (though not always charitable or wise) phrases like "macular degenerates" to describe less fortunate inhabitants of her assisted living community. What these people share is intact memory and the gift of gab—but this really has little to do with overarching wisdom. When asked by Alford to fill out a questionnaire indicating the happiest time of his life, Albee responds, "Now, always." Please. People spout such platitudes because that is what the therapeutic culture tells them they are supposed to say—in the same way that everyone who claims to have had a "near-death experience" reports the presence of a bright light, with or without intimations of relatives and friends already enveloped by the radiance. Thanks to blogs and made-for-television movies, we all know what a near-death experience is supposed to feel like—just as we all know that we're not supposed to live in the past or the future but in the "now." Statements like Albee's are strongly influenced by the social prescription that successful aging means being at peace with oneself. It was a great relief to me when, in the middle of the interview with Alford, Albee suddenly shifted from his above-it-all shtick and began railing at critics who gave his plays bad reviews years ago. That sounds like the man who wrote *Who's Afraid of Virginia Woolf?*—not like the peaceful senior citizen who claims that these are the best years of his life.

In a fashion resembling Goldberg's assertion that a rich intellectual life is like a coat of armor when entering old age, Alford finally observes, "My looks will fade, my power will wane, my money will be spent or diminished by rampant inflation, my wit will grow softer, my hipness will grow stale. But I will still have my mind. This gives me a great feeling of security; it's like knowing that even once you run out of sea-soaked saltines, you can still eat the boat."[27] (Actually, you will die much faster if you've eaten dehydrating sea-soaked saltines; you may not live long enough to try eating the boat.) The conviction that one will always have one's mind is based on and is designed to promote a false sense of security, because no one can know at any point whether he or she will still have a functioning brain in old age. The old-age wisdom canon is essentially a defense against the knowledge of the terrible fates that lie ahead for so many of us before we actually die. I may and do hope that I will retain my intellectual powers—whether anyone considers me wise or not—into old old age, but the fact that people like Philip Vellacott and Harold Bloom managed to do so tells me absolutely nothing about the odds of my winding up in the dementia-free half of the very old population. And simply being free of dementia is no guarantee of being considered a wise old woman rather than a cranky one. Crankiness—which might be called righteous anger in the young or middle-aged—is something that old people, and especially old women, display at their peril. If you're a woman in your eighties who expresses displeasure when a waiter patronizingly calls you "young lady," you will immediately be classified as a cranky old bitch instead of a sweet old lady.

But there is much more to the exaltation of old-age wisdom than the simple, understandable desire to believe that something worthwhile awaits us in the closing stages of life even if we have lost our looks, our health, our wealth, and our standing in the world. Erikson's triumph of "ego integrity over despair" and Levinson's inner-directed integration of work and play depend on a high level of detachment from the strivings of earlier adult life, from competition in both work and love. We can achieve wisdom only when we have overcome our desire for validation from others, when we have retired from the fray. Needless to say, it is extremely convenient for the young if the old decide to aspire to a higher, detached level of consciousness instead of to make more demands on the rest of society.

The most trenchant analysis of the presumed relationship between wisdom and detachment comes not from a psychologist or sociologist but from an English professor, Kathleen Woodward, whose essay "Against Wisdom: The Social Politics of Anger and Aging" makes a powerful case that the invocation of old-age wisdom is both a conscious and unconscious strategy to defuse the anger of the old at both their personal and social fates. Woodward, who heads the Walter Chapin Simpson Center for the Humanities at the University of Washington, draws a provocative comparison between G. Stanley Hall's 1922 book *Senescence* and Betty Friedan's *The Fountain of Age,* published more than seven decades later. While Hall's approach to old age is based on a century-old male model, Friedan's views are channeled through feminism—specifically, through her own role as the founding mother of the second wave of American feminism that emerged in the 1960s. The two share the conviction—which I find dubious but Woodward does not judge—that there must be some sort of evolutionary purpose for the extra decades of life granted to middle-class people by the economic progress and medical advances of the twentieth century. Hall and Friedan, like the social Darwinists of the late nineteenth century, both confuse evolution in nature with evolution in society: it is futile to look to either Darwin or God for the "purpose" of longevity. Thinking that because more of us are living to old old age there must be some good reason—dictated by either evolution or a divine creator—for our still being on this earth is just another form of the persistent human desire to place ourselves at the center of all nature. That many of the old now wish to embrace this understandable exaggeration of human importance undermines rather than supports the idea that some special wisdom must be associated with advanced age.

Woodward's most important insight, particularly regarding Friedan, is that the feminist founder cannot reconcile her anger at actually being old with her claim that society's need for wisdom represents the real, "evolutionary" purpose of longevity—especially female longevity. Hall envisioned wise old men as advisers to the world (rather like Eldertopia), while Friedan envisions both men and women (but especially old women, since there are so many more of them) as meeting "the growing need for . . . wisdom transcending narrow expertise in every field."[28] Friedan undermines her own example by citing the longevity of many Supreme Court justices over the past fifty years as proof of the wisdom of old age. While I considered John Paul Stevens the wisest member of the Supreme Court before his retirement at age ninety, I shudder to think about the possibility of Antonin Scalia serving on the Court until his late eighties. Supreme Court members are generally long-lived not because they have any special wisdom but because they belong to a social class that earns a good deal of money and receives first-rate health care benefits; not least, they command the services of numerous law clerks to ease the burdens of demanding work at an advanced age. Friedan even suggests that there should be a third house of Congress, drawn from Eldertopia and uncorrupted by the need to raise money for reelection, "whose sole function is to ask the larger questions."[29] Nattering on about the "freedom from youthful competitive compulsion" that can "more than compensate for whatever losses of muscle power or memory also come with age," Friedan begins by acknowledging her depression about growing older but ends by supposedly transcending anger with wisdom.[30] She talks about old age as a social construct, defined by ageist perceptions, instead of as a reality that poses huge difficulties for many of the old themselves. Such an approach demands that the oldest old—many of whom may be physically or mentally incapable of contributing anything to the work of the world—be left out of the picture entirely. But Betty Friedan was a very angry woman at many stages of her adult life. Without her anger, she never would have written *The Feminine Mystique*. *The Fountain of Age* is propelled by anger too—but Friedan can't own up to it because of her need to embrace a mythical noncompetitive detachment as the key to wisdom. She is particularly angry at her own marginalization within the women's movement, which she attributes largely to her age (younger women care too much about abortion and not enough about menopause, or too much about menopause and not enough about developing new living arrangements for the old). It is only through the posture of superior wisdom—of having risen above old hurts and passions—that Friedan can provide an evolutionary justification for old age. So she concludes her book with a magisterial, utterly unconvincing description of her old-age liberation from the angry woman she has been. "I recognized my own compelling need now to transcend the war between the sexes," she writes, "the no-win battles of women as a whole sex, oppressed victims, against men as a whole sex, the oppressors. . . . The unexpectedness of this new quest has been my adventure into age. . . . *I am myself at this age*."[31] So who was that fighting feminist whose book changed so many women's lives, the tough-minded woman who named the problem that had no name? I don't recognize Friedan as a contemplative, equable old lady, searching for some evolutionary justification, via wisdom, for her own existence. Woodward, by contrast, says flatly that "there is absolutely no need to have to justify—through the lens of wisdom—the extraordinary extension of life expectancy that has been gained over this century."[32] She further argues that the myth of "older is wiser" actually interferes with the work that needs to be done, by people of all ages, to make old old age less difficult than it now is.

> It is time to declare a moratorium on wisdom. . . . Wisdom carries the connotation of detachment, hence . . . the extreme difficulty of putting it together with engagement, or re-engagement. Wisdom justifies the disengagement theory of aging—that older people "naturally" withdraw from their social roles so as to make their ultimate disappearance—death—far less difficult for the smooth functioning of society. Wisdom carries the connotation of dignified behavior, hence, the further difficulty of its association with a rhetoric of protest [against ageism].[33]

I agree, but I consider it significant that so many people do feel a need to justify longevity by redefining old age as a highly desirable stage of life instead of as a period fraught with difficulties that must be addressed by society as a whole as well as by individuals. The myth of old-age wisdom, which requires freedom from youthful desires, acts as an uneasy and frequently hostile bedfellow to the myth of young old age, which falsely suggests that "age is just a number" and that successful aging is defined by the capacity of the old to behave as if they were young—or at least in a younger fashion than any previous generation has had to behave in order to attain social acceptance.

CHAPTER NINE

Endings

> It was part of the decency of Death that he should come unheralded with his face covered and his hands concealed at the hour when he was least expected. He should come slowly, like his brother Sleep—or swiftly and violently like the consummation of the act of love, so that the moment of surrender would be a stillness and a satiety instead of a wrenching separation of spirit and flesh.
>
> The decency of Death. It was the thing men hoped for vaguely, prayed for if they were disposed to pray, regretted bitterly when they knew it would be denied them.
>
> —Morris West, *The Devil's Advocate*

If a decent death is defined by the absence of extended suffering, an American who lives into advanced old age in the twenty-first century probably has less chance of receiving that mercy than the poorest peasant did in the fourteenth century. The peasant would likely have succumbed to an infectious disease, possibly in terrible pain but in short order, without the prolonged agony, devolving into pointless limbo, of modern medicalized death. It took no more than seven days from the date of infection, for example, for the Black Death to claim its victims. And the peasant would probably have died in his home, however humble—at least if family members were still alive—and would have been comforted by the hope of salvation and eternal life.

In the United States today, only about 20 percent of us die at home, although public opinion surveys repeatedly have shown that 90 percent of Americans—whether or not they subscribe to the hope of immortality—would prefer to end their lives in their own beds. Until the middle of the twentieth century, most Americans really did die at home rather than in medical or long-term care institutions. This was often true of the young as well as the old, unless the imminent threat was something that might be addressed by a surgeon.* More than half of Americans now die in hospitals, and an astonishing 20 percent spend their final days in intensive care units, hooked up to machines that do nothing but prolong the inevitable and isolate the dying person from family and friends. As the French historian Philippe Ariès observes in his magisterial work *The Hour of Our Death* (1981), people throughout the developed world became less tolerant with each decade of the twentieth century of "the sights and smells that in the early nineteenth century were part of daily life, along with suffering and illness."[1] The sanitization of death was an inevitable part of this decreasing tolerance for evidence of physical decay, and America led the world in the process of segregating the dying. Ariès notes that the circle of participation in the care of the dying "steadily contracted until it was limited to the closest relatives or even to the couple, to the exclusion of children. Finally, in twentieth-century cities, the presence of a terminal patient in a small apartment made it very difficult to provide home care and carry on a job at the same time."[2] Not only hospitals but other institutions are the houses of death for Americans. Around 25 percent, usually those with irreversible dementia, die in nursing homes. A tiny percentage die in hospices, which offer palliative care to ease pain but not aggressive technological or surgical intervention to prolong a terminal disease. The American way of death costs a fortune. One-third of the entire Medicare budget is spent on care in the final year of life. According to a study by the Dana-Farber Cancer Institute, a staggering one-third of these last-year dollars are spent on care—much of it in ICUs—in the final month of life.[3] Whether they die at home or in an institution, the oldest old usually die after a long period of suffering from chronic, incurable conditions that finally become unmanageable. Death rarely has the decency to strike them down with a heart attack on the street

* Doubters should take a look at death scenes from movies of the 1930s and 1940s. They almost always take place at home, unless someone has been gunned down in the streets. In the 1945 classic *Mildred Pierce,* with the title role played by Joan Crawford, Mildred's daughter expires of pneumonia in an impromptu oxygen tent set up by a doctor in the home of Mildred's estranged husband's mistress. This is not exactly dying in one's own bed, but the mistress offered a haven to the sick child because Mildred herself was unavailable as the result of an amorous dalliance. No one apparently thought about going to the hospital. It is worth noting that this movie was made before penicillin—which saved many soldiers' lives in battlefield hospitals during World War II—became generally available to civilians in the United States.

while they are still able to walk about freely, or to take them unexpectedly in their sleep and allow them, as the young Keats wrote, "to cease upon the midnight with no pain." The novelist Richard Dooling, who worked as a respiratory therapist in ICUs in the 1980s, recalls "marveling, along with the young doctors and nurses I worked with, over how many millions of dollars were spent performing insanely expensive procedures, scans and tests on patients who would never regain consciousness or leave the hospital." When Medicare or supplemental insurance stopped paying, Dooling remembers, families would sign over a lien on their houses to the hospital to continue futile care, sometimes spending "their entire savings so Grandma could make yet another trip to the surgical suite on the slim-to-none chance that bypass surgery, a thoracotomy, an endoscopy or kidney dialysis might get her off the ventilator and out of the hospital in time for her 88th birthday."[4]

Family battles around hospital deathbeds are common. My mother, Irma B. Jacoby—whose specific task as a volunteer for twenty years at Sparrow Hospital in Lansing, Michigan, was to help families deal with such issues—would watch in amazement as members of some families threw punches at one another in the critical care unit's lobby. "More than once, I'd see eyeglasses smashed and flying across the room," she recalls. "Usually, it was because the kids disagreed over what Mom or Dad would have wanted. And Mom or Dad had never exactly made it clear, and could no longer speak for themselves. There would be adult children who obviously felt guilty because they hadn't had the best relationship with their parent, and they were trying to make up for it by keeping Mom or Dad alive, to no point, for as long as possible." The gap between the way Americans actually die and the way they say they want to die is due, in part, to procrastination about legal planning that would reduce the number of family fights in the waiting rooms of intensive care units. And procrastination is inseparable from a refusal to face the fact of our own mortality. By the time we reach the age when our contemporaries start dying in significant numbers, we are still reluctant to squarely acknowledge what the obituary pages have been telling us, with a growing insistency, for decades.

It starts in your forties or, if you are lucky, in your fifties. You open the newspaper (or you did, back in the day when literate people read print editions of newspapers), and you see the name of someone you know—someone near your own age—on the obituary page. Death, usually in the form of cancer or a heart attack, has come to claim a man or woman much too early, in what is generally considered the prime of adult life. You feel a definite sense of shock, even if the person was not a friend, because he or she was born around the same time you were. But you get over the shock quickly because, after all, the death of anyone in his or her forties or fifties is now a relatively rare event—and you can file it away in the portion of your memory reserved for being struck by lightning or choking to death on a fortune cookie. If you are particularly susceptible to fears aroused by the misfortunes of others, you may schedule your annual physical a few months early.

In your sixties—even though health statistics and personal experience indicate that most middle-class people have many years of active life ahead of them—the obituary pages become harder to shrug off. This time, the public record of the dead may include someone you know well—even a close friend. A friend's vital, active husband drops dead of a heart attack while playing tennis. A writer whose work you admire—didn't she survive breast cancer in her forties?—has a recurrence and cannot be saved, even though chemotherapy has improved in the past two decades. Although these people still seem much too young to die—for are you not too young to be worried about life's inevitable end?—they no longer fall into the category of freak accidents. They are, rather, shadows of a future that no longer seems—because in fact it is not—as far away as death seemed when you were in the middle of your adult life. Still, you try to figure out what they did wrong to damage their health. Did they smoke? If they quit smoking, when did they quit? Were they overweight? Were they couch potatoes? Did they drink too much? Anything to separate them from you, to tell yourself that what happened to them could not happen to you anytime soon. Something else starts to happen in your sixties, however, and it makes this kind of self-protective rationalization more difficult. The mentors of your youth—people ten, fifteen, twenty years older than you are—begin to appear on the obituary pages with an almost metronomic regularity. Your favorite college professor, the one who sparked your interest in Russia, is gone. When you were a student, he was in his forties. Now that you are sixty, why should you be surprised to hear about his death? But you are. And whether your parents are still alive or not, there is a relentlessness to the progression that cannot be denied. This sensation of inevitability sharpens every year, until a friend writes you a letter on an August day and remarks, "It seems almost a miracle that I haven't attended a funeral since May."

It is not that old people become obsessed with death but that, with each passing year and decade, death becomes a more conscious presence in everyone's life, however pleasurably and fully life may be proceeding. The losses mount up. The blows may cease for a season, but they keep on coming. And still, only a minority make plans for the ending that will eventually be described, often in vague terms, on the obituary page. There are essentially four approaches for mentally competent people to take when contemplating the manner in which they would prefer to live out whatever time is left. First, there is the "do everything" ethic, in which the full resources of medical technology are ordered into action without regard for either the likelihood of recovery or the quality of life to be recovered. The first pathway to end-of-life care requires a minimum of planning, because "do everything" is the inherent bias of our medical system in the absence of a patient's explicit instructions or explicit guidance from the next of kin. The second and, I suspect, by far the most common approach is really a nonapproach: people hope that when the time comes, either they will be able to make a last-minute decision about continuing or discontinuing treatment themselves or that their closest relatives (usually a spouse or children) will do the right thing. The second approach—or, as I see it, the avoidance of decision making about the process of dying—assumes that our closest relatives will be able to read our minds at the appropriate moment. It also assumes that relatives will have our best interests at heart. The third approach might be described as "Do everything possible only if there is a realistic hope that I can emerge as a functioning, mentally competent human being. Then stop and let me die." This approach requires extensive planning, including advance written directives that may or may not be followed, and difficult conversations with a spouse or children. Given the inherent human predilection for putting off discussions about unpleasant realities that may lie far in the future, it is not hard to understand why so many Americans spend the last weeks of their lives in a hospital that has nothing to offer in the way of healing—in spite of the fact that only 22 percent believe that medical personnel are always obliged to do everything possible to save a patient's life.[5] The fourth and, as we know, extremely rare approach is suicide or assisted suicide when confronted with an irreversible disease that may, nevertheless, take months or even years to finish its work.

The most consistent finding of public opinion polls on this subject is the inconsistency between Americans' expressed wishes about wanting to exert control over their medical care at the end of life and their actual willingness to take responsibility for making their preferences clear beforehand, in writing as well as by talking, in the event that they are unable to express their views in the final weeks, months, or, in the case of dementia sufferers, years of life. This inconsistency was demonstrated strikingly by the irrational furor over an innocuous proposal in the Obama administration's health care reform bill to allow Medicare to pay, once every five years, for voluntary discussions about end-of-life care between doctors and patients. The fury and fear were certainly stoked by the far right, which wanted to torpedo any health care reform legislation, but the anger was definitely not confined to the lunatic fringe. The rationality-challenged but cleverly opportunistic fringe was represented by the shameless hustler Sarah Palin, who—blogging away viciously after walking away from her job as governor of Alaska—transformed entirely voluntary consultations into "death panels" that would decide whether old people and children like her son with Down syndrome would continue to receive medical care. (Palin's exploitation of her Down syndrome child was a particularly vile tactic, because when her son grows up, he will be eligible for federal Social Security payments for the disabled—payments that I seriously doubt the anti-government Palin will turn down.) But her ravings struck a chord with ordinary people who, whatever their own views on aggressive medical intervention at the end of life, were scared by the very phrases "government bureaucrats" and "death panels." Many political analysts attributed the bogus controversy entirely to the reflexive American fear of any government involvement in individual decisions, and that certainly did play a role (albeit an ironic one for people over sixty-five, who happily depend on the government to pay for most of their health care). But I think that much of the fear was also generated by a distaste for the very idea that individuals should exercise more affirmative responsibility in planning for death. Although nearly 30 percent of Americans have living wills specifying their wishes about care at the end of life, most have never provided their doctors with a copy of the documents. The Dana-Farber Institute study estimated that American medical costs could be reduced by $75 million a year if more cancer patients discussed living wills with their families or doctors before they could no longer speak for themselves.[6] That's a drop in the ocean, but the savings would be immeasurably greater if all older Americans explored the subject with their physicians as well as their family members and legal representatives. The fact that 70 percent of Americans do not have living wills, in spite of the publicity devoted to the subject over the past two decades, surely indicates the majority's aversion to thinking about or planning for the end of life.

A study published in 2006 by the Pew Research Center for the People and the Press provides some fascinating insights into the complexity and ambivalence of Americans' attitudes toward all issues surrounding death and dying. This opinion poll was conducted long before the surge of passion created by the political debate over health care reform. Nearly 70 percent of married people say they have had a conversation with their husband or wife about the spouse's wishes for end-of-life care.[7] But the pollsters did not ask people about the content of those conversations. That only 30 percent of Americans have actually written down their wishes, while 70 percent claim to have talked about what they want, may suggest that people have more trust in their loved ones than in written documents—or that most people want to leave a lot of wiggle room for future changes of opinion.

Another likely possibility is that such discussions tend to be vague rather than unambiguous. I have one friend, for example, whose husband simply told her, "Just don't let me linger too long if there's really no hope." If I were this man's wife, having known him thirty years, I would probably interpret his statement as "Don't put me on a ventilator if I'm unconscious and my brain is never going to work again." But it would be a tougher call if my husband could breathe without a ventilator, yet his doctors told me there was no chance of his ever regaining consciousness or resuming a normal life. Removing a feeding tube is much more difficult for most people than simply ordering that artificial life support be turned off. I would be much more comfortable as a wife with a specific document asking that hydration and nutrition be withheld in such circumstances. Yet this man—who is a lawyer—has not spelled out his wishes in writing in a way that would free his wife of the burden of making the decision without knowing what her husband really wanted. Of those surveyed by the Pew Center, only 57 percent with living parents had spoken about the subject with their mother and fewer than half with their father. (Adult children are obviously counting on Mom to make the decisions for Dad.) For baby boomers—and especially for women, who overwhelmingly make up the old old—there are many disturbing implications about a marriage-centered approach to planning for life's end. If there are no children, there is no obvious candidate to step forward and attend to the decent death of a ninety-year-old woman whose husband (or ex-husband) died long ago. It is imperative for both men and women, if they have no partner and no children, to speak with a close friend about their wishes and take the additional steps needed to ensure that a friend may act in the legal capacity that is automatically allowed a spouse or child. As many gay couples learned under the worst possible circumstances, when AIDS first appeared in the 1980s, even a distant, angry family member has more of a say in end-of-life care than someone who does not have the legal status of a blood relative or spouse. And there is a significant gap between people's general statements about the individual's right to refuse medical treatment and their preferences about their own care. Although only 22 percent say that doctors should always do everything to save a patient's life, 34 percent say that they themselves would tell their doctor to "do everything"—even if their illness was terminal and they were in great pain. However, that is not the majority viewpoint: most Americans say that they would choose to stop medical treatment if they had a painful terminal illness. That's fine if a person is able to speak for himself or herself at the end, or if there is a close, preferably a first-degree, relative on the spot. But the growing number of Americans like me, living alone and lacking children, are in a very different and more difficult position. My brother is only three years younger than I am and, judging from the life expectancy statistics, it is likelier that I will outlive him than that he will outlive me. The beloved man to whom I had assigned my health care proxy, and who fully understood and agreed with my views about this subject, is now dead. When I draw up a new will (only half of Americans have any written will, by the way), I must find a friend who is willing to act as a backup for my brother. I do have nieces, whom I love and respect, but they are only in their twenties—too young, in my view, to be entrusted with such a crucial responsibility. I probably should, and will, have a conversation with them about this issue (certainly after the publication of this book), but I suspect that my reluctance to intrude on their youth with talk about death may be shared by many parents who, like me, fall in the young old category and do not expect to die anytime soon.

It is natural that the young, as a group, should have much more faith in medical technology than the old do. Asked in 2005 whether they would like to live to one hundred, the only group that produced a majority—55 percent—of would-be centenarians was between ages eighteen and twenty-nine. Asked the same question in 1990, only 44 percent of people in that age group said they wanted to live to one hundred. Among Americans over sixty-five today, only 37 percent say they want to live that long.[8] It seems that the marketers of longevity have been most effective at convincing young adults that their old age will be very different from that of their own grandparents. Still, it is significant that more than a third of those over sixty-five—a group presumably most familiar with the problems associated with old old age—also want to live to the centennial landmark. Baby boomers are just as eager—in the case of young boomers, more eager—to survive to one hundred as older Americans are. The published Pew poll does not indicate how many of those who want to live to the century mark also want everything possible done to sustain life under any circumstances, but it makes sense that people who see old old age as desirable would be most aggressive in their use of medicine and medical technology. The question, as the over-sixty-five and the over-eighty-five population swells during the next thirty years, is whether our society can afford attempts to gratify the desire of so many people for a greatly extended life span. One may hope that the 55 percent of Americans under thirty who say they want to become centenarians will, as they age themselves, become more aware of the drawbacks to advanced old age, because it is truly staggering to contemplate the economic and social consequences if living to one hundred becomes a widely held goal and a realistic possibility for the majority of Americans rather than an idle wish. If Americans, as a people, avoid planning for and thinking about death, they probably have also failed to take a hard look at what will be needed financially, and from whom, to live decently in their tenth, much less their eleventh, decades of life.

I have emphasized that planning is not required to produce an expensive death in an intensive care unit, and that is generally true under Medicare as it operates today. The default medical position, particularly in specialties treating patients for cancer and heart disease—the two most common causes of death among the old—is to keep fighting with all of the resources of modern medicine. That is also the default position for emergency medical technicians, in the absence of a specific written directive to the contrary, if they are called to attend an old person who has collapsed after a stroke or heart attack. The eighty-nine-year-old sister of an eighty-five-year-old friend of mine was "saved" by a medic alert system that brought assistance within eight minutes to her Manhattan apartment after she suffered a massive heart attack. The technicians went to work, as they are required to by law, and the woman was taken to a hospital. She had no living will and had not authorized anyone to make medical decisions for her. Although she never regained consciousness, she survived in an intensive care unit for more than two weeks, at a cost to Medicare of more than $100,000. The sister pleaded with doctors to turn off the ventilator, but they refused to do so until all brain activity ceased and she could be declared legally dead. My own friend, shocked by the sequence of events, went to see a lawyer the day after her sister's funeral and had him draw up a health care proxy assigning her nephew the right to make the decision to turn off a ventilator if there was no hope of recovery. "I don't believe my sister would have wanted this waste of effort and medical care and money," says my friend, "but the fact is, she didn't talk to me or anyone else about what she did want. And I didn't press her on it." As the executor of the will, the sister had to sell cherished antique jewelry to pay for expenses that Medicare did not cover. "I know she wanted her nieces to have this jewelry," my friend says, "because she specified it in her will. But there was too much that Medicare didn't pay for, and selling the heirloom jewelry was the only way to pay the bill. The last weeks of her life were a total waste—there's no other way to put it. It was an urgent wake-up call for me. The easiest thing is just to do nothing."

It is unlikely, however, that "do everything" will remain the health care system's default position as the huge baby boom generation ages. That is the kernel of rationality in the fears of some older Americans who, while they do not believe the extreme right's rhetoric about "death panels," do fear that universal health coverage for Americans of every age would inevitably mean cuts in previously sacrosanct Medicare entitlements. Without massive tax increases for everyone, we cannot afford to continue to keep eighty-nine-year-olds alive in ICUs after they have suffered irreversible heart or brain damage. We certainly cannot afford to go on doing this by default for people who might not even have wanted such care if they were asked but were too fearful of death to deal straightforwardly with the limited alternatives that await everyone at the end of life. That is why the politically motivated attack on Medicare financing of voluntary consultations about end-of-life care between doctors and seriously ill patients is so irrational and antirational. Simply encouraging doctors and patients to talk about the taboo subject, as the Dana-Farber Institute study demonstrated, would save money by giving people who do *not* want "everything done" a clear picture of their choices as well as the opportunity to state their wishes. And doctors would be forced to take a hard look at their own assumptions about what patients want. The day after Massachusetts senator Edward M. Kennedy lost his battle with brain cancer, I heard an incredible conversation between Dr. Nancy Snyderman, a medical correspondent for NBC News, and a specialist she was interviewing about brain cancer. The average survival rate for patients with Kennedy's type of brain tumor is twelve to eighteen months (the senator survived for fifteen months after his diagnosis), but the specialist said that he always emphasizes that such statistics reveal nothing about an individual patient's chances. He and Snyderman assured each other that there was no reason why any patient shouldn't hope to be in the 1 percent who live longer. To hear a highly respected neurologist say that survival statistics mean nothing on an individual basis is to understand that many doctors, probably because they view death as a professional defeat, conspire to deprive patients of information about the real odds they face.

Average survival statistics certainly do mean something, and they are particularly meaningful to the old. Senator Kennedy, a man who, at seventy-six, was still hard at work and clearly felt that he had a great deal more to do, chose surgery. At eighty-six, or ninety-six, he might have made an entirely different decision based on the same information.

But we can be certain that Kennedy, whose wealth and position as the Senate's leader on health care issues gave him access to all of the top specialists in the country, did not make his decision based on false hope offered by the kind of doctors who pretend that survival statistics ought to mean nothing to individuals. Furthermore, during the last months of his life—when it became clear that aggressive treatment could do nothing more to stop the tumor's growth—the senator opted for palliative care. He chose to spend his last weeks not in an intensive care unit but at his home, surrounded by family and presumably receiving a dosage of pain medication that kept him comfortable while still enabling him, according to his friends, to spend meaningful time with those he loved. Two weeks before he died, he went sailing with his wife.[9] His choice was clearly the one I describe as "Do everything possible until there is no longer any chance that I can survive as a competent human being." It seems absolutely clear that such choices ought to be encouraged at every level of the health care system. By "encouraged," I do not mean that people should be forced to stop medical care if they want to continue it but that they should be offered information—preferably when they are in good health—that will lead them to think about both their values and the practical choices available to the terminally ill. If something is not done to persuade more old people to make active choices about what they want done medically at the end of their lives—regardless of the lies that pandering politicians may tell their aging constituencies—at some point economics will dictate the kind of health care rationing that simply says no to individuals who want the kind of high-tech medical care that cannot provide any meaningful quality of life and can only delay an inevitable death. The default position will then shift to "do nothing beyond a certain point or beyond a certain age." And age-based rationing, as opposed to decisions based on the condition of and outlook for individuals, is the crudest, most ethically dubious—albeit the most cost-effective and the most likely—outcome of upholding social and medical customs that encourage patient passivity about end-of-life care.

A willingness to face the fact of death is, then, the first essential requirement for the good ending that nine out of ten Americans say they want but that only two out of ten actually experience. Wealth—certainly not the kind of wealth the Kennedy family possessed—is not essential, although enough money for home health care aides is. Anyone who has ever helped someone die at home knows that both Medicare and supplemental insurance policies are maddeningly inconsistent on the matter of what care they will pay for outside an institutional setting, although Medicare will pay and pay and pay to keep a comatose patient alive in an ICU. What is crucial, however—as important as money for home health care and the willingness of the individual to face death—is a loving caretaker. And that caretaker, as it was for Ted Kennedy, as it was for my father, is almost always a wife. Without my mother, my father could not have died at home, because both my brother and I lived more than a thousand miles away.

The last time I saw my father, Robert Jacoby, as a healthy man was in the summer of 1985, when he was diving into swimming pools, taking morning walks that sometimes began at four-thirty, and making his special gazpacho to distribute to his neighbors. He was only seventy-one, and having been blessed (and sometimes cursed) with extraordinary restless energy throughout his life, he seemed two decades younger than he was. In October, I flew off to England on a magazine assignment and stopped at the legendary Fortnum & Mason store in London to order a special Christmas present for Dad—a package that included some of his favorite Scottish shortbread and clam chowder. Fresh clams, like most of the seafood my father loved, were unavailable in Michigan, so he was always eager to find high-quality canned clam chowder. Dad was something of an Anglophile, and I anticipated his delight at opening a package with a label from Fortnum & Mason, purveyors to Her Majesty. I did not know that by Christmas, my father would be so nauseated from chemotherapy that he would scarcely be able to stand the sight of any food, fresh or canned. The phone call came from my father himself in November, and what he had to say could not have surprised me more than an announcement of plans for a trip to Mars. He had been diagnosed with lung cancer metastasized to the bone; all of the years of smoking unfiltered Camels had caught up with him. He managed to quit—too late—only in his mid-sixties. But Dad said he was going to "beat this thing." He was about to enter the hospital for a round of chemotherapy; there were new drugs; lung cancer wasn't always an immediate death sentence. At that time, however, there really were no drugs that could prolong the life of a patient in such an advanced stage of cancer. When a compassionate oncologist told my father there was no point in putting himself through a second round of chemo, he came home to die. My mother recalls, "We stopped on a corner just outside the hospital and I turned to Bob and said, 'Oh, I'm so glad you're coming home.' He turned to me and said, 'I'm not exactly glad to be coming home *today*'—meaning that he knew his leaving the hospital meant nothing else could be done."

One of the dirty little secrets about why so many people die in hospitals is that many of their partners do not want the serious and painful responsibility of seeing someone they love through his last months, weeks, or days. When a loved one's closing time on this earth is spent in a hospital, we are protected from the brutal physical reality of a life that is ebbing. Someone intubated in an ICU does not cry "Help" pitifully from the bedroom and leave a caretaker shattered by the realization of exactly how little she can do to help. In the hospital, urine and feces are removed by sanitary tubes and catheters; the sheets do not have to be changed. Nurses do the sedating and administer pain medication. My father's oncologist, unlike many in his specialty, did not abandon patients when there was nothing more he could offer to save their lives. He saw to it that my father had all the morphine he needed to blunt the pain that would increase before he died. He told my mother not to call 911 for at least a half hour after my father seemed to have stopped breathing, so that there would be no chance of emergency medical technicians trying to resuscitate him and take him back to the hospital. Mom gave my dad morphine every time he asked and knew that she was doing the right thing, but she still struggled with guilt because she also knew that she was hastening his death. "You can't escape the guilt," she says, "even though you know, and I did, that he did not want to go on living in this condition. To the very end, when I knew he had stopped breathing, I actually had to restrain myself from calling 911. It's a situation in which doing the right thing, the right thing for the other person, goes against your own selfish instincts."

I do not know whether any death can truly be called good, decent, or dignified. For me, the physical reality of the end, the flickering out, whether slow or fast, of brain neurons that have communicated with one another so brilliantly to form the life experience of one member of our species—one beloved member—overwhelms everything else. To an atheist, death—whether it comes as a thief in the night or through a sudden, violent confrontation—is no more and no less than the fate all humans share. Take away supernatural hopes and one is left with nature, which is neither decent nor indecent. The difference between "do everything" and "do everything—but stop when there is no more to be done" lies not in any spurious distinction between the "unnatural" (ventilators and tubes) and the "natural" (palliative care at home or in a hospice) but in the recognition that human intelligence itself is a part of and not the master of nature. Acceptance of the point at which intelligence and its inventions can no longer battle the ultimate natural master, death, is a true affirmation of what it means to be human. And if loving caretakers and a medical system informed by more humility cannot endow death with dignity or decency, they can at least offer a final forum in which human beings may talk to one another in ways that, for whatever reasons, were not possible in the past. In one of my last conversations with my father, he said, "The one thing I wish is that I could go knowing that you have a good man to love and take care of you." This comment hurt me (although I know he did not intend to be hurtful), because I would have given anything to fulfill my father's dying wish. But then my father added a coda that was one of the most important things he ever said to me: "You have to be willing to show people you need them. Don't be too proud to do that." This was deathbed advice I could use—and something I truly needed to hear and contemplate. "I'll really try, Daddy," I promised—and those were the last words I said to him. I cannot imagine such a conversation taking place had my father been hooked up to tubes in a hospital room, with strangers walking in and out and attending to his physical needs. To my mother, my father said in his last days, "I could never have made it without you." She cherishes the memory of that sentence, and she was the one who made it possible for him to say what he wanted to say, in a place where he was still Bob Jacoby and not only a helpless, dying patient.

If I could choose the manner of my death, it would resemble my father's and Ted Kennedy's endings. But one cannot assume the existence of a loving partner at one's side. One cannot assume that one's final illness will lend itself to palliative care that eases pain without destroying the mind weeks or even months in advance of death. And that is why I believe that physician-assisted suicide should be legal and available to the minority of people who want, in certain circumstances, to end their own lives. Suicide, the least chosen way of ending, requires even more thought and planning (sometimes with the collaboration of a caretaker and sometimes not) than a "natural" death at home in the United States. It cannot be said frequently enough that suicide is rare—though somewhat more common among the old than among younger adults. In a fact sheet on suicide, the National Institute of Mental Health reports that although people over sixty-five make up only 12 percent of the U.S. population, they account for 16 percent of suicide deaths. This sounds alarming, until one considers the rarity of all suicide; the overall suicide rate works out to 10.9 per 100,000 in the general population and 14.2 per 100,000 in the over-sixty-five population.[10] Most mental health authorities treat this disparity as if it were a scandal, but I would be astonished if the suicide rate among the old, given that many of them suffer from debilitating, incurable, and painful diseases, was *not* higher than it is among the young.* But the mental health establishment, for the most part, does not believe there is such a thing as a "rational" suicide; instead, most of the professionals attribute suicide—even by those who are terminally ill—to clinical depression that can and should be treated. In a long 1991 newspaper article on depression and suicide, Dr. Aaron Beck, a psychiatrist at the University of Pennsylvania, expressed what was then—and still is—the dominant medical view. "When people are facing death from illness, only a small percentage are suicidal," he said. "And what makes them suicidal is the depression, not the physical condition." The first part of this statement is true; the second is a professional and personal value judgment. Beck went on to argue that depressed patients are unable to see other ways out of their suffering and added, "Clinically, we find it's possible to correct these misperceptions with therapy. Afterward, these same patients who were so intent on suicide tell you they're grateful they're still alive."[11] I find this a presumptuous statement, because it assumes that suicidal depression is always irrational and that outsiders—specifically, professional outsiders—are always in a better position than the individuals

* These overall figures for broad age groups over and under sixty-five have not changed significantly, but between 2005 and 2007, the Centers for Disease Control reported a statistically noticeable rise in the suicide rate in the forty-five to fifty-five age group—from 16.3 to 17.6 per 100,000 Americans. Between ages seventy-five and eighty-five, the rate was 16.4 per 100,000. These figures—the most recent available—cannot be attributed to the economic crisis that became apparent in 2008, and experts have no real explanation. Some have speculated that the baby boomers' use of mind-altering prescription drugs may play a role, but that is only speculation. No one knows whether the rise in the middle-aged suicide rate will continue or whether suicide will become even more prevalent among Americans over sixty-five as the boomers age.

themselves to judge what depths of suffering a human being ought to be willing to tolerate to be considered a person of sound judgment. Individuals differ enormously in their tolerance for pain—both physical and emotional—throughout their lives. Who is a doctor to judge how much loss another person should tolerate before saying, "No more"? There are certainly many instances in which irrational depression leads to suicide—among young and old—and medical professionals, family, and friends should make every attempt to intervene. Some people, for example, interpret a diagnosis like cancer or multiple sclerosis as a death sentence—while others comprehend that their disease may be manageable and treatable for many years. In suicidal people who can enjoy a good quality of life with treatment, the leap to regarding a diagnosis as an immediate death sentence does represent distorted, depressed thinking. But sometimes a death sentence is just that—a death sentence. And depression, whether it leads to suicide or not, is a perfectly rational response to a terrible situation that cannot be changed. Nor do I think that terminal illness is the only rational reason for suicide. Alzheimer's, for example, is not terminal under the definition of Oregon's, Washington's, or Montana's assisted suicide laws—only these states permit physician-assisted suicide in the nation—but anyone diagnosed in the early stages of the disease faces the prospect of irreversible brain degeneration that may well take years to end in death. It is, in my view, much more rational to contemplate suicide at a time when one still has the capacity to act than it is to simply deny the terrible fate that awaits everyone with Alzheimer's, thereby condemning oneself through inertia to months or years of institutional care. If there is no one who loves you enough to take care of you even in the intermediate stages of the disease—and, make no mistake, only love makes it possible to tenderly look after the needs of someone whose mind is dying—a terrible choice must be made by an individual in the early stages of Alzheimer's. I am not suggesting that most people would or should commit suicide, even in these arduous circumstances, but that it is utterly irrational not to carefully consider the choice. Ideally, we would all have someone who loves us enough to accompany us through the valley of the shadow. In the real world, many people are denied this ultimate grace.

In the past fifty years, religious attitudes toward suicide have partaken of the medicalization of what used to be considered a mortal sin in Christian tradition. Indeed, most Protestant denominations and the

Roman Catholic Church, which once denied a Christian burial to suicides, have acceded to this medicalization in order to treat the families of suicides with more compassion. Whenever members of the faithful kill themselves, most churches now charitably assume that the balance of their minds must have been disturbed and that the dead cannot be damned for their actions. The dominant psychiatric interpretation of suicide as the outcome of pathological depression lends support to liberal religious forces that wish to absolve the suicide of moral culpability. The traditional Christian prohibition against suicide derives from the belief that only God has the power of life and death; therefore, the man who takes his own life is usurping God's prerogative.*

One of the most dubious denunciations of suicide, whether made from a religious or a therapeutic perspective, is that it represents the "easy way out." Not that I think there is anything morally wrong with taking the easy way out of irremediable suffering, but it is clear that suicide, if it really were easy, would be much more common than it is. Seneca was right in his famous catalog of all of the opportunities for suicide that lie close at hand, but, as a Stoic, he underestimated the degree to which the human desire to go on living makes it impossible for most people to avail themselves of such opportunities—even in the direst of circumstances. "Wherever you look," he wrote, "there is an end to your troubles. Do you see that precipice? That way you can drop to freedom. Do you see that sea, that river, that well? Liberty sits in their depths. Do you see that tree—stunted, blighted, and barren? Release hangs from its branches. Do you see your throat, your gullet, your heart? They are all escape-routes from servitude. Are the exits I show you too difficult, requiring too much courage and strength? Do you ask what is the straight route to freedom? Any vein in your body." As it happens, people find it just as difficult—maybe more—to cut open their veins as to jump off cliffs. Guns had not been invented in Seneca's day, but in the United States they are almost as common as veins and are the preferred weapon of suicide for men. (Men's greater familiarity with and willingness to use guns is considered the main reason why the suicide rate for American men is much higher than for women in all age groups.

* Right-wing Christian apologists for the death penalty, like U.S. Supreme Court Justice Antonin Scalia, get around the prohibition against man usurping the life-and-death power of God by asserting that the state, in imposing the death penalty, derives its power from God. An individual who commits suicide, however, must be either crazy or a sinner.

Women attempt suicide twice as frequently as men, but they are less likely to succeed because the method they prefer—usually an overdose of prescription drugs—is less certain.) One of the reasons why there is a movement in favor of physician-assisted suicide, however, is that most human beings, in the past and today, are reluctant to inflict the pain of violent suicide on themselves even if they are already in pain. The other reason is that even with a sophisticated array of pharmaceuticals, there is a good chance that a person, acting without professional help, will get it wrong and wind up, still alive, with a damaged brain. Taking a not-quite-lethal dose of drugs can be the equivalent of jumping off a cliff, landing in a tree, and winding up paralyzed instead of dead.

Oregon's Death with Dignity Act, which legalizes physician-assisted suicide (advocates of the law prefer to call it physician-assisted dying), was the result of a citizen initiative passed by a margin of 51 to 49 percent in 1994. After a long legal battle, the law went into effect in October 1997. In November of that year, voters ratified the act by a much wider margin, 60 to 40 percent. The law allows physicians, under extremely strict conditions, to prescribe a lethal dose of medication to be taken by a terminally ill patient (but not administered by the doctor) whose life expectancy is less than six months. In the thirteen years since the law went into effect, fewer than four hundred people have chosen to end their lives—another testament to the rarity of the desire to kill oneself, even in life's worst circumstances. It is not easy for a patient to qualify for the assistance of a doctor under the law. First, a physician must certify that the patient's life expectancy is no more than six months. The patient must then request the lethal dose on two separate occasions, separated by fifteen days, and must provide a written request, signed in the presence of two witnesses (at least one of them not related to the patient). A second doctor must confirm the patient's diagnosis and prognosis and ability to speak for himself or herself. Finally, a psychological consultation is required if the patient's physician suspects that he or she may be mentally impaired. But psychological consultations are not required in all cases, and that is one of the main arguments used against Oregon's system by those (especially psychiatrists) who oppose all laws permitting physician-assisted suicide.

American attitudes about suicide, spouse-assisted suicide, and physician-assisted suicide have undergone major changes in the direction of patient autonomy during the past four decades. Sixty-two percent of Americans under sixty-five say that individuals have a moral right to end their own lives if there is no hope of recovery. Only among evangelical Protestants is there a majority—57 percent—who say there is no right to commit suicide under any circumstances. Sixty percent of Roman Catholics, 73 percent of mainline Protestants, and 78 percent of secularists believe in a moral right to suicide. Over age sixty-five, the force of traditional religious prohibition is much stronger. Even so, 50 percent uphold a moral right to suicide for those who are terminally ill. What I find somewhat surprising is that 67 percent of Americans say that a spouse is either "sometimes" or "always" morally justified in helping a terminally ill husband or wife commit suicide, but the public is almost evenly split—46 percent in favor, 45 percent against—on the issue of physician-assisted suicide.[12] One wonders how the public thinks a spouse can assist in a suicide without the help of a physician willing to prescribe enough lethal drugs. It is a good deal easier to imagine helping a person commit suicide by handing him pills than by placing a gun in his hand. The disparity between support for physician-assisted suicide and spouse-assisted suicide may be attributed to a combination of distrust of the medical and legal establishment and respect for the traditionally privileged status of marriage. Furthermore, although there is majority support for both an individual's right to suicide and for spouse-assisted suicide at the end of life, only about a third of Americans say that they can actually imagine themselves committing such actions. Americans may trust their own decisions—however illegal they may be in the case of assisted suicide—more than they trust any public and legally sanctioned mechanism. Juries during the past thirty years have been generally lenient in cases where spouses have been tried for killing a desperately ill husband or wife—or a partner in the end stages of Alzheimer's. But jurors have also been lenient in the rare cases when doctors have been tried for assisting suicides. Juries in conservative Oakland County, Michigan, refused many times to convict Jack Kevorkian, whose medical license was revoked by the State of Michigan for having assisted people in committing suicide. Only when Kevorkian (known to his critics as Dr. Death) actually administered a lethal injection himself, instead of having the patient perform the act, was he tried for and convicted of homicide. Even then, he had to spell out the details of the case on *60 Minutes* before he was finally convicted. (The patient, a victim of amyotrophic lateral sclerosis, popularly known as Lou Gehrig's disease, was mentally competent but physically unable to do so much as push a button. ALS is a neuron motor disorder that eventually paralyzes its victims, leaving them with a functioning brain until they die of suffocation.) Kevorkian went to jail in 1999 and was paroled after serving only eight years and two months of a ten- to twenty-five year sentence for second-degree murder.

Throughout the late 1980s and 1990s, the growing mainstream interest in a right to die was demonstrated on many fronts. *Final Exit,* in effect a how-to manual on suicide and euthanasia by Derek Humphry, founder of the Hemlock Society, topped the *New York Times* best-seller list in 1991. The book is believed to have played an important role in raising consciousness of end-of-life issues, and a second edition was issued in 1997, the year Oregon's assisted suicide law went into effect. Under President George W. Bush, Attorney General John Ashcroft attempted to use federal drug laws to prosecute Oregon doctors who provided lethal prescriptions under the state's law. However, the U.S. Supreme Court, by a 6–3 vote in 2006, rebuked Ashcroft and the Bush Justice Department and upheld a Ninth U.S. Circuit Court of Appeals ruling that Ashcroft had made a "unilateral attempt to regulate general medical practices historically entrusted to state lawmakers" in an attempt to interfere with "the democratic debate about physician-assisted suicide."[13]

The most cogent assembly of arguments against assisted suicide—if you begin with the premise that suicide is always a tragedy—is presented in a volume titled *The Case Against Assisted Suicide: For the Right to End-of-Life Care* (2002), edited by Dr. Kathleen Foley, a neurologist and expert on palliative care, and Dr. Herbert Hendin, a noted psychiatrist and founding director of the American Foundation for Suicide Prevention. In their analysis of the Oregon law, Foley and Hendin seem particularly indignant about the fact that patients who are turned down by one doctor when they request a lethal prescription can then go to another physician who is more favorably disposed toward assisted suicide in general. But I fail to see why permitting people to choose a doctor who agrees with their values is unethical from a medical standpoint or mentally unbalanced from a patient's perspective. If I wanted an abortion, I would go to a Planned Parenthood clinic—not to a prenatal clinic run by the Roman Catholic Church. And if I were contemplating ending my life, I would go not to Hendin or Foley but to a physician who believes that suicide, in some cases, can be a rational decision. But Hendin and Foley denounce the Oregon Health Division, the state agency required to file reports on the Death with Dignity Act, for not interviewing physicians whose patients sought another doctor after the first doctor had refused their assisted suicide request. "To fairly evaluate the adequacy of the end-of-life care provided these patients," the authors argue, "OHD investigators would have needed to interview these [initial] physicians as well as those who participated in the assisted suicide. Instead, the OHD report treats physicians who declined to assist patients' suicides as though their opinions reflected a personal bias rather than perhaps a considered but different medical opinion."[14] But doctors have considered, differing medical opinions on many questions. As a patient, I pick the doctor whose opinion seems most sound to me medically and most in accord with my values. Why should physicians' differing opinions about writing a lethal prescription be placed in an entirely separate category from physicians' differing opinions about, say, the value of surgery versus oncology and radiation for a particular cancer patient? If I choose to limit my treatment to chemotherapy and radiation and die in short order, the state health department does not hold a hearing and ask my physicians to answer for my refusal to have an operation. As a mentally competent patient, I have the final word if I do not want surgery or any other form of treatment. Opponents of physician-assisted suicide argue that suicide falls within an entirely different ethical category because taking a lethal dose of drugs is an irreversible action, with the outcome known in advance. This is unquestionably an ethical issue for doctors, who may understandably consider any participation in assisted suicide a violation of their Hippocratic oath to give "no deadly potions." Yet doctors do prescribe deadly potions all the time (as my father's doctor did) in the knowledge that they may hasten death, but the primary intention is to relieve pain, not to cause death. (In theology, this is known as the principle of the double effect, originating in Thomas Aquinas's justification, laid out in the *Summa Theologica,* for killing in self-defense.) Certainly no health professional should ever be required to facilitate a suicide if such assistance violates his moral convictions—and no doctor is required to do so in Washington, Oregon, or Montana. But it is quite a different matter for doctors who oppose assisted suicide to insist that doctors with different moral and medical views should be prohibited from living out their own values. Like the majority of voters who have approved assisted suicide laws, I view statutes legalizing assisted suicide as a matter of the individual patient's autonomy, and the freedom of physicians to act as they see morally fit is an issue only when *all* doctors are prohibited—or required—to assist a patient in this process.

The psychiatric case against assisted suicide—and it is a case strongly influenced by Freudian determinism—is that there is no such thing as patient autonomy in this matter, because most people (actually, all people) who want to commit suicide are either badly informed or totally in thrall to their neurotic, depressive needs, including an excessive need for control of their own lives and deaths. This assumption—and it is very close to an a priori assumption for physicians with classical psychoanalytic training—leads to several conclusions. First, total opposition to assisted suicide privileges the professional judgment of those doctors who see depression and distorted mental processes in every would-be suicide. This notion of superiority as a result of professional training is highly suspect, since all psychiatrists and psychologists are trained—and rightly so—to see a suicide on their watch as a personal failure. That psychiatric training should drum this idea into future doctors is understandable: it *is* tragic when someone who may have many healthy years of life ahead of him commits suicide, because he sees no other way out of his emotional pain. But the situation is quite different for men and women who already have most of life behind them and who face a painful and inevitable death, whether in six months or a year. One of Hendin and Foley's objections to the Oregon suicide law is that no doctor can predict with pinpoint accuracy whether a person will die within six months. That is certainly true, but it is hard to see why it matters if someone chooses to commit suicide six months, eight months, or a year before he or she would have died.

Hendin and Foley also contend that seriously ill patients who seek assisted suicide have much in common psychologically with suicidal patients who are not ill. This may be true, but what suicidal patients of every age and state of health have in common psychologically is less important than the vast disparities in their physical conditions and in their prospects for a meaningful life over time. "Not all patients who want to die, with or without assistance, are clinically depressed," the authors concede. "Yet whether or not they are depressed, patients who request assisted suicide are similar to other suicidal patients in that they are usually ambivalent about their desire to die and are often expressing an anguished wish for help. When this ambivalence is not heard and such requests to die are taken literally and concretely, an assisted suicide can occur with the patient in a state of unrecognized terror."[15] In this view, even if patients do not meet the psychiatric criteria for clinical depression, they really don't mean it when they say that they want to die. Instead, they are expressing their terror of death by trying to set the time for and the conditions of their own dying. Doctor knows best. Serious illness deprives everyone of control. For such patients, Foley and Hendin say, "knowledge that they are going to end their lives or will be helped to do so can have a calming influence . . . that masks their depression and anxiety."[16] And this is wrong—why? Finally, the authors argue that because a "majority of those who request assisted suicide or euthanasia are not primarily motivated by current pain or suffering but by dread of what will happen to them in the future," palliative care is the real remedy for suicide among the ill. I absolutely agree that most people who seek out assisted suicide are motivated by fear of what will happen in the future rather than by what is happening to their bodies in the present. By the time pain becomes unbearable, people are unable to marshal their forces, think about what they would prefer, and assert their will—and must therefore rely on the kindness of strangers or relatives. I also agree that better access to palliative care for most patients—and the assurance that they will not be deprived of pain-relieving drugs—would prevent many suicides, assisted or not. I have the highest regard for palliative care and for those who provide it, professionally or personally. The two men I loved most in the world both died at home, with all of the palliative care needed to relieve their pain. But providing enough medication to completely relieve pain results in the eventual suppression of nearly all mental functioning—and while that seems a merciful trade-off for people who, like my father, retained the ability to talk and think until a few days before death, it can seem like a very bad trade-off if an individual lies comatose, or in a state of near unconsciousness, for weeks or even months. That is one reason why so many people die in hospitals or long-term care institutions instead of at home. As Ariès observes, death in a hospital offers the family a way out of observing the fate of a loved one suspended indefinitely between life and death, even though no extreme measures have been taken to preserve life. "Although it is not always admitted," he notes, "the hospital has offered families a place where they can hide the unseemly invalid whom neither the world nor they can endure. It also gives them a good excuse to let someone else deal with all those awkward visitors, so that they can continue to lead a normal life."[17] One reason many people cite for considering assisted suicide is that they do not want their families to witness the excruciating late stages of an illness that will inevitably end in death. Foley and Hendin dismiss such statements as "I don't want to be a burden to my family" as indicators of depression; what suffering patients need, the authors say, is "assurance that they are still wanted."[18] But in some instances, what a dying man or woman truly wants is not an exhortation to go on fighting but permission from loved ones to give up the struggle to live. Those who oppose assisted suicide in all cases refuse to concede that even though a dying patient may have full access to palliative care, he or she might prefer suicide—especially if a sympathetic lifelong partner agrees—to an uncertain ending in which it may not be possible to relieve pain without destroying the mind for a significant period of time. Foley and Hendin set up a false dichotomy in the title of their book. One does not have to be *against* assisted suicide to be *for* the right to decent end-of-life care. Opponents of legal assisted suicide also warn darkly of evil adult children who will be only too happy to hasten their parents' demise in order to free themselves of caretaking responsibilities and hasten the arrival of an inheritance. This is certainly a real possibility in some cases; history, literature, and police blotters tell us so. And so there must be strict legal safeguards, wherever assisted suicide is legal. But it makes about as much sense to criminalize all assisted suicide because there are some people who are willing to speed their parents' departure for financial reasons as it does to make all painkillers illegal because some patients abuse them.

There is yet another horror experienced by many relatives of the dying—an agonizing inability to respond to requests for help, in the form of an overdose of drugs, out of fear of legal consequences. A friend of mine still grieves, twenty years after the fact, over his failure to act when his longtime partner, Mark, was dying of AIDS and asked repeatedly if his lover couldn't give him "something" to hasten his end. "I was afraid of being prosecuted," says my friend, who was a medical writer at the time and knew exactly what drugs were needed. "There was a lot of anger toward me on the part of his family; his parents and brother never admitted he was gay until he was dying of AIDS. The right thing, the loving thing, was to get the drugs Mark wanted and give them to him. But I put my fears of legal jeopardy above everything else." The reporter Betty Rollin made a different choice when her mother, Ida Rollin, was dying of ovarian cancer and asked her daughter to use her investigative skills to find out what drugs, in what combination, would end her suffering. Ida had fought hard to live, going through a long course of aggressive chemotherapy. She was prepared to endure more when her doctor, realizing (though not explicitly saying) that nothing more could be done, sent her home from the hospital. She could afford the best possible palliative care at home, and her daughter and equally devoted son-in-law ("Don't call him my son-in-law, he's my son," Ida always said) lived nearby, but there came a time when palliative care no longer palliated anything. As Betty recounts in her book *Last Wish* (1985), by the time Ida asked her daughter to find out what combination of drugs would end her life, she was incontinent, in severe pain (in spite of the drugs she was taking), too nauseated to eat, and unable to leave her apartment. She told Betty, "Everything makes me sick now. This isn't life. If I had life I'd want it. I don't want this." Yet it was entirely possible that Ida might live several more months. "Mother," Betty asked, "is that what you really want—to die?" Ida replied firmly, "Of course I want to die. Next to the happiness of my children, I want to die more than anything in the world."[19] Betty found out what mix of drugs would enable her mother to end her life, and Ida took the pills herself. Her last words, as she drifted into sleep with Betty and her son-in-law, Ed, at her side, were:

> I want you to know that I am a happy woman. I made a man happy for forty years, and I gave birth to the most wonderful child, and late in life I had another child whom I love as if I had given birth to him too. No one has been more blessed than I. I've had a wonderful life. I've had everything that is important to me. I have given love and I have received it. . . . Remember, I am the most happy woman. And this is my wish. I want you to remember . . .[20]

Ida was most concerned that Betty and her husband not place themselves in legal jeopardy, and she planned every detail to avoid that possibility. Even so, when *Last Wish* was published, there was talk that Betty might be prosecuted for aiding a suicide. Manhattan's district attorney, Robert Morgenthau, a sensible and sensitive man, quickly put an end to the speculation by declining to prosecute. Ida Rollin's last words don't sound like the thoughts of a depressed or irrational woman; she sounds like a woman who was satisfied with what life had given her and who looked at a future she no longer wanted to endure with clear-eyed realism and with what might truly be called the wisdom of old age. Ida was in no doubt that she was loved deeply, and I think it is disgusting and disrespectful for anyone to suggest that what her daughter should have done, in response to her mother's explicit, sober, and carefully considered request for help in dying, was to send her off to a mental health professional to be evaluated for depression. Betty Rollin's mother was not asking for reassurance that she was wanted; she was asking for an exit from a life that, to her, was no longer worth living.

A very public suicide in 2009 by a 102-year-old St. Louis civic leader—unassisted by any doctor or relative—spoke directly to the issue of whether there is anything unbalanced about wanting to control the manner and time of one's own death. Isadore E. Millstone was not terminally ill, but he was clearly tired of a life in which he required a constant caretaker and could no longer do most of the things he enjoyed. He had been a builder, philanthropist, and leader in civil rights causes at a time when St. Louis, in the 1940s, was still very much a Southern city in its racial attitudes. One day, this determined man took the keys to his live-in caretaker's car, drove to the bank of the Missouri River, and jumped off a heavily traveled bridge. A star swimmer and diver in high school, Millstone had remained active athletically until his nineties—but various physical problems, including a shoulder injury, had left him unable to pursue the sports he loved. He had outlived two wives and both of his children. He left letters for several of his relatives, and only five weeks before his death, he had delivered a long speech, without notes, about his extraordinary life and the gratitude he felt for all that he had been given. Looking back after Millstone's suicide, many of his friends concluded that he had delivered his own eulogy. Millstone founded a construction company shortly after graduating from college, and he built many of the most famous landmarks in St. Louis. He directed much of his philanthropy toward the Jewish community and the needs of poor minorities. As the head of a construction company, he had refused to sign contracts in the 1940s and 1950s unless unions admitted African Americans. He started vocational schools for black men who wanted to enter skilled trades, such as bricklaying and welding, that had long been for whites only. After his memorial service, his grandson,

Mike Kuhn, said simply of his grandfather, "He was in charge of his life, and he was in charge at the end."[21] The suicide of a man who was so respected within the community, and who was not in imminent danger of dying, generated widespread discussion about the "right to die." As Bill McClellan, a columnist for the *St. Louis Post-Dispatch,* noted, it would have occasioned little comment if Millstone had chosen to die quietly at home by washing down an overdose of pills with a drink. People would have said he made a mistake, if anyone questioned the death of a 102-year-old at all. Instead, Millstone chose to leave no doubt about his intentions. "Maybe he didn't feel like 30," McClellan wrote. "Maybe he hadn't felt like 30 since he was 65. But maybe he felt like 80. Which is to say, he felt all right but not great. Limited. Or maybe he thought that life was like a banquet. He could remember his early days at the table with his parents and his siblings. Then in the fullness of life, his own family was at the table, his wife and his children. Then they left. Finally, despite the love of dining, he was ready to leave the table. . . . Enough, he said."[22] No doubt a psychiatrist could have been found to prescribe antidepressants to help this centenarian deal with his "unrecognized terror" of death. No doubt a social worker (had Millstone not had devoted grandchildren and enough money to stay out of the more authoritarian precincts of the "helping professions") could have been found to declare that the 102-year-old patriarch needed to be watched constantly so that he would not be in charge at the end. I think that the judgment of a man like Isadore Millstone and a woman like Ida Rollin should be respected. And I don't think that an old person who wants to say "Enough" should have to do so by jumping off a bridge or entreating a daughter to break the law in order to write a longed-for ending. We talk about the need to respect the wisdom of the old, yet we treat them like children who could not possibly know what is best for them. Outsiders—and they include members of the therapeutic priesthood as well as representatives of orthodox religion—have no right to impose their definition of a decent death on any human being. That less shock is engendered by the suicide of a centenarian than by the suicide of a young adult is not a manifestation of ageism but a realistic recognition that someone who has already lived to one hundred is going to die soon in any case and that he is perfectly within his rights to prefer death by a final dive to a slow death monitored by a professional caregiver and characterized by increasing incapacity.

Let us be honest with the old, and with their relatives, about what can and cannot reasonably be expected from medical treatment near the end of life. Let us offer palliative care liberally in nonhospital settings, so that people who do not want to die hooked up to machines are not forced to do so. But let us also respect the wishes of the few old people who have had enough and want to end their own lives on their own terms. Let us not insult them by dismissing their justified fear of lingering too long as a mental disorder. It is outrageous for opponents of assisted suicide to suggest that the only proper response to a loved one's expressed wish to die is to assure him that he is still needed. My lover and best friend did not ask me, or anyone else, to help him commit suicide when he was battling both cancer and Alzheimer's—and I don't think he would have done so even if his mind had not been clouded. But if he had asked, I hope that I would have had the courage not to turn away. And when he did say simply, and only in the last few weeks of his life, "I want to die," it would have been cruel and utterly selfish to reply, "Don't leave me. I still need you." And so I said, "You've fought harder than I thought anyone could. You can rest now." I assured him that I would always love him, and that I would remember him in my last lucid moment on earth. "But I won't know that," he replied, with a faint smile and a flash of the ironic humor that still dwelled in some synapse of his failing brain.

CHAPTER TEN

The Ethics of Longevity: An Argument in Search of Facts

And nothing 'gainst Time's scythe can make defence
Save breed, to brave him when he takes thee hence.

—William Shakespeare, Sonnet 12

I don't want to achieve immortality through my work. . . .
I want to achieve it through not dying.

—Woody Allen

If 90 could really become the new 50, there is no logical reason—apart from the problem of what to do with so many more people occupying space on a crowded planet—why anyone should object to scientific research that might extend the average human life span to, say, 120, thereby putting off uncomfortable questions about old-age poverty, the likelihood of dementia, end-of-life care, living wills, and assisted suicide for several decades. Strange as it may seem to boomers with immediate concerns about whether they will outlive their savings even without taking anti-aging drugs, an intense debate is being conducted, mainly among scientists, bioethicists, and theologians (the two latter groups sometimes indistinguishable to a lay observer), about whether it is morally right to engage in basic scientific research aimed solely or primarily at extending the outer limits of the current life span rather than targeting specific diseases.

It is tempting to dismiss the argument over anti-aging research as nothing more than an "elitist" pastime: one can only imagine the public response if an American president, in his next State of the Union address, were to propose launching a "war on death before 120," as President Nixon declared a "war on cancer." Age 120 is an arbitrary figure, but it is in the ballpark of estimates by serious scientists of feasible extended life spans. Richard A. Miller, the University of Michigan gerontologist who has suggested that anti-aging science might be able to extend the average life span by up to 40 percent (see p. 88), also notes, apparently with a straight face, that claims in the mass media suggesting that people might live two hundred to six hundred years are not backed up by scientific evidence. This lamentable lack of evidence, he adds, even applies to claims "by accredited gerontologists."[1] And I was so sure that any claim made by an "accredited gerontologist" must be true! In any event, whether the putative American president had been talking about living to 114, 120, or 200, psychiatrists would surely jam the airwaves and the blogosphere the day after his speech with warnings that the chief executive's sanity must be evaluated under the provisions of the Twenty-fifth Amendment (although, given the advanced age of some powerful members of the House and Senate, the willingness of Congress to remove such a president from office is far from a foregone conclusion).

The seemingly abstract debate over the ethics of longevity extension is, however, closely related to many of the practical social dilemmas created by our ambivalent attitudes about old age and death in the present, not the future. The myth of the new old age provides both a precondition for and the backdrop against which arguments play out for and against research that might one day enable genetic manipulation of longevity. Without the hype promoting the idea that it is possible not merely to improve one's health and sense of well-being but also to vanquish aging itself by strict monitoring of health habits in young adulthood, it is hardly likely that more than half of Americans under thirty, and more than a third of older adults, would want to live to one hundred—much less beyond. That is why Americans spend billions of dollars each year on anti-aging dietary supplements, at best neutral placebos and at worst downright harmful. The ubiquitous "clinically proven effective" line in commercials is one of the more clever deceptions in advertising. Products unregulated by the Food and Drug Administration cannot make the assertion that they are "scientifically proven effective" because they have not been tested in double-blind clinical trials—that is, trials overseen by researchers under controlled medical conditions in which one group is administered a drug and one a placebo. The adjective "clinical" in advertising means something different; it simply indicates that people who have taken the supplements believe that the products work. Thus, the term "clinically proven" in a tagline for a commercial means that the product in question has *not* been evaluated in a scientific clinical trial. For an American public already eager to believe in the value of scientifically untested anti-aging formulas, it is even easier to invest excessive hope in real scientific research dedicated to the premise that within this generation's life span, there may be true, scientifically kosher miracle drugs, targeted to a particular aging gene or genes, that will enable everyone to live not only a much longer but also a much healthier life.

It is not always easy and it may be impossible to separate the quest for longevity from the age-old human longing for immortality. Arthur Caplan, director of the Center for Bioethics at the University of Pennsylvania, observes that longevity is frequently confused with immortality in ethical arguments about anti-aging research. "No technology is available or even foreseeable that will make immortality possible anytime in the lives of anyone reading this, or their kids, or their kids' kids. Live a lot longer? Maybe. Live forever? Not a chance anytime soon. The debate is really about living a lot longer than we now do, not living forever."[2] I am not at all sure, though, that immortality is ever really off the emotional agenda (even if that agenda is unacknowledged) of either scientists or the general public. MSNBC put the catchy headline "It's Not Immoral to Want to Be Immortal" above Caplan's article; "It's Not Immoral to Want to Live Longer" would have failed to pack the same punch. Another peculiar aspect of the debate, especially in the United States, is the contradiction between Americans' desire to live ever-longer lives and their stated religious convictions that a better life is waiting, in the words of the old spiritual, in the sweet by-and-by. More than three-quarters of Americans say that they believe in life after death; with characteristic American optimism, many more believe in heaven than in hell. Death, for these religious believers, still has a sacred meaning as the door to eternal life. It is strange, however, that Americans can simultaneously embrace the immortality of the human soul and commit themselves to getting every last bit of bodily mileage out of medical technology and Big Pharma. Believers from the most conservative precincts of Christianity are among the strongest opponents of research focusing directly on the extension of longevity, because they see the anti-aging battle as a hubristic attempt to interfere with

God's prerogatives. Yet in this scheme of thought, keeping brain-dead people technically alive with machines is not a violation of God's plan, because turning a machine off is an affirmative human decision and—who knows?—maybe prayer will effect a miracle. Americans with a secular orientation are most likely to leave living wills opposing the use of technology to prolong physical existence if there is no hope of recovery. Secular arguments against pro-longevity research—at least they are framed in terms that appear secular—substitute nature for God. Because aging and death are characteristic of all plant and animal species, tampering with generally known limits to the life expectancy of humans is seen by some secular philosophers as a violation of nature's plan. But, as Caplan notes, "nature has no interest in how long any species lives—as long as it lives long enough to reproduce."[3] Humans, by contrast, are extremely interested in how long they are going to live. Nature may be indifferent to us, but we are not indifferent to what nature inevitably (*not* inevitably, say the researchers who want to extend longevity) does to us. That is why I do not think the lure of physical, as distinct from spiritual, immortality can truly be separated from the ideal of pain-free, decrepitude-free extended old age with a much more distant terminus. Nearly every writer (including bioethicists) who considers the subjects of aging and immortality eventually gets around to the poignant scene from *The Odyssey* in which Odysseus decides to take his leave of the alluring goddess Calypso to return to his human wife, Penelope. He tells Calypso:

> *Don't be angry my lady goddess.*
> *I know that gentle Penelope is no match for you*
> *In beauty and grace, for she is a mortal woman,*
> *Unlike you, a goddess*
> *Who will never grow old and die.*
> *Even so, I long for the day that I can return home.*
> *And if some god overturns me on the wine-dark sea,*
> *I will endure this fate too,*
> *For I have suffered much on the sea and in battle.*
> *Let one more trial be added to my story.*[4]

Odysseus's return to the travails of suffering humanity and his rejection of infinite pleasure among the immortals are seen as the morally superior choice not only by conservative bioethicists but by nearly all writers in the Western classical tradition. The novelist Robert Hellenga uses the exchange between Odysseus and Calypso in a scene in which college students are asked by their professor to consider the drawbacks of immortality. The teacher tells his class that "it's a question of what attitude we take towards our fantasies, towards our deepest wishes. We want sexual gratification; we want to escape death. That seems to be the bottom line. But then we find another line below that one. And to me this is the most important thing of all. Better to live out your life with a real woman, or a real man, than with a sex god or goddess."[5] Yes, but Odysseus was faced with a clear-cut choice. His decision to go home would have been easier had he been offered a choice between certain immortality on Calypso's island and returning to a Penelope who might not grow old or die anytime soon—who would possess, as would Odysseus himself, the kind of conditional immortality that is the paradoxical promise of anti-aging drugs.

"Why must we die?" is the anguished question that resurfaces throughout Western literature; it is the question that separates humans from the other species supposedly entrusted to our inept dominion by the God of the Bible. This is a very different question from "Why must we die so soon?" The traditional Christian answer—that we are mortal because we ignored the warning of the God of Genesis and ate of the fruit of the tree of knowledge—has been transformed into the secular injunction to accept the indifferent mandate of nature. Odysseus's response is closer to the post-Darwinian natural imperative than it is to the Christian answer. But humans in every era have been no more disposed to accept the rule of nature than the one rule laid down by God in Eden, so the question of whether aging as we know it today is "natural" is the first mistaken turn in the ethical debate about longevity. The human species has always intervened in nature—wisely and unwisely; sometimes supported and sometimes opposed by either civil or religious authorities; and always with unintended as well as intended consequences. It hardly seems useful to quarrel about whether attempting to intervene in the aging process itself differs in any ethically significant way from the invention of the wheel or the smallpox vaccination or the manufacture of penicillin. The question of whether aging is "natural" or ought to be scientifically classified as a disease (after all, what is more natural than disease?) seems to me much less important, from an ethical as well as a practical standpoint, than whether the battle for the extension of longevity ought to be a social priority. In exploring that issue, almost as little guidance can be expected from the serious science dealing with longevity as from the hype generated by the bogus "anti-aging" industry of untested and unregulated dietary supplements; Internet sites encouraging microscopic scrutiny of every health habit; "age-defying" cosmetics; and plastic surgery that turns wrinkled old people into unwrinkled (for a moment in time) old people who can barely smile or frown. The only thing to be said, with complete certainty, is that an almost unimaginable amount of money will be made by the first company to come up with a longevity extension drug thought to be based on science rather than fantasy.

The State of the Science

The real science of anti-aging is relatively new, and there is considerable disagreement among scientists themselves, even without introducing ethical questions into the mix, about the significance of the results of investigations into longevity that have already been conducted in other species. It has been known for some years that certain rodents live longer when placed on a severely restricted diet, in which they take in 30 percent fewer calories than laboratory rats and mice fed an ordinary diet. Since it would be futile to expect humans to cut their caloric intake by that much, one of the major focuses of pro-longevity research today is the development of a drug or drugs that would imitate, in the human body, the anti-aging effects of caloric restriction in laboratory experiments. The fact that many drugs found effective in rodents do not work in the more complex human organism has produced a good deal of the skepticism that exists within the scientific community about the potential effectiveness of anti-aging drugs that might one day make it to market. Biologists do not even agree on the meaning of twenty-year studies in rhesus monkeys, a primate species much closer to *Homo sapiens* than mice are to men. A study begun more than twenty years ago at the University of Wisconsin showed that monkeys fed 30 percent fewer calories died at about one-third the rate from causes associated with old age as those fed a normal diet. (Since monkeys live an average of twenty-seven years and a maximum of forty, the results are not all in yet. The Wisconsin researchers expect the calorie-restricted monkeys to live 10 to 20 percent longer than the nondieting monkeys.) Richard Weindruch, professor of medicine at the University of Wisconsin, says the study means that "much of the biology of caloric restriction is translatable into primates, which makes it more likely it would apply to humans."[6] Not so fast, say other biologists. It seems that the Wisconsin researchers, in their monkey death total, excluded all deaths not thought to result from aging—such as from endometriosis (a condition in which tissue similar to the uterine lining grows in other parts of the body) or under anesthesia while a blood sample was being taken. As is well known from many studies on humans, anesthesia-related deaths and severe surgical complications in general are more common in the elderly than in young adults. "Ultimately the results seem pretty inconclusive at this point," said Steven Austad, a biologist at the University of Texas Health Science Center. "I don't know why they didn't wait longer to publish." Austad also pointed out that some of the deaths may have been due to the severe caloric restriction itself.[7]

Caloric restriction was the area of research described by Harvard's David Sinclair in his 2008 comments that so excited the standing-room-only audience at the World Science Festival session on whether ninety might become the new fifty. As already noted (see p. 8), Sinclair's company, Sirtris Pharmaceuticals, is now conducting clinical trials in humans of drug formulations—the particular compounds being tested are called sirtuin activators—to assess their impact on diabetes. The sir-2 gene was discovered as a result of research conducted by Sinclair and Leonard P. Guarente, of the Massachusetts Institute of Technology, in a project attempting to identify genes that might prolong the life span of the familiar single-cell organism yeast. It turns out that both mice and humans possess sir-2 genes, which produce proteins, called sirtuins, that seem to be activated when energy reserves in a cell have fallen to a low level—a process that occurs naturally in the body if calories are severely restricted.

Should Sirtris's drugs prove effective in the treatment of diabetes or any other disease, the question is whether most of the drugs would be prescribed for specific illnesses or for the off-label use of "defying" old age. I would be willing to bet that any drug rumored to have anti-aging properties—once approved by the FDA to treat a specific disease—will soon be prescribed more frequently to people who simply want to remain forever young than to patients with a particular illness. I can envisage a commercial saying something like, "You've heard about the chemical that makes mice live longer—but now we know it can help treat people suffering from _____." Fill in the blank with anything the FDA considers a disease. The main advertisement would be followed by the usual caveats required by law, including a statement that "there is no evidence that this drug has anti-aging benefits in humans." Wink, wink. It cannot be said often enough that it is impossible in a clinical trial that lasts, at most, a few years to demonstrate that any drug intervention increases longevity. But that is certainly not going to stop millions of people who already spend huge amounts on anti-aging products with no scientific pedigrees at all from doing everything possible to get their hands on a drug that at least has a scientific imprimatur for another purpose. Moreover, the primary contention of the most enthusiastic anti-aging researchers is that it is more efficient to target genes that control the overall aging process than to search for the genes that provide pathways to specific age-related diseases. Therefore, more money ought to be spent on anti-aging science. This argument was articulated most forcefully by Miller in 2002:

> If we—the good guys who favor preventive medicine and medical research—accept the idea that it would be worthwhile to prevent late-life illness and thus prolong the period of healthy active life, then we ought to note that researchers are very far from developing any method that can, even in laboratory rodents, prevent cancer, osteoporosis, immunosenescence, heart or kidney disease, cataracts, or indeed any other of the troublesome concomitants of old age. We can, however, routinely retard *all* of those tribulations at the same time, at least in laboratory mammals, by well-validated methods. We do not know how these interventions work and are not likely to figure this out without a substantial investment of money and brainpower.[8]

One might infer from this passage that researchers devoting all of their time to specific diseases are "the bad guys." This is partly an argument about money and competitiveness within the scientific community—

a not-so-subtle plea for the government and private foundations to transfer some of the research dollars now dedicated to finding cures for specific diseases into the laboratories of those doing basic research on aging. But even if scientists like Miller are right—and aging is the Disease, with a capital *D,* responsible for all other diseases that attack the old—it is certainly possible that a greatly extended life span would simply put off the mental and physical illnesses that afflict so many of the old old in the last decades of life now. Whether it would benefit humanity if, instead of developing Alzheimer's at eighty and living to ninety, more people developed Alzheimer's at ninety and lived to one hundred is certainly an arguable question. Are ten more years of life that precious if the final act plays out in the same agonizing way? This is not a rhetorical question for individuals or for the human species, and the answer is not as obvious as it appears to those whose initial response is, "Whoopee, ten more years is ten more years." At first glance, the issue seems like a no-brainer: extra years without Alzheimer's would be an unequivocal good. But if one is still fated to develop Alzheimer's, even at a later stage, it is not at all unreasonable to wish for death from another cause before the brain begins to decay. I, personally, would rather see the discovery of an effective treatment or preventative for the scourge of Alzheimer's than a significant increase in life expectancy. This is, however, an entirely theoretical and possibly a false choice. We may get neither or both outcomes. Or one. And if the one turned out to be increased life expectancy with brain degeneration at the end, I would argue that science has done us no favor. But the tantalizing possibility held out by pro-longevity researchers is that people might live much longer *and* remain healthy until the end. The great advantage enjoyed by those promoting this theory is that by the time any scientist can declare, on the basis of a controlled clinical trial, that a drug thought to have general anti-aging properties as well as specific disease-fighting capabilities has actually extended life by more than a few healthy years, subjects who are now in their fifties will have to have lived, in disproportionate numbers, into their tenth and eleventh decades of life. But no one would ever know how difficult the longevity hypothesis is to test from the excited tone of the news accounts that always appear when some substance is found to extend the life span of mice.

There was tremendous excitement in the general press, for instance, when it was announced that the drug rapamycin—used in humans as an immunosuppressant to prevent organ rejection after transplants—had been shown to increase the life span of mice by 9 percent in males and 13 percent in females.[9] In human years, the mice were around sixty when the drug was first administered—a significant finding, because one of the major obstacles to manipulation of the aging process is that many interventions found effective in laboratory animals work only if they begin in young adulthood or sooner. (Even in humans, theoretically aware of their own mortality, it would surely be much easier to get a sixty-year-old to take an anti-aging drug than to get a twenty-year-old to do so. Persuading people with no symptoms of illness to take drugs—even if a symptomless, life-threatening condition like high blood pressure has been unequivocally diagnosed—is a chronic problem in medical practice.) The results of the rapamycin study are part of an ongoing effort, financed by the National Institute on Aging, to monitor possible anti-aging drug testing on mice. A *New York Times* roundup article on longevity research, published ten days after the rapamycin results were documented in *Nature* magazine, was accompanied by a huge picture of two hands—one gnarled and liver spotted, the other as plump, youthful, and filled with natural collagen as any hand used to sell nail polish or anti-aging creams in advertisements by cosmetic companies. The article was excellent and accurate, but the visual portrayal of hands, in terms of fueling fantasies about eternal youth, was worth several thousand words.[10] When one considers the purpose for which rapamycin is actually used in human medicine now—to mute the normal responses of the immune system in order to prevent transplant rejection—the difficulties of administering any similar drug to an older population, more vulnerable to infections than the young, are obvious. Even if the drug turned out to be one of the minority of medications that work as well in men as in mice, it would seem a bad bargain to gain pink young skin and then to be carried off by pneumonia because a weakened immune system was unable to fight off the common cold. The ground rules for clinical trials ensure against any possibility that the immunosuppressant as currently formulated would ever be tested widely on healthy humans. Nevertheless, it is devoutly to be hoped that only a minuscule number of the millions of Americans who want to live to one hundred have access to rapamycin, because some fountain of youth enthusiasts would surely attempt to test the drug's potential anti-aging properties on themselves.*

One of the major dilemmas inherent in all basic research attempting to identify the role of specific genes in individual diseases or in the overall process of aging—and this phenomenon is familiar throughout the history of science—is that the more scientists learn, the more they learn about what they do not know. Since the human genome was fully decoded seven years ago, researchers throughout the world have been comparing the genomes of sick people and healthy people in an effort to target genes implicated in common diseases. Scientists had theorized that only a small number of genes, carried by large numbers of people, were responsible for the most prevalent serious illnesses, but the reverse has turned out to be the case. After more than one hundred genome decoding projects conducted by research teams studying thousands of patients in many countries, several widespread gene variants have been found—but they explain only a small percentage of the total genetic risk for diseases. Writing in a special issue of *The New England Journal of Medicine* on the state of genomic research, the Duke University geneticist David B. Goldstein argues that large numbers of genetic variants—hundreds or even thousands—may be implicated in common diseases like Type 2 diabetes. "In pointing at everything," Goldstein writes, "genetics would point at nothing." Only extremely rare diseases, such as Huntington's and early-onset Alzheimer's, are caused by one specific gene mutation. "The apparently modest effect of common variation on most human diseases and related traits probably reflects the efficiency of natural selection in prohibiting increases in disease-associated variants in the general population," Goldstein suggests.[11] As genetic researchers focusing on Alzheimer's have discovered, the much more common late-onset Alzheimer's is influenced by a wide variety of "susceptibility genes." A study headed by Bruce Yankner at Harvard Medical School has identified at least 440 genes in the brain's frontal cortex—which controls complex learning as well as long-term planning—that begin to work less efficiently after age forty. The study's ultimate goal—which

* Indeed, the rapamycin researchers do not even know how the drug works to slow aging in mice; they know only that it inhibits a protein called TOR (target of rapamycin). The scientists do not know exactly how the TOR pathway might be implicated in the progression of age-related disease.

is nowhere in sight for researchers now—is to find out which genes play the most important role in determining who makes it through old age without severe dementia.[12] Most of the *New England Journal* commentaries were bad news for biotech companies trying to market "personal genomic testing" as a way for individuals to assess their future risk for serious but extremely common diseases. If genomic testing can identify only those genes responsible for a tiny proportion of a person's total genetic risk of a disease, the tests may produce either false reassurance or excessive worry—with no means of prevention—for the average person. In *The New England Journal,* two geneticists caution:

> One argument in favor of using the available genetic predictors is that some information must be better than no information, and we should not let the perfect be the enemy of the good by refusing to make use of our knowledge until it is more complete. Why not begin testing for common genetic variants whose associations with susceptibility to disease have been established?
>
> The answer lies in the stability of the current risk estimates. Genetic variants conferring the highest relative risks are almost certainly overrepresented in the first wave of findings from genome-wide association studies, since considerations of statistical power predict that they will be identified first. *However, a striking fact about these first findings is that they collectively explain only a small proportion of the underlying genetic contribution to most studied diseases.* (italics mine)[13]

Debate over whether the breakdown of the body in old age is inevitable can, at times, seem ridiculous to nonscientists—with the exception of those who believe, with a near-religious fervor, that a "cure" or "treatment" for human aging itself is imminent. Most (though not all) evolutionary biologists contend that there is a rate of aging intrinsic to each species, depending on its complexity and adaptation to its environment. They agree with most cultural historians and historians of science that the near doubling of average life expectancy since the middle of the nineteenth century is due largely to modifications of an environment that used to be more hostile to human life. The nineteenth-century discovery that many diseases are transmitted by bacteria, followed by fundamental improvements in sanitation systems, had nothing to do with the biology of aging or the intrinsic susceptibility of humans to disease. Some of the greatest medical advances of the twentieth century, including antibiotics and vaccines, simply provided the body with a defense against infectious diseases that it could not mount on its own. Most evolutionary biologists and geneticists believe it unrealistic to expect that the fundamental process of aging, and all of its associated diseases, can be affected by pharmacological intervention in a single gene. Writing in *Nature* magazine, Jan Vijg, chairman of the genetics department at the Albert Einstein College of Medicine of Yeshiva University, and Judith Campisi, senior scientist at the Lawrence Berkeley National Laboratory, argue that while the biology of aging is similar in species as different as yeast and humans, "the response of simple organisms to interventions might not be predictive [of extended life expectancy] when complexity increases, or when physiology deviates significantly from humans." Thus, they assert, the hope of using a drug in humans to produce the same effect as severe caloric restriction in mice "may be an illusion."[14] They caution that "there are still enormous gaps in our knowledge about how metabolic pathways operate and interact; serious side effects may constrain the effectiveness of pharmacological interventions."[15] The evolutionary biologists generally believe that, regardless of how many cures are found for numerous diseases, there is still a continuing buildup of damage to DNA over time. This wear and tear, in turn, disrupts the genetic instructions that help most of the young maintain much healthier bodies than most of the old. The internal instructions that say "No you don't" to a developing cancer cell, for instance, become less and less effective with age. In this view, progressive damage to DNA is, in the long term, irreversible—although that does not rule out the possibility of somewhat longer life spans.

These conclusions return the argument, in circular fashion, to the question of why humans must die at all. The English biologist Thomas Kirkwood, quoted in the *Times* article accompanied by dramatic pictures of a tired old hand and a perky young hand, says that old people die eventually because of the constant effort required to keep body cells operating. "This [effort], in the long run," he contends, "is unwarranted—in terms of natural selection, there are more important things to do." That is simply another way of stating that nature does not care how long we live if we live long enough to reproduce. Such cautionary talk inflames the competitive juices of researchers dedicated to extending the human life span. The experimental biologist Gary Ruvkin of Massachusetts General Hospital, one of the lead investigators on a study of longevity extension in roundworms, says tartly, "My rule of thumb is to ignore the evolutionary biologists—they're constantly telling you what you can't think."[16] So there, take that, you wrongheaded pessimists. There is no doubt that aging researchers will continue to ignore the evolutionary biologists—and there is no scientific reason why they should listen to other scientists who are telling them that their life's work is unlikely to succeed anytime soon. The acknowledgment that we must all die eventually is neither a convincing scientific nor ethical argument against research designed to prolong life before death. And scientists like Vijg, Campisi, and Kirkwood are not saying their colleagues should refrain from research aimed at extending the human life span; they are saying that it's not going to be easy. The biogerontologists seem angrier at the evolutionary biologists than vice versa—probably because challenges to the feasibility of developing an effective, safe, single-bullet anti-aging drug are more likely than any high-flown ethical arguments to forestall the expansion of government funding for biogerontological research. The more speculative the science seems and the more distant and uncertain the payoff, the less likely it is that serious aging research will receive enough public money to fairly test its hypothesis that healthier, longer living through chemistry is not only possible but attainable within the near future.

But Is It Right?

The investment of passion in an ethical debate about the applied science or technology of the future is a relatively rare phenomenon. Educated people in New England in the eighteenth century, like the future president John Adams and his wife, Abigail, were already using an early form of smallpox immunization, known as variolation, on their children when Puritans who still clung to the doctrine of strict predestination asserted that failing to submit to smallpox was an insult to divine hegemony.* Anesthesia had already been administered effectively (most

* In fact, some Puritans—most notably the fire-breathing preacher Cotton Mather—supported even the earliest methods of immunization and encouraged their use throughout New England. The method used by the Adams family—called variolation (after the Latin word *varus,* for the disfiguring marks left by smallpox) or inoculation—involved the injection of tiny amounts of

notably, to Queen Victoria for the delivery of her eighth and ninth children in 1853 and 1857) when some fire-and-brimstone preachers began decrying the use of chloroform and ether as a violation of God's injunction to the disobedient Eve that "in sorrow thou shalt bring forth children." The efficacy of the birth control pill had already been demonstrated when the spiritual descendants of both Puritans and "papists" began decrying the new method of contraception as a spur to promiscuity. In general, even the most judgmental people tend to shy away from pronouncements about the morality of scientific research in the absence of practical results that, in any case, probably lie far in the future. The all-too-human tendency to put off thinking about anything that has not already occurred is not necessarily a good thing: those who tried to sound an early tocsin about the hidden time bomb of bad debt propping up the American economy at the turn of the millennium were ignored, not only by the public but by financial leaders, until the housing market crashed in 2008.

The ethics of aging research, however—like the ethics of any stem cell research that hints at human cloning—are a conspicuous exception to the rule that even intellectuals find it hard to work themselves into a state of high moral dudgeon over something, good or bad, that has not yet happened. In the case of aging research, part of what inflames the ethical chattering classes is the inordinate amount of publicity devoted to any scientific project that involves the promise of longer life. Every time someone finds a new way to extend the life span of mice, worms, or fruit flies, the discovery is translated by the mass media into the idea that very soon we will all be able to get an anti-aging shot along with

---

smallpox virus under the skin of nonimmune individuals. The inoculator usually poked the skin with a lancet dampened with fresh pus taken from a smallpox victim, and the person being inoculated would hopefully endure only a mild case of smallpox. In spite of the primitive and somewhat risky nature of the procedure (children who had been inoculated were isolated to prevent their transmitting fresh cases of smallpox to others and were sick for several weeks), the death rate was ten times lower among those who had been inoculated than among people who caught smallpox "the natural way" during an epidemic. In 1796, the great British scientist and physician Edward Jenner developed the much safer method of vaccinating children with pus from infected cows. The fluid from cows produced a mild case of pox and provided immunity in humans from future infection by the much more deadly strain of human smallpox. Unlike earlier inoculation, Jenner's cowpox vaccination procedure carried little risk of death or spreading infection, and within twenty years had replaced variolation. One of the earliest success stories in what can be considered modern medicine, Jenner's experiments are considered the basis of immunology.

our annual flu shot. And just as predictably, a heavyweight bioethicist will find it necessary to remind us sententiously that dying is a part of living and ask where we would be today if no one had ever died. Then another influential bioethicist—one more favorably disposed toward immortality—will weigh in and point out that we've managed to get along all right as human life expectancy has doubled over the past century and a half and that we can surely figure out what to do if, in the next century, it becomes necessary to change the lyric "Over the river and through the woods to Grandmother's house we go" to "Over the river and through the woods to Great-great-grammy's house we go." (Figuring out how to make that lyric scan will be one of the challenges of the ageless society.)

The titillating power of longevity and immortality stories, however, is not the whole explanation for the ethical brouhaha over anti-aging research. Like the debate over stem cell research that could facilitate human cloning, the prospect of a greatly (as distinct from a slightly) expanded life span raises some basic fears about a forced redefinition of what it means to be human. A core Western (particularly American) value is that the individual is unique, irreplaceable, and unreproducible: cloning would pose a direct challenge to the exaltation of individuality. In similar fashion, the awareness of all humans, in every culture, of their own mortality is a core characteristic that separates the human species from all others. Anything that raises the possibility of a much more plastic human life span calls into question a wide variety of institutions, customs, and beliefs. The most important threatened belief is the conviction that death—a literal deadline—is what gives life meaning. To be sure, Caplan is right when he says that living much longer, not living forever, is the only real issue in the laboratory now. But the prospect of living decades longer than most people do today produces an existential anxiety that, for some, is even more powerful than the fear of death. Who would I be if I could expect to live not another twenty or thirty years but another half century? What would I be doing? What would I be able to do? What would the world be like? Would my loved contemporaries be alive too, or would an anti-aging drug work for only some members of my generation? Would there, for the first time, be a lot more old people than young people walking around, and what would that mean? These are extremely disturbing questions—perhaps all the more so because their unsettling nature does not in any way negate the powerful individual desire to cheat death as long as possible.

Conservative ethicists, who see pro-longevity research as a dangerous business, rarely base their arguments on religion, but there is a distinctly theological cast to their contention that some aspects of human experience, and of nature itself, ought to be left alone by scientists too inquisitive for their own good. Leon Kass, chairman of the President's Council on Bioethics under George W. Bush, has said and written frequently that "the finitude of human life is a blessing for every individual, whether he knows it or not." Even if that is true, there is no evidence that finitude at eighty, if people did not succumb as early as they do now to degenerative diseases, is more of a blessing than finitude at ninety or one hundred. What seems to concern Kass is not so much the length of life as the temerity of researchers who wish to manipulate the process of aging and give themselves credit, in God-like fashion, for the extension of longevity. "Killing the creature made in God's image is an old story," Kass says. "Redesigning him after our own fantasies: That's what's really new."[17] One of Kass's weirder scenarios is that people would be less likely to have children if the average life span increased significantly. For someone who believes in an intrinsic "human nature," it seems odd to suspect that humans would stop wanting to reproduce simply because they thought they might live to 100 or 120 rather than 80. If there is any immutable natural urge built into our species, it is the urge to reproduce our own kind. It hardly seems likely that most people start having children in their twenties because they are worried about their own mortality—*Honey, let's start our family because the average life expectancy deadline is just sixty years from now.* Almost no men and women in their twenties, unless they have been touched by early illness or an out-of-order death in their families, have enough fear of death to rule out even the most imprudent risk taking. They already think they are going to live forever, so the prospect of adding another twenty or thirty years to an unimaginable terminus would hardly prompt them to delay child-bearing for decades—even if it were possible to do so. And none of the scientists involved in aging research have been talking about delaying puberty—the only imaginable scenario in which either sex or reproduction could be put off, for the vast majority of people, much beyond the fertility window that now extends, roughly, from the mid-teens to the early forties. For Kass, the desire to extend youth (or young old age) is nothing more than "an expression of a childish and narcissistic wish to eat one's life and keep it"—a wish that is "incompatible with devotion to posterity." Such a desire, he emphasizes, "is in principle hostile to children, because children, those who come after, are those who will take one's place; *they* are life's answer to mortality, and their presence in one's house is a constant reminder that one no longer belongs to the frontier generation."[18] Kass, in his mid-seventies, presumably does not regard his own desire to continue living as hostile to his children and grandchildren "in principle." And I would be willing to bet, should Kass retain his mental faculties and live another twenty years, he will make an open-ended exemption for himself from an arbitrary deadline while continuing to relentlessly criticize those who do not share his lofty, dispassionate acceptance of the finitude of life. In principle, to be sure. It is perfectly all right, in this view, to live as long as possible—undergoing all of the bypass surgeries, chemotherapy, and hip replacements that Medicare will pay for—as long as you do not avail yourselves of any specific drugs that may materialize with the specific purpose of retarding the aging process.

The question that the conservative bioethicists are raising really amounts to, What are men and women going to do with all that extra time and freedom? The suspicion that people might, and probably would, use their extra time frivolously and badly is rooted in the deep conservative fear of anarchy. Conservatism distrusts anyone who proposes that it is possible to live wisely without constraining rules originally imposed from the outside—whether by a divine creator, an impersonal nature, or a social and political authority. It is the idea of human choice unfettered by humility that bothers the most conservative ethicists. Kass, for example, is a longtime opponent of living wills. He argues that "it's preposterous to think that we can have the kind of foreknowledge to cover the myriad circumstances in which we may find ourselves. Nor can you accurately pass judgment on how you're going to feel about your life in a different circumstance. . . . No kind of legal approach and no kind of medical approach are going to take the place of a loving, prudent caregiver on the spot."[19] That many people may not have loving or prudent caregivers when they are old seems not to occur to Kass. (Perhaps it would if he were a woman.) I certainly trust my imperfect judgment as it exists right now, based on more than four decades of adult life and on what I have learned from the deaths of many I love, more than I do anyone else's judgment. And if I am not able to speak for myself at the end, and the loving and prudent caregiver does not materialize (and few people are graced with such devotion more than once in a lifetime), my doctors will have to make do with my wishes, as they are today and have been for many years, rather than their own. On the one hand, ethicists like Kass do not want people to live "forever" through the vainglorious efforts of human science. On the other hand, they do not want fallible humans to plan ahead and use their own best judgment in an effort to avoid living too long in suffering or unconsciousness. Any argument, whether against longevity-extending efforts or attempts to exert some influence on the manner of one's own death, is bound to fail if it is based on the obvious fact of human imperfection. We are all we have.

But Kass does not only argue against agelessness. He also argues against the more limited goal of banishing the diseases that make advanced old age a living hell for so many people. He actually sees value in "senility, crippling arthritis, the need for hearing aids and dentures, and the degrading dependencies of old age." Without enduring the degenerative disease of old age, he insists, people would be even more afraid and reluctant to die than they are now. "Would not death become even more of an affront?" he asks. "Would not the fear and loathing of death increase in the absence of its harbingers? We could no longer comfort the widow by pointing out that her husband was delivered from his suffering. Death would always be untimely, unprepared for, shocking."[20] I have news for Kass: death is always untimely and unprepared for, even when it is no surprise. And being told what anyone who has ever cared for a suffering loved one already knows—that he has been delivered from suffering—is no comfort. That a man's suffering is worthwhile because its end can be used to console a widow is one of the most worthless ethical principles ever formulated—along with the social constructivists' suggestion that the presence of the demented may be beneficial to the rest of us because we can learn some unspecified lessons from people with damaged minds. There is also something decidedly akin to the views of the Puritans in Kass's ideas about the meaning in suffering at the end of life. His statement is all the more surprising because Kass is a Jew, and these thoughts were first delivered at a lecture sponsored by the Shalem Center, an academic institute in

Jerusalem devoted to research on Jewish social issues, values, and philosophy. Christianity is founded on a belief in the redemptive nature of suffering, as exemplified by the death of Jesus on the cross, but the idea that suffering has intrinsic moral value—as opposed to being something one attempts to endure with as much dignity as possible—is very, well, un-Jewish. When my partner said, with the last energies of his failing mind, that he wanted to die, it was a statement not of acceptance but of exhaustion and well-justified despair. If his cancer had not overtaken his Alzheimer's, if he had lived months or years longer, he would no longer have had any awareness of the possibility of his own death. Only someone who is still among the young old, as Kass is, could have the lack of discrimination to talk about senility in the same breath as dentures, hearing aids, and arthritis.

Daniel Callahan, cofounder of the Hastings Center—one of the first bioethics think tanks—essentially shares Kass's view on longevity-extending research, but he does not deliver sermons on the virtues of suffering and decrepitude. "We need not tolerate a heart attack in an eighty-year-old," he writes. "The attack can be averted and, even if it takes place, angioplasty or a bypass procedure can save the person suffering it from a once certain death. What, then, are the 'unalterable, unmanageable facts' about our illnesses? Surely not that they are inevitable and unavoidable. Not one could be counted theoretically unconquerable. This is the heroic part of medicine." Yet Callahan goes on to argue that "in our own lives we cannot make a self of that kind of heroism. We will die, and we will die of something not yet conquered, *whatever* it is that is not yet conquered. We cannot live a life, or shape a self, based on the visions of scientific medicine."[21] I agree with Callahan's last assertion, but the conviction that it is impossible to shape or define the self around a scientific or medical model has little to do with the question of whether living longer lives would place science in charge of everything. If eighty-year-olds need not accept death after heart attacks, it is not logical to suggest that nonagenarians and centenarians should bow meekly to the same fate. The question of whether the self—by which I presume Callahan means the emotional, intellectual, and (for a religious man) spiritual qualities that differentiate humans from other species—can be shaped by science is yet another dead end if one accepts the degree to which science has already been absorbed into the self-definition of men and women of the twenty-first century.

Bioethicists and scientists who strongly support anti-aging research come in two varieties—those who already have a financial stake in the new biotechnology and those who do not. The arguments of the former ought to be regarded with considerable skepticism, because one of the chief aims of biotech entrepreneurs is to create an aura of inevitability about genetic intervention in advance of the real methods of intervention. Thus, when the means arrive, the debate over ends will already be over. The laudatory publicity about longevity extension in laboratory animals prepares the way for future huzzahs about longevity extension in humans. "Death," says William Haseltine, CEO of Human Genome Sciences, "is a series of preventable diseases."[22] Note, in his statement of breathtaking certitude, that Haseltine uses the word "death" rather than "aging." Because biotech company executives raise capital from private investors and do not have to worry about the political and cultural sensibilities of legislators or those in charge of disbursing government research funds, they reveal open-ended goals more readily than scientists who depend on public money. Gregory Stock, former director of the UCLA Program on Medicine, Society and Technology (and now CEO of Signum Biosciences), goes just as far in his book *Redesigning Humans: Our Inevitable Genetic Future* (2002). Stock, who might have been invented as a nemesis by Kass and Callahan, is not merely enthusiastic about limited interventions such as the development of drugs to target genetic pathways involved in age-related diseases. He is also supportive of everything from the possibility of embryo selection aimed at improvement of the human species to direct modification of sperm and egg cells. Stock proposes a war on aging; if death is simply a series of preventable diseases, aging is no more than one of those curable pathologies. He calls for a straightforward acknowledgment that "what we really desire is not shorter morbidity at the end of life but a life that is both healthier *and* longer."[23] It seems self-evident that people who stand to make a great deal of money from sophisticated genetic engineering, if and when it becomes possible, are not in the best position to raise questions about either the ethical or the social consequences of their experiments. I have no quarrel with scientific businessmen profiting from discoveries that benefit humanity, but they can hardly be objective judges of whether what they are doing is in fact a benefit to humanity. And, as the ethicist Harry Moody (who coined the terms *wellderly* and *illderly* to describe different categories of old people) observes, an entire school of futurist philosophers and scientists who call themselves transhumanists "have explicitly rejected the idea that humanity represents a value to be celebrated or cherished as a pinnacle of cosmic evolution."[24] Although I am as addicted to being human as anyone else, I can contemplate the possibility that humanity might not be the end of evolution with equanimity. While I do cherish the idea that some scholars of the future may find something useful or pleasurable in my books—as I have found it a meaningful experience to read the works of scholars and historians of the past—I do not find it inconceivable or demeaning to imagine that another, higher species might also be interested in a record of human history. It might even be worth becoming immortal in order to find out what a more intelligent species would make of the history that *Homo sapiens* presumes to consider the summa of summae. In any event, whether humanity might one day evolve into or be forcibly replaced by another species does not seem relevant to the issue of whether it is a good idea to work on extending the human life span.

Academic bioethicists who favor pro-longevity research, like the Canadian feminist philosopher Christine Overall, tend to ask some of the same questions as ethicists like Kass and Callahan about the meaning of longer lives, but the pro-longevity philosophers naturally come up with different answers. Overall comes down on the side of longevity not because she regards it as a self-evident good but because the debate has the potential to "motivate us to rethink social arrangements and the limits now placed on the development of human potential."[25] One of the more puzzling aspects of her argument is that longer lives would somehow provide the opportunity to redress the injustices and frustrations endured by people from disadvantaged groups in their younger years.[26] But the most effective way to increase the life expectancy of the poor is by beginning at the beginning of life and endowing all Americans with the economic and educational opportunities conferred upon the upper-middle class from birth. The last years of life—whatever the efficacy of anti-aging drugs that might be developed—hardly provide the opportunity for human development that is inherent in the first years. Moreover, it is naïve to think that drugs to delay aging would be any more available to the poor than any other form of medical care offered by a society that worships free-market idols. The good chance that such drugs would be very expensive and would therefore provide yet another advantage for the already advantaged is largely ignored by pro-longevity bioethicists who, in considering the philosophical and moral questions inherent in longer lives, simply dismiss huge questions of social justice and adopt a we-can-work-it-out posture. But, as I have argued throughout this book, our society has to this point failed miserably in attempts to work out the serious social and economic problems experienced by the old old in the present. There is little chance that simply increasing the numbers of the old relative to the rest of the population—even if the oldest old were healthier than they are now—will force us to radically rethink our approach to such issues as old-age poverty, intergenerational responsibility, the social and sexual isolation of so many old women, or the moral value of personal autonomy. To cite a powerful and intractable example, it is hard to imagine that gender-related age issues could be dealt with except through a radical form of genetic engineering. The answer of longevity enthusiasts, I suspect, is that part of genetic reengineering of the species will be the extension of the male life span so that it approximates that of females. But that won't help heterosexual old women much, unless the hardwired tendency of old men to be attracted to younger women can also be reengineered. But then, perhaps old women who have been heterosexual all their lives can be reengineered as lesbians, which would take care of any remaining gender gap in life span as well as the desires of old men for young mates. This is, to be sure, a hyperbolic scenario—but no more so than the hyperbole of those scientists who expect us to accept the proposition that greater longevity is such an obvious good that dwelling on any attendant social ills is merely a hobgoblin of little minds. To the charge of irrational, antiscientific stupidity, Richard Miller levels an additional accusation of "gerontologiphobia" at anyone who regards the prospect of extending life by many decades as, at best, a mixed blessing. Miller argues that "the current, alarming population crisis and depletion of nonrenewable resources has come about without the slightest aid from biogerontologists, who have not yet discovered anything that actually improves public health or prevents disease. . . . Proposals that do address the root causes of the problem—solutions based on access to birth control information and hardware, strong incentives for resource conservation, and changes in social attitudes toward optimal family size, the scheduling of reproductive effort, and the proper role of the human female—typically elicit strong opposition from powerful religious, economic, and political factions." Therefore, Miller concludes, the "fashionable concern about the hypothetical ill effects of hypothetical future advances in biogerontology seems, from this perspective, a diversionary tactic to draw attention away from those authentic malefactors whose political connections are better than those of lowly biogerontologists."[27] Note the implication that anyone who is reluctant to get on board the pro-longevity bandwagon must be a right-wing religious nut or a supporter of untrammeled free-market conservatism. Miller concludes with a flourish of sarcasm:

> Perhaps there are some who, after sober and deliberate contemplation, feel that our Malthusian ills are best addressed by strategies that constrain the productive life span of healthy adults rather than by controlling the supply of new people. Were I a member of such a group, I would suggest that it devote its energies to removing seat belts from automobiles, insulin and antibiotics from pharmacies, and antismoking campaigns from schools, because compared with these interventions, picking on biogerontologists has a pretty low yield. The gerontologiphobic position . . . seems to me indefensible, but it is common enough to present a formidable obstacle to progress in aging research.[28]

The accusation of gerontologiphobia, used in this fashion, is essentially a conversation stopper, the equivalent of racism or communism or fascism rather than a fair description. What it means in this context is, "I want your money for my research, and you're a bad, bad person who hates and fears old people if you don't want to give it to me." Perhaps there should be another term—say, gerontologimania—to describe those who are convinced not only that their research will produce older generations in which people are healthy and vigorous until the day they die but that it is completely within the realm of human ingenuity to maintain a population much more heavily weighted than it is today in favor of those who have long since finished with their evolutionary task of reproduction. For such a scenario to be feasible economically, one must have absolute faith in the scientific possibility of producing generations of the old who can work (and, under capitalism) shop till they drop. If new biogerontological interventions, instead of curing the "preventable" diseases of old age, simply put them off another decade or two, that will be no concern of those rich enough to afford anti-aging drugs, but it will definitely concern younger adults expected to support a much larger population to a much more advanced age.

In an important sense, on both sides, the debate about whether it is ethical to conduct research that might lead to genetic engineering for the purpose of "vanquishing age" is a diversion from the discussion we ought to be having about the real problems of the old today and in the near future. Many scientists and bioethicists, with very different views about anti-aging research, have been drinking the same Kool-Aid as starry-eyed believers in a future where not only aging but death itself will succumb to the conquest of one preventable disease after another. I have often argued with ardent supernaturalists who claim that science is just another religion. But ethical debate over scientific issues certainly sounds like religion when it is based on conclusions far in advance of scientific evidence: the furious philosophical and scientific infighting has about as much relevance as debates about the Holy Trinity to the lives of boomers already in midlife or among the young old. We will almost certainly—maybe tomorrow, maybe a few years from now—find that some drugs containing substances found to extend the lives of laboratory animals have some applicability to human illnesses. But these drugs will not help us deal with the urgent questions raised by the forthcoming retirement of the boomers.

As an atheist and a secularist, I do not share Kass's and Callahan's view that death is what endows life with purpose. In *The Denial of Aging,* Dr. Muriel Gillick asserts, with a common sense that is lacking in many of these debates, "My contention is not that it is good to be mortal because it promotes productivity, but rather that mortality is simply a reality."[29] Whether the average life span is seventy or one hundred, human beings are always going to want more life not because they have something more to contribute to the grand scheme of nature but simply because our species wants what it wants—in this case, to stick around as long as possible—and, unlike mice or monkeys, has the intelligence to at least pursue that goal. With a few exceptions like Gillick, there is a missing perspective in this debate—the vantage point of a pragmatic humanism that neither disdains nor exalts the human desire to extend our allotted temporal arc, as individuals and as a species. The issue is not whether it is morally wrong to want to live longer but whether it makes sense for a society to assume the costs that will inevitably be associated with a longer period of old age for more of its members. Nevertheless, I support anti-aging research in spite of the exaggerated claims of many of its leading practitioners and proponents. There is certainly a possibility that such research may one day yield treatments for diseases that everyone can agree to define as diseases and thereby reduce human suffering. If the short-term potential of such research has been oversold, that is no reason not to invest in the long term out of fear that the bogeymen of indolence, hedonism, and boredom will descend (even more frequently than they do already) on a humanity that cannot be trusted to order its own affairs in the absence of a proximate rather than a distant death sentence. This does not mean, however, that anti-aging research ought to have any special or preeminent claim on public resources.

The allocation of money for health care and for scientific research is essentially a political decision—and that is why the ethical debate over immortality and longevity is posing the wrong questions about aging. Would longer lives benefit the human species, as opposed to gratifying the biologically hardwired individual desire to thwart death as long as possible? Regardless of how one answers that theoretical question, it is much less urgent than the practical question of how best to balance the needs of different generations. Compared with the need to muster the political will to address questions of social justice for every generation, anti-aging research is far down on my list of what ought to be America's priorities. Specifically, the search for cures for "preventable" diseases that strike most harshly and frequently in the last decades of life does not have a greater claim than the implementation of public health programs of proven effectiveness in the first years of life. The debate about whether it is immoral to want to be immortal does exactly nothing to advance either our understanding of tangible problems that affect and afflict the old today or our willingness to imagine and finance a better future for those who will, inevitably, find themselves among the old throughout all of our tomorrows.

CHAPTER ELEVEN

Necessary Bedfellows: Bridges Between Generations, Old-Age Autonomy

In the course of writing this book, I turned sixty-five—a welcome milestone that I once thought would be depressing. I greeted this birthday with relief because it made me eligible for Medicare, and I am no longer obliged to spend 15 percent of my after-tax income on health insurance premiums. I can choose my own doctors, instead of being stuck with physicians who participate in a miserly managed care program—the only insurance I could get as a self-employed writer—that has become a byword for bureaucratic indifference and inefficiency among both patients and doctors in New York City. Nothing about my life has changed except that, solely because of my age, I am entitled to a government benefit that greatly alleviates the financial stress I have labored under for most of my adult life in order to provide for my own medical care.

This is plain wrong. If decent health care should be a right in a modern society—and I believe that it should—it ought to be a right for everyone and not only for Americans sixty-five and over. It is simply unjust to subsidize medical care for people in one age group and leave nearly everyone else to fend for themselves. The remedy for this social injustice, however, is not to gut Medicare but to work out a new, fairer, and more inclusive social contract designed to address the needs of every generation. Unfortunately, political discourse has taken exactly the opposite tack during the debate in Washington over the rising federal deficit. Instead of talking about social justice for everyone, Washington bloviators talk only about the need to "reform entitlements." In the same Orwellian fashion that has made *liberal* a dirty word since the rise of the New Right in the 1980s, the old meaning of entitlement—something one has earned through particpation in society—has been turned on its head and is commonly used to describe something to which Americans are supposedly unentitled.

The chief obstacles to reaching a new intergenerational consensus are not greedy geezers and bloated Medicare entitlements, as political conservatives constantly insist (although every one of them is just as eager to sign on to Medicare at sixty-five as liberals are), but the nation's continuing failure to acknowledge the limits of individual approaches to broad social problems. The existence of a small proportion of geezers who are not only greedy but rich by the standard of Americans of any age is much less important than the fact that the longer most people live, the more economic struggles they will face. Health care is by no means the only necessary element of a new intergenerational contract, but it is central to the task of lightening all other economic burdens that weigh most heavily on the poor and dependent in every generation—including the oldest old. It is within the power of baby boomers, by virtue of the sheer size of their generation, to point the way toward social changes that will benefit the young as well as the old. If boomers do not lead the way, no one will. This effort will demand nothing less than a radical rethinking of the cherished American myth that individuals should be capable of maintaining their economic independence throughout their lives. The failure of American boomers to live out this myth has left many of us trembling on the verge of what was supposed to be retirement; the absence of this myth in most of Europe has left my European contemporaries, who have already paid their dues in taxes, looking to the future with equanimity. In the United States, the forging of a more just intergenerational contract will require, paradoxically, not only a new and deeper respect for the social responsibilities of generations to one another but also for the importance of individual autonomy to the old. Boomers will need to plan in a more systematic way for old age even as—also paradoxically—they begin to cast off delusions about their capacity to exercise complete control over the circumstance of their final years. The older boomers—those born between 1946 and 1957—must confront these issues while they are still among the vigorous ranks of the young old rather than the needier ranks of the old old, and they would do well to study the role of some of their more intransigent elders in the recent health care debate.

The potential for generational warfare inherent in America's current social contract was demonstrated during the health care reform debate of 2009 by the opposition of a large majority of the old—including members of the "greatest generation"—to reforms that might lead to expanded health care for the young and, in the process, pose a threat to current levels of Medicare benefits. The angriest old may not be greedy or rich, but they are scared. The cost of the health care bill passed in 2009 was supposed to be offest by cutting Medicare fraud and waste. What older voters heard, however, was a threat to what they already had, and their awareness that many of them would be broke and/or sick without Medicare did not make them more willing to extend a helping hand to those younger Americans who are already broke and sick without access to affordable health care. A *New York Times*–CBS News poll conducted at the height of the health care debate found that only 31 percent of Americans over sixty-five supported universal health care for anyone but themselves.[1] If the older boomers, already entering the Medicare system, adopt the same me-before-everyone-else posture, they are apt to be in for a rude surprise. What is at stake is nothing less than the implicit and explicit intergenerational contract that has financed Social Security since the 1930s and Medicare since the 1960s. As long as American families in their thirties and forties are just one serious illness away from bankruptcy under our current profit-driven insurance system, young- and middle-aged adults will be in no mood to expand old-age health insurance—or even maintain it at the present level—for seventy- and eighty-something boomers.

In September 2009, the forty-million-member AARP, whose membership is about evenly divided between those between ages fifty and sixty-five and those over sixty-five, launched a series of meetings across the country in an effort to bridge the generation gap within its own ranks. Although AARP officials tried to minimize the generational division over the Obama administration's health care efforts, what they heard at their community meetings only underlined the clash of interests between those old enough for Medicare and those still struggling with the private health insurance system. Don Nichols, a retired eighty-five-year-old, interrupted a neighbor at a meeting in a small town in Wisconsin and declared that young and middle-aged Americans had no right to complain about the cost of health insurance. "If they quit their smoking and drinking," he said, "they would be able to afford it." Nichols was responding to fifty-eight-year-old Karen Rasmussen, who had told the AARP audience that she and her husband were deeply in debt because of medical bills to treat his cancer. "We're hoping the government can do something because this is just breaking our backs," she said. That's when the selfless representative of the greatest generation spoke up about the smoking and drinking that supposedly makes young Americans unable to pay their medical bills.[2] The term "ageism" has long been used to describe the negative feelings of the young about their elders, but—as the self-protective response from many older voters at health care forums around the country demonstrated—prejudice based on age and on the interests of one's own age group can cut both ways. In all age groups, women were much more likely than men, and the poor and lower-middle-income earners much more likely than the rich, to support expansion of health benefits. But these disparities only underline a social reality that holds true at every age: women are more likely to be poor than men, and the less money people have, the more likely they are to support public programs. There is no question that the health care debate—which essentially tried to tinker at the edges of a broken system—brought out the worst in a great many older Americans who have something others don't and are determined to hang on to it, their children and grandchildren be damned.

Furthermore, another perilous age divide on social spending—between the older and younger demi-generations of boomers—is also beginning to manifest itself. Despite the common cultural influences shared by both halves of the boomer generation, the younger boomers came of age not during the late 1960s but during the Reagan era: they have spent much of their adult lives in a society dedicated to eschewing collective responsibility for social welfare and reviving Gilded Age notions of rugged individualism. Such an ethos penalizes those who are either too young or too old to meet their own needs without help. An exemplary specimen of this thinking on the part of younger boomers can be found in the writings of Tyler Cowen, a gadfly libertarian conservative professor of economics who has made his reputation arguing that the free market is good for culture because it pushes institutions to provide more of the cultural products people want. His position is roughly equivalent to that of an economist who believes that the market is good for nutrition because it produces more of the sugary food products that Americans want. Cowen (when he is not congratulating those who have made a marketable commodity out of the public's shortened attention span) has also identified Medicare as the nation's chief budgetary problem. In a memorable *New York Times* piece (memorable because it was published just about six weeks before the collapse of the financial markets in the autumn of 2008), Cowen made the dire prediction, plucked out of air, that income taxes would rise to 60 to 80 percent if Medicare benefits were not sharply cut. Cowen, born in 1962, would have the United States avoid the imaginary fate of an 80 percent income tax rate by cutting Medicare benefits for those who have high lifetime earnings, which are "relatively easily measured and hard to game, rather than to one's income or assets in any current year." He argues that tying benefits to lifetime income "reflects an ethic of individual responsibility—namely, that people who have earned well throughout their lives should be expected to take care of themselves, precisely so that the truly unfortunate can be helped." Cowen acknowledges that the system wouldn't be perfect. "What if you lose or squander all your savings, for example, just before you retire?" he asked in a question that might have been intended rhetorically but became all too real when the value of tax-deferred retirement accounts and housing—the savings of the older boomers—tanked along with the stock market in September 2008.[3]

But the recent economic crisis is not the only, or even the primary, flaw in any proposal to sharply cut Medicare benefits for those who have been well off for much of their lives. A high lifetime earner might have a child, say, with Down syndrome and allot most of his earnings, year after year, to savings plans designed to ensure that the child would be taken care of after the parents died. Some high earners are putting four children through college and, again, are much less able to save money for their own future than a parent with one or two children. Perhaps, in a mythical world of benefits linked to earnings, people would be penalized for having more than one or two children by losing Medicare benefits. One can only imagine what an outcry such a proposal would bring from the Catholic Church and the Protestant Christian right. Finally, our hypothetical high lifetime earner, even without taking anti-aging nostrums, might outlive his (or, more likely, her) savings. There would have to be numerous exceptions to the general premise that high earners should receive much less in public old-age benefits, so there would have to be a new government agency to determine which old people deserve exemptions from draconian cuts. Pity that agency and all who work within its cubicles. The idea of linking public benefits to a Puritan concept of private rectitude, paradoxically coupled with reliance on good luck, simply does not work in the real world. Talk about cutting Medicare and Social Security benefits for high-income earners, and the average American probably thinks about Bill Gates, Warren Buffett, and Michael Bloomberg. To really make a dent in entitlement programs, high-income earners would probably mean everyone in the middle and upper-middle class. The adjunct college professor who never received health insurance from his employer. The single mother with a professional job and what looks like an excellent income on paper, with a third of her earnings allotted to child care. The small business owner who did really well for years but was wiped out in the Crash of '08. The self-employed contractor who, for his entire working life, has had to pay both the employer's and the employee's share of Social Security—double what people who are on someone else's payroll must contribute. You. The title of Cowen's most recent book, *Create Your Own Economy: The Path to Prosperity in a Disordered World* (2009), says it all as far as excessive faith in rugged individualism is concerned. As long as Americans continue to believe in the myth that each of us possesses the power to create our own economy, we will be paralyzed, as a society, in our effort to meet the huge challenges to our institutions posed by the impending old age, and old old age, of the boomers.

As in every other stage of life, both individual and social factors shape the reality of people's lives in old age and the way they interpret those realities. Health, as the young old metamorphose into the more frail and more dependent old old, is the prime example of a reality that becomes less subject to individual choice and manipulation and more dependent on social arrangements, which in turn depend partly on the political will of a society. To pretend that people in their twenties and thirties can be induced to voluntarily devote a large proportion of their disposable income to insuring themselves against penury in their eighties and nineties is to ignore everything that is known about the way Americans have behaved since the dawn of the republic. As is evident from the tax rolls of New England towns, many people did not save enough for their old age in the early nineteenth century: they worked until they died. That might be viewed as rational behavior, given the average life expectancy of the time, were it not for the fact that when it comes to aging and death—whether average life expectancy is forty or eighty—everyone tends to believe that he or she will be the exception. In the early twentieth century—before Social Security but after forced retirement and an industrial labor system made it impossible for people to work until they died—Americans still did not save enough, even though many more of them were already living beyond the age when they were capable of earning a decent wage. The willingness of people to save for the distant future depends much more on the exigencies of life in the present than on the expectation or likelihood of future government benefits. No one is going to choose saving for old age over making a mortgage payment. No conscientious parent is going to choose saving for retirement over sending children to college. No one is going to save for medical bills that might come due at age ninety if a stack of medical bills has piled up this month. Using a calculator and drawing on the skills of a friend who is a statistician, I discovered that, absent my large private health insurance premiums, I could have paid 25 percent more in taxes *and* still saved twice as much as I have during my prime earning years. That might explain why Europeans, who pay much higher taxes than Americans, nevertheless have a much higher rate of personal savings. If those who want to slash Medicare benefits for what they consider "high lifetime earners" have their way, a good many of the 8.5 million Americans who will be over eighty-five in the year 2030 will be ill-clothed, ill-housed, and ill-fed—and if they have dementia, they will be warehoused in the deplorable nursing homes reserved for those who have exhausted their assets.

I would love to believe that I will always remain sharp as a tack, that I will continue to write until I draw my last breath and drop dead in front of my computer while working on my next book, and that I will always remain self-sufficient in the apartment where I have lived nearly my entire adult life. I place a high value on personal autonomy, and this perception is not only a generational trait but a predisposition shared by most people in my lonely profession. But my hope, as an individual, is significantly at odds with what I know to be the reality of old old age for women who live as long as the women in my family generally do. There is, to be sure, an important role for individuals and families in shaping a new vision of old age based on reality rather than on fantasies of eternal youth. However, the first task of the young old boomers is to distinguish between aspects of old age that can be influenced, if not entirely controlled, by individual will and those susceptible only to collective political action.

The two overwhelming problems of real old age in the United States today are health, which generally worsens over time, and the tendency of all but the richest Americans to grow poorer as they grow older. Within these general categories lie a host of specific issues that can be addressed only through collective action. A short list would include:

- Medicare bias in favor of high-tech and surgical procedures instead of preventive health care. This bias also discourages psychotherapy and ordinary doctor-patient consultations in which older patients might get a chance to talk about their health concerns instead of being hustled out the door with a new prescription. Medicare, as currently constituted, generally pays for a scan costing thousands of dollars but not for a fifteen-minute talk that might reduce the need for aggressive medical interventions.
- The dearth of paid social services, provided at home or in community centers, that might keep many more of the frail elderly in their own homes and out of both expensive assisted living facilities and even more expensive nursing homes.
- Failure to subsidize long-term care for those who need it and must therefore exhaust all of their assets before they can qualify for Medicaid, which generally provides the lowest quality of nursing home care for those who cannot afford to pay.
- A you're-on-your-own government policy toward caretakers who want to keep family members in their homes but cannot bear the burden alone.
- A severe shortage, in many areas of the country, of affordable, accessible housing for healthy old people who have too much income to qualify for subsidies but not enough to pay market rate rents. Assisted living facilities are extremely expensive and are not even needed by many old people whose disabilities are minor and whose needs might be met simply by moving to an apartment—if they could afford the rents.
- Failure to use the skills of healthy old people who are able and

willing to work either full time or part time—thereby easing their own financial burdens and continuing to contribute to society.

If one looks beneath the surface of these issues, it is clear that they are of great importance to Americans of all ages. Medicare's orientation toward procedures rather than human services that promote health, toward the treatment of rather than the prevention of disease, is shared by the entire American health care system. Our approach to Type 2 diabetes, which generally declares itself in middle age (although doctors are now diagnosing diabetes in record numbers in overweight children and teenagers), is a prime example of the connection between the health of young and old. Americans who already have full-blown diabetes today in their thirties, forties, and fifties will be tomorrow's seventy- and eighty-something diabetics, driving up the cost of Medicare and producing all of the complications associated with late-stage diabetes—including blindness, serious heart disease, and circulatory problems that can lead to gangrene and amputation of blood-starved lower limbs. There is a direct connection between the suffering and medical bills of aging diabetics and the failure of both government and the private insurance system to finance effective preventive programs aimed at children as well as young adults. In similar fashion, the absence of public subsidies for home care is an issue for adults of all ages. Middle-aged children who would like to help their parents remain in their own homes are often as frustrated as the old themselves by their inability to afford some special service—say, a helper who would buy groceries and cook meals—that can mean the difference for the elderly between largely independent living and institutionalization.

Providing preventive medical care and a better social safety net for people of all ages would certainly cost much more than what is now being spent on Social Security and Medicare—and that would be the case even if new health and social services lead to savings in old-age entitlements. Fiscal conservatives are right when they say that we cannot expand the social safety net, while maintaining taxes at the same level, without driving up federal and state deficits. The conservatives' answer is that individuals, whether they make $50,000 or $50 million a year, must discipline themselves throughout young adulthood and middle age to save for old age—however long that old age may be. And they must do it for the foreseeable future, whatever their personal responsibilities and however they may be buffeted by upheavals in the economy. In the world where real people struggle mightily with money problems, however, there are only two choices about the way society takes economic care of, or does not take care of, the old. We can sharply cut Medicare and Social Security expenditures either by cutting services across the board or through some cockamamie scheme like basing Medicare reimbursement on what a person's income was in his or her prime earning years. Or we can tax all income, including that of people over sixty-five, at a level necessary to maintain the kind of social safety net that exists in every other developed country—which would include comprehensive health insurance for the young as well as benefits for the old. Boomers who are still working—whether they are over or under sixty-five—are likely to exert the greatest influence in the process of deciding whether Americans are going to hope for the best and cling to the current system or work out an arrangement of broader social welfare programs that will give both young and old adults a stake in a new social contract. In *The Denial of Aging,* Muriel Gillick describes thc stakes for the old in clear-cut terms:

> The baby boomer generation has a choice to make. We can stumble into old age, hoping that our physicians will have the wisdom to treat us appropriately, given our degree of vigor or of infirmity, and expecting to accept their beneficence. . . . We can remain optimistic because we believe that abiding by the latest dietary recommendations and adhering to a regular exercise regimen will suffice to keep us healthy and strong until, at age 100, we die in our sleep.
>
> Alternatively, the baby boomers can decide individually and collectively to do our utmost to shape our future. Since passivity has not been a characteristic widely attributed to the generation born between 1946 and 1964, it is surprising that acquiescence is precisely what we've seen to date. Perhaps our reticence arises from our terror at the prospect of death, which is after all the culmination of aging. . . . Maybe the acknowledgment that before death comes a no-man's-land in which many people merely exist—unproductive, unvalued, and often unwell, but alive—is just too mind-boggling to consider. We need to act to landscape

that terrain so that it is not barren and desolate, but rather a period of fulfilled yearning, triumphant aspiration, but also sadness and grief—much like all the other phases of life.[4]

That is a tall order. Gillick goes on to talk about the necessity for Medicare reform, but what she means is an expansion of Medicare to provide continuing care for old people outside hospitals and long-term care institutions as well as inside them. What conservative cost cutters mean by Medicare reform is compressing, not expanding, the scope of old-age entitlements. When Obama, born near the end of the baby boom, talks about the need for entitlement reform, he often sounds more like a conservative than a liberal. That emphasis may be partly attributable to his relatively young age: a president in his forties, whatever his politics, is naturally attuned to the economic concerns of adults in midlife.

We did not have the health care debate we should have had, in the last few years, despite all the sound and fury, because the entire discussion was based on a combination of liberal and conservative fallacies. The liberal fallacy, which I cannot imagine that either President Obama or his economic advisers really believed, was that it is possible to extend health insurance to forty million uninsured Americans without everyone being asked to sacrifice a certain amount of self-interest (a.k.a. money) for the common good. Liberal politicians, beginning with Obama, felt obliged to promise that health care reform would not require anyone's taxes, excepting those making more than a quarter of a million dollars a year, to go up at all. And the Democrats tried to soothe angry older voters with the pledge that only "fraud and waste" would be cut. Conservatives were equally dishonest with the riled-up elderly. They presented themselves as the defenders of Medicare—a ludicrous stance that seemed to work among people who have forgotten that there would have been no Medicare in the first place if the Republican Party (which was much more moderate in the 1960s than it is today) had had its way. The Republican right offered the disingenuous promise that Medicare benefits can stay the same, Americans under sixty-five can continue to absorb crushing increases in private insurance costs, taxes can be cut even further, and there will be no revolt down the road as young, badly insured Americans are asked to pay for the health costs of a mushrooming population of the old and the old old. What will really happen if there is no serious health care reform is that the right will lead the push to slash Medicare benefits, including the prescription drug plan that a Republican-controlled Congress passed during President George W. Bush's administration, without raising taxes to pay for the new entitlement. Indeed, that is exactly what happened in 2011, as Republicans threatened to push the U.S. government into default by refusing to raise the national debt limit. "Entitlement reform" was to be enacted at gunpoint, and everything from raising the retirement age to charging much higher Medicare premiums for affluent old people was proposed. The Tea Party legislators who had campaigned in 2010 by warning about "death panels" changed their tune, while attempting to pacify Americans over sixty-five by promising that proposed cuts would only affect the future of people under fifty-five. What was never on the table, of course, was raising taxes—not only to ensure the solvency of Medicare and Social Security but to provide better health insurance for Americans under sixty-five and ease the potential for generational warfare. Moreover, the underlying assumption that most boomers will enjoy a "new," much healthier old age than their parents—thereby making Medicare and Social Security less important—was never challenged.

One factor that could move the debate in another, more reality-based direction is the recognition of younger boomers that they too are getting older. It will not be too long before boomers now in their forties become as worried as older boomers about what lies ahead for them economically in old age. The 1997 Yankelovich report on generational spending habits characterized boomers as "the generational cohort active in the consumer marketplace today *that grew up with the expectations, life skills, and values created by the unbridled economic growth of their formative years*." The authors minimized the differences between older and younger boomers and concluded that economic, not cultural or political, experiences are what ultimately unite the boomers who came of age during the Reagan era with the boomers whose coming-of-age experiences took place in the late 1960s and early 1970s. In the view of the market researchers, both consumer groups "shared a confidence that the progress and prosperity would never stop, which created the Boomer generational sense of expectation and entitlement."[5] This was certainly a valid analysis in the late 1990s, at least for upper-middle-class boomers, but the shared confidence of those at both ends of the boomer generation has been replaced by a shared anxiety engendered by the Crash of '08.

From the standpoint of those, like me, who wish to see a new intergenerational contract that covers social welfare needs for Americans of all generations, the disruption of boomer expectations is not necessarily a bad thing. But it is not necessarily a good thing, either: the strident tone of the health care debate is only the most recent historical demonstration that people who feel personally threatened by change are frequently less, not more, cognizant that the satisfaction of their own needs depends on the satisfaction of others' needs. People who have already lost one dream are not apt to easily accept the loss or reduction of benefits that they have always included in their image of their future. The now-receding dream of early retirement—very much a part of the thinking of upper-middle-class boomers who were looking forward to doing a lot more playing than working in their sixties and seventies—is not likely to make disappointed people in their sixties embrace the inevitable forthcoming proposals to raise the age at which one can work and still collect full Social Security benefits. I suspect that the AARP, if it continues to support social reforms that benefit those under sixty-five as well as those over sixty-five (as it has historically), will have a battle that will make the town hall meetings look like models of civility. It remains to be seen whether either the younger or the older cohorts of the boomer generation have the political inclination or will to challenge a social contract that has, for nearly fifty years, placed the health of the old in an entirely different category from the health of the young. Boomers voted for both Ronald Reagan and Bill Clinton, for George W. Bush and Barack Obama: their representatives in the media bloviate on both MSNBC and Fox News. It is possible that, once they have old-age entitlements of their own to protect, boomers will mimic those among their elders who consider Medicare a just reward for a lifetime of work, while dismissing government-subsidized health care for children and young adults as socialism.

Still, I continue to derive a certain amount of hope from the dose of economic reality that boomers have received over the past three years. Memories of the unbridled economic growth of our formative years, as the Yankelovich report put it, have been tempered by the reality of lost homes, lost jobs, and lost health care and by the insecurity of those who have retained their houses and health care but are struggling to pay for them—and to keep working as long as possible. Only a thoroughgoing fool in his or her fifties or early sixties today can fail to grasp the fact that we are going to need every penny of our Social Security checks, and every bit of coverage from Medicare, to maintain a decent standard of living even if we have substantial savings and even if longevity does not increase significantly in our lifetime. And if we recognize the possibility that we will need public help in our old age, how can we turn a blind eye to the needs of those who must pay the bill? The chief obstacle to renegotiating America's intergenerational contract is not boomer narcissism or shortsightedness but the historical distaste of many Americans for any proposal that they should sacrifice a good deal more of their personal money in the furtherance of public good. Yet public opinion polls, even at the height of the deficit debate and Tea Party obstructionism, showed that the majority of Americans today are willing to pay higher taxes themselves to maintain Social Security and Medicare. Mystifyingly, Obama and the Democrats seemed unable to take advantage of this sentiment, while the far right brilliantly exploited the historic American distaste for a big government and higher taxation (except, of course, when Americans face the loss of their own government benefits).

It would be a mistake, to conclude that money, and the often excessive American faith in rugged individualism as the answer to everything—are the only obstacles to creative thinking that might establish better conditions for old age. The central emotional challenge of advanced old age, as distinct from financial issues, is the establishment of a livable balance between autonomy and dependency. Losing control over their lives is the deepest fear of mentally competent old men and women, and any sound social policy must be based on recognition of that fact. A great deal has been written recently—not much of it by the old themselves—about the need for the old to gracefully accept their increasing need for help from others. Mary Pipher, a psychologist, suggests in a book of essays on aging that the word "dependency" should be replaced with the words "mutuality" or "interdependency."[6] This kind of thinking about old age is especially prevalent in the "helping professions," which many old people see as a conspiracy to render them helpless. It is undoubtedly true that an objectively better quality of life—regular meals, better and quicker access to health care, opportunities for socializing (not socialism)—can be provided in communal rather than individual settings. But that is not what all, or even most, old people want for themselves. Objective factors affecting quality of life can usually be measured; they include a person's state of health, the degree to which ill health causes functional disability, and the presence or absence of enough money to provide for both necessities and pleasure. But subjective quality of life, which includes just about everything else that makes a person happy or unhappy at any age, is a more complicated matter. If people do not like force-fed interdependency and see it as pure dependency, having their physical needs met does not feel like a fair trade-off for the loss of independence. One might look, for example, at a ninety-year-old man—I'll call him Jake—of my acquaintance and conclude that he has little to complain about. He is mentally alert, able to navigate with a walker, and housed in his own apartment in the "independent living" section of a well-kept Manhattan assisted living complex. Jake is the object of constant attention from his female neighbors, who outnumber him twenty to one. But he is also a man who always placed a high value on privacy, and he is driven mad by frequent exhortations to join in sing-alongs, bridge games, and a host of communal activities compelling a sociability that has never been one of his distinguishing characteristics. He still mourns for his wife, who died of Alzheimer's two years ago, and has no interest in the women trying to get him to participate in activities in which he never had any interest when he was younger. His grief is seen as depression because it has lasted "so long" (as one of his sons puts it), and both the assisted living staff and his children seem to think that two years is long enough to "snap out of it" after a fifty-year marriage. The children also consider their father unrealistic to long for the apartment he originally left so that he could help care for his demented wife in a setting that provided professional help and to want another apartment of his own. It does not seem to occur to Jake's sons and daughter that living in an environment of his own choosing might revive their father's spirit, which is slowly being crushed by the knowledge that his offspring will not support him in his desire to live independently—in large part because they would worry about his physical safety more and have to assume more responsibility for his welfare. Money is not a problem for Jake, and he could easily afford the kind of home services, from aides to help him bathe to deliveries of precooked meals, that would enable him to live on his own. What he is not capable of doing is overseeing the complicated financial arrangements for a return to his own apartment and organizing the care he would need. Without active help from his children, he will remain in an institutional setting where he is compelled to eat bland food he does not enjoy, stay indoors most of the time on clear days when he is perfectly capable of pushing his own walker down the street (because the rules require him to be accompanied by an aide), and generally abandon control over his everyday activities. "I should have planned better," he tells me. "But I just didn't realize how difficult it would be to get myself out of here once I moved in for my wife's sake." Yes, he should have planned better. What he probably should have done was rent his former apartment instead of selling it—which would have facilitated his return to the outside world after his wife died. But he was overwhelmed and thinking only of her, and he sought the quickest way to obtain the professional care she needed in a place where he could remain by her side. Because Jake chose *not* to take the easy way out and institutionalize his wife in a nursing home, while diminishing his role to that of a visitor to her narrowing world, he lost his own autonomy. And there is no social system in place to support him in his desire to regain part of the life he lost when he accompanied his wife on her final journey into darkness. The assisted living facility does not want to lose a paying customer. The children do not want to involve themselves in a complicated rearrangement of their father's finances that would enable him to live in a manner more consistent with his personality and his tastes. Hiring a lawyer, which this man has thought about doing, would mean fighting his flesh and blood. And he does not have the energy to fight alone.

There is a lesson for fifty- and sixty-something boomers in my ninety-year-old friend's experience, which underlines the importance of thinking about and planning for various possibilities, including worst-case contingencies, when we are strong enough and healthy enough to resist pressure from others. The children in this relatively common family drama are not terrible people: their father's independence is simply not the priority for them that it is for him. Acknowledgment of generational interdependency may be crucial to any attempt to deal with large health care and economic issues on a social and political level, but it is useless on an individual and familial level unless it includes real respect for an old person's desire for as much autonomy as possible. My friend is mentally and physically capable of handling a significantly greater degree of independence, but it is more convenient for his children to foster his continued dependency in a place that frees them from anxiety about his falling and not being able to summon help quickly enough. But safety is not necessarily the most important thing in life. Not at any age.

Much of the criticism of the ideal of autonomy has focused on the boomer generation, and much of it is still rooted in antagonistic reactions to the social legacy of the 1960s and 1970s. The idea that an excessive emphasis on self-determination is a characteristic exclusive to boomers ignores the historical fact that independence and individuality, for better as well as for worse, have been ingrained in American DNA since the beginning. If one looks at what old people themselves have written about the experience of old age (as opposed to what middle-aged people write about what they think old age ought to be and how the old ought to behave), there is nothing to indicate that the loss of independence was any less bitter for those who lived to be old hundreds of years ago than it is today. Beginning with the backlash in the 1970s against the disturbing social movements of the 1960s, a series of social critics—Christopher Lasch's sweeping indictment in *The Culture of Narcissism* (1978) comes to mind—have taken the boomers to task for being disrespectful of tradition, too focused on themselves, and unconcerned about the larger good of society. No sensible person could disagree with the position that the culture of excessive autonomy is at its worst when dealing with the needs not only of the very old but of the very young. That does not mean, however, that it is in the best interests of the old for other people—whether children, doctors, or representatives of the therapeutically oriented helping professions—to decide how much autonomy is too much autonomy. When I think about the struggles in old age of the people closest to me, I cannot fail to see that their loss of independence, both real and perceived, has been the most painful experience of their adult lives. And while some diminution of autonomy is inevitable in advanced old age—a complete loss is inevitable for those with terminal dementia—it is not inevitable for everyone. In many instances, the fading away of control over one's own life seems inevitable only because other people—often much loved people—tell the old that it must be so. They are not always right.

CONCLUSION

> We never look enough, never exactly enough, never passionately enough.
>
> —Colette, age seventy-nine

I HAVE THREE SNAPSHOTS of myself, at different stages of my life, with the three long-lived women from whom I am directly descended on the maternal side of my family. In the first photo, taken in 1948 by my forty-nine-year-old grandmother, I am three years old and holding a balloon while sitting on the steps of Gran's house. My great-grandmother Christina Roethenhoeffer, in her mid-eighties, is sitting beside me, her white hair swept up in a bun that was already going out of style even for very old women. She was called Howdy, because, in her state of good-natured dementia, that was just about the only word she said to anyone. To the extent that I thought of Howdy as a person, I thought of her as my gran's responsibility—as Gran herself did. Howdy was a gentle soul, who—my grandmother would tell me much later—had borne nine children and endured a great deal of abuse from her drunkard of a husband. Gran would never have thought of putting Howdy in a nursing home, in part because her mother had inserted her own body between her children and her husband's fists. From Howdy's blank stare in the picture, it is clear that by the middle of the twentieth century, she was beyond remembering what had happened to her as a young woman.

Fast-forward to the summer of 1998, when I spirited Gran away from her nursing home and took her for a picnic lunch by the Grand River, which runs through southern Michigan. I am fifty-three, and she is ninety-nine. In a snapshot taken by an obliging teenager, I have my arm around Gran, and I look like a giant beside her frail form. Her body shriveled from bone loss and the inactivity of life in a nursing home, Gran—unlike her mother—retained a functioning mind in her old age. "I feel like I've been let out of prison," she told me. "It's been so long since I've just watched little children playing." Then she talked about how useless she felt. I asked myself why this fate had befallen my grandmother, but I already knew. I was fit and healthy, and it took all of my strength to help her physically from the car to the riverbank and back into the car. My mother, having lost most of her strength in one arm because she was unlucky enough to be diagnosed with breast cancer when surgeons were still doing muscle-excising radical mastectomies on every woman, could never have managed it. I had worked and lived in New York City for most of my adult life, and I was not about to give up my life to help my mother take care of my grandmother.

There is a third picture, of my mother and me, taken in the early 1990s, when I was in my forties and she, in her seventies, was still able to travel without difficulty. We are in Rockefeller Plaza in front of the Christmas tree, and we both appear to be in a lighthearted holiday mood. Mom loved New York: in the early 1990s, she was able to walk and climb stairs and do all of the things there are to do in a great city. She loved the theater and eating out in the restaurants she read about in *New York* magazine, to which she subscribed and still does. Most of all, she loved people-watching in Central Park. But she had a life of her own in East Lansing. Her friends and her volunteer work were there, and so was Gran, who was not yet in a nursing home but needed a good deal of help from Mom to continue living in her own apartment. Today I look at the Rockefeller Plaza picture frequently and reflect on my mother's trips to the city, because I know that she will never be able to travel here again. At eighty-nine, she is too frail, her energy level too low, her thinning bones too painful, for her to walk without a cane, to climb stairs, or, even in a wheelchair, to negotiate the gantlet of post-9/11 airports. She has a vital mind, but her body has failed her. Mom needs help, but I can no more give up my life now—or, to be honest, I am no more willing to give up my life—than I was fifteen years ago. Nor was my mother willing to give up her life so that she could provide her own mother the kind of full-time care that Gran provided for my great-grandmother. My grandmother, unlike my mother and unlike me, never worked outside her home after marriage, and she was of a generation and economic class in which a woman always placed her family's interests above her own. She wanted to go to high school, but her education ended in eighth grade, in 1913, when she went to work to help support her younger brothers and sisters. Her first job was picking onions on farms that still existed in what are now the suburbs of Chicago. My grandmother kept her eighth-grade diploma for the rest of her life, with its elegant script and signature by the Cook County superintendent of schools. It hangs on the wall of my office today, as a tribute to what was a real achievement in the early years of the twentieth century and a reminder of the possibilities that women were once expected to give up unquestioningly—not once upon a time, but just two generations ago—in service to their families. That was the way it was for the rest of Gran's life: everyone else came first. When Howdy became incapable of looking after herself, there was no question about who would be her caretaker. Did Howdy therefore have a better old age than my grandmother or my mother? I have no idea. It is entirely possible that when she first moved into Gran's house, Howdy was as reluctant to be displaced from her own home as the widows of New England were in the eighteenth century. My great-grandmother's life was so different from mine—although, for a brief time, our existence on this earth coincided—that I can hardly imagine what might have improved, or worsened, her final years.

My grandmother and my mother, however, occupy an arc in time that is much more comprehensible to me. I think frequently about what society might have done for them, or what they might have done themselves, to experience a better—not a new, but a better—old age. And I think about this with full knowledge that, in comparison with the closing years of life for many in this country, my grandmother's last decade and my mother's ninth decade were not all that bad. Yet my grandmother suffered deeply from the loss of her autonomy in the last years of her life, as my mother is suffering now. In spite of their very different histories—one of the most important differences being that my mother went to college and has had more opportunities than my grandmother did—dismay at their loss of independence is the shared issue of their old age. I think a good deal about what, if anything, I might do to make the last years of my life more satisfying than the lives of the women who preceded me.

Many well-meaning friends—nonfiction writers who are thoroughly acquainted with the public's insatiable appetite for self-help prescriptions that dispense assurances of our ability to control our lives—have advised me to end this book on a hopeful note, filled with specific positive suggestions for boomers on the cusp of the invisible divide between late middle and young old age. Like every other generation of our species, we are about to enter a zone that, if the chart of aging were a medieval map, would be inscribed with the warning "Here Be Dragons." One of those dragons, I suspect, must be a creeping realization of the ultimate ineffectiveness of the defenses—the "positive" measures—by which all of us attempt to keep the demons of old old age at bay.*

As may be inferred from the previous chapter, I believe that a number of much-needed social policy changes could provide more opportunities for people to live out their old age in conditions that would expand their arena of personal choice. My grandmother's quality of life, for example, would have been greatly enhanced, long before she required any sort of nursing care, had there been a decent public transportation system in East Lansing, Michigan—one that did not require her to walk blocks to a bus stop in order to avoid calling on her daughter every time she needed to do the smallest errand. How oppressive it must be to know that you can never leave the house spontaneously, on your own feet, and go out for an ice cream cone on a hot summer afternoon! That was the restrictive reality of daily life for my gran, as it is in all but a small number of cities in the United States today for anyone who can no longer drive.

Many practical obstacles to the autonomy of the old were created by entrenched institutional and social structures, engendered by the post–World War II migration from cities to suburbs, and therefore cannot be changed by individual acts of will. One of the few worthwhile pieces of positive advice for people contemplating retirement and relocation

* Actually, the legend "Here Be Dragons" appears in Latin (*hic sunt dracones*) on only one well-known medieval globe. It seems that "Here Be Lions" (*hic sunt leones*) was the common medieval designation for unknown areas and unknown dangers. The transformation of lions into dragons in the modern imaginative construct of maps has been the subject of numerous scholarly essays. Since lions are now a part of the known world, and we all have a good idea of what to expect from them, I'll stick with dragons as a more appropriate metaphor for the uncharted perils that lurk in the region of old age.

is that they move to an apartment in a city with taxis and decent public transportation instead of moving to either the Hurricane Belt or the Sun Belt, where life without a car is not life at all. Some will surely accuse me of what Russians call *gorodski patriotizm* (which literally translates as "city patriotism" but probably ought to be translated as "civic boosterism"), but there is no doubt in my mind that the greatest place to grow old in the United States is my hometown, New York City. In this amazing city, frail octogenarians and nonagenarians—many of whom would be sitting in their condos watching television in Sun City, Arizona, or in East Lansing—are taking their dogs to the park in the morning (even if the leash is attached to a wheelchair or walker), using the lifts provided for the disabled on every city bus, and setting off for concerts, museums, restaurants, or, yes, Bloomingdale's. Anyone lucky enough to be a New Yorker is already a resident of an assisted living community. The cleaner, the drugstore, and the liquor store all offer free delivery for young and old alike. It's just considered part of the cost of doing business, and if you're a longtime customer living on a fixed income, no one sneers at a small tip. What grocery stores charge for delivery amounts to less than the cost of gas, much less car maintenance and insurance. And there are many other, smaller cities, from Seattle to Boston, that offer similar amenities. One of the big advantages of living in a walkable city is that walking is good for your health. While average life expectancy in the United States has increased by two and a half years since 1990, the life expectancy of New Yorkers has increased by more than six years. Eleanor Simonsick, a Baltimore-based epidemiologist who has studied the effect of walking, found that walking not only increases life expectancy but that the faster people walk, the longer they live.[1] Not only are New Yorkers famous for their pace on the sidewalks but they also walk to parks—and they spend more time in parks than other Americans because they do not have to drive to them.

In most of the nation's suburban and exurban sprawl, however, these choices do not exist—and that's something aging boomers ought to think about before contemplating retirement to some sunny, sprawling clime that turns into a trap for those who can no longer drive themselves to the golf course in order to ride on their golf carts. If you want to stay active and engaged with the world around you, forget about *Money* magazine's annual list of the best places in America to retire. Topping the list for 2009 were Port Charlotte, Florida; Palm Springs, California; and Traverse City, Michigan.[2] Traverse City is the only place that doesn't quite fit on this list, since it is delightful in summer but a slippery winter nightmare for anyone not quite as steady as she used to be. Perhaps *Money* assumes that its readers have enough money for two retirement homes in very different climate zones. I've been to all of the so-called best towns for retirement, and they have many attractions. But if you can't drive and aren't rich enough to have someone else drive you where you want to go, you're stuck in your air-conditioned condos (during the endless summers in Florida and Arizona) and in your centrally heated houses, preferably in front of a fireplace (when the winter winds blow in off Grand Traverse Bay).

Right up there with the concept of retirement to a resort community as nirvana is the exaltation of retirement itself. I confess that I cannot understand the appeal of unlimited "free time," and one does not need to be a workaholic to question the advisability of too much leisure. Being forced to work longer, or to think about developing new skills to augment an inadequate retirement income, might turn out to be an invigorating kick in the pants for boomers rather than a life sentence at hard labor. One study indicates that of all Americans, those still working over age sixty-five have the highest levels of job satisfaction. Approximately 71 percent said they were "very satisfied" with their jobs.[3] It is likely that Americans interviewed for this survey had always liked their jobs and did not want to retire—certainly not at sixty-five—and that future research will uncover more dissatisfaction among those who, as a result of the lingering depressed economy, must keep working to pay their bills. But that expectation might just as easily turn out to be mistaken, given that it is based on the idea of retirement as not only a right but a glorious way to spend the last two or three decades of life. Retirement is undoubtedly a cherished and much-needed goal for people whose bodies are marked by decades of hard physical labor or for white-collar workers who have always hated their jobs, but it is a passport to boredom and purposelessness for many old men and women who like to work and are healthy enough to do so. Work, both paid and volunteer, makes people feel useful, and the sense that one is no longer of use—voiced so poignantly by my grandmother when we saw each other for the last time—is one of the most fundamental losses experienced by too many among the old. And that just about sums up my "positive advice": live in a place that forces you to stay on your feet, and look for work wherever and whenever you can find it.

Maintaining a sense of dignity and a sense of purpose in the final stages of life is, however, much more complicated than simply picking the right place to live and hoping for good health—or good enough health—to be of use in society. For too many Americans like my grandmother, old age—especially advanced old age—means a sharp and unwanted transition from a sense of themselves as people valued by family and community to a diminished sense of themselves as burdens who serve no purpose. It is a shift from active to passive, from being a caretaker to being a care recipient, from independence to dependence, and it is experienced as a personal loss at the deepest internal level, regardless of outer circumstances. This unwanted transition can be delayed but not denied, unless one dies in vigorous young old age, in full command of one's life. I am not counting on any of my supposedly age-defying health habits (lots of exercise, lots of vegetables, moderate drinking, and lifelong nonsmoking) to serve as a talisman against an enforced late-life transition to dependency. If these habits keep me healthier longer, well and good. And if they don't, and my appointed fate is a drawn-out ordeal, the way I treat my body makes my life better now. I am certainly not counting on pro-longevity science to serve as my deus ex machina if I live as long as my mother, grandmother, and great-grandmother. Should scientific breakthroughs against the most fearsome diseases of old age become realities, I will greet them as welcome surprises, in the same way that I will greet a passionate late-life love affair or a financial bonanza. But I am not counting on being the fortunate exception in any of these areas. And no amount of psychological jargon about interdependence can obscure the negative emotional character of old-age dependency for people who, regardless of their level of engagement with others, have always rejoiced in their autonomy.

If the old must accept the physical limits that deteriorating health places upon their independence, the same cannot be said about yielding to the psychological demands of emotional correctness—which presents an image of successful aging as a progression toward a calm, detached state of wisdom. The old are told, repeatedly, that a good adjustment to their stage of life requires the attainment of a peace of mind rising above temporal passions, the adoption of a sub specie aeternitatis view of human affairs, and the internalization of an altogether more equable view of whatever used to generate out-of-control emotions. Psychologists suggest that in this calmer universe the old conduct "life reviews" and ask themselves such questions as, "How did my life matter?" "What can I look back on with pride?" and "Did I love the right people?"[4] Something bothers me about this image of old men and women tallying up a life's balance sheet; after all, once you start adding up the score, the test is over. (In any case, "Did I love?" seems more germane than "Did I love the right people?") I don't want to become one of those ancient scorekeepers. I absolutely refuse to accept this definition of successful aging. Inherent in that refusal, for all who stand on the threshold of old age, is a determination to lay claim to a future defined, insofar as possible, not by those who want us to fit their image of the old but by our own values. First among these values is a recognition that there is no one "right" way to experience old age. Those whose goal is to become sages, embodying peace of mind and serving as examples to others, are welcome to it. I intend to be an angry old woman, a discontented work in progress, as long as my mind continues to function. One of my most cherished old friends, the Washington, D.C., civil rights figure Julius W. Hobson, used to say, "I sleep mad." The last time I saw him—he was as mad about dying young (or, rather, middle-aged) as he had always been about the poor quality of public schooling for black children in the nation's capital—he said, "Remember, hold on to your anger."

Refusing to conform to the emotionally correct image of old age as a time of placid contemplation is an affirmation of self. Realistic acceptance of the possibility of future dependency, whether as a result of physical disability or the disintegration of one's mind, does not mean that anyone should be required to cede one iota of control over her own life to others until she chooses to do so—or until there is no other choice. That our bodies may prove unable to maintain our autonomy until death, that our disintegrating brains may one day deprive us of the consciousness that distinguishes us as individuals and as a species, increases rather than diminishes the importance of insisting on one's own values as long as possible.

In addition to the promotion of peace of mind, the most common prescription for successful aging is optimism. Unless one falls naturally among the group of human beings who might be classified as nature's cheerleaders, this is bad medicine for anyone who wants to maintain a sense of self-worth. There is no question that it is easier for everyone else—from adult children to doctors—to relate to old people who present an image of hopefulness and good cheer rather than crankiness and depression. But that tells us nothing about whether optimism, unless it is genuine rather than feigned for public consumption, is good for old people themselves. As Barbara Ehrenreich notes in *Bright-sided: How the Relentless Promotion of Positive Thinking Has Undermined America* (2009), the American social directive to adopt positive thinking as the answer to every life crisis applies to people of all ages in our society. On no group, however, does the positive thinking edict descend with greater coercive force than on the old.

The General Social Survey, conducted every year since 1972 by the National Opinion Research Center, asks Americans of every age whether they are "very happy," "pretty happy," or "not too happy." And every year, articles based on the survey report that people over sixty-five are the happiest Americans. The headlines proclaim: "Grow Older and Happier," "Aging Seen As Key to Happiness," and "Older Americans Happier Than Younger Ones." But the findings of the General Social Survey run counter to other studies, which show that older people are at high risk for depression. One possible explanation may be that the researchers combined "very happy" and "pretty happy" into one happy category—which may be as misleading as lumping sexagenarians and nonagenarians in the same "over-sixty-five" group for purposes of calculating the risk of Alzheimer's. In fact, the original study did not show that the reported level of happiness increases with age but that it increases in *young* old age and drops among the oldest survivors. Although people who were in their sixties and seventies between 2000 and 2004 were more likely to consider themselves "very happy" than younger Americans, those in their eighties and nineties were much less likely to report a high level of happiness than either the middle-aged or the young old.[5] None of the stories on the study in the mass media mentioned this finding in their glowing accounts about how older means happier.

I encountered a similar problem in analyzing the results of two national sex studies for the AARP some years ago. These studies showed a high level of satisfaction with their sex lives on the part of the old—but the catch was that "very satisfied" was combined with "satisfied" for purposes of reaching a cheerful conclusion. It seems to me that "satisfied"—like "pretty happy" in the happiness studies—can mean almost anything. It takes a lot less honesty in this society to check off "pretty happy" and "satisfied" instead of "not too happy" and "unsatisfied." Telling the stranger (in this case, the researcher) what he wants to hear is a time-honored way of dealing with intrusive questions, and in this case it makes a much better story. Another possible explanation for the contradiction between reported levels of happiness and the susceptibility of the old to depression is that many of the "positive" emotions reported by the elderly—such as contentment and serenity—are considered "passive" emotions by psychologists. Negative feelings like loneliness are also considered passive. "The reason we think the elderly have higher levels of depression is not because they have higher levels of negative emotions but that they have higher levels of passivity," said Catherine Ross, coauthor of a study on emotions and aging. "The sadness part may not be a negative emotion but a manifestation of the energy level."[6]

Yet the media are relentless in promoting the idea that aging boosts happiness—even when they have to ignore the data within the studies. Only last year, *The New York Times* reported, "A large Gallup poll has found that by almost any measure, people get happier as they get older, and researchers are not sure why." The Gallup poll, unlike the General Social Survey, did not include anyone over eighty-five. By leaving out those in their late eighties and nineties, researchers can be certain that they are never confronted with people in the age groups at highest risk for mental and physical decline. Furthermore, a telephone poll all but guarantees that the pollster will not be hearing from people, whatever their age, who are too ill or are too demented to talk on the phone. The poll reported that stress declines beginning at age twenty-two, reaching its lowest point at eighty-five. Sadness was said to reach its highest point at age fifty, declining until seventy-three, and then rising again slightly by eighty-five.[7] I am not certain why the media are so determined to push the idea that old age brings happiness, but it does seem that the deliberate exclusion of the oldest old from the calculus—both by pollsters and the press—argues powerfully for the determination of American society to define all of the old as the young old.

There is also something insidious about the equation of happiness with contentment, accompanied as often as not by physical exhaustion, in the old. My mother, after a knockout course of intravenous antibiotics to clear up an infection, had the temerity to complain about her fatigue to a visiting nurse. "Why don't you just be good to yourself and lie in bed all day and watch TV?" was the nurse's helpful reply. As it happens, staying in bed and watching television is not my mother's idea of a meaningful, fulfilling day. It doesn't make her "very satisfied" or even "satisfied" with her life. My mother is not contented. The difference between her and these passively happy (but also potentially depressed) old people in studies is that she doesn't pretend to be contented. I admire her for that.

It is not surprising that boomers approaching retirement age have already been well schooled in the received opinion that you're not getting older, you're getting happier. Moreover, boomers are even more disposed than their parents to accept the idea that depression and negative thinking can make you sick and that positive thinking can make you well—so much so that many women, as Ehrenreich notes, blame their own "bad attitude" for recurrences of breast cancer. Many cancer patients have heard so much propaganda about the importance of a positive attitude that they are unaware of recent research indicating that there is absolutely no relationship between a patient's pessimism or optimism and survival.* As people age, they can naturally expect more and more losses—from the death of a spouse to serious illness—over which they have no control. And Americans are told constantly that even if they cannot control their objective circumstances, they can

* A large Australian study of breast cancer patients, presented in 2008 at the annual meeting of the American Society of Clinical Oncology in Chicago, found that a patient's attitude—from despair to the most radiant optimism—had absolutely no effect on the chance of recurrence. Kelly-Anne Phillips, one of the lead researchers, told American cancer specialists that while a positive attitude may indeed improve a woman's overall quality of life, it has no statistically significant effect on the length of survival after an initial diagnosis of breast cancer "and we can now tell them it would not have improved their outcome."

change their attitude toward what is happening—and the only acceptable change is to accentuate the positive. A classic example of positive attitude propaganda, titled "The Secrets of Resilient People," appeared in the AARP magazine, which reaches more Americans over fifty than any print media outlet in the United States. What defines people who are successful at handling the many losses of aging? They view the glass as half full. They find the silver lining. They "actively seek solutions" (unlike those who presumably refuse to get out of bed in the morning). They're spiritual. They're playful. There is no hope here for a serious atheist who looks at a cloud and sees a cloud. (Like the AARP articles I used to write, this piece quotes only one person over age sixty.) Deborah Robinson, whose fifty-seven-year-old husband was diagnosed with early-onset Alzheimer's in 2002, survives the inevitable progression of her husband's disease, and his death, by "reframing the situation in the most positive terms possible." She decides that "we would rise above it, and it would be our finest hour."[8] The articles goes on to present a formula for positive change to those whose dark view of life prevents them from thinking about an Alzheimer's diagnosis as an opportunity for personal growth. "Experts say that negative thinking is just a bad habit," the article assures readers, "though it may take some work to change your mind-set. The first step: Observe the spin you put on your own experiences. When you catch yourself thinking negatively, challenge yourself to frame the situation in more positive terms. For instance, when you open your 401(k) statement, think: 'If I change my investment strategy, I'll do better' instead of 'I'll never recoup my losses.' " The article does not explain exactly how one would apply that sleight of mind to Alzheimer's.

The only hope for a pessimist in this alternate universe known as Eldertopia is to twist herself into a pretzel to change her lifelong bad habit of negative thinking. There is nothing wrong with adhering to the gospel of optimism for people who have demonstrated a capacity, throughout their lives, to reframe even the most hopeless situations in more positive terms. It may well be true that optimistic people have happier lives not only in old age but in youth and middle age. But it seems to me a highly dubious proposition that "successful aging" can be achieved by trying to change one's personality in a fundamental way—by, in a deep sense, denying the values of the person one has always been. Some research scientists have concluded that optimism and pessimism are, to a considerable extent, innate tendencies that manifest themselves even in infancy, and I find this viewpoint persuasive. That makes it even more puzzling when geriatricians, social workers, and hovering friends and relatives try to turn pessimists into optimists as they face the inevitable losses of advancing age. The American cultural approval of cheerfulness, and disapproval of negativity, also force the old to present an equable response that would not be demanded, even in our boosterish culture, from a younger person. My ninety-year-old friend who lost his wife to Alzheimer's was compelled to endure constant comments about how good it was that her suffering had ended and how he wouldn't have wanted her to go on "living that way." Well, of course he did not want her to go on with her extended death-in-life—but no one seemed to understand that he was grieving for the woman she had been when she was in her right mind, not for the lost self she had been for the last years of her life. If anyone had told me that helping to care for a beloved man with Alzheimer's would give me a chance to experience my "finest hour," I probably would have smashed some inanimate object in order to avoid punching the Job's comforter in the nose.

The phenomenon of becoming a better person through adversity has been described by psychologists as post-traumatic growth syndrome. I am not making this up: post-traumatic growth syndrome is the ultimate "positive reframing" of post-traumatic stress disorder. This sort of talk is fundamentally disrespectful both to the stricken and to their caretakers and fellow sufferers. It forces many old people to buy into the equation of optimism with resilience, if only because acknowledging their true feelings of anger and despair may alienate those who have the power to help or harm them. People have a right to their grief, anger, and, yes, depression—and never more so than when they have already endured the blows of a lifetime and the blows still keep on coming. The assertion of this right seems to me to afford far better preparation for suffering and loss than donning a fanciful coat of emotional armor based on the notion that something good always comes out of something bad. In a beautiful memoir about the illness and death of his mother, Susan Sontag, David Rieff writes that "the ways in which she parsed her own despair could themselves appear like a subspecies of hope." After Sontag's death from a virulent form of blood cancer in 2004, at age seventy-one, Rieff found an entry in a journal she had written in her forties, when she received her first cancer diagnosis (of the breast that time).

One sentence leaped off the page: "Despair shall set you free." Rieff initially thought his mother had been making a morbid joke but, as he read further, learned that she had been entirely serious. "I can't write," Sontag noted, "because I don't (won't) give myself permission to voice the despair I feel. Always the *will*. My refusal of despair is blocking my energies."[9] What is intriguing about this passage is its acknowledgment of the sheer effort required to battle despair. It suggests that the conscious refusal of despair is a very different phenomenon from the psychobabbling optimism that sees unimaginable pain and sorrow as an opportunity for personal growth. Laying claim to the right to feel rotten about what is happening can free up energy for the fight to live as well as possible through whatever life hands out as we grow older.

I have asked myself repeatedly why I feel so strongly that the myth and marketing of young old age are harmful not only to society but to individuals who must live through real old age. The case against the propagation of this myth is much clearer when considering large social issues in an aging society, because faith in the future victory of science over old age and its discontents is bound to divert energy and money from the urgent task of devising new institutions and strategies to meet the needs of the old as they are now. But it is more difficult to make the case, on an individual basis, against the elixir of hope for a new old age of sexy skydiving centenarians. Even if there is little fact-based justification for this hope, there is still an argument to be made that belief in agelessness is no more deleterious to adults than belief in Santa Claus is to children. To this I reply that adults are not children. The old are not children, even though they are often treated as children. Hope is not incompatible with realism, but it is incompatible with the expectation that things are going to turn out well if we only conduct ourselves well. Inflated expectations about successful aging, if the body imposes a cruel old age, can lead to real despair. I have heard genuine bitterness rather than irony in the voices of old people, facing some new bodily catastrophe, who whisper "the golden years" under their breath in a tone that sounds like a curse.

The myth of young old age spreads a miasma that obscures the intensity of memory and vision—not wisdom—that is the gift of sentience if one is fortunate enough to remain aware until the end. It is impossible to look enough, to look exactly enough, to look passionately enough while rejecting reality in favor of fantasy. On our last day together, my grandmother did not only mourn for her usefulness. This poet with an eighth-grade education also said, taking a long, last look at the river, "It's good to know that the beauty of the world will go on without me." If I can say that, in full knowledge of my rapidly approaching extinction, I will consider my life a success even though I will have failed, as everyone ultimately does, to defy my old age.

Acknowledgments

First, I wish to thank my mother for agreeing to be interviewed, formally and informally, about the reality of "old old" age. I have learned much more from her about the vicissitudes of advanced old age than I would have learned otherwise—sometimes more than I wanted to know. I would also like to thank her friends Martha Seaman and Mary Ann Ross for their wit and insights.

This is the fourth book I have written in the last decade based largely on my research in that indispensable institution, the New York Public Library. Much of my work has been accomplished in the Frederick Lewis Allen Room, an "office" for nonfiction writers. I especially wish to thank Jay Barksdale, who is in charge of the administration of the Allen Room and its literary denizens—a job comparable to herding cats.

I am particularly grateful to the late Dr. Robert N. Butler and Dr. Muriel R. Gillick for sharing their insights and overview of old age in all of its aspects—positive and negative.

To my friends Angeline Goreau and Mark Lee, thank you for reading portions of my manuscript in advance and talking me through some of the hard spots.

I cannot express enough gratitude to Dan Frank for being the serious editor he is in a frivolous time. I am also indebted to everyone at Pantheon who worked on this book, including Jill Verrillo, Kate Freeman, and Kim Thornton.

As always, thanks to Georges and Anne Borchardt, my literary agents for nearly all of my adult life.

Notes

Notes based on online documents are followed by (W). They may be accessed by entering the title and date in a search engine. URLs are usually omitted because they move too frequently to serve as reliable reference points for the reader.

CHAPTER ONE. NEVER SAY OLD

1. Robert N. Butler, *Why Survive? Being Old in America* (New York, 1975), p. 421.
2. Quoted in Eleanor Blau, "Gray Panthers Out to Liberate Aged," *The New York Times,* May 5, 1972.
3. Interview with the author, July 26, 2008.
4. Alzheimer's Association, "Alzheimer's Disease Facts and Figures 2010." (W)
5. Muriel R. Gillick, *The Denial of Aging: Perpetual Youth, Eternal Life, and Other Dangerous Fantasies* (Cambridge, Mass., 2006), p. 123.
6. Caryn Eve Murray, "How Long Will You Live?" *Newsday,* June 28, 2008.
7. See Dick Smillie, "A Headache for Dr. Oz," *Forbes,* June 16, 2009.
8. In Stephanie Clifford, "Online Age Quiz Is a Window for Drug Makers," *The New York Times,* March 26, 2009.
9. John Updike, *Villages* (New York, 2004), p. 318.
10. Sherwin B. Nuland, *How We Die: Reflections on Life's Final Chapter* (New York, 1994), p. xviii.
11. Betti Jane Levine, "The Sky's the Limit," *Los Angeles Times,* February 5, 1998.
12. Majia Azzati et al., "The Reversal of Fortunes: Trends in County Mortality and Cross-county Mortality Disparities in the United States," *PLOS Medicine,* April 2008. (W)
13. Quoted in Jane E. Brody, "In Act 2 of Life, Doing Work That Matters," *The New York Times,* July 8, 2008.
14. Emma Brown, "Donors Aid Man, 107, at Risk of Losing Housing," *The Washington Post,* July 9, 2009.
15. Bob Pool, "Woman, 97, Has a Front Seat to Homelessness," *Los Angeles Times,* October 16, 2009.

16. Quoted in Anemona Hartocollis, "Rise Seen in Medical Efforts to Improve Very Long Lives," *The New York Times,* July 18, 2008.
17. Robert N. Butler, *The Longevity Revolution: The Benefits and Challenges of Living a Long Life* (New York, 2008), p. 61.

CHAPTER TWO. YOUTH CULTURE: AN AMERICAN TRADITION

1. Ken Dychtwald, *Age Power: How the 21st Century Will Be Ruled by the New Old* (New York, 1999), p. 6.
2. David Hackett Fischer, *Growing Old in America* (New York, 1977), p. 27.
3. Benjamin Wadsworth, "Death is certain, the time when uncertain" (1710). *Early American Imprints,* Series 1, no. 1492 (American Antiquarian Society and News Bank, 2002).
4. Increase Mather, *Two discourses shewing, I. That the Lords ears are open to the prayers of the righteous. II. The dignity & duty of aged servants of the Lord. Also, a preface in which the Congregational discipline of the churches in New-England is vinidcated, with the authors dying testimony there-unto* (Boston, 1716). *Early American Imprints,* Series 1, no. 1838 (American Antiquarian Society and News Bank, 2002).
5. Thomas Paine, *The Rights of Man,* in *The Thomas Paine Reader,* ed. Michael Foot and Isaac Kramnick (New York, 1987), p. 204.
6. J. E. A. Smith, *The History of Pittsfield, Massachusetts,* vol. 2 (Boston, 1869–76), p. 312; Susan Kurland, "A Political History of Concord" (Unpublished senior thesis, Brandeis University, 1972), p. 148, in Fischer, *Growing Old in America.*
7. Lawrence Stone, "Walking over Grandma," *The New York Review of Books,* May 12, 1977.
8. Kevin C. Fleming, Jonathan M. Evans, and Darryl S. Chutka, "A Cultural and Economic History of Old Age in America," *Mayo Clinic Proceedings,* vol. 78 (2003), p. 916. (W)
9. Paula A. Scott, *Growing Old in the Early Republic: Spiritual, Social, and Economic Issues, 1790–1830* (New York, 1997), p. xiv.
10. Eliphet Williams to William Williams, February 9, 1803, Williams Family Papers, Connecticut Historical Society, in ibid., p. 147.
11. Timothy Stephens, August 1, 1820, Hartford County Court Records, Revolutionary Pension Applications, 1830–1832, in Scott, *Growing Old,* p. 193.
12. Eunice Stone to Abigail Williams, September 2, 1824, Abigail Williams Papers, Connecticut Historical Society, in Scott, *Growing Old,* p. 195.
13. Scott, *Growing Old,* p. 160.
14. Thomas Paine, *Agrarian Justice,* in *The Thomas Paine Reader,* p. 483.
15. John Adams and Thomas Jefferson, *The Adams-Jefferson Letters,* vol. 2, ed. Lester J. Cappon (Chapel Hill, N.C., 1959), p. 578.
16. Ibid., p. 579.
17. Stanley Griswold, *The Good Man's Prospects in the Hour of Death* (Litchfield, Conn., 1801), p. 15, in Scott, *Growing Old,* p. 25.

18. Isaac Bickerstaffe, *He Would If He Could; or, An Old Fool Worse Than Any* (New York, 1808), p. 5, in Scott, *Growing Old,* p. 48.
19. Caroline M. Kirkland, *The Evening Book; or, Fireside Talk on Morals and Manners* (New York, 1852), p. 251.
20. Ibid., pp. 257–58.
21. Henry D. Thoreau, *"Walden" and "Resistance to Civil Government,"* ed. William Rossi (New York, 1992), p. 5.
22. Ralph Waldo Emerson, "Circles" (Boston, 1841) *Harvard Classics* (W); "Old Age," *The Atlantic Monthly,* January 1862. (W)
23. W. Andrew Achenbaum, *Old Age in the New Land: The American Experience Since 1790* (Baltimore, 1978), p. 20.
24. Ibid.
25. Burton J. Hendrick, "The Superannuated Man," *McClure's,* no. 32, December 1908.
26. Charles Darwin, *The Descent of Man* (New York, 1948), p. 501.
27. William Osler, "The Fixed Period," in *Aequanimitas: With Other Addresses to Medical Students, Nurses, and Practitioners of Medicine* (Philadelphia, 1910), pp. 391–411.
28. "Osler Writing Essay on Man's Crisis at 40," *The New York Times,* February 25, 1905.
29. "Suicide Heard Osler Speech," *The New York Times,* February 26, 1905.
30. In Glenda Laws, "'The Land of Old Age': Society's Changing Attitudes Toward Urban Built Environments for Elderly People," *Annals of the Association of American Geographers* (December 1993).
31. William Graebner, *A History of Retirement: The Meaning and Function of an American Institution, 1885–1978* (New Haven, Conn., 1980), pp. 7–8.
32. "Fight the Old Age Limit," *Chicago Daily Tribune,* October 18, 1905.
33. "Age Limit Stirs Gray Haired Men," *Chicago Daily Tribune,* October 19, 1905.
34. Dominic Gagliardo, *American Social Insurance* (New York, 1955), in Fischer, *Growing Old in America,* p. 142.
35. U.S. Bureau of Economic Analysis (Washington, D.C., 1973), pp. 212–14, in Fischer, *Growing Old in America,* p. 142.
36. William Graebner, *A History of Retirement,* p. 13.
37. *The Inland Printer,* no. 47 (July 1911), in Graebner, *A History of Retirement,* p. 22.
38. Graebner, *A History of Retirement,* p. 26.
39. Michael B. Katz, *In the Shadow of the Poorhouse: A Social History of Welfare in America* (New York, 1986), p. 202.
40. Harvey Lehman, "The Age of Eminent Leaders, Then and Now," *American Journal of Sociology,* no. 52 (1947), p. 345.
41. Herbert Spencer, *Social Statics* (New York, 1864), p. 415.
42. Felix Adler, *The Spiritual Attitude Toward Old Age* (New York, 1906), p. 6.
43. Ibid., p. 11.
44. G. Stanley Hall, *Senescence: The Last Half of Life* (New York, 1922), p. 383.

CHAPTER THREE. BOOMER BEGINNINGS AND AGE-DEFYING DENIAL

1. George Orwell, "James Burnham and the Managerial Revolution," www.george-orwell.org/James_Burnham_and_the Managerial_Revolution/0.html. (W)

2. Herman Brotman, "Income Resources of the Elderly," *Aging,* May 1970, p. 25. (W)

3. Arthur Schlesinger Jr., *The Age of Roosevelt,* vol. 2, *The Coming of the New Deal* (Boston, 1957), p. 315.

4. Ibid., p. 24.

5. Michael Harrington, *The Other America: Poverty in the United States* (New York, 1962), pp. 5–6.

6. National Council on Aging, *The Golden Years: A Tarnished Myth,* a report prepared for the Office of Economic Opportunity, 1970, p. 4. (W)

7. Laura Miller, "The Golden Age of Self-Help," *The New York Times Book Review,* June 20, 2004.

8. Thomas A. Harris, *I'm OK, You're OK* (New York, 1969), p. xvii.

9. Ibid., p. 264.

10. Quoted in Michael Winerip, "Doc, Make Me New Again," *The New York Times,* February 13, 2009.

11. In ibid.

12. Quoted in Thomas Boswell, "How Can You Tell the Dancer from the Dance?" in *How Life Imitates the World Series* (Garden City, N.Y., 1982), p. 252.

CHAPTER FOUR. MIRACLES OF MODERN MEDICINE AND OTHER HALF-TRUTHS

1. See "The History of Polio: A Hypertext Timeline," posted by Edmund Sass. (W)

2. In Gina Kolata, "In Long Drive to Cure Cancer, Advances Have Been Elusive," *The New York Times,* April 24, 2009.

3. U.S. Census Bureau, "65+ in the United States: 2005," March 9, 2005. (W)

4. Vicki A. Freedman, Linda G. Martin, and Robert F. Schoeni, "Recent Trends in Disability and Functioning Among Older Adults in the United States: A Systematic Review," *The Journal of the American Medical Association,* vol. 288, no. 24 (December 25, 2002).

5. Ibid.

6. Robert F. Schoeni, Vicki A. Freedman, and Linda G. Martin, "Why Is Late Life Disability Declining?" *The Milbank Quarterly,* vol. 86, no. 1 (March 2008).

7. Diane Swanbrow, "Disability Rates Dropping Among Older Americans," in University of Michigan Institute for Social Research, March 10, 2008. (W)

8. Dana E. King, Arch G. Mainous, and Mark Carnemolla, "Adherence to Healthy Lifestyle Habits in U.S. Adults, 1988–2006," *The American Journal of Medicine,* vol. 122, issue 6 (June 2009).

9. Quoted in Roni Caryn Rabin, "Bad Habits Asserting Themselves," *The New York Times,* June 9, 2009.

10. Interview with the author, July 26, 2008.

11. S. Jay Olshansky, Leonard Hayflick, and Bruce A. Carnes, "No Truth to the Fountain of Youth," *Scientific American,* June 2002.
12. Richard A. Miller, "Extending Life: Scientific Prospects and Political Obstacles," *The Milbank Quarterly,* vol. 80, no. 1 (2002), p. 164.
13. Alice Park, "How to Live 100 Years," *Time,* February 22, 2010, p. 61.
14. In ibid., p. 66.
15. Quoted by Jason Pontin, "An Age-Defying Quest (Red Wine Included)," *The New York Times,* July 8, 2007.
16. In ibid.
17. In ibid.
18. Quoted in Susan Jacoby, "Stem Cells: The Rush Is On," *AARP Bulletin,* July 8, 2005.
19. Interview with the author.
20. William A. Haseltine, "Regenerative Medicine: A Future Healing Art," *The Brookings Review,* Winter 2003. (W)
21. In Jon D. Miller, "Breaking News or Broken News: A Brief History of the 'First Cloned Human Embryo' Story," *Nieman Reports,* vol. 56 (Fall 2002), p. 184.
22. Joannie Fischer, "The First Clone," *U.S. News & World Report,* December 3, 2001.
23. Gina Kolata, "Company Says It Produced Embryo Clones," *The New York Times,* November 26, 2001.
24. Gina Kolata, "Cloning Creates Human Embryos," *The New York Times,* February 12, 2004.
25. Nicholas Wade and Choe Sang-Hun, "Human Cloning Was All Faked, Koreans Report," *The New York Times,* January 10, 2006.
26. Muriel R. Gillick, *The Denial of Aging,* pp. 6–7.

CHAPTER FIVE. A MIND IS A TERRIBLE THING TO LOSE

1. Susan Sontag, *Illness As Metaphor* (New York, 1978), p. 3.
2. Greg A. Sachs, "Dying from Dementia," *The New England Journal of Medicine,* vol. 361, no. 16 (October 15, 2009), pp. 1595–96.
3. National Institute of Mental Health, "The Numbers Count: Mental Disorders in America," 2010; Alzheimer's Foundation of America, "About Alzheimer's: Statistics." (W)
4. In Susan Dominus, "Astor Legacy Now a Victim of Indignity," *The New York Times,* July 4, 2009.
5. Lennart Mucke, "Alzheimer's Disease," *Nature,* vol. 461, no. 15 (October 2009).
6. Alessandra Stanley, "The Alzheimer's Project: The Disease That Steals Your Self," *The New York Times,* May 8, 2009.
7. In John Hoffman and Susan Froemke, *The Alzheimer's Project: Momentum in Science* (New York, 2009), pp. xi–xii.
8. Quoted in Denise Grady, "Minimal Benefit Is Seen in Drugs for Alzheimer's," *The New York Times,* April 7, 2004.

9. "Alzheimer's Drugs: Summary of Recommendations," http://www.consumerreports.org/health/best-buy-drugs/alzheimers.htm. (W)

10. Alzheimer's Foundation of America, "About Alzheimer's: Treatment." (W)

11. Interview with the author, July 26, 2008.

12. Quoted in Gina Kolata, "After Years of Study, No Magic Bullet Against Alzheimer's," *The New York Times,* August 29, 2010.

13. Edmund G. Howe, "Caring for Patients with Dementia: An Indication for 'Emotional Communism'" *Journal of Clinical Ethics,* no. 9 (1998) pp. 3–11.

14. T. M. Kitwood, *Dementia Reconsidered: The Person Comes First* (Philadelphia, 1997), p. 144.

15. T. M. Kitwood and Kathleen Bredin, "Towards a Theory of Dementia Care," *Journal of Clinical Ethics,* no. 9 (1998), p. 273.

16. See Marta Turner, Gabrielle Barby, and Andrew Bailey, "The Biochemical Basis of Autism Spectrum Disorders," *Molecular Biology Today* vol. 6, issue 6 (June 2000).

17. Jesse F. Ballenger, *Self, Senility, and Alzheimer's Disease in Modern America: A History* (Baltimore, 2006), p. 3.

18. Thomas Jefferson to John Adams, October 12, 1823, *The Adams-Jefferson Letters,* vol. 2, ed. Lester J. Cappon (Chapel Hill, N.C., 1959), p. 599.

19. Jefferson to Adams, January 8, 1925, in ibid., p. 695.

20. Jefferson to Adams, June 1, 1822, in ibid., p. 577.

21. Frederick Law Olmsted to John Olmsted, May 10, 1895; to Frederick Jr., October 15, 1895, Papers of Frederick Law Olmsted, Library of Congress, in Dorie McCullough Lawson, *Posterity: Letters of Great Americans to Their Children* (New York, 2004), pp. 241–43.

22. Karen A. Lyman, "Bringing the Social Back In: A Critique of the Biomedicalization of Dementia," *The Gerontologist,* vol. 29, no. 5 (1989), p. 603.

23. Ibid.

24. Claudia Cooper, Gill Livingston et al., "The CARD Study—Abuse of People with Dementia by Family Carers," *British Medical Journal,* January 23, 2009.

25. "Who Buys Long-Term Care Insurance," America's Health Insurance Plans, April 2007. (W)

26. Susan L. Mitchell et al., "The Clinical Course of Advanced Dementia," *The New England Journal of Medicine,* vol. 361, no. 16 (October 15, 2009), pp. 1529–38.

CHAPTER SIX. WOMEN: EVENTUALLY THE ONLY SEX

1. Robert N. Butler, *The Longevity Revolution* (New York, 2008), table 1.1, p. 404.

2. Ibid., p. 127.

3. Bill Hendrick, "Disability Gender Gap for Seniors," WebMD Health News, May 5, 2009. (W)

4. S. Jay Olshansky, Leonard Hayflick, and Bruce A. Carnes, "No Truth to the Fountain of Youth," *Scientific American,* June 2002.

5. Women's Institute for a Secure Retirement, "Minority Women and Retirement Income," November 15, 2002. (W)

6. Abraham Moisisa and Steven Hipple, "Trends in Labor Force Participation in the United States," *Monthly Labor Review,* October 2006, pp. 35–57.

7. Timothy Smeeding and Susanna Sandström, "Poverty and Income Maintenance in Old Age: A Cross-National View of Low Income Older Women," *Luxembourg Income Study Working Papers Series,* Working Paper No. 398, January 2005. (W)

8. Sylvia Ann Hewlett, *Off-ramps and On-ramps: Keeping Talented Women on the Road to Success* (Boston, 2007), p. 45.

9. Ibid., p. 43.

10. Sharon R. Cohany and Emy Sok, "Trends in Labor Force Participation of Married Mothers of Infants," *Monthly Labor Review,* vol. 130, no. 2 (February 2007).

11. Meg Wolitzer, *The Ten-Year Nap* (New York, 2008), p. 13.

12. Ibid., p. 353.

13. Hewlett, *Off-ramps and On-ramps,* pp. 50–51.

14. Ibid., p. 34.

15. Betty Friedan, *The Fountain of Age* (New York, 1993), p. 299.

16. Ibid., p. 151.

17. Susan Jacoby, "Appearance Anxiety," *The New York Times,* August 28, 1988.

18. Nora Ephron, "A Few Words About Breasts," in *Crazy Salad* (New York, 1975), pp. 3–12.

19. Letty Cottin Pogrebin, *Getting Over Getting Older: An Intimate Journey* (New York, 1996), pp. 128–29.

20. Robert McG. Thomas Jr., "Shirley Polykoff, 90, Ad Writer Whose Query Colored a Nation," *The New York Times,* June 8, 1998.

21. J. Walker Smith and Ann Clurman, *Rocking the Ages: The Yankelovich Report on Generational Marketing* (New York, 1997), p. 227.

22. In Ruth La Ferla, "Over 60: Fashion's Lost Generation," *The New York Times,* December 3, 2000.

23. In ibid.

24. Philip Roth, *The Dying Animal* (New York, 2001), p. 34.

25. Susan Jacoby, "Sex in America," *AARP : The Magazine,* July–August 2005.

26. Colette, "Under the Blue Lantern," trans. by Roger Senhouse, in *Earthly Paradise,* ed. Robert Phelps (London, 1966), p. 495.

27. Colette, *Belles Saisons: A Colette Scrapbook,* ed. Robert Phelps (New York, 1978), p. 272.

CHAPTER SEVEN. GREEDY GEEZERS AND OTHER HALF-TRUTHS

1. Henry Fairlie, "Talkin' 'Bout My Generation," *The New Republic,* March 28, 1988.

2. Ibid.

3. Patrick Purcell, "Income of Americans Aged 65 and Older, 1968 to 2008," Congressional Research Service, November 4, 2009, p. 15. (W)

4. Robert N. Butler, *The Longevity Revolution* (New York, 2008), p. 46.

5. Purcell, "Income of Americans," figures 9 and 10, p. 19. (W)

6. Ibid., p. 12.

7. Cited in Stephen Gandel, "Why It's Time to Retire the 401(k)," *Time,* October 9, 2009.

8. Dean Baker and David Rosnick, *The Housing Crash and the Retirement Prospects of the Late Baby Boomers,* Center for Economic and Policy Research (Washington, D.C., 2008), updated March 2010. (W)

9. Ibid., executive summary.

10. Edmund L. Andrews, *Busted: Life Inside the Great Mortgage Meltdown* (New York, 2009), p. 37.

11. Ibid., pp. 6–7.

12. In Gandel, "Why It's Time."

13. In Jack Healy, "Back into the Deep End," *The New York Times,* September 11, 2009.

14. Carole Fleck, "No Rest for the Weary," *AARP Bulletin,* September 2009.

15. Quoted in ibid.

16. In Michael Luo, "Years After Layoffs, Many Still Struggle to Match Old Salaries," *The New York Times,* August 4, 2009.

17. Till von Wachter, Jae Song, and Joyce Manchester, "Long-term Earning Losses Due to Mass Layoffs During the 1982 Recession," April 2007. (W)

18. In Luo, "Years After Layoffs."

19. Quoted in Steven Greenhouse, "65 and Up and Looking for Work," *The New York Times,* October 24, 2009.

20. In ibid.

21. Henry Morgenthau, *Diaries,* Henry Morgenthau Jr. Papers, vol. 3, pp. 58–60, Franklin D. Roosevelt Library, Hyde Park, N.Y., quoted in William Graebner, *A History of Retirement* (New Haven, Conn., 1980), p. 256.

CHAPTER EIGHT. THE "WISDOM OF OLD AGE"

1. Paul P. Baltes et al., "Wisdom: One Facet of Successful Aging," in *Late Life Potential,* ed. Marion Perlmutter (Gerontological Society of America, 1990), p. 75.

2. Elkhonon Goldberg, *The Wisdom Paradox: How Your Mind Can Grow Stronger As Your Brain Grows Older* (New York, 2005), p. 71.

3. Ibid.

4. William Thomas, "What Is Old Age For?" *Yes!* Fall 2005. (W)

5. Henry Fairlie, "Talkin' 'Bout My Generation," *The New Republic,* March 28, 1988.

6. "50 Reasons to Love Being 50+," *AARP: The Magazine,* September–October 2008.

7. Monika Ardelt, "Wisdom and Life Satisfaction in Old Age," *The Journals of Gerontology: Series B: Psychological Sciences and Social Sciences,* vol. 52B (January 1997). (W)

8. Daniel J. Levinson, *The Seasons of a Man's Life* (New York, 1978), p. 36.

9. Adam Hochschild, *Half the Way Home: A Memoir of Father and Son* (New York, 1987), p. 198.

10. Jimmy Carter, *The Virtues of Aging* (New York, 1998), p. 8.

11. Henry A. Kissinger, *Crisis: The Anatomy of Two Major Foreign Policy Crises* (New York, 2003), p. 535.

12. Anthony Lewis, "The Kissinger Doctrine," *The New York Times,* February 25, 1975.

13. Kissinger, *Crisis,* p. 544.

14. Rita Levi-Montalcini, *In Praise of Imperfection: My Life and Work,* trans. Luigi Attardi (New York, 1988), p. 5.

15. Ibid., p. 38.

16. Ibid., p. 205.

17. Goldberg, *The Wisdom Paradox,* p. 13.

18. Ibid., p. 234.

19. Ibid.

20. David N. Anderson, "Treating Depression in Old Age: The Reasons to Be Positive," *Age and Ageing: The Journal of the British Geriatrics Society,* vol. 30 (2001). (W)

21. Interview with the author, November 3, 2009.

22. Goldberg, *The Wisdom Paradox,* p. 273.

23. Ibid., p. 291.

24. Ibid., p. 64.

25. Ibid., p. 288.

26. Henry Alford, *How to Live: A Search for Wisdom from Old People* (New York, 2009), p. 3.

27. Ibid., p. 179.

28. Betty Friedan, *The Fountain of Age* (New York, 1993), p. 244.

29. Ibid.

30. Ibid., p. 326.

31. Ibid., p. 638.

32. Kathleen Woodward, "Against Wisdom: The Social Politics of Anger and Aging," *Journal of Aging Studies,* vol. 17, no. 1 (February 2003), p. 63. (W)

33. Ibid.

CHAPTER NINE. ENDINGS

1. Philippe Ariès, *The Hour of Our Death,* trans. Helen Weaver (New York, 1981), p. 170.

2. Ibid.

3. Baohui Zhang et al., "Health Care Costs in the Last Week of Life: Associations with End-of-Life Conversations," *Archives of Internal Medicine,* vol. 169, no. 5 (March 9, 2009), pp. 480–88.

4. Richard Dooling, "Health Care's Generation Gap," *The New York Times,* August 17, 2009.

5. Pew Research Center for the People and the Press, "Strong Public Support for Right to Die," January 5, 2006. (W)

6. Zhang et al., "Health Care Costs."

7. Pew Research Center, "Strong Public Support."

8. In ibid.

9. See Mark Leibovich, "After a Grim Diagnosis, Determined to Make a 'Good Ending,'" *The New York Times,* August 27, 2009.

10. National Institute of Mental Health, "Suicide in the U.S.: Statistics and Prevalence," 2006 (last year for which statistics are available). (W)

11. In Daniel Goleman, "Missing in Talk of Right to Die: Depression's Grip on a Patient," *The New York Times,* December 4, 1991.

12. Pew Research Center, "Strong Public Support."

13. *Gonzales v. Oregon,* 546 U.S. 243.

14. Kathleen Foley and Herbert Hendin, eds. *The Case Against Assisted Suicide: For the Right to End-of-Life Care* (Baltimore, 2002), pp. 164–65.

15. Ibid., p. 313.

16. Ibid., p. 314.

17. Ariès, *Hour of Our Death,* pp. 570–71.

18. Foley and Hendin, *Case,* p. 313.

19. Betty Rollin, *Last Wish* (New York, 1985), p. 150.

20. Ibid., p. 236.

21. Quoted in Michelle Munz, "Millstone Tribute Sheds Light on Likely Suicide," *St. Louis Post-Dispatch,* June 1, 2009.

22. Bill McClellan, "Final Gift from Man Who Embraced Life," *St. Louis Post-Dispatch,* June 10, 2009.

CHAPTER TEN.
THE ETHICS OF LONGEVITY: AN ARGUMENT IN SEARCH OF FACTS

1. Richard A. Miller, "Extending Life: Scientific Prospects and Political Obstacles," *The Milbank Quarterly,* vol. 80, no. 1 (2002), p. 164.

2. Arthur Caplan, "It's Not Immoral to Want to Be Immortal," MSNBC.com, April 25, 2008. (W)

3. Interview with the author, 2008.

4. In Robert Hellenga, *The Fall of a Sparrow* (New York, 1998), p. 182. Translation by the author.

5. Ibid., p. 183.

6. Nicholas Wade, "Dieting Monkeys Offer Hope for Living Longer," *The New York Times,* July 10, 2009.

7. In ibid.

8. Miller, "Extending Life," p. 174.

9. David E. Harrison et al., "Rapamycin Fed Late in Life Extends Lifespan in Genetically Heterogeneous Mice," *Nature,* no. 460 (July 8, 2009), pp. 392–95.

10. Nicholas Wade, "Tests Begin on Drugs That May Slow Aging," *The New York Times,* August 18, 2009.

11. David B. Goldstein, "Common Genetic Variations and Human Traits," *The New England Journal of Medicine,* April 23, 2009.

12. In Alice Park, "How to Live 100 Years," *Time,* February 22, 2010, pp. 62, 65.

13. Peter Kraft and David J. Hunter, "Genetic Risk Prediction—Are We There Yet?" *The New England Journal of Medicine,* April 23, 2009.

14. Jan Vijg and Judith Campisi, "Puzzles, Promises and a Cure for Aging," *Nature,* no. 454 (August 28, 2008), pp. 1065–71.

15. Ibid.

16. Quoted in Wade, "Tests Begin on Drugs."

17. Quoted in Bret Stephens, "Soul Man," *The Wall Street Journal,* January 7, 2006.

18. Leon Kass, "L'Chaim and Its Limits," *First Things: A Journal of Religion and Public Life,* May 2001.

19. Ibid.

20. Ibid.

21. Daniel Callahan, *The Troubled Dream of Life: Living with Mortality* (New York, 1993), p. 125.

22. Quoted in Lawrence M. Fisher, "The Race to Cash in on the Genetic Code," *The New York Times,* August 29, 1999.

23. Gregory Stock, *Redesigning Humans: Our Inevitable Genetic Future* (Boston, 2002), p. 80. Also, see pp. 78–88.

24. Harry R. Moody, "Intimations of Prolongevity," *The Gerontologist,* vol. 44, no. 3 (2004).

25. Christine Overall, *Aging, Death, and Human Longevity: A Philosophical Inquiry* (Berkeley, Calif., 2003), p. 40.

26. Ibid., p. 194.

27. Miller, "Extending Life," p. 171.

28. Ibid.

29. Muriel R. Gillick, *The Denial of Aging* (Cambridge, Mass., 2006), p. 224.

CHAPTER ELEVEN. NECESSARY BEDFELLOWS: BRIDGES BETWEEN GENERATIONS, OLD-AGE AUTONOMY

1. In Eduardo Porter, "Think About the Grandkids," *The New York Times,* October 11, 2009.

2. Quoted in Gardiner Harris, "A Heated Debate Is Dividing Generations in AARP," *The New York Times,* October 4, 2009.

3. Tyler Cowen, "Means Testing for Medicare," *The New York Times,* July 20, 2008.

4. Muriel R. Gillick, *The Denial of Aging* (Cambridge, Mass., 2006), pp. 255–56.

5. J. Walker Smith and Ann Clurman, *Rocking the Ages: The Yankelovich Report on Generational Marketing* (New York, 1997), p. 45.

6. Mary Pipher, "Another Country," in *Aging in America,* ed. Olivia J. Smith (New York, 2000), p. 152.

CONCLUSION

1. Quoted in Clive Thompson, "Why New Yorkers Last Longer," *New York,* August 13, 2007.

2. "Best Places to Retire 2009," CNNMoney.com. (W)

3. Tom W. Smith, "Job Satisfaction in America: Trends and Socio-demographic Correlates," General Social Survey, National Opinion Research Center at the University of Chicago, August 27, 2007. (W)

4. Mary Pipher, "Another Country," in *Aging in America,* ed. Olivia J. Smith (New York, 2000), p. 140.

5. Yang Yang, "Social Inequalities in Happiness in the United States, 1972–2004: An Age-Period-Cohort Analysis," *American Sociological Review,* vol. 73, no. 2 (April 2008), table 1.

6. Quoted in Shankar Vedantam, "Older Americans May Be Happier Than Younger Ones," *The Washington Post,* July 14, 2008.

7. Nicholas Bakalar, "Happiness May Come with Age, Study Says," *The New York Times,* May 31, 2010.

8. Quoted in Beth Howard, "The Secrets of Resilient People," *AARP: The Magazine,* November–December 2009.

9. David Rieff, *Swimming in a Sea of Death: A Son's Memoir* (New York, 2008), pp. 139–40.

Selected Bibliography

Achenbaum, W. Andrew. *Old Age in the New Land: The American Experience Since 1790*. Baltimore: Johns Hopkins University Press, 1978.

Adams, John, and Thomas Jefferson. *The Adams-Jefferson Letters*. Edited by Lester J. Cappon. Chapel Hill: University of North Carolina Press, 1959.

Adler, Felix. *The Spiritual Attitude Toward Old Age*. New York: Ethical Culture Society, 1906.

Alford, Henry. *How to Live: A Search for Wisdom from Old People*. New York: Hachette, 2009.

Andrews, Edmund L. *Busted: Life Inside the Great Mortgage Meltdown*, New York: Norton, 2009.

Angel, Ronald J., and Jacqueline L. Angel. *Who Will Care for Us: Aging and Long-term Care in Multicultural America*. New York: New York University Press, 1997.

Ariès, Philippe. *The Hour of Our Death*. Translated by Helen Weaver. New York: Knopf, 1981.

Ballenger, Jesse F. *Self, Senility, and Alzheimer's Disease in Modern America: A History*. Baltimore: Johns Hopkins University Press, 2006.

Boswell, Thomas. *How Life Imitates the World Series: An Inquiry into the Game*. New York: Penguin, 1983.

Bourne, Randolph S. *Youth and Life*. Boston: Houghton Mifflin, 1913.

Briggs, Rick. *Caregiving Daughters: Accepting the Role of Caregiver for Elderly Parents*. New York: Garland, 1998.

———. *The Longevity Revolution: The Benefits and Challenges of Living a Long Life*. New York: Public Affairs, 2008.

Butler, Robert N. *Why Survive? Being Old in America*. New York: Harper, 1975.

Butler, Robert N., and Kenzo Kiikuni, eds. *Who Is Responsible for My Old Age?* New York: Springer, 1993.

Callahan, Daniel. *False Hopes: Why America's Quest for Perfect Health Is a Recipe for Failure*. New York: Simon and Schuster, 1998.

———. *The Troubled Dream of Life: Living with Mortality*. New York: Simon and Schuster, 1993.

Carter, Jimmy. *The Virtues of Aging*. New York: Ballantine, 1998.

Cary, Cynthia. *A Foxy Old Woman's Guide to Living with Friends*. Freedom, Calif.: Crossing Press, 1998.

Cather, Willa. *The Old Beauty and Others*. New York: Knopf, 1948.

Cicero. *On the Art of Growing Old*. Translated by Herbert Newell Couch. Providence, R.I.: Brown University Press, 1959.

Cole, Thomas. *The Journey of Life: A Cultural History of Aging in America*. New York: Cambridge University Press, 1992.

Colette. *Belles Saisons: A Colette Scrapbook*. Edited by Robert Phelps. New York: Farrar, Straus and Giroux, 1978.

———. *Earthly Paradise*. Edited by Robert Phelps. London: Secker and Warburg, 1966.

Cowen, Tyler. *Create Your Own Economy: The Path to Prosperity in a Disordered World*. New York: Penguin, 2009.

Dychtwald, Ken. *Age Power: How the 21st Century Will Be Ruled by the New Old*. New York: Jeremy P. Tarcher/Putnam, 1999.

Ehrenreich, Barbara. *Bright-sided: How the Relentless Promotion of Positive Thinking Has Undermined America*. New York: Metropolitan Books, 2009.

Emerson, Ralph Waldo. *Emerson's Essays*. New York: Harper Colophon, 1951.

Ephron, Nora. *Crazy Salad: Some Things About Women*. New York: Knopf, 1975.

———. *I Feel Bad About My Neck and Other Thoughts on Being a Woman*. New York: Knopf, 2006.

Ferguson, Niall. *The Ascent of Money: A Financial History of the World*. New York: Penguin, 2009.

Fischer, David Hackett. *Growing Old in America*. New York: Oxford University Press, 1977.

Foley, Kathleen and Herbert Hendin, eds. *The Case Against Assisted Suicide: For the Right to End-of-Life Care*. Baltimore: Johns Hopkins University Press, 2002.

Friedan, Betty. *The Fountain of Age*. New York: Simon and Schuster, 1993.

Gardam, Jane. *Old Filth*. New York: Europa Editions, 2006.

Gaylin, Willard, and Bruce Jennings. *The Perversion of Autonomy: The Proper Uses of Coercion and Constraints in a Liberal Society*. New York: Free Press, 1996.

Ghilarducci, Teresa, ed. *What You Need to Know About the Economics of Growing Old (but Were Afraid to Ask)*. South Bend, Ind.: University of Notre Dame Press, 2004.

Gillick, Muriel R. *The Denial of Aging: Perpetual Youth, Eternal Life, and Other Dangerous Fantasies*. Cambridge: Harvard University Press, 2006.

Goldberg, Elkhonon. *The Wisdom Paradox: How Your Mind Can Grow Stronger As Your Brain Grows Older*. New York: Gotham Books, 2005.

Graebner, William. *A History of Retirement: The Meaning and Function of an American Institution, 1885–1978*. New Haven, Conn.: Yale University Press, 1980.

Harrington, Michael. *The Other America: Poverty in the United States*. New York: Macmillan, 1962.

Harrison, Barbara Grizzuti. *Off Center*. New York: Dial Press, 1980.

Hawthorne, Nathaniel. "Dr. Heidegger's Experiment." In *Little Masterpieces,* edited by Bliss Perry. New York: Doubleday, Page & Co., 1906.

Hellenga, Robert. *The Fall of a Sparrow*. New York: Scribner, 1998.

Hewlett, Sylvia Ann. *Off-ramps and On-ramps: Keeping Talented Women on the Road to Success*. Boston: Harvard Business School Press, 2007.

Hirshman, Linda. *Get to Work: A Manifesto for Women of the World*. New York: Viking, 2007.

Hochschild, Adam. *Half the Way Home: A Memoir of Father and Son*. New York: Penguin Books, 1987.

Jacoby, Susan. *The Age of American Unreason*. New York: Pantheon, 2008.

Kirkland, Caroline M. *The Evening Book; or, Fireside Talk on Morals and Manners*. New York: Scribner, 1852.

Kissinger, Henry A. *Crisis: The Anatomy of Two Major Foreign Policy Crises*. New York: Simon and Schuster, 2003.

Kitwood, T. M. *Dementia Reconsidered: The Person Comes First*. Philadelphia: Open University Press, 1997.

Lasch, Christopher. *The Culture of Narcissism: American Life in an Age of Diminishing Expectations*. New York: Norton, 1978.

Lawson, Dorie McCullough. *Posterity: Letters of Great Americans to Their Children*. New York: Broadway Books, 2004.

Levi-Montalcini, Rita. *In Praise of Imperfection: My Life and Work*. Translated by Luigi Attardi. New York: Basic Books, 1988.

Levinson, Daniel J. *The Seasons of a Man's Life*. New York: Knopf, 1978.

———. *The Seasons of a Woman's Life*. In collaboration with Judy D. Levinson. New York: Knopf, 1996.

Moody, Harry. *Ethics in an Aging Society*. Baltimore: Johns Hopkins University Press, 1992.

Nuland, Sherwin B. *How We Die: Reflections on Life's Final Chapter*. New York: Vintage, 1997.

Osler, Sir William. *Aequanimitas: With Other Addresses to Medical Students, Nurses, and Practitioners of Medicine*. Philadelphia: P. Blakiston's Son, 1910.

Overall, Christine. *Aging, Death, and Human Longevity: A Philosophical Inquiry*. Berkeley: University of California Press, 2003.

Paine, Thomas. *The Thomas Paine Reader*. Eds. Michael Foot and Isaac Kramnick. New York: Penguin Books, 1987.

Pogrebin, Letty Cottin. *Getting Over Getting Older: An Intimate Journey*. New York: Little, Brown, 1996.

Putnam, Robert D. *Bowling Alone: The Collapse and Revival of American Community*. New York: Simon and Schuster, 2000.

Rieff, David. *Swimming in a Sea of Death: A Son's Memoir*. New York: Simon and Schuster, 2008.

Rollin, Betty. *Last Wish*. New York: Linden Press/Simon and Schuster, 1985.

Roth, Philip. *The Dying Animal*. Boston: Houghton Mifflin, 2001.

———. *Everyman*. Boston: Houghton Mifflin, 2006.

———. *Exit Ghost*. Boston: Houghton Mifflin, 2004.

———. *The Humbling*. Boston: Houghton Mifflin, 2009.

———. *Reading Myself and Others*. New York: Penguin, 1985.

Sarton, May. *After the Stroke: A Journal*. New York: Norton, 1988.

Schlesinger, Arthur. *The Age of Roosevelt*. Vol. 2, *The Coming of the New Deal*. Boston: Houghton Mifflin, 1957.

Scott, Paula A. *Growing Old in the Early Republic: Spiritual, Social, and Economic Issues, 1790–1830*. New York: Routledge, 1997.

Shulman, Alix Kates. *To Love What Is: A Marriage Transformed*. New York: Farrar, Straus and Giroux, 2008.

Smith, J. Walker, and Ann Clurman. *Rocking the Ages: The Yankelovich Report on Generational Marketing*. New York: Harper Business, 1997.

Smith, Olivia J., ed. *Aging in America*. New York: H. W. Wilson, 2000.

Sontag, Susan. *Illness As Metaphor*. New York: Farrar, Straus and Giroux, 1978.

Stanton, Elizabeth Cady. *Eighty Years and More: Reminiscences, 1815–1987*. Boston: Northeastern University Press. 1993.

Stock, Gregory. *Redesigning Humans: Our Inevitable Genetic Future*. Boston: Houghton Mifflin, 2002.

Thoreau, Henry David. *Walden;* and *Resistance to Civil Government: Authoritative Texts, Thoreau's Journal, Reviews, and Essays in Criticism*. Ed. William Rossi. New York: Norton, 1992.

Updike, John. *My Father's Tears and Other Stories*. New York: Knopf, 2009.

———. *The Poorhouse Fair*. New York: Knopf, 1958.

———. *Villages*. New York: Knopf, 2004.

Wolitzer, Meg. *The Ten-Year Nap*. New York: Riverhead Books, 2008.

Index

AARP, 19, 93–4, 150–1, 157, 158, 291
health care debate and, 267–8, 277
AARP: The Magazine, 187, 293
AARP Bulletin, 18, 87, 93–4
Achenbaum, W. Andrew, 40, 41
"acting one's age," 37–8
Adams, Abigail, 252
Adams, John, 30, 34, 35–6, 117–18, 252
ADL (activities of daily living) disabilities, 83–5
Adler, Felix, 52–3
Advanced Cell Technology (ACT), 96–8
advance directives, 214
Africa, saying about wisdom of old age attributed to, 180n
African Americans, 20, 62–3, 64, 69, 130, 236
"Against Wisdom" (Woodward), 206–7
age discrimination, in workplaces of Gilded Age, 47–51
ageism, 17, 18–19, 195, 207, 208, 268
coining of term, 7
Hall's repudiation of, 54–5
Osler's valedictory address and, 44–8
selective diminution of, 7–10
see also youth culture
Age of Reason, The (Paine), 34
aging:
defined, 88
diseases related to, 8, 16–17, 87–9, 246–7; *see also* Alzheimer's disease
distinction between mental and physical deterioration in, 35–6, 40, 43–4, 117–18
as euphemism for "old," 6
happiness and, 290–1
progressive damage to DNA and, 251
rate of, intrinsic to each species, 250
Agrarian Justice (Paine), 34
AIDS, 217, 234–5
Albee, Edward, 204, 205
alcohol intake, 75, 85
Alford, Henry, 203–5
Allen, Woody, 239
Alliance Defense Fund, 93n
Alzheimer's Association, 112
Alzheimer's disease, 8, 9, 12, 16, 17, 24, 82, 83, 84, 88, 89, 91, 100 26, 293
abusive caregivers and, 121–2
age as chief risk factor for, 109, 110
anti-aging research and, 247
at-home care for, 122–3, 124–5
author's personal experience with, 103–4, 120, 121, 122, 294
awareness of one's own helplessness in, 100–1, 113
biomedical model of, 113–15, 116, 119, 122
denial of risk of, 102–3, 104, 110
diagnosis of, 108–9, 110–11
early-onset, 106, 108–9, 249
education level and, 104

Alzheimer's disease *(continued)*
embryonic stem cell research and, 92, 93, 95, 105
gender difference in, 128
genetic pathways to, 105–6, 109, 129, 249–50
government policies and, 122–6
health habits and, 114–15, 129
junk thought and, 116–17, 119, 120
media portrayals of, 102–3
need for long-term care facilities and, 99, 125–6
nursing home placement and, 111–12, 123–5
painful medical interventions and, 123–4
pharmaceuticals marketed for prevention or slowing of, 17–18, 111–12, 115
physiological and neurological mechanisms in, 107–8
prevalence of, 101–3, 113–14
Reagan's presidency and, 182–3
social constructivist model of, 115–22
social shame and stigma surrounding, 103–5, 113
suicide and, 226, 229
time lapse between basic research and usable treatment for, 99, 106, 107, 109–10
treatment prospects for, 106–7, 108, 109–10, 111–12, 113
Alzheimer's Foundation of America, 111, 112, 113
Alzheimer's Project, The, 103, 106, 107, 109–10, 111, 124–5
American Express, 51
American Revolution, 29–31, 32, 34, 35
"American Scholar" (Emerson), 38
amyloid protein, 108
Andrews, Edmund L., 164
anesthesia, 252–3
antebellum era, 36–41
Anti-Age Limit League, 48–9
anti-aging products:
class and access to, 260–1
clinical trials and, 8–9, 246
dietary supplements, 240–1, 244
marketing of, 90–2, 245–6
rapamycin and, 248–9
resveratrol and, 8–9, 15, 91–2
anti-aging research, 87–99, 184, 239–64
academic bioethicists' support for, 260–3
aging process and, 87–9, 251
allocation of money for, 264
biotech entrepreneurs and, 259–60
conservative Christians' opposition to, 241–2
dying as part of living and, 251, 254, 263
embryonic stem cell research and, 8, 24, 92–5, 105
ethical debate about, 239–44, 252–64
evolutionary biologists' perspective on, 251–2
existential anxieties and, 254–8
feasible extended life spans and, 89, 239–40
gerontologiphobia accusations and, 261–2
human longing for immortality and, 89, 241, 242–3
Kass's arguments against, 255–8
media hype and, 96–8, 247–8, 253–4
in other species, 244–5
secular arguments against, 242
state of science of, 244–52
targeting overall aging process vs. specific age-related diseases in, 246–7
and time lapse between basic research and usable treatment, 94–5
use for extra time and, 256–7
vigor of extended lives and, 90, 247
anti-government philosophy, 35
Aquinas, Thomas, 231
Aricept, 17–18, 111–12
Ariès, Philippe, 211, 233–4
arthritis, 15, 21, 35, 81, 84
gender difference in, 128
obesity and, 129
artificial life support, 216, 242
Ashcroft, John, 230

assets, preserved by old Europeans, 177, 178
asset transfers, Medicaid and, 109
assisted living, 153–4, 272, 278–80
Astor, Brooke, 12, 102, 103, 105, 203
athletic capacity, 76–8
Austad, Steven, 245
autism, 116–17
autonomy, criticism of ideal of, 280–1
autonomy in old age, xii, 27, 271, 278–81
  author's personal experience with family members' loss of, 3–4, 282–4
  best places for, 285–7
  decline in disability rates and, 83–5
  labor-saving devices and, 84–5
  loss of, as trade-off for having physical needs met, 278–80
  obesity and, 128–30
  public subsidies for home care and, 272, 273
  social policy changes and, 272–3, 285
  transition to dependency from, 288, 289

baby boomers, 56–79
  African American or poor, 62–3
  convinced that age can be defied, 66, 68, 74–9
  disruption of expectations of, 276–7
  economic expectations of, 59–60, 61–2, 276, 277
  generational conflicts and, 59, 157, 265–8, 274–8
  Gillick's call for collective action by, 274–5
  health habits of, 86–7
  impact of Crash of '08 on, 162–71, 269, 276, 277–8
  impending retirement of, 155–7, 158, 171, 176, 179, 263
  linear life and career paths rejected by, 58, 61–2, 66–7
  low rate of personal savings of, 162, 167–8, 171
  marketing geared to, 14–16
  medical miracles in formative years of, 80–2
  need for intergenerational contract and, 265–8, 274–8
  older vs. younger, 60–1, 268–9, 276
  predictions on aging of, 4–5
  retirement as envisioned by, 59–60, 168
  retirement postponed by, 168, 277
  self-help ethos of, 57, 66–74
"baby bust" generation, 62
Baker, Dean, 162, 164
Ballenger, Jesse F., 117
bankruptcy, 22
  corporate, pensions lost due to, 169, 178
Baryshnikov, Mikhail, xiii
Bass, Anne, 145
Bazell, Robert, 6
Beck, Aaron, 225
Beethoven, Ludwig van, 47
being at peace with oneself, 200, 201, 205
Berger, Bessie Mae, 23–4
Berman, Jennifer, 151
Berne, Eric, 70
Bickerstaffe, Isaac, 37
Bill (homeless man in New York City), 32–3
Bing, Rudolf, 102
birth control pill, 253
bladder cancer, age and successful treatment of, 18
Bloom, Harold, 204, 205
bodily functions, preoccupation with, 186
Bond, Julian, 188
Boniva, 13–14
boomers, *see* baby boomers
brain, balance of power between hemispheres of, 200
breast cancer, 21, 105, 129, 283, 292
Bredin, Kathleen, 116
Bright-sided (Ehrenreich), 290
Broderick, Minnie (author's grandmother), 3–4, 6, 10, 25–6, 78, 85, 143, 152, 282–4, 287–8, 296
Brookings Review, 95
Browning, Robert, 180–1
Buchanan, James, 41
Buffett, Warren, 160

Bureau of Labor Statistics, 168, 172
Bush, George W., 19, 56, 92, 230, 276, 277
Busted (Andrews), 164
Butler, Robert N., 4–5, 9, 27, 86, 114–15, 130

Callahan, Daniel, 258, 263
caloric restriction, anti-aging effects of, 244–5, 251
Cambodia, extension of Vietnam War into, 195–6
Campisi, Judith, 251, 252
cancer, 81, 88, 92, 102, 103, 105, 129, 216, 219, 222–3, 251
  health habits and, 129
  positive attitude and, 292
  responses to diagnosis of, 226
  treatment vs. cure for, 82–3
Caplan, Arthur, 241, 242, 254
cardiovascular disease, 84, 129
Carnegie, Andrew, 43–4
Carnes, Bruce A., 88–9
Carter, Elliott, 10
Carter, Jimmy, 194–5, 196
Carter, Rosalynn, 194
Case Against Assisted Suicide, The (Foley and Hendin), 230–4
cataract surgery, 84
CBS News, 267
Census, U.S., 4, 28, 42, 49
Census Bureau, U.S., 83, 174
centennial landmark, desire to reach, 218, 240
Center for Economic and Policy Research (CEPR), 162–5, 171
Centers for Disease Control, 225n
Certner, David, 173
character, continuity of, 192–4, 196–9
Chicago Daily Tribune, 48
childbearing:
  delaying of, 66, 67–8
  longevity extension and, 255–6
child care, taking time off from work for, 130–6
Childhood and Society (Erikson), 181
childhood mortality, 48, 49
children, severely disabled, public support for, 175–6
choice feminism, 133–4
cholesterol, 86
Christianity, 186, 243, 258, 269
  "Jesus freaks" and, 72
  suicide and, 226–7
  see also Protestantism
Christian right, 68, 92, 93n, 227n, 241–2
Churchill, Winston, 182
cities, growing old in, 286
civil rights, Obama's election and, 188–9
Civil War, 35, 42
Clairol, 143–4
class, social or economic, 51
  economic expectations and, 62
  health habits and, 86–7
  impact of Crash of '08 and, 164–5
  longevity increases and, 19–20, 53–4, 260–1
  as predictor of financial status in old age, 171
  prospect of reaching old age and, 49
"clinically proven," use of term, 240–1
Clinton, Bill, 277
Clinton, Hillary, 135, 143, 144
cloning, human, 96–8, 253, 254
clothes, 144, 146, 161
CNN, 96, 98
cognitive function, exercises for improvement of, 200, 202
cognitive impairment:
  of world leaders, 181–3
  see also Alzheimer's disease; dementia
Cohen, Mendes, 52
Coleman, Janet, 18
Colette, 84, 153, 282
college education, 58, 61, 175, 271
colonial era, 28–9
Common Sense (Paine), 30, 34
Congress, U.S., 35, 48, 51, 207
Congressional Research Service, 159, 160, 171
Consumer Reports, 111
co-op conversions, 166

Copland, Aaron, 102
Corlett, Candace, 146
cosmetic surgery, 75–6, 141, 147
Cowen, Tyler, 268–70
crankiness, 205–6
Crash of '08, *see* financial collapse of 2008
Create Your Own Economy (Cowen), 270
cults, in 1970s, 72–3
Culture of Narcissism, The (Lasch), 281

Dana-Farber Cancer Institute, 211, 216, 220
Darwin, Charles, 43, 52, 53, 149, 206–7
Davigius, Martha L., 115
death, 210–38
  belief in life after, 241
  as deliverance from suffering, 257–8
  discussions with loved ones about, 216–18
  doctors' views on survival statistics and, 220–1
  "do everything" approach and, 214–15, 217, 219–20, 224
  "do everything possible until there is no longer any chance that I can survive as a competent human being" approach and, 214, 221, 222–4
  dying process and, 17
  endowing with decency and dignity, 223–4
  family battles and, 212
  of friends, 140, 213–14
  at home, 210–11, 222–3, 224
  in hospital, families insulated by, 233–4
  legal planning and, 212, 214–18, 256–7
  literary depictions of, 40
  loving caretaker and, 222–3, 224
  modern medicalized, prolonged agony of, 210, 211–12, 214–15, 219
  nature's imperatives and, 223–4, 242, 243
  obituary pages and, 212–14
  palliative care and, 211, 223, 224, 231, 233, 234, 235
  as part of living, 251, 254, 263
  and proximity to eternal life, 29, 36, 37, 52, 53
  spending on care in final year and month before, 211, 212
  of spouse or partner, 138, 139, 216
  see also suicide
"death clock" sites, 14
Death of Ivan Ilyich, The (Tolstoy), 40
"death panels," 26, 215, 220
death penalty, 227n
DeBakey, Michael, 10
decision making, 181–2
de la Renta, Annette, 145
dementia, 12, 16, 100–26, 180, 183, 200, 257, 271, 281, 282
  ADL disabilities and, 83
  depression and, 201
  despite learnedness, intelligence, and even genius, 203
  dying and, 211, 215
  gender difference in, 128
  palliative care for pain and, 101, 124
  in previous centuries, 117–19
  reversible causes of, 110
  social constructivist model of, 115–17
  see also Alzheimer's disease
Democratic Party, 157, 169, 268, 275
denial, 75, 203
  of Alzheimer's risk, 102–3, 104, 110
  of one's own mortality, 212–14
Denial of Aging, The (Gillick), 12–13, 263, 274–5
depression, xii, 6, 183, 207, 279, 290, 291, 292
  dementia and, 110, 201
  in hospitalized elderly, 201
  at odds with happy talk promoting myth of new old age, 200–2
  suicide and, 225–6, 227, 232, 233, 234, 236
Depression, Great, 57, 60, 63, 175
despair, conscious refusal of, 294–5
Devil's Advocate, The (West), 210
diabetes, 8–9, 13, 20, 86, 95, 114, 176, 245
  gender difference in, 128
  obesity as risk factor for, 130

diabetes *(continued)*
poverty and, 130
reform in health care system's approach to, 273
Dickens, Charles, 40
dietary supplements, anti-aging, 240–1, 244
disability rates, 83–5
gender difference in, 128–9, 130
obesity and, 128–30
poverty and, 130
disabled children, public support for, 175–6
discrimination:
age, in workplaces of Gilded Age, 47–51
sex, 70
see also ageism
Disraeli, Benjamin, 46
divorce, 125
economic impact on women of, 131–2, 136
DNA, progressive damage to, 251
"Dr. Heidegger's Experiment" (Hawthorne), 190–2, 199
Dooling, Richard, 212
double effect, principle of, 231
Downey, James F., 48
Do You Remember Love?, 103
drug addiction, 105
Duke University Medical Center, 128, 129
Dying Animal, The (Roth), 150

early republican era, 30–7
dread of age-related mental deterioriation in, 36, 117–18
economic hardships of old age in, 31–2, 33–5
New England meetinghouse shift in, 30–1
Paine's proposal for old-age pension in, 34, 35
saving for retirement in, 270–1
economic class, *see* class, social or economic
economic inequality, 19–20
Edison, Thomas, 43
education:
college, 58, 61, 175
life expectancy and, 19–20
Ehrenreich, Barbara, 290, 292
"elderly, use of word, 6
elderly poor, 63–6, 159, 176
commercial establishments' hostility toward, 64–5
in current times, 22–4, 32–3
in early republican period, 31–2, 33
invisibility of, 64–5
Paine's proposal for old-age pensions and, 34, 35
in sixties, 63–4
as women's issue, 130–6
Eldertopia, 184–6
Eli Lilly, 106, 108
embryo cloning, 96–8
embryonic stem cell research, 8, 24, 92–5, 105
government policies and, 92–3
and time lapse between basic research and usable treatment, 94–5
Emerson, Ralph Waldo, 38, 39–40, 42, 71
emotional correctness, 5–6, 288–9
emotions of old people:
right to expressiveness and, 54–5, 289
studies on, 291–2
emphysema, 129
Enjoli, 133
Enlightenment, 29
Enron, 178
Eons.com, 14
Ephron, Nora, 142
Eppig, John, 97
equality among generations, 30
Erhard, Werner, 72
Erikson, Erik H., 181, 192, 206
Ertegun, Mica, 144
Esquire, 69n
EST (Erhard Seminars Training), 72–3
Europe, social safety net in, 177–8, 266
evangelicalism, 36
evolution, 260
Darwin's theory of, 43, 52, 53, 149; *see also* social Darwinism
purpose of longevity and, 206–7

evolutionary biologists, 251–2
Exelon, 111–12
exercise, 75–8, 85, 86, 135
to boost mental functioning, 200, 202
cognitive effect of, 114–15
orthopedic surgeries and, 76–7, 78
experience, learning from, 184, 188–90
extraordinary older persons, idealization of, 9–10

Fairlie, Henry, 155–6, 187
falls, irreversible physical decline after, 87–8
feeding tubes, 216–17
Feminine Mystique, The (Friedan), 208
feminism, 70, 197, 206, 208
choice, 133–4
issues of old age ignored by, 140
Field, Sally, 13–14
"50 Reasons to Love Being 50+," 187
Final Exit (Humphry), 230
financial collapse of 2008, 61, 125, 136, 159, 253
boomers affected by, 162–71, 269, 276, 277–8
gender gap in layoffs during, 131
increased rate of savings after, 175
job losses in, 170, 171, 172–3
low- and lower-middle-income households most affected by, 164–5
real estate values and, 161–2, 163–7, 168
retirement savings accounts reduced by, 125, 162, 167–8
financial ignorance, 172
Finucane, Thomas, 111
Fischer, David Hackett, 30–1
Fisher Center for Alzheimer's Research Foundation, 102n
"Fixed Period, The" (Osler), 44–8, 52
Foley, Kathleen, 230–4
Fonda, Jane, 143
Food and Drug Administration (FDA), 8, 17, 111, 240, 245–6
Foote, Cone & Belding, 143–4
Ford, Betty, 105
Fountain of Age, The (Friedan), 11, 140–1, 206–8
fountain of youth, Hawthorne story based on, 190–2
401(k)s, 162, 167–8
Fox, Michael J., 93
Franklin, Benjamin, 30, 46, 68–9
free markets, 35
free radicals, 88
Friedan, Betty, 11, 140–1, 147, 206–8
friendships, losses of aging and, 138, 139, 140
fruits and vegetables, 85, 86

Gallup polls, 291–2
Games People Play (Berne), 70
gender differences:
in attitudes toward work, 135
in disability rates, 128–9, 130
in earnings, 131, 135
in life expectancy, 122, 127, 261
General Social Survey, 290–1
generational conflicts:
contemporary, 157, 265–8, 274–8
need for intergenerational contract and, 265–8, 274–8
in 1960s and early 1970s, 59
generational interdependency, 280
generational segregation, 63, 64–6
Generation Xers, 61, 67, 176
genetic engineering, 259, 261, 263
genetics:
Alzheimer's disease and, 105–6, 109, 129, 249–50
of exceptional people, 90
longevity manipulation and, 240
risk for diseases and, 249, 250
genomic testing, 250
GI Bill, 57–8
Gilded Age, 42–53
discrimination against older workers in, 47–51
pensions in, 51
rise of industrial capitalism in, 42–3, 47–8
social Darwinism in, 42–8, 51–2

Gillick, Muriel R., 12–13, 99, 201, 263, 274–5
Gilman, Daniel Coit, 52
girdles, 145
Gladstone, William, 47
Glamour, 67–8
GlaxoSmithKline, 91
God, 243
  interfering in prerogatives of, 227, 241–2, 255
Goldberg, Elkhonon, 104, 110, 181–2, 200, 201–3, 205
"golden years," 60
Goldstein, David B., 249
Graebner, William, 47, 50
grandparenting, 193–4
gray hair, 144, 146
Gray Panthers, 7, 66
Great Expectations (Dickens), 40
Great Society, 159
greedy geezer stereotype, 155–62, 265–6
  Fairlie's article and, 155–6
  homeownership and, 161–2
  incomes of Americans over sixty-five and, 159–60
  needs of old people and, 160–1
  opposition to health care reform and, 157–8
  payment of Social Security benefits to rich seniors and, 160
Greenberg, Steven M., 25, 26
Griswold, Stanley, 37
Growing Old in America (Fischer), 30–1
Guarente, Leonard P., 245
Gumbiner, Barry, 94–5, 98

hair coloring, 143–4
Half the Way Home (Hochschild), 193–4
Hall, G. Stanley, 54–5, 206–7
Hamilton, Alexander, 30
Hancock, John, 30
happiness, age related to, 290–1
Harrington, Michael, 64
Harris, Thomas A., 70–2
Harris Interactive, 132
Harrison, Barbara Grizzuti, 73n
Harrison, William Henry, 40–1
Harvard Medical School, 249–50
Harvard University, 124
Haseltine, William A., 95–6, 259
Hasidic sects, 72, 73
Haubner, Larry "Curly," 23, 24
Hawthorne, Nathaniel, 40, 190–2, 199
Hayflick, Leonard, 88–9
HBO, *see Alzheimer's Project, The*
health care, 86
  Alzheimer's disease and, 122–6
  rationing of, 221
  social justice for every generation and, 264, 265–8, 274–8
  universal, 26, 175, 220, 265–8
  see also medicine
health care proxies, 219
health care reform, 157–8, 179, 215, 216, 220, 275–7
  liberal and conservative fallacies in debate over, 275–6
  older Americans' opposition to, 220, 266–8
health habits and lifestyle factors:
  Alzheimer's disease and, 114–15
  in anti-aging efforts, 240, 244
  of boomers, illusions about, 87
  disability in old age and, 84, 128–30
  impact of, 75
  with negative impacts, 85–6
  "real age" vs. biological age and, 14–15, 75
  "young old" and, 19
health insurance, 22, 265, 267, 271, 276
  workplace benefits and, 131, 169, 207
  see also Medicaid; Medicare
heart attacks, 12, 81, 128, 211–12, 219, 258
heart disease, 81, 83, 86, 88, 219
Hellenga, Robert, 243
Hendin, Herbert, 230–4
Henry V (Shakespeare), 141
Heraclitus, 192

heredity, *see* genetics
Hewlett, Sylvia Ann, 132, 135
"He Would If He Could" (Bickerstaffe), 37
Hidden Brain Drain Task Force, 132–4, 135
high blood pressure, 86
Hirshman, Linda, 133
Hispanics, 62, 130
History of Retirement, A (Graebner), 47, 50
Hobson, Julius W., 289
Hochschild, Adam, 193–4
Hochschild, Harold, 193–4
Hodes, Richard J., 111
Holocaust Memorial Museum, U.S., 189–90
home care, 11, 25, 177
  for Alzheimer's disease, 122–3, 124–5
  dying at home and, 221–2
  public subsidies for, 272, 273
homelessness, 32–3
Homer, Hazel, 25, 26
homosexuality, 68
Hopkins, Harry, 63, 173–4
Horn & Hardhart cafeterias, 65
hospice benefits, of Medicare, 124
hospices, 211
Hour of Our Death, The (Ariès), 211, 233–4
housing for healthy old people, 272
How to Live (Alford), 203–5
human cloning, 96–8, 253, 254
human genome, 105, 249
Humphrey, Hubert H., 6
Humphry, Derek, 230
Hurlburt family, 90

Illness As Metaphor (Sontag), 100
immigrants, 42
immortality, 52, 89, 241, 242–3
immunosuppressants, 95, 96, 248–9
I'm OK, You're OK (Harris), 70–2
income:
  of Americans over sixty-five, 159–60, 161, 171
  high lifetime, Medicare benefit cuts for, 269–70, 271, 274
  inequality in, 162
  insufficient to save money, 22, 24, 174, 273–4
independence in old age, *see* autonomy in old age
individual variations in aging process, 53
industrial capitalism, 42–3, 47–8
infectious diseases, improved defenses against, 250–1
inheritance, 34, 41
Inland Printer, The, 50
In Praise of Imperfection (Levi-Montalcini), 197–9
intensive care units (ICUs), 211, 212, 219, 220, 222
intergenerational contract, 265–8, 274–8

Jackson, Reggie, 77
Jacoby, Irma B. (author's mother), 4, 25–6, 57, 58, 74–5, 80, 143, 152–3, 156, 186, 204, 212, 283, 284, 292
  husband's death and, 222–3, 224
Jacoby, Robert (author's father), 57, 58, 74, 222–3, 224, 231, 233
Javits, Jacob, 69
Jefferson, Thomas, 29, 34–6, 117–18
Jenner, Edward, 253n
Johns, Stephen Tyrone, 190
Johnson, Lyndon, 59, 63, 158, 159
joint replacement surgery, 76, 81, 84, 95
Journal of Regenerative Medicine, 96
Journal of the American Medical Association (JAMA), 83–4
junk thought, Alzheimer's disease and, 116–17, 119, 120

Kant, Immanuel, 203
Kass, Leon, 255–8, 263
Keats, John, 212
Kekes, John, 188
Kennedy, Edward M., 195, 220–1, 222, 224
Kennedy, John F., 59
Kevorkian, Jack, 229–30
Khmer Rouge, 195–6

King, Dana E., 86
Kirkland, Caroline, 37–8
Kirkwood, Thomas, 251, 252
Kissinger, Henry A., 195–6
Kitwood, Tom, 116
Kolata, Gina, 97
Koop, C. Everett, 13
Koufax, Sandy, 77
Kuhn, Maggie, 7, 11, 66, 147
Kuhn, Mike, 237

laborsaving devices, 84–5, 86
Lancet, 17n, 111
Lanza, Robert, 97
Lasch, Christopher, 281
Last Wish (Rollin), 235
Lau, Charley, 77
layoffs:
  gender gap in, 131
  long-term effects of, 170, 171
  of workers nearing retirement age, 169
letting oneself go, 143–7
  see also physical attractiveness
Levi-Montalcini, Rita, 197–9
Levinson, Daniel J., 192–3, 206
Levinson, Judy, 192
life after death, belief in, 241
life expectancy, *see* longevity and life expectancy
lifestyle factors, *see* health habits and lifestyle factors
Lincoln, Abraham, 40, 41, 46
Linotype machine, 50
Little House on the Prairie series (Wilder), 41–2
Livingto100.com, 14
living wills, 216, 217–18, 219, 242, 256–7
loneliness, xii
  of old women, 136–40
longevity and life expectancy, 156, 271
  capacity for procreation related to, 203–4
  class and increases in, 19–20, 53–4, 260–1
  in colonial era, 28–9
  and desire to live to one hundred, 218
  economic and social consequences of advanced old age and, 218–19
  economic outcomes of continued increases in, 176–7
  environmental improvements and, 7, 49, 250–1
  extending boundaries of, 152, 239–64; *see also* anti-aging research
  extreme, skepticism about virtues of, 25–6
  gap between dignified, socially valued life and, 54–5
  gender gap in, 122, 127, 261
  good health habits and, 75
  medical care and, 7, 8–9, 15, 17
  middle-aged workers and, 48
  of New Yorkers, 286
  obesity and diabetes and outlook for, 176–7
  predictions of, 14–15
  race, education, and class and, 19–20
  retirement age and, 168, 172–4
  in revolutionary era, 29–30
  wisdom of old age and, 180–1, 184, 203–4, 206–7, 208, 209
Long Life Family Study (LLFS), 90
long-term care insurance, 123
Los Angeles Times, 19, 23–4
losses of aging, 6
  acknowledging true feelings of anger and despair and, 294–5
  loneliness and, 138–40
  positive attitude and, 292–3, 294
  women's financial resources and, 159–60
Lowell, James Russell, 38
lung cancer, 129, 222–3
Lyman, Karen, 120–1

MacDonald, Jay, 76
Madison, James, 30
Mad Men, 144, 159
Madoff, Bernard, 171–2
makeup, 143

Maltby, Timothy, 32
Mancini, Joe, 168
marital property, 33
marketing, medical and pharmaceutical, 13–16, 87
  agelessness of actors and celebrities in, 13–14
  anti-aging science and, 90–2
  for Aricept, 17–18
  to older women, 146
  to undiagnosed at-risk patients, 15–16
marriage:
  economic advantage conferred on women by, 130–2
  gender differences in, from age sixty-five on, 140
  see also divorce
Marshall, Anthony, 12, 105
masturbation, 147
Mather, Increase, 29, 252n
McCain, John, 183
McClellan, Bill, 237
McClure's, 43
McDonald's, 65
Medicaid, 23, 123, 124, 272
Medicare, 7, 10–11, 19, 22, 25, 34, 56, 128, 155, 160, 171
  Alzheimer's disease and, 123–4
  benefit cuts for high lifetime earners and, 269–70, 271, 274
  creation of, 158
  Democratic and Republican positions on, during health care debate, 275–6
  end-of-life care and, 124, 211, 212, 215, 219, 220, 221–2
  intergenerational contract and, 265–8, 274–8
  oriented toward procedures rather than human services, 272, 273
  political pressure for benefit cuts in, 158, 162–3, 276
  prescription drug plan and, 276
  tax rates and, 179, 220, 269, 271, 273, 274
medicine, 80–99
  advances of 1950s and 1960s in, 80–2
  age and success of procedures, 18–19
  anti-aging research and, 89–99, 239–64; *see also* anti-aging research
  boomers' faith in, 74
  cancer and, 81, 82–3
  decline in disability rate and, 83–5
  embryonic stem cell research and, 8, 24, 92–5, 105
  faith in, among young vs. old, 218
  longevity increases related to advances in, 7
  media hype and, 96–8
  regenerative, 95–6
  time lapse between basic research and usable treatment and, 94–5, 98–9, 106
  see also health care
Meet the Press, 96
Melville, Herman, 40
memoirs and autobiographies:
  of former government officials, 194–6
  of Levi-Montalcini, 197–9
menstrual periods, heavy, 15–16
middle age, 68
  defining of, 14
  employment discrimination and, 47–9
midlife transitions, 199–200
Mikulak, Andy, 15
Mildred Pierce, 211n
Miller, Richard A., 89, 240, 246, 247, 261–2
Millstone, Isadore E., 236–7
Mirabella, 146
Mitchell, Susan L., 124
mitochondria, 88
Moby-Dick (Melville), 40
Money, 286–7
Montana, law on physician-assisted suicide, 231
Moody, Harry R., 11, 259–60
Morgenthau, Henry, Jr., 173–4
Morgenthau, Robert, 235–6

mortality, 255, 256, 263
  acceptance of, 199, 212, 221, 242–3
mortgages, 160, 161, 163, 164, 165, 166, 170, 271
  interest rates of, 58, 61
motherhood, taking time off from work for, 130–6
MSNBC, 241, 277
Mucke, Lennart, 106–7
multiple sclerosis, 226
Munnell, Alicia, 168

Natansohn, Linda, 14
National Council on Aging, 64–5
National Institute of Mental Health, 225
National Institute on Aging, 84, 113, 248
National Institutes of Health (NIH), 84, 92, 128
National Opinion Research Center, General Social Survey conducted by, 290–1
National Public Radio (NPR), 97
natural selection, 43, 149, 249, 251
Nature, 107, 248, 251
NBC News, 96, 98
neuropsychiatric research, 181
New Deal, 51, 56
New England Journal of Medicine, 249, 250
New England meetinghouses, seating arrangements in, 30–1
new old age, *see* young old age, myth of
New Republic, 155–6
Newton, Isaac, 104, 117, 203
New York City, growing old in, 286
New York Times, 21, 25, 45–6, 48–9, 70, 76, 77, 92, 96, 97, 105, 107, 146, 164, 168, 173, 230, 248, 251, 267, 269, 291
Nichols, Don, 267
Ninth U.S. Circuit Court of Appeals, 230
Nishi, Setsuko, 204
Nixon, Richard M., 59, 69, 82, 196
NPD Group, 144
Nuland, Sherwin B., 16–17
nursing homes, 3–4, 12–13, 211, 271, 272

Obama, Barack, 68, 82, 156
  election of, 69, 92, 153, 188–9, 277
  health care reform and, 157, 179, 267, 275
  stem cell research and, 92, 93n
  as younger baby boomer, 61–2, 66
Obama, Michelle, 61, 66, 68
obesity, 20, 85–6, 114, 176
  defined, 128
  poverty and, 130
  as risk factor for age-related diseases, 128, 129–30
obituary pages, 212–14
O'Brien, Stephen J., 76
Ochs family, 49
"Ode: Intimations of Immortality from Recollections of Early Childhood" (Wordsworth), xiii
Odyssey, The, 242–3
old age:
  literary depictions of, 40
  see also old old age; young old age, myth of
Old Age in the New Land (Achenbaum), 40, 41
old-age pensions, 34
Older Women's League (OWL), 156
old old age, 26, 63, 66, 87
  centennial landmark and, 218, 240
  commonness of Alzheimer's in, 102–3
  facing reality of, 5, 6, 12
  as women's issue, 127, 140; *see also* women in old age
"old," use of word, 5–6, 11, 13
Olmsted, Frederick Law, 118–19, 203
Olshansky, S. Jay, 88–9
Oprah Winfrey Show, The, 15, 69
optimism:
  as innate tendency, 293–4
  successful aging and, 290, 293
Oregon, Death with Dignity Act in, 226, 228, 230–2
organ transplants, 81, 95, 248
orthopedic surgeries, 76–7, 78
Orwell, George, 59, 165
Osler, William, 44–8, 49, 52, 53, 54, 59, 156n

osteoarthritis, 15
osteoporosis, 74, 78, 81
  drugs for prevention of, 13–14
Other America, The (Harrington), 64
Overall, Christine, 260
Oxford English Dictionary, 188
oxidation, 88
Oz, Mehmet, 14–15

Packman, Harry, 76–7
pain, 152–3, 186
  palliative care and, 211, 223, 224, 231, 233, 234, 235
  undertreatment of, in dementia patients, 101, 124
Paine, Thomas, 30, 34–5
Palin, Sarah, 135, 183, 215
Parkinson's disease, 92, 93, 201
part-time jobs, 21, 131, 132, 135, 273
pattern recognition, 181–3, 189
Pelosi, Nancy, 143, 144
pensions, 49
  breach of contracts for, 169, 178
  defined-benefit plans, 162, 167
  401(k)s, 162, 167–8
  old-age, Paine's proposal for, 34, 35
  private, 34, 51, 60, 130, 131, 160, 167, 169
  for war veterans, 32, 35, 51
  see also Social Security
Perelman, Ron, 136
"The personal is political" slogan, 70
personality, continuity of, 192–4, 196–9
pessimism, as innate tendency, 293–4
Pew Research Center for the People and the Press, 216
pharmaceuticals:
  Medicare prescription drug plan and, 276
  promise of extended youth and, 8–9
  see also marketing, medical and pharmaceutical
Phillips, Kelly-Anne, 292n
physical attractiveness, 141–8
  age-related changes and, 141–2
  body-shaping garments and, 145–6
  clothes and, 144, 146
  hair coloring and, 143–4
  makeup and, 143
  standards for older men and, 146–7
  Vogue's issues on older women and, 144–5
physician-assisted suicide, 224, 228–34
Pierce, Franklin, 40
Pipher, Mary, 278
Max Planck Institute, 181, 184
Playtex, 145
Pogrebin, Letty Cottin, 142
polio, 80–1
Polykoff, Shirley, 143–4
positive attitude, 288–95
  cancer survival and, 292
  demands of emotional correctness and, 288–9
  losses of aging and, 292–3
  surveys on happiness of older Americans and, 290–2
posttraumatic growth syndrome, 294
potency-enhancing drugs, 13, 150–1
poverty, 20
  gender difference in, 130
  health habits and, 86
  War on Poverty and, 63
  see also elderly poor
"prehypertensive," marketing and, 16
prescription drug plan, 276
presidential cabinet members, ages of, 51
presidential election of 2008, 153, 183, 188–9
presidents:
  ages of, 40–1, 183
  decline of mental faculties and, 182–3
Pressman, Peter I., 21
Pritchett, Rees, 105
procreation, life span related to, 203–4
pro-longevity science, *see* anti-aging research
Protestantism, 28–9, 36–7, 53, 226–7, 229
public transportation, 285, 286
Puritans, 28–9, 36, 52, 53, 186, 199, 252, 253

race, life expectancy and, 19–20
Rampling, Charlotte, 144–5
rapamycin, 248–9
Rasmussen, Karen, 267–8
Reagan, Nancy, 93, 105, 113
Reagan, Ronald, 16, 19, 56, 61, 93n, 102, 105, 155, 194, 268, 276, 277
  in early stages of Alzheimer's disease during his presidency, 182–3
RealAge.com, 14–15
real estate, Crash of '08 and, 161–2, 163–7, 168
recessions:
  of mid-1970s and early 1980s, 61
  see also financial collapse of 2008
recombinant DNA technology, 95
Redesigning Humans (Stock), 259
Reeve, Christopher, 93
regenerative medicine, 95–6
religion:
  bigotry in early republican era and, 36
  extremist movements of 1970s and, 72, 73
  junk thought and, 116
  see also Christianity; Protestantism
Remsen, Ira, 52
Republican Party, 169, 268, 275–6
respect for one's elders, 36
responsibility, individual vs. collective, 175–6, 265, 268–9
resveratrol, 8–9, 15, 91–2
retirement, 54, 55, 59–60
  best places for, 285–7
  boomers' conception of, 59–60
  compulsory, 50
  exaltation of, 287
  impending, of boomers, 155–7, 158, 171, 176, 179, 263
  Levinson's speculation about transition after, 192–3
  as opportunity for relaxation and leisure activities, 60
  pre-twentieth-century statistics on, 49
  saving for, *see* saving for retirement
  working after, 60, 168–9, 172–3, 273, 287–8
retirement age, 6
  for blue-collar vs. white-collar workers, 20–2
  life expectancy and, 168, 172–4
  Social Security eligibility and, 20–2, 146, 277
revolutionary era, 29–31
rhesus monkeys, calorie-restricted, 244–5
Rieff, David, 294–5
Rights of Man, The (Paine), 30
Rockefeller, John D., 43
Rocking the Ages, 145
Roethenhoeffer, Christina "Howdy" (author's great-grandmother), 282, 283
Rollin, Betty, 235–6
Rollin, Ida, 235–6, 237
Roman Catholic Church, 227, 229
Roosevelt, Franklin D., 173
Rosnick, David, 162
Ross, Catherine, 291
Roth, Philip, 40, 150
Russert, Tim, 96
Ruvkin, Gary, 252

Sachs, Greg A., 101, 124
St. Louis Post-Dispatch, 237
Salk polio vaccine, 80–1
Savidge, Martin, 96
saving for retirement, 22–3, 58, 174–6
  Crash of '08 and, 125, 162, 167–8
  incomes too low for, 22, 24, 174, 273–4
  mandatory taxation and, 174–5
  outliving one's savings and, 23
  since dawn of Republic, 270–1
  Social Security as supplement to, 34
  women's own 401(k)s separate from their husbands' and, 135
  in young adulthood, 174–5, 270–1, 273–4
savings:
  Americans' low rate of, 175
  boomers' low rate of, 162, 167–8, 171
  European tax rates and, 178
  401(k)s and, 162, 167–8
  of young adults, 174–5, 176

Scalia, Antonin, 207, 227n
Scandinavia, social safety net in, 177–8
Schellenberg, Gerard D., 109, 110
Schlesinger, Arthur, Jr., 10, 60
Schoeni, Robert F., 85
Scholl's cafeterias, 65, 66
Science, 97, 98
Scientific American, 88–9
scientific research:
  dominance of young in, 47
  see also anti-aging research
Scott, Paula A., 31–2, 33
Seasons of a Man's Life, The (Levinson), 192–3
Sebelius, Kathleen, 144
second careers, 21
Second Great Awakening, 36
Self, Senility, and Alzheimer's Disease in Modern America (Ballenger), 117
self-help ethos, 57, 66–74
  belief in mutability of objective reality and, 73–4
  conviction that age can be defied and, 66, 68, 74–9
  EST and, 72–3
  extremist religious movements of 1970s and, 72, 73
  transactional analysis and, 70–2
Senate Special Committee on Aging, 63
Seneca, 227
Senescence (Hall), 54–5, 206–7
sex, 6–7, 37, 147–52
  men's desire for younger women and, 148–50, 261
  old men's opportunities for, 148–51
  of old men with women somewhere near their own age, 150–1
  old women's lack of opportunities for, 136, 140–1, 147–9, 151–2
  potency-enhancing drugs and, 13, 150–1
  studies on old people's level of satisfaction with, 291
sex discrimination, 70
Shahid, Sam, 146
Shakespeare, William, 141, 239
Sharp, Phillip A., 91–2
Shaywitz, David A., 94, 98
Shriver, Maria, 103
Shriver, Sargent, 203
Simonsick, Eleanor, 286
Simpson, Alan, 156, 158
Sinclair, David, 8–9, 91, 94, 245
Sirtris Pharmaceuticals, 8–9, 91–2, 245–6
sirtuin activators, 245
sir-2 genes, 245
Skelly, Florence, 145
smallpox immunization, 252–3
Smith, Ruth Proskauer, 10
smoking, 20, 74, 75, 85, 129, 135, 222
Snyderman, Nancy, 220
social class, *see* class, social or economic
social constructivist theorists, 115–22
  caregivers critiqued by, 115–17, 119–22
  historical record at odds with, 117–19
social Darwinism, 42–4, 51–2, 53, 60, 206
  Osler's valedictory address and, 44–8, 52
social safety net, in Europe vs. U.S., 177–8, 266
Social Security, 19, 22, 34, 56–7, 60, 128, 130, 135, 215, 267, 270, 273, 274, 277
  age and dependency on, 171
  benefit calculations and, 63–4
  boomers' views on paying taxes for, 56–7, 156
  creation of, 173–4
  divorce and, 131–2
  greedy geezer stereotype and, 155–62
  impending retirement of baby boomers and, 155–7, 158, 171
  inadequate for financing of retirement years, 23–4, 58, 169–70, 173
  loss of husband and, 160
  mandatory nature of contributions to, 174–5
  needs of old people and, 160–1
  political pressure for benefit cuts in, 162–3
  raising age of eligibility for, 20–2, 146, 277
  right's opposition to, 178
  taxable income maximum for, 157

Social Security *(continued)*
work history and, 131, 132, 136
working to supplement income from, 168–9
Sontag, Susan, 100, 294–5
Spanx, 145–6
Spencer, Herbert, 43, 52
spinal cord injuries, 92, 93
Spiritual Attitude Toward Old Age, The (Adler), 52–3
Spock, Benjamin, 7, 59
Stalin, Joseph, 181–2
standard of living, improvements in, 7, 57
Steinem, Gloria, 140
stem cells, 97n
adult, 93, 95
see also embryonic stem cell research
Stephens, Timothy, 32
Stevens, Ann Huff, 170
Stevens, John Paul, 207
Stewart, Dugald, 117
Stock, Gregory, 259
Stone, Eunice, 33
Stone, Lawrence, 30–1
strokes, 88, 128, 129, 201, 219
student loans, 163
suburbs, as retirement destinations, 285, 286–7
suffering, intrinsic moral value ascribed to, 185–6, 257–8
suicide, 46, 215, 224–38
Alzheimer's disease and, 226, 229
assisted, fear of prosecution and, 234–5
assisted, Oregon's, Washington's, and Montana's laws on, 226, 228, 230–2, 234
assisted, psychiatric training and, 232
assisted by spouse or other family member, 228–9, 234–6, 237
depression and, 225–6, 227, 232, 233, 234, 236
as "easy way out," 227
Foley and Hendin's arguments against, 230–4
methods of, 227–8
of Millstone, 236–7
physician-assisted, 224, 228–34
public opinion on moral right to, 228–9
religious attitudes toward, 226–7, 229
statistics on, 225
Supreme Court, U.S., 207, 230
surgeries:
cosmetic, 75–6, 141, 147
joint replacement, 76, 81, 84, 95
organ transplants, 81, 95, 248
orthopedic, 76–7, 78
Swift, Jonathan, 117, 203

taxes, 34, 167, 171, 174, 175, 176, 275, 276
Europeans' social safety net and, 177, 178, 266, 271
Medicare and, 179, 220, 269, 271, 273, 274
Social Security, 56–7, 156, 157, 160
Taylor, Zachary, 41
Ten-Year Nap, The (Wolitzer), 134–5
thinness, exaltation of, 128, 129
Thomas, William H., 184–6
Thoreau, Henry David, 38–9, 53, 55, 192
three-generation households, 27, 33, 62
Time, 90
Today, 174
Tolstoy, Leo, 40, 47
transactional analysis (TA), 70–2
transhumanists, 260
Trollope, Anthony, 44, 45
Tyler, John, 41

unemployment, 169, 170, 172–3
Unitarianism, 37
United Presbyterian Church, 7, 147
universal health care, 26, 175, 220, 265–8
University of Illinois, 114
University of Wisconsin, 244–5
Updike, John, 16, 40
U.S. News & World Report, 96, 98

Vellacott, Philip, 196–7, 205
Viagra commercials, 13, 144, 147–8
Victoria, Queen, 253

Vietnam War, 58, 59, 63, 65, 69, 195–6
Vijg, Jan, 251, 252
violence, 71–2
Virtues of Aging, The (Carter), 195
Vogue, 144–5
von Brunn, James W., 189–90

Wachter, Till von, 170
Walden (Thoreau), 38–9
walking, life expectancy and, 286
Wallace, Mike, 147
Walters, Barbara, 147
War on Poverty, 63
Washington, George, 30, 34
Washington, law on physician-assisted suicide in, 226, 231
Washington Post, 23, 56, 63, 65, 96, 97
Weaver, Sigourney, 144
Web sites, for boomers who want to increase their odds of living longer, 14–15
weight control, 85, 129–30, 135
  see also obesity
Weindruch, Richard, 245
Weiss, Rick, 97
wellderly-illderly distinction, 11–12, 13
West, Morris, 210
Westphal, Christoph, 91
westward migration, 41–2
White, E. B., 102
White House Diary (Carter), 194
Why Survive? Being Old in America (Butler), 4–5
widows, personal and social loneliness of, 138, 139
Wilder, Laura Ingalls, 41–2
Wilkinson, Frank, 169
Williams, Rev. Eliphet, 32
Wilson, Alpheus W., 52
Winder, William S., 46
wisdom of old age, 180–209, 237
  acceptance of mortality and, 199
  balance of power between hemispheres of brain and, 200
  basic elements to canon of, 184
  continuity of character and personality and, 192–4, 196–9
  detachment from strivings of earlier adult life and, 184, 192–6, 198, 206, 208, 209, 288–9
  exercises to boost mental functioning and, 200, 202
  Hall's ambivalence about, 54–5
  Hawthorne's "Dr. Heidegger's Experiment" and, 190–2
  industrial capitalism and, 42–3
  learning from life experience and, 184, 188–90
  meaning of "wisdom" and, 187–8
  memoirs by former government officials and, 194–6
  in mid-nineteenth century, 38–40
  pattern recognition and, 181–3
  as "purpose" of longevity, 203–4, 206–7, 208, 209
  reflectivity and perceptiveness assertions and, 184–8
  reputed veneration of, in halcyon past, 27, 28, 29
  Thomas's Eldertopia and, 184–6
Wisdom Paradox, The (Goldberg), 104, 110, 181–2, 200, 201–3, 205
Wolitzer, Meg, 134–5
women, 54, 66–7
  Anti-Age Limit League and employment of, 48
  attitudes toward work among, 134–5
  as caretakers for family members, 124, 125, 282–4
  childbearing delayed by, 66, 67–8
  economic advantage conferred by marriage on, 130–2
  economic impact of divorce on, 131–2, 136
  gender gap in earnings and, 131
  hostility toward ambition in, 135
  interrupted career patterns of, 130–6
  poverty throughout lifespan among, 130
  retirement savings of, 135

women in old age, 58, 127–54
crankiness of, 205–6
diminished sense of physical attractiveness of, 141–8
disability risk and, 128–30
economic consequences of decisions made in younger adulthood by, 130–6
gender difference in life expectancy and, 122, 127
loneliness of, 136–40
loss of spouse and, 138, 139, 159–60
as majority of Social Security recipients, 156
obesity in younger adult lives and, 128–30
Osler's views on, 46
pension benefits for widows and, 51
poorer than old men, 33
poverty and, 130–6
sexual opportunities of, 136, 140–1, 147–52
white vs. minority, 130
without caretakers, 127–8
women's movement, *see* feminism
Woodward, Joanne, 103
Woodward, Kathleen, 206–7, 208
Wordsworth, William, xiii
work:
after retirement, 60, 168–9, 172–3, 273, 287–8
gender differences in attitudes toward, 134–5
gender gap in earnings and, 131, 135
part-time, 21, 131, 132, 135, 273
women's interrupted career patterns and, 130–6
workday, shortening of, 50
World Science Festival (New York City, 2008), 5, 8–9, 91, 94, 245
World War II, 57, 58, 155, 157, 159, 204, 211n

Yankelovich Partners, 145, 276, 277
Yankner, Bruce, 249–50
Young, Andrew, 188
young old age (or new old age), myth of, xi–xiii, 5, 11–27, 132, 209, 240, 292, 295
efforts to deal pragmatically with problems of real old age hindered by, 22–4, 179
euphemisms and coy terms in, 11–12
extending life at any cost and, 25–6
marketing campaigns and, 13–16, 17–18
race, education, and economic differences ignored in, 19–22
realities of aging at odds with, 12–13, 16–17, 26
selective ageism and, 18–19
Web sites catering to boomers and, 14–16
youth culture, 28–55
ages of presidents and, 40–1
in antebellum era, 36–41
decorum proscribed for older people and, 37–8
in early republican era, 30–7
first generation of great American writers and, 38–40
in Gilded Age, 42–53
industrial capitalism and, 42–3, 47–8
influx of immigrants and, 42
in 1960s, 39, 64
Osler's valedictory address and, 44–8, 52
in revolutionary era, 29–31
social Darwinism and, 44–8
westward migration and, 41–2

Zinn, Howard, 10

ALSO BY SUSAN JACOBY

"Forceful. . . . Cogently argued. . . . An intellectual journey of the first order." —Chicago Tribune

THE AGE OF AMERICAN UNREASON
Revised and Updated

A cultural history of the last forty years, *The Age of American Unreason* focuses on the convergence of social forces—usually treated as separate entities—that has created a perfect storm of anti-rationalism. These include the upsurge of religious fundamentalism, with more political power today than ever before; the failure of public education to create an informed citizenry; and the triumph of video over print culture. Sparing neither the right nor the left, Jacoby asserts that Americans today have embraced a universe of "junk thought" that makes almost no effort to separate fact from fiction.

History/Current Affairs